THE NEW PALGRAVE

THE INVISIBLE HAND

THE NEW PALGRAVE

THE INVISIBLE HAND

EDITED BY

JOHN EATWELL · MURRAY MILGATE · PETER NEWMAN

MACMILLAN
REFERENCE

© The Macmillan Press Limited, 1987, 1989

All rights reserved. No part of this publication
may be reproduced or transmitted, in any form or by any means,
without permission.

First published in
The New Palgrave: A Dictionary of Economics
Edited by John Eatwell, Murray Milgate and Peter Newman
in four volumes, 1987

Published in the United Kingdom by
THE MACMILLAN PRESS LIMITED, 1989
London and Basingstoke
Associated companies in Auckland, Delhi, Dublin, Gaborone,
Hamburg, Harare, Hong Kong, Johannesburg, Kuala Lumpur, Lagos,
Manzini, Maseru, Melbourne, Mexico City, Nairobi, New York,
Singapore, Tokyo.

The New Palgrave is a trademark of The Macmillan Press Limited

British Library Cataloguing in Publication Data

The New Palgrave: the invisible hand.
   1. Free economics
   I. Eatwell, John   II. Milgate, Murray
   III. Newman, Peter
   330.12′2

   ISBN 0-333-49532-2
   ISBN 0-333-49533-0 Pbk

Sep 89

Printed in Hong Kong

Contents

General Preface   vii
Preface   xi

Adam Smith	Andrew S. Skinner	1
Anarchism	George Woodcock	43
Claude Frédéric Bastiat	R.F. Hébert	50
Jeremy Bentham	Ross Harrison	53
Collective action	Mancur Olson	61
Common law	P.S. Atiyah	70
Constitutional economics	James M. Buchanan	79
Economic freedom	Alan Peacock	88
Economic harmony	Israel M. Kirzner	94
Economic laws	Stephano Zamagni	99
Equilibrium: development of the concept	Murray Milgate	105
Adam Ferguson	Nicholas Phillipson	114
William Godwin	Peter Marshall	116
Friedrich August von Hayek	Roger W. Garrison and Israel M. Kirzner	119
Thomas Hobbes	C.B. Macpherson	131
David Hume	Eugene Rotwein	134
Francis Hutcheson	Andrew S. Skinner	143
Individualism	C.B. Macpherson	149
Interests	Albert O. Hirschman	156
Invisible hand	Karen I. Vaughn	168
Law and economics	David Friedman	173
Liberalism	Ralf Dahrendorf	183
Liberty	Alan Ryan	188
John Locke	Karen I. Vaughn	192

Contents

Bernard Mandeville	N. Rosenberg	196
John Stuart Mill	Alan Ryan	199
John Millar	Nicholas Phillipson	211
Moral philosophy	R.S. Downie	213
Natural law	N.E. Simmonds	223
Property	Alan Ryan	227
Property rights	Armen A. Alchian	232
Scottish Enlightenment	John Robertson	239
Self-interest	D.H. Monro	245
Social cost	J. de V. Graaf	251
Utilitarianism	C. Welch	257
Utopias	Gregory Claeys	271
Contributors		278

General Preface

The books in this series are the offspring of *The New Palgrave*: *A Dictionary of Economics*. Published in late 1987, the *Dictionary* has rapidly become a standard reference work in economics. However, its four heavy tomes containing over four million words on the whole range of economic thought is not a form convenient to every potential user. For many students and teachers it is simply too bulky, too comprehensive and too expensive for everyday use.

By developing the present series of compact volumes of reprints from the original work, we hope that some of the intellectual wealth of *The New Palgrave* will become accessible to much wider groups of readers. Each of the volumes is devoted to a particular branch of economics, such as econometrics or general equilibrium or money, with a scope corresponding roughly to a university course on that subject. Apart from correction of misprints, etc. the content of each of its reprinted articles is exactly the same as that of the original. In addition, a few brand new entries have been commissioned especially for the series, either to fill an apparent gap or more commonly to include topics that have risen to prominence since the dictionary was originally commissioned.

As *The New Palgrave* is the sole parent of the present series, it may be helpful to explain that it is the modern successor to the excellent *Dictionary of Political Economy* edited by R.H. Inglis Palgrave and published in three volumes in 1894, 1896 and 1899. A second and slightly modified version, edited by Henry Higgs, appeared during the mid-1920s. These two editions each contained almost 4,000 entries, but many of those were simply brief definitions and many of the others were devoted to peripheral topics such as foreign coinage, maritime commerce, and Scottish law. To make room for the spectacular growth in economics over the last 60 years while keeping still to a manageable length, *The New Palgrave* concentrated instead on economic theory, its originators, and its closely cognate disciplines. Its nearly 2,000 entries (commissioned from over 900 scholars) are all self-contained essays, sometimes brief but never mere definitions.

Apart from its biographical entries, *The New Palgrave* is concerned chiefly with theory rather than fact, doctrine rather than data; and it is not at all clear how theory and doctrine, as distinct from facts and figures, *should* be treated in an encyclopaedia. One way is to treat everything from a particular point of view. Broadly speaking, that was the way of Diderot's classic *Encyclopédie raisonée* (1751–1772), as it was also of Léon Say's *Nouveau dictionnaire d'économie politique* (1891–2). Sometimes, as in articles by Quesnay and Turgot in the *Encyclopédie*, this approach has yielded entries of surpassing brilliance. Too often, however, both the range of subjects covered and the quality of the coverage itself are seriously reduced by such a self-limiting perspective. Thus the entry called '*Méthode*' in the first edition of Say's *Dictionnaire* asserted that the use of mathematics in economics 'will only ever be in the hands of a few', and the dictionary backed up that claim by choosing not to have any entry on Cournot.

Another approach is to have each entry take care to reflect within itself varying points of view. This may help the student temporarily, as when preparing for an examination. But in a subject like economics, the Olympian detachment which this approach requires often places a heavy burden on the author, asking for a scrupulous account of doctrines he or she believes to be at best wrong-headed. Even when an especially able author does produce a judicious survey article, it is surely too much to ask that it also convey just as much enthusiasm for those theories thought misguided as for those found congenial. Lacking an enthusiastic exposition, however, the disfavoured theories may then be studied less closely than they deserve.

The New Palgrave did not ask its authors to treat economic theory from any particular point of view, except in one respect to be discussed below. Nor did it call for surveys. Instead, each author was asked to make clear his or her own views of the subject under discussion, and for the rest to be as fair and accurate as possible, without striving to be 'judicious'. A balanced perspective on each topic was always the aim, the ideal. But it was to be sought not *internally*, within each article, but *externally*, between articles, with the reader rather than the writer handed the task of achieving a personal balance between differing views.

For a controversial topic, a set of several more or less synonymous headwords, matched by a broad diversity of contributors, was designed to produce enough variety of opinion to help form the reader's own synthesis; indeed, such diversity will be found in most of the individual volumes in this series.

This approach was not without its problems. Thus, the prevalence of uncertainty in the process of commissioning entries sometimes produced a less diverse outcome than we had planned. 'I can call spirits from the vasty deep,' said Owen Glendower. 'Why, so can I,' replied Hotspur, 'or so can any man;/ But will they come when you do call for them?' In our experience, not quite as often as we would have liked.

The one point of view we did urge upon every one of *Palgrave*'s authors was to write from an historical perspective. For each subject its contributor was asked to discuss not only present problems but also past growth and future prospects. This request was made in the belief that knowledge of the historical development of any theory enriches our present understanding of it, and so helps to construct better theories for the future. The authors' response to the request was generally so positive that, as the reader of any of these volumes will discover, the resulting contributions amply justified that belief.

John Eatwell
Murray Milgate
Peter Newman

Preface

Although he mentioned it only twice, Adam Smith introduced into the language of economists a metaphor as powerful as any used before or since: the invisible hand. The meaning that Smith imparted to the phrase remains much the same today. Every individual, acting solely in the pursuit of private gain, is 'led by an invisible hand to promote an end which was no part of his intention' (*Wealth of Nations*, 1776, Book IV, Chapter II), that end being 'the publick interest'.

The idea lying behind the invisible hand, though not the metaphor itself, belongs to Bernard de Mandeville and his *Fable of the Bees* (1714). In political economy that idea and the doctrine of *laissez faire* have always been closely related, intertwined in various guises until their contemporary manifestations – intellectually powerful but ideologically pallid – as the relations between Pareto efficiency and competitive equilibrium. For the metaphor captured in one strikingly memorable phrase the belief that, however individuals perceive their own situations, certain systematic forces – primarily those of competition – are always at work in the economy as a whole, persistent and regular in their action in a wide variety of settings.

The deployment of the invisible hand to provide a moral gloss to competitive capitalist behaviour was the provenance of the Scottish moral philosophers. However, its application to moral philosophy has been of little lasting significance compared to its life in economics. It is easy enough to see why. Since the metaphor directed one to contemplate the unintended consequences of individual action, inquiry into the moral character of agents – in a world where outcomes were invariably different from anything those agents actually intended – hardly mattered. Scottish moral philosophy died out. Its 'best heads joined to the best hearts', to borrow Smith's description of prudent behaviour, were replaced by utilitarian calculators or Kantian moral agents. Scottish economics, on the other hand, continued to thrive.

The idea of unintended consequences was not an exclusively Scottish invention.

Contents

It was also the standard fare of the French Physiocrats, who spoke of social and economic outcomes as being governed by forces 'independent of the wills of men'. It is with their expression of the idea that one can begin to understand the apparent paradox that in economic analysis the invisible hand has acted as a sponsor of the centrality of both agency and structure. Indeed, it might be said that structuralists of all kinds conceive the very task of their discipline to be that of rendering visible the invisible hand.

The essays in this volume deal with some of the themes and issues in economics upon which the invisible hand has left its mark. The essays do not exhaust the field of its influence; they do, however, capture the diversity and power of its legacy.

The Editors

Adam Smith

ANDREW S. SKINNER

Adam Smith (1723–1790) was born in Kirkcaldy, on the east coast of Scotland, and baptized on 5 June, 1723. He was the son of Adam Smith, Clerk to the Court Martial and Comptroller of Customs in the town (who died before his son was born) and of Margaret Douglas of Strathendry.

Smith attended the High School in Kirkcaldy, and then proceeded to Glasgow University. He first matriculated in 1737, at the not uncommon age of fourteen. At this time the university, or more strictly the college, was small. It housed only twelve professors who had in effect replaced the less specialized system of regents by 1727. Of the professoriate, Smith was most influenced by the 'never-to-be-forgotten' Francis Hutcheson (Corr., letter 274, dated 16 November 1787). Hutcheson had succeeded Gerschom Carmichael, the distinguished editor of Pufendorf's *De Officio Hominis et Civis*, as Professor of Moral Philosophy.

Smith left Glasgow in 1740 as a Snell Exhibitioner at Balliol College to begin a stay of six years. The atmosphere of the college at this time was Jacobite and 'anti-Scotch'. Smith was also to complain: 'In the university of Oxford, the greater part of the publick professors have, for these many years, given up altogether even the pretence of teaching' (WN, V. i. f. 8). But there were benefits, most notably ease of access to excellent libraries, which in turn enabled Smith to acquire an extensive knowledge of English and French literature, which was to prove invaluable.

Smith left Oxford in 1746 and returned to Kirkcaldy without a fixed plan. But in 1748 he was invited to give a series of public lectures in Edinburgh, with the support of three men – the Lord Advocate, Henry Home; Lord Kames; and a childhood friend, James Oswald of Dunnikier.

The lectures, which are thought to have been primarily concerned with rhetoric and belles lettres, brought Smith £100 a year (Corr., letter 25, dated 8 June 1758). They also seem to have been wide-ranging.

Smith's reputation as a lecturer brought its reward. In 1751 he was elected to the Chair of Logic in Glasgow University, again with the support of Lord Kames.

According to John Millar, Smith's most distinguished pupil, he devoted the bulk of his time to the delivery of a system of rhetoric and belles lettres, which was based on the conviction that the best way of

> explaining and illustrating the various powers of the human mind, the most useful part of metaphysics, arises from an examination of the several ways of communicating our thoughts by speech, and from an attention to the principles of those literary compositions which contribute to persuasion or entertainment (Stewart, I. 16).

Smith continued to teach the main part of his lecture course on logic after he had been translated to the Chair of Moral Philosophy in 1752. A set of lecture notes, discovered by J.M. Lothian in 1958, relate to the session 1762/3. The notes correspond closely to Millar's description of the course given more than a decade earlier, in that they are concerned with such problems as the development of language, style and the organization of forms of discourse which include the oratorical, narrative and didactical. Smith was primarily concerned with the study of human nature and with the analysis of the means and forms of communication. He no doubt continued to lecture on these subjects to students of moral philosophy because he rightly believed them to be important (see J.M. Lothian, 1963; W.S. Howell, 1975).

Smith's lectures on language were published in expanded form as *Considerations Concerning the First Formation of Language*, in the *Philological Miscellany* for 1761. They were reprinted in the third edition of the *Theory of Moral Sentiments* in 1767.

Smith's teaching from the Chair of Moral Philosophy fell into four parts and in effect set the scene for the major published works which were to follow. Again on the authority of John Miller, it is known that Smith lectured on natural theology, ethics, jurisprudence and 'expediency', or economics, *in that order*. The lectures on natural theology (a sensitive subject at the time) have not yet been found. But Millar made it clear that the lectures on ethics form the basis for the *Theory of Moral Sentiments* and that the subjects covered in the last part of the course were to be further developed in the *Wealth of Nations* (Stewart, I. 20). As to the third part, on jurisprudence, Millar noted that:

> Upon this subject he followed the plan that seems to be suggested by Montesquieu; endeavouring to trace the gradual progress of jurisprudence, both public and private, from the rudest to the most refined ages, and to point out the effects of those arts which contribute to subsistence, and to the accumulation of property, in producing correspondent improvements or alterations in law and government (Stewart, I. 19).

Illustration and confirmation of this claim proved impossible until 1896 when Edwin Cannan published an edition of the *Lectures on Jurisprudence*. The notes edited by Cannan are dated 1766, although they were taken in the session 1763/4. This was Smith's last session in Glasgow, so that these lectures, where 'public' (broadly constitutional law) precedes 'private' jurisprudence (concerning man's rights as a citizen), *may* reflect a preferred order. A second set of notes, this time relating to the previous session, were also found by J.M. Lothian as recently as 1958 and are here styled LJ (A).

Academically, the major event for Smith was the publication of the *Theory of Moral Sentiments* in 1759. The book was well received by both the public and Smith's friends. In a delightful letter Hume reminded Smith of the futility of fame and public approbation, and having encouraged him to be a philosopher n practice as well as profession, continued:

> Supposing therefore, that you have duely prepared yourself for the worst by these Reflections; I proceed to tell you the Melancholy News, that your Book has been most unfortunate: For the Public seem disposed to applaud it extremely (Corr., letter 31, dated 12 April 1759).

The book was to establish Smith's reputation. There was a second revised edition in 1761 and further editions in 1767, 1774, 1781 and 1790.

Charles Townshend was among those to whom Hume had sent a copy of Smith's treatise. Townshend had married the widowed Countess of Dalkeith in 1755 and was sufficiently impressed by Smith's work to arrange for his appointment as tutor to her son, the young Duke of Buccleuch. The position brought financial security (£300 sterling p.a. for the rest of his life), and Smith duly accepted, formally resigning his chair early in 1764.

Smith and his party left almost immediately for France to begin a sojourn of some two years. At the outset, the visit was unsuccessful, causing Smith to write to Hume, with some humour, that 'I have begun to write a book in order to pass away the time. You may believe I have very little to do' (Corr., letter 82, dated 5 July 1764, Tolouse).

But matters improved with Smith's increasing familiarity with the language and the success of a series of short tours. In 1765 Smith, the Duke, and the Duke's younger brother Hew Scott, reached Geneva, giving Smith an opportunity to meet Voltaire, whom he genuinely admired as 'the most universal genius perhaps which France has ever produced' (Letter 17). The party arrived in Paris in mid-February 1766, where Smith's fame, together with the efforts of David Hume, secured him a ready entré to the leading *salons* and, in turn, introductions to *philosophes* such as d'Alembert, Holbach and Helvetius.

During this period Smith met François Quesnay, the founder, with the Marquis de Mirabeau, of the Physiocratic School of economics (Meek, 1962). By the time Smith met Quesnay, the latter's model of the economic system as embodied in the *Tableau Economique* ([1757], trans. in Meek, 1962) had already been through a number of editions. Quesnay was then working on the *Analyse* (trans. in Meek, 1962), while it is also known that A.R.J. Turgot was currently engaged on his *Reflections on the Formation and Distribution of Riches* (trans. in Meek, 1973).

Smith, who had already developed an interest in political economy, had arrived in Paris at the very point in time that the French School had reached the zenith of its influence and output. The contents of Smith's library amply confirm his interest in this work (Mizuta, 1967).

Smith's stay in Paris had been enjoyable both socially and in academic terms. But it was marred by the developing quarrel between Hume and Rousseau and sadly terminated by the death of Hew Scott. Smith returned to London on 1 November 1766.

Smith spent the winter in London, where he was consulted by Townshend and engaged in corrections for the third edition of the *Theory of Moral Sentiments*. By the spring of 1767 (the year in which Sir James Steuart published his *Principles of Political Oeconomy*) Smith was back in Kirkcaldy to begin a study of some six years. It was during this period that he struggled with the *Wealth of Nations*. Correspondence of the time amply confirms the mental strain involved. But by 1773 Smith was ready to return to London, leaving his friends, notably David Hume, under the impression that completion was imminent. As matters turned out, it took Smith almost three more years to finish his book; a delay which may have been due in part to his increasing concern with the American War of Independence and with the wider issue of the relationship between the colonies and the 'mother country' (WN, IV. vii).

An Inquiry into the Nature and Causes of the Wealth of Nations was published by Strahan and Cadell on 9 March 1776, and elicited once more a warm response from Hume:

Dear Mr. Smith: I am much pleas'd with your Performance, and the Perusal of it has taken me from a State of great Anxiety. It was a Work of so much Expectation, by yourself, by your Friends, and by the Public, that I trembled for its Appearance; but am now much relieved. Not but the Reading of it necessarily requires so much Attention, and the Public is disposed to give so little, that I shall still doubt for some time of its being at first very popular (Corr., letter 150, dated 1 April 1776).

In fact, the book sold well, with subsequent editions in 1778, 1784, 1786 and 1789.

1776 was marred for Smith by the death of David Hume, after a long illness, and by his concern over the future of the latter's *Dialogues Concerning Natural Religion*. This work, together with Hume's account of 'My Own Life' had been left in the care of William Strahan, to whom Smith wrote expressing the hope that the *Dialogues* should remain unpublished, although Hume himself had determined otherwise.

But Smith proposed to 'add to his life a very well authenticated account' of Hume's formidable courage during his last illness (Corr., letter 172, dated 5 September 1776). The letter was published in 1777, and as Smith wrote later to Andreas Holt, 'brought upon me ten times more abuse than the very violent attack I had made upon the whole commercial system of Great Britain' (Corr., letter 208, dated October 1780).

In 1778 Smith was appointed Commissioner of Customs, due in part to the efforts of the Duke of Buccleuch. The office brought an income of £600, in addition to the pension of £300 which the Duke refused to discontinue (Corr., letter 208). Smith settled in Edinburgh, where he was joined by his mother and a cousin, Janet Douglas.

During 1778 Alexander Wedderburn sought Smith's advice on the future conduct of affairs in America. Smith's 'Thoughts on the State of the Contest with America' were written in the aftermath of the battle of Saratoga. The Memorandum was first published by G.H. Guttridge in the *American Historical Review* (vol. 38, 1932/3).

In this document, Smith rehearsed a number of arguments which he had already stated in WN (IV. vii. c). He advocated the extension of British taxes to Ireland and to America, provided that representatives from both countries were admitted to Parliament at Westminster in conformity with accepted constitutional practice. Smith noted that 'Without a union with Great Britain, the inhabitants of Ireland are not likely for many ages to consider themselves as one people' (WN, V. iii. 89). With respect to America, he observed that her progress had been so rapid that 'in the course of little more than a century, perhaps, the produce of American might exceed that of British taxation. The seat of the empire would then naturally remove itself to that part of the empire which contributed most to the general defence and support of the whole' (WN, IV. vii. c. 79).

But Smith also repeated a point already made in WN; namely, that the opportunity for union had been lost, and proceeded to review the bleak options, now all too familiar, which were actually open to the British Government. Military victory was increasingly unlikely (WN, V. i. a. 27) and military government, even in the event of victory, unworkable (Corr., 383). Voluntary withdrawal from the conflict was a rational but politically impracticable course, given the probable impact on domestic and world opinion (ibid.). The most likely outcome, in Smith's view, was the loss of the thirteen united colonies and the successful retention of Canada – the worst possible solution since it was also the most expensive in terms of defence (Corr., 385).

Smith worked hard as a Commissioner, and to an extent which, as he admitted, affected his literary pursuits (Corr., letter 208). But in this period he completed the third edition of WN (1784), incorporating major developments which were separately published as 'Additions and Corrections'. The third edition also features an index and a long concluding chapter to Book IV entitled 'Conclusion of the Mercantile System'.

After 1784 Smith must have devoted most of his attention to the revision of TMS. The sixth edition of 1790 features an entirely new Part VI, which includes a further elaboration of the role of conscience, and the most complete statement which Smith offered as to the complex *social* psychology which lies behind man's broadly economic aspirations.

In addition to the essay on the 'Imitative Arts', which is mentioned in his letter to Andreas Holt (Corr., letter 208), Smith observed that 'I have likewise two other great works upon the anvil; the one is a sort of Philosophical History of all the different branches of Literature, of Philosophy, Poetry and Eloquence; the other is a sort of theory and History of Law and Government' (Corr., letter 248 dated 1 November 1785, addressed to the Duc de la Rochefoucauld).

Smith's literary ambitions also feature in the Advertisement to the 1790 edition of TMS, where he drew attention to the concluding sentences of the first edition of 1759. In these passages Smith makes it clear that TMS and WN are parts of a single plan which he hoped to complete with a published account of 'the general principles of law and government, and of the different revolutions which they had undergone in the different ages and periods of society'. Smith's 'present occupations' and 'very advanced age' prevented him from completing this great work, although the approach is illustrated by LJ (A) and LJ (B), and by those passages in WN which can now be recognized as being derived from them (most notably WN, III and V. i. a, b).

Smith died on 17 July 1790, having first instructed his executors, Joseph Black and James Hutton, to burn his papers, excepting those which were published in *Essays on Philosophical Subjects* (1795).

In what follows, Smith's system will be expounded in terms of the order of argument which he is known to have employed as a lecturer; namely, ethics, jurisprudence and economics. Each separate area of analysis may be represented as highly systematic; all are interdependent, forming in effect the component sections of a greater whole.

THE THEORY OF MORAL SENTIMENTS

The Theory of Moral Sentiments shows clear evidence of a model, and of a form of argument which is in part designed to explain how so self-regarding a creature as man succeeds in erecting barriers against his own passions.

In Part VII of TMS, Smith reviewed different approaches to the questions confronting the philosopher in this field, basically as a means of differentiating his own contribution from them.

In Smith's view there were two main questions to be answered: 'First, wherein does virtue consist?', and secondly, 'by what means does it come to pass, that the mind prefers one tenour of conduct to another'? (TMS, VII. i. 2). In dealing with the first question, Smith described all classical and modern theories in terms of the emphasis given to the qualities of propriety, prudence and benevolence. In each case, he argued that the identification of a particular quality was appropriate, but rejected what he took to be undue emphasis on any one. He criticized those who found virtue in propriety, on the ground that this approach emphasized the importance of self-command at the expense of 'softer' virtues, such as sensibility. He rejected others who found virtue in prudence because of the emphasis given to qualities which are useful, thus echoing his criticism of David Hume in TMS, Part IV. In a similar way, while he admired benevolence, Smith argued that proponents of this approach (notably Francis Hutcheson) had neglected virtues such as prudence.

Smith's criticism of Hutcheson's teaching is remarkable for the emphasis which he gave to self-interest and his denial of Hutcheson's proposition that self-love 'was a principle which could never be virtuous in any degree or in any direction' (TMS, VII, ii. 3.12). Smith also rejected the argument of Mandeville, whose fallacy it was 'to represent every passion as wholly vicious, which is so in any degree' (TMS, VII. ii. 4.12). Smith contended that 'The condition of human nature were peculiarly hard, if these affections, which, by the very nature of our being, ought frequently to influence our conduct, could upon no occasion appear virtuous, or deserve esteem and commendation from anybody' (TMS, VII, ii. 3.18).

'A further distinctive element in Smith's approach emerges in his treatment of the second question. He accepted Hutcheson's argument that the perception of right and wrong rests not upon reason but 'immediate sense and feeling' (TMS, VII. iii. 2.9). But Smith rejected Hutcheson's emphasis on a special sense, the moral sense, which was treated as being analogous to 'external' senses, such as sight or touch. But in so doing Smith in effect elaborated on the argument of his teacher, who had already presented moral judgements as being disinterested and based upon sympathy or fellow-feeling. Smith also enlarged on the role of the *spectator*, which had been a feature of the work done by Hutcheson and Hume.

Smith argued that the spectator may form a judgement with respect to the activities of another person by visualizing how he would have behaved or felt in similar circumstances. It is this capacity for acts of imaginative sympathy which permits the spectator to form a judgement as to the propriety or impropriety of the conduct observed, and as to the 'suitableness or unsuitableness, the proportion or disproportion which the affection seems to bear to the cause or object which excites it' (TMS, I. i. 3.6).

'Since we can 'enter into' the feelings of another person only to a limited degree, Smith was able to identify the 'amiable' virtue of sensibility with the quality of imagination, and that of self-command with a capacity control expressions or feeling to such an extent as to permit the spectator to comprehend, and thus to 'sympathize', with them.

The argument was extended to take account of those actions which have consequences for other people, in suggesting that in such cases the spectator may seek to form a judgement as to the propriety of the *action* taken and of the *reaction* to it. The sense of *merit* 'seems to be a compounded sentiment, and to be made up of two distinct emotions; a direct sympathy with the sentiments of the agent, and an indirect sympathy with the gratitude of those who receive the benefit of his actions' (TMS, II. i. 5.2). Conversely, a sense of *demerit* is compounded of 'antipathy to the affections and motives of the agent' and 'an indirect sympathy with the resentment of the sufferer' (TMS, II. i. 5.4).

Smith further contended that 'Nature, when she formed man for society, endowed him with an original desire to please, and an original aversion to offend his brethren' (TMS, III. 2.6).

But this general disposition is not of itself sufficient to ensure an adequate degree of control. The first problem which Smith confronted is that of *information*, a problem which arises from the fact that the actual spectator of the conduct of another person is unlikely to be familiar with his *motives*.

Smith solved this problem by arguing that we tend to judge our own conduct by trying to visualize the reaction of an imagined or 'ideal spectator' to it; that is, by seeking to visualize the reaction of a spectator, who is necessarily fully informed, with regard to our own motives. Smith gave more and more attention to the role of the ideal spectator in successive editions as an important source of control; that is, to the voice of 'reason, principle, conscience ... the great judge and arbiter of our conduct' (TMS, III. 3.4). Looked at in this way, the argument depends on man's desire not merely for praise, but praiseworthiness (TMS, III. 2. 32)

The second problem arises from the fact that Smith, following Hume, presents man as an active, self-regarding being, whose legitimate pursuit of the objects of ambition, notably wealth, can on some occasions have hurtful consequences for others. The difficulty here is that of *partiality* of view, even where we have the information which is needed to arrive at accurate judgements. When we are about to act, 'the eagerness of passion will seldom allow us to consider what we are doing with the candour of an indifferent person', while after we have acted, we often 'turn away our view from those circumstances which might render ... judgement unfavourable' (TMS, III. 4.3–4). The solution to this particular problem is found in man's capacity for generalization on the basis of particular experience:

It is thus that the general rules of morality are formed. They are ultimately founded upon experience of what, in particular instances, our moral faculties, our natural sense of merit and propriety, approve, or disapprove of. ... The general rule ... is formed, by finding from experience, that all actions of a certain kind, or circumstanced in a certain manner, are approved or disapproved of (TMS, III. 4.8).

It is these rules that provide the yardstick against which man can judge his actions in all circumstances; rules which command respect by virtue of the desire to be praiseworthy and which are further supported by the fear of God (TMS, III. 5. 12).

Smith thus offered an explanation of the way in which men were fitted for society, arguing in effect that they typically erect a series of barriers to the exercise of their own (self-regarding) passions, which culminate in the emergence of generally accepted rules of behaviour.

The rules themselves vary in character. Those which relate to justice 'may be compared to the rules of grammar; the rules of the other virtues, to the rules which critics lay down for the attainment of what is sublime and elegant in composition. The one, are precise, accurate and indispensable. The other, are loose, vague, and indeterminate' (TMS, III. 6.11).

But Smith was in no doubt that the rules of justice were indispensable. Justice 'is the main pillar that upholds the whole edifice' (TMS, II, ii. 3.4). Smith added that the final precondition of social order was a system of positive law, embodying current conceptions of the rules of justice and administered by some system of magistracy:

As the violation of justice is what men will never submit to from one another, the public magistrate is under the necessity of employing the power of the commonwealth to enforce the practice of this virtue. Without this precaution, civil society would become a scene of bloodshed and disorder, every man revenging himself at his own hand whenever he fancied he was injured (TMS, VII. iv. 36).

Smith's ethical argument forms an integral part of his treatment of jurisprudence precisely because it is concerned to show how particular rules of behaviour emerge. In LJ the focus is narrower than in TMS, but it is still the spectator that is of critical importance, whether Smith is discussing accepted standards of punishment or of law. Attention has also been drawn to the role of the magistrate in this connection (Bagolini, 1975) and of the Legislator (Haakonssen, 1981).

Smith's emphasis in TMS is interesting. He chose to concentrate on the means by which the mind forms judgements as to what is fit and proper to be done or to be avoided, as distinct from trying to formulate specific rules of behaviour. He had recognized that while the *processes* of judgement might claim universal validity, *specific* judgements must be related to experience.

No one living in the age of Montesquieu could fail to be aware of variations in standards of accepted behaviour in different societies at the same point in time, and in the same societies over time. The point at issue seems to have been grasped by Edmund Burke in writing to Smith: 'A theory like yours founded on the Nature of man, which is always the same, will last, when those that are founded upon his opinions, which are always changing, will and must be forgotten' (Corr., letter 38, dated 10 September 1759).

But Smith did not deny that common elements could be found on the basis of experience. Although he did not complete his intended account of the 'general principles' involved (TMS, VII. iv. 37), Smith did provide an argument which related the discussion of private and public jurisprudence to four broad types of socio-economic *environment*, the stages of hunting, pasture, farming and commerce. The importance of the argument in the present context is that it was designed in part to explain the origin of government, thus solving a problem which was only noted in TMS. At the same time the historical dimension throws light on the causes of change in accepted rules of behaviour. As part of the same exercise, Smith supplied a successful account of the emergence of the stage of commerce, the stage with which he, as an economist, was primarily concerned.

THE HISTORY OF CIVIL SOCIETY

The first stage of society was represented as the 'lowest and rudest', such 'as we find it among the native tribes of North America' (WN, V. i. a. 2). In this case life is supported by gathering the fruits of the earth, by hunting and fishing. As a result, Smith suggested that such communities would be small and characterized by a high degree of personal liberty. He also noted that disputes between different members of the community would be limited in the absence of private property, and that 'there is seldom any established magistrate or any regular administration of justice' (WN, V. i. b. 2) in this situation.

The second stage, that of pasture, is represented as a 'more advanced state of society, such as we find it among the Tartars and Arabs' (WN, V. i. a. 3). Here the use of cattle is the dominant economic activity, indicating that communities would be larger in size and nomadic in character. But the key feature of the second stage was found in the emergence of a form of property which could be accumulated and transmitted from one generation to another. It is property which 'necessarily requires the establishment of civil government' (WN, V. i. b. 2). Elsewhere he noted that 'Civil government, so far as it is instituted for the security of property, is in reality instituted for the defence of the rich against the poor' (WN, V. i. b. 12). In another passage where Smith associated the emergence of government with the stage of pasture, he drew the attention of his auditors to the proposition that 'Laws and government may be considered in this and indeed in every case as a combination of the rich to oppress the poor' (LJ (A), iv. 22–3).

At the same time, Smith noted that the prevailing form of economic organization must lead to a high degree of dependence, since those who do not own the means of subsistence have no way of earning it save through personal service:

> The second period of society, that of shepherds, admits of very great inequalities of fortune, and there is no period in which the superiority of fortune gives so great an authority to those who possess it. There is no period accordingly in which authority and subordination are more perfectly established (WN, V. i. b. 7).

In effect, Smith used *contemporary* evidence regarding the Arabs, Tartars and North American Indians to illustrate the socio-economic stages through which the nations which overran the Western (Roman) Empire had probably passed. It is in this and in this sense only that the term 'conjectural history' accurately reflects Smith's purpose (Stewart, II. 48).

The German and Scythian nations had already attained what is in effect a higher form of the second stage, with some idea of agriculture and property in *land*. Smith argued that these nations would naturally use existing institutions in their new situation, and that their first act would be a division of the conquered territories (WN, III. ii. 1). In this way, Smith traced the movement from the second to the third stage, that of agriculture. Here property in land is the source of power and distinction, although the basic pattern of subordination remains the same.

But the feature on which Smith concentrated most attention was that of *political* instability: 'In those disorderly times, every great landlord was a sort of petty prince. His tenants were his subjects. He was their judge, and in some respects their legislator in peace, and their leader in war' (WN, III. ii. 3). The first historical response to this situation led to the emergence of the feudal system, which Smith represents as involving a complex of agreements for mutual service and protection. But even here: 'The authority of government still continued to be, as before, too weak in the head and too strong in the inferior members, and the excessive strength of the inferior members was the cause of the weakness of the head' (WN, III. iv. 9).

10

The second response was the most critical and is illustrated by the support given by monarchs to cities, partly as a means of enabling their inhabitants to protect themselves, but largely with a view to forming a new tactical alliance (WN, III. iii) which could offset the power of the aristocracy. Cities emerged as 'a sort of independent republicks' with important powers of self-government which brought 'along with them the liberty and security of individuals' (WN, III. iii. 8, 12).

The institution of the self-governing city was to satisfy a basic precondition of economic growth (as it had done in classical Greece), especially where it was supported by ease of access to the sea. Growth was based on foreign trade, and Smith proceeded to trace a general pattern which was based upon particular examples, such as Venice, Genoa and Pisa. This pattern initially involved the importation of foreign manufactures in exchange for limited surpluses in primary products, to be followed by the development of domestic manufactures based on foreign materials, and then by a process of refinement of those 'coarse and rude' products which were domestic in origin. Such developments, Smith continued, made it quite possible for the city to 'grow up to great wealth and splendor, while not only the country in its neighbourhood, but all those to which it traded, were in poverty and wretchedness' (WN, III. iii. 13).

But in the next part of the analysis, Smith outlined the way in which the pattern of economic growth based on the city would impinge on the agrarian sector. He argued that economies based upon manufacture and trade inevitably provided the great proprietors of land with a means of expending their surpluses, thus giving an incentive to maximize them (WN, III. iv. 10). This led to the gradual dismissal of retainers and to a proces of modification in the pattern of leaseholding; a process which witnessed a move away from the use of slave labour to the metayer system, and eventually to the appearance of farmers properly so called, 'who cultivated the land with their own stock, paying a rent certain to the landlord' (WN, III. ii. 14).

As a result of these two trends, the great proprietors slowly lost their authority, until a situation was reached where 'they became as insignificant as any substantial burgher or tradesman in a city' (WN, III. iv. 15). Smith was able to conclude:

> commerce and manufactures gradually introduced order and good government, and with them, the liberty and security of individuals, among the inhabitants of the country, who had before lived almost in a continual state of war with their neighbours, and of servile dependence upon their superiors. This, though it has been the least observed, is by far the most important of all their effects. Mr. Hume is the only writer who, so far as I know, has hitherto taken notice of it (WN, III. iv. 4).

The argument as a whole provides one of the most dramatic examples of Smith's doctrine of unintended social outcomes (WN, III. iv. 17). The *historical* analysis of the third book of WN is highly polished in part because Smith perceived that it could be presented as a model and in part because the argument had been rehearsed over many years. But the lectures add a further dimension. The treatment of 'public jurisprudence' sets out to provide a philosophical or scientific account of developments which began in Athens and end in modern Europe. But within this broad sweep, more and more attention is given to what was in effect a 'Historical View of the English Government' – significantly, the title of John Millar's major work, first published in 1786.

Attention was drawn to the nature of the English constitution and the claims to liberty, an argument which is conveniently summarized in LJ (A) (iv. 165 – v. 15). Smith drew on this analysis in WN when giving attention to the 'admirable' structure of the courts in England, and to the importance of a separation of powers:

> In order to make very individual feel himself perfectly secure in the possession of every right which belongs to him, it is not only necessary that the judicial should be separated from the executive power, but that it should be rendered as much as possible independent of that power (WN, V. i. b. 25).

In the same way, Smith drew attention to the need for, and dangers of, a standing army, while indicating that in England a solution close to the ideal had been found where: 'the military force is placed under the command of those who have the greatest interest in the support of the civil authority' (WN, V. i. a. 41).

Equally important was the gradual shift in the balance of power which had elevated the House of Commons to a superior degree of influence as 'an assembly of the representatives of the people who claim the sole right of imposing taxes' (WN, IV. vii. b. 51). This was the system which had been 'perfected by the revolution' (WN, IV. v. b. 43), and which could only be fully understood by reference to underlying economic trends. Yet Smith insisted that England alone had escaped from absolutism (LJ (A), iv. 168), a circumstance which he attributed to the fact that a solution had been found to the Scottish problem, to the natural fertility of the soil, and to Britain's position as an island. Smith added to this list the peculiarities of sovereigns, such as Elizabeth I, who, being childless, sold off crown lands and thus weakened the position of her successors (LJ (A), iv. 171). He also drew attention to the character of the Stuart kings, a family which 'were set aside for excellent reasons' at the time of the Revolution (LJ (B), 82).

But Smith was aware of the fact that England was not unique, that her institutions had been deliberately exported to the American colonies in a more republican form, thus short-circuiting the historical process and contributing to a rapid rate of economic development (WN, IV. vii. b. 51) in the West.

Expediency (*Economics*). As Smith moved to the last section of his course, his students would be well aware of the relevance of the materials just considered. His treatment of the stage of commerce makes it clear that the usual features of dependence and subordination would be found in this, as in all other, types of social organization. But here wealth only commands respect and thus deference (TMS, I. iii. 2.3), while dependence relates to the forces of the market rather than to individuals. In this context: 'Each tradesman or artificer derives his subsistence from the employment, not of one, but of a hundred or a thousand different customers. Though in some measure obliged to them all, he is not absolutely dependent upon any one of them' (WN, III. iv. 12). The stage of commerce is one where goods and services command a price, and where the 'great commerce of every civilised society, is that carried on between the inhabitants of the town and those of the country' (WN, III. i. 1).

Smith's students would also be aware that many of the psychological judgements which Smith deployed in TMS were peculiarly relevant to a situation where the institutional impediments to economic growth had been largely removed. It was in this context that he drew attention to the deception involved in the pursuit of wealth; a deception which 'rouses and keeps in continual motion the industry of mankind' (TMS, IV. 1. 10). In another notable passage, which draws upon the analogy of the Invisible Hand, Smith drew attention to the fact that the 'rich', in expending their surpluses, contribute 'to make nearly the same distribution of the necessaries of life, which would have been made, had the earth been divided into equal portions among all its inhabitants' (TMS, IV. 1. 10).

But perhaps the most striking passages are those in which the reader is reminded of the proposition that self-interested actions, including economic actions, have a 'social' reference. From whence, Smith enquired, 'arises that emulation which runs through all the different ranks of men, and what are the advantages which we propose by that great purpose of human life which we call bettering our condition?' He answered: 'To be observed, to be attended to, to be taken notice of with sympathy, complacency, and approbation' (TMS, I. iii. 2. 1). Smith went further in suggesting that a person 'appears mean-spirited' who does not pursue the 'more extraordinary and important objects of self-interest', contrasting the 'man of dull regularity' with the 'man of enterprise' (TMS, III. 6. 7).

Later in the argument Smith stated that men tend to approve of the *means* adopted to attain the *ends* of ambition. Hence 'that eminent esteem with which all men naturally regard a steady perseverance in the practice of frugality, industry and application, though directed to no other purpose than the acquisition of fortune'. In a further passage Smith was to argue that it 'is the consciousness of this merited approbation and esteem which is alone capable of supporting the agent in this tenour of conduct', since normally the 'pleasure which we are to enjoy ten years hence interests us so little in comparison with that which we may enjoy today' (TMS, IV. i. 2. 8).

ECONOMIC THEORY

Smith's writings on economics (apart from two fragments on the division of labour styled FA and FB in the Glasgow edition) are contained in the lecture notes for 1762/3 and 1763/4 together with the document first discovered by W.R. Scott and described by him as an '*Early Draft*' of WN (Scott, 1937). The first set of lectures is less complete than the second, and omits the discussion of Law's Bank, interest, exchange and the causes of the slow progress of opulence. On the other hand, those topics with *are* covered in LJ (A), and which correspond to sections 1–12 of Part 2 in Cannan's edition of LJ (B) are typically handled with much more elaboration. LJ (B) is not only more complete, at least in terms of coverage, but also more highly finished.

Each version of Smith's early analysis shows an interest in major themes, which are developed in an order which owes much to Hutcheson (Scott, 1900, ch. 11), most notably the discussion of the division of labour and its implications, and the treatment of price and allocation. Smith departs from Hutcheson, and discloses a debt to Hume, in developing a third topic; namely, the critique of the mercantile 'fallacy' (Stewart, IV. 24).

But the later work reveals a smooth, progressive, analytical development, as compared to LJ. In WN the treatment of the division of labour assumes its most elaborate form, while the theory of price features for the first time a clear distinction between factors of production (land, labour, capital) and categories of return (rent, wages, profit). These distinctions enabled Smith to give new meaning to his earlier grasp of the general interdependence of economic phenomena and to proceed to an account of a macroeconomic model which owed much to the teaching of Quesnay. Although some commentators have suggested that Smith's treatment of physiocratic teaching in WN (IV. ix) was slighting, the fact remains that his assessment of the contribution of the school accurately reflects its purpose and provides details of the more sophisticated model associated with 'revisionists' such as Turgot (Meek, 1962). There is no reason to doubt the truth of Dugald Stewart's assertion that 'the intimacy in which he lived with some of the leaders of that sect, could not fail to assist him in methodizing and digesting his speculations' (Stewart, III. 5). Stewart also noted that 'If he had not been prevented by Quesnay's death, Mr. Smith once had an intention (as he told me himself) to have inscribed to him his 'Wealth of Nations' (Stewart, III. 12). Stewart also recorded that the division between rent, wages and profit may have originally been suggested to Smith by his old friend James Oswald (Works, 1856, ix. 6).

Division of labour. Although Smith's model, in its post-physiocratic form, has several distinct elements, the feature on which he continued to place most emphasis was the *division of labour*. In terms of the content of the model outlined in the previous section, a division of labour is of course implied in the existence of distinct *sectors* or types of productive activity. But Smith also emphasized the fact that there was specialization by types of employment, and even within each employment. To illustrate the basic point, Smith chose the celebrated example of the pin, a very 'trifling manufacture' which none the less required some eighteen distinct processes for its completion.

Smith was at pains to point out that the division of labour (by rocess) helped to explain the relatively high productivity of labour in modern times – a phenomenon which he ascribed to the increase in 'dexterity' which inevitably results from making a single, relatively simple operation 'the sole employment of the labourer'; to the saving of time which would otherwise be lost 'in passing from one species of work to another'; and to the associated use of machines which 'facilitate and abridge labour, and enable one man to do the work of many' (WN, I. i. 6–8). Although Smith was later to claim that agriculture was the most productive area for investment, he pointed out that the scope for the division of labour was more limited in this field than in manufactures (WN, I. i. 4; see below, p. 28).

Four important points followed. First, Smith associated the division of labour with the process of *invention* (technical change);

> A great part of the machines made use of in those manufactures in which labour is most subdivided, were originally the inventions of common workmen, who, being each of them employed in some very simple operation, naturally turned their thoughts towards finding out easier and readier methods of performing it (WN, I. i. 8).

He also drew attention to the contribution of the 'makers of machines', and to the work of

> those who are called philosophers or men of speculation, whose trade it is, not to do any thing, but to observe every thing; and who, upon that account, are often capable of combining together the powers of the most distant and dissimilar objects. In the progress of society, philosophy or speculation becomes, like every other employment, the principal or sole trade and occupation of a particular class of citizens (WN, I. i. 9).

Secondly, Smith argued that the division of labour is limited only by the extent of the market (WN, I. iii), drawing attention in this context to the importance of the means of communications, such as good roads, and of access both to the sea and to navigable rivers. The latter point bears directly on Smith's historical analysis (see above, p. 9); the former was taken up in his treatment of public works (see below, pp. 31–3). The same argument was to be developed in terms of Smith's plea for freedom of trade (see below, pp. 29–30) and serves as a reminder that the division of labour would both contribute to, and be sustained by, the process of economic growth (which is analysed in WN, II). Thirdly, Smith contended that the institution of the division of labour helped to explain not only the enormous increase in the productivity of labour in modern times, but also an improvement in the level of material welfare of such an order that the accommodation of the 'frugal peasant' now 'exceeds that of many an African king, the absolute master of the lives and liberties of ten thousand naked savages' (WN, I. i. 11). Smith also observed that the consumer who purchases a single commodity acquires, in effect, the separate outputs of a 'great variety of labour' (WN, I. i. 11). 'The woollen coat, for example, which covers the day labourer, as coarse and rough as it may appear, is the produce of the joint labour of a great multitude of workmen' (WN, I. i. 11).

However, the aspect of this discussion which is most immediately relevant is the light it throws on the necessity of *exchange*. As Smith observed, once the division of labour is established, our own labour can supply us with only a very small part of our wants. He thus noted that even in the barter economy the individual can best satisfy the whole range of his needs by exchanging the surplus part of his own production, receiving in return the products of others. Where the division of labour is *thoroughly* established, it is then to be expected that each individual is in a sense dependent on his fellows, and that 'Every man thus lives by exchanging, or becomes in some measure a merchant' (WN, I. iv. 1).

Smith argued, indeed, that:

As it is by treaty, by barter, and by purchase, that we obtain from one another the greater part of those mutual good offices which we stand in need of, so it is this same trucking disposition which originally gives occasion to the division of labour (WN, I. ii. 3).

Value. These observations brought Smith directly to the problem of *value*, and it is noteworthy that in order to simplify the analysis he used the *analytical* (as distinct from the *historical*) device of the barter economy.

In dealing with the *rate* of exchange, Smith argued that 'the proportion between the quantities of labour necessary for acquiring different objects seems to be the only circumstance which can afford any rule for exchanging them for one another' (WN, I. vi. 1). Thus he suggested that if it takes twice the labour to kill a beaver than it does to kill a deer, then 'one beaver should naturally exchange for or be worth two deer'. This is one way of looking at the problem of exchange value, but Smith seems to have treated it, not as an end in itself, but as a means of elucidating those factors which govern the value of *the whole stock of goods* which the individual creates, and which it is proposed to use in exchange.

Looking at the problem in *this way*, Smith went on to argue that:

The value of any commodity ... to the person who possesses it, and who means not to use or consume it himself, but to exchange it for other commodities, is equal to the quantity of labour which it enables him to purchase or command. Labour, therefore, is the real measure of the exchangeable value of all commodities (WN, I. v. 1).

Smith's meaning becomes clear when he remarks that the exchangeable value of a *stock* of goods must always be in proportion to

the quantity ... of other men's labour, *or, what is the same thing, of the produce* of the other men's labour, which it enables him to purchase or command. The exchangeable value of everything must always be precisely equal to the extent of this power (WN, I. v. 3; italics supplied).

In other words, Smith is here arguing that the real value of the goods which the workman has to dispose of (in effect, his income) must be measured by the quantity of goods which he receives once the whole volume of (separate) exchanges has taken place.

Now, if, as Smith suggested, the *rate* of exchange between goods is always equal to the ratio of the labour *embodied* in them, then it follows that the labour embodied in the stock of goods used in exchange must be equal to the labour embodied in the goods received. The argument has two important features. First,

Smith suggests that in the barter economy, the labour which the individual expends, and which is embodied in the goods *he* creates, must exchange for, or command, an equal quantity. In short, labour embodied equals labour commanded. But it is also evident, in the modern economy, that labour is no longer the sole factor of production, and that in 'this state of things, the whole produce of labour does not always belong to the labourer' (WN, I. vi. 7). The equality between labour embodied and labour commanded appears to be relevant to the barter economy and to no other.

A clear difference between the barter and modern economies is to be found in the fact that, while in the former, goods are exchanged for goods, in the latter, goods are exchanged for a sum of money, which may then be expended in purchasing other goods. Under such circumstances, the individual, as Smith saw, tends to estimate the value of his receipts (received in return for undergoing the 'fatigues' of labour) in terms of money rather than in terms of the quantity of goods he can acquire by virtue of his expenditure. But Smith was at some pains to insist that the real measure of our ability to satisfy our wants is to be found in 'the money's worth' rather than the money, where the former is determined by the quantity of products (labour 'commanded') which either individuals or groups can purchase. Smith went on to distinguish between the nominal and the real value of income, pointing out that if the three original sources of revenue in modern times are wages, rent and profit, then the real *value* of each must ultimately be measured 'by the quantity of labour which they can, each of them, purchase or command' (WN, I. vi. 9).

The determinants of price. Smith's emphasis on exchange also focused attention on the issue of demand, which had already been elaborated in TMS, most notably in Part IV ('Of the beauty which the appearance of UTILITY bestows upon all the productions of Art'.) In LJ Smith contrasted the demand for commodities of immediate use, such as those related to subsistence and shelter, with a desire for refinement which was based on the 'delicacy' of body and the 'much greater delicacy' of mind (LJ (B), 208; cf. LJ (A), iv. 1–30). In this connection, he drew attention to man's 'taste of beauty, which consists chiefly in the three following particulars, proper variety, easy connection and simple order', before going on to note that 'These qualities, which are the ground of preference and which give occasion to pleasure and pain, are the cause of the many insignificant demands which we by no means stand in need of' (LJ (B), 209).

The argument is given further point by Smith's handling of the famous paradox; namely, that the 'things which have the greatest value in use (e.g. water) have frequently little or no value in exchange; and, on the contrary, those which have the greatest value in exchange (e.g diamonds) have frequently little or no value in use' (WN, I. iv. 13).

Smith's handling of the first part of the problem is based on his recognition that both goods are considered to be 'useful'. In the former case (water) a value is placed upon the good because it can be used in a practical way, while in the latter case (diamonds) the good appeals to our 'senses', an appeal which, as

Smith observed, constitutes a ground 'of preference', 'merit' or 'source of pleasure'. He concluded: 'The demand for the precious stones arises altogether from their beauty, they are of no use, but as ornaments' (WN, I. xi. c. 32).

At the same time, Smith appreciated that merit (value) is a function of scarcity: 'the merit of an object which is in any degree either useful or beautiful, is greatly enhanced by its scarcity' (WN, I. xi. c. 31). Even more specifically, he remarked: 'Cheapness is in fact the same thing with plenty. It is only on account of the plenty of water that it is so cheap as to be got for the lifting, and on account of the scarcity of diamonds (for their real use seems not yet to be discovered) that they are so dear' (LJ (B), 205–6). The argument can be extended to the problem of particular commodities in a way which is consistent with the negatively sloped demand curve, which his formal analysis of the determinants of price effectively employs.

On the supply side, Smith assumes the existence of given 'ordinary' or 'average' rates of wages, profit and rent; rates which may be said to prevail within any given society or neighbourhood, during any given (time) period (WN, I. vii. 1). The assumption is important for three reasons: first, it indicates that in dealing with the problem of price, Smith may be seen to have used the analytical device of a static system. Secondly, it should be noted that these rates determine the supply price of commodities and establish in effect the *position* of the (horizontal) supply curve. Thirdly, the argument suggests that the price of commodities may be established by 'adding up' the component parts of wages, profit and rent.

With these three points forming Smith's major premises, he proceeded to examine the determinants of price and may be seen to have produced a discussion which involves two distinct but related problems. First, he set out to illustrate those forces which determine the prices of particular commodities (Blaug, 1962, p. 42). Secondly, he appears to have used the analysis as a means of elucidating the phenomenon of *general interdependence* already hinted at in the *Lectures* (Hollander, 1973, p. 114).

In dealing with the first aspect of the problem, Smith examined the case of a commodity manufactured by a number of sellers, opening the analysis by confirming the distinction between 'natural' and 'market price' already established in LJ. *Natural price* is now defined as that amount which is 'neither more nor less than what is sufficient to pay the rent of the land, the wages of the labour, and the profits of the stock ... according to their natural rates' (WN, I. vii. 4). Where the natural price prevails, the seller is just able to cover his costs of production, including a margin for 'ordinary or average' profit. By contrasts, *market price* is defined as that price which may prevail at any given point in time, being regulated 'by the proportion between the quantity which is actually brought to market, and the demand of those who are willing to pay the natural price of the commodity' (the 'effectual demanders'; WN, I. vii. 8). The two 'prices' are interrelated, the essential point being that while, in the short run, market and natural price may diverge, in the long run they will tend to coincide. Natural price thus emerges as an *equilibrium* price, which will obtain when the commodity in question is sold at its cost of production. The latter point may be illustrated by examining the consequences of a divergence between the two prices. For example, if the quantity offered by the seller was less than that which the consumers were prepared to take at a particular (natural) price, the consequence would be a competition among consumers to procure some of a relatively limited stock. Under such circumstances, Smith argued that the 'market' will rise above the 'natural' price, the extent of the divergence being determined by the 'the greatness of the deficiency' and varying 'according as the acquisition of the commodity happens to be of more or less importance' to the buyer (WN, I. vii. 9). In making the latter point, Smith took note of the fact that where a relative shortage occurs of goods which are 'necessaries' of life, the extent of the divergence between the two prices (in effect the demand and supply prices) would be greater than that which would occur in other cases (for example, luxuries).

Under such circumstances, the price received by the seller must exceed the natural price (cost of production), with the result that rates of return accruing to factors in this employment (notably wages and profit) also rise above their 'ordinary' level. The consequence of such a divergence between the returns paid in a particular employment and the 'natural' rates prevailing must then be an inflow of resources to this relatively profitable field, leading to an expansion in the supply of the commodity, and a return to that position where it is sold at its natural price. Given a relative shortage of the commodity in the market, Smith concluded: 'The quantity brought thither will soon be sufficient to supply the effectual demand. All the different parts of its price will soon sink to their natural rate, and the whole price to its natural price' (WN, I. vii. 14). In short, the 'natural price' emerges as the equilibrium or 'central' price 'to which the prices of all commodities are continually gravitating' (WN, I vii. 15).

The first stage of the discussion establishes that in the case of any one commodity, equilibrium will be attained where the good is sold at its natural price, and where each of the (relevant) factors is paid for at its natural rate. It is evident that if this process, and this result, holds good for all commodities taken separately, it must also apply to all commodities 'taken complexly', at least where a competitive situation prevails. *Over the whole economy*, a position of equilibrium would be attained where each different type of good is sold at its natural price, and where each factor in each employment is paid at its natural rate. The economy can then be said to be in a position of 'balance', since where the above conditions are satisfied there can be no tendency to move resources within or between employments. Where a position of 'balance' is disturbed (for example, as a result of changes in tastes) it will naturally tend to be re-established as a result of (simultaneous) adjustments in the factor and commodity markets. Departure from, and reattainment of, a position of equilibrium depends upon the essentially self-interested actions and reactions of consumers *and* producers. Smith's treatment of price and allocation thus provides one of the best examples of his emphasis on 'interdependence' and a further example of his thesis of the Invisible Hand.

THE NATURAL RATES OF FACTOR PAYMENT

Smith's theory of price was built upon the assumption of given rates of factor payment. His next task was to elucidate the forces which determine the *level* of ('ordinary or average') rates of return during any given time period, or over time. He applied the simple 'demand and supply' type of analysis just considered, while taking pains to differentiate between different types of factor payment (WN, I. vi).

Wages constitute payment for the use of the factor labour. The payment is made by those classes who require the factor (undertakers, farmers) and accrues to those who effectively sell their labour power. The process of wage determination may then be viewed as a kind of bargain or contract (WN, I. viii. 11) where the balance of advantage generally lies with the 'masters'; the reason being that while contemporary legislation permitted their 'combinations', it prevented those of the workers. But Smith also pointed out that the bargaining strength of the two parties would itself be affected by demand and supply relationships, irrespective of legal privileges (WN, I. viii. 17).

Wage rates may be relatively high or low, depending on the available supply of labour and the size of the fund (or capital stock) available for its purchase. Smith did not in fact set out to define some upper limit for wages, but he did suggest that the lowest limit, in the long term, must be determined by the needs of *subsistence* (WN, I. viii. 15). The importance of the 'subsistence wage' lies in the fact that it constitutes the long-run supply price of labour, the argument being in effect that over time labour may be produced at constant cost, leading to the conclusion that the subsistence wage could be regarded as a kind of 'natural' or equilibrium rate. Smith made use of three cases to illustrate an argument which is analogous to the previous treatment of equilibrium price.

In a position of long-run equilibrium the demand for, and supply of, labour must be such that the workforce is in receipt of a subsistence wage. Under such circumstances, a position of equilibrium is established in the sense that there can be no tendency for population to increase or diminish, a condition which will obtain so long as there is no change in the size of the wages fund. This is Smith's example of the stationary state, as illustrated by the experience of China (WN, I. viii. 24). Secondly, Smith examined a case where there is a fall in the demand for labour either in any one year or continuously over a number of years. Under such circumstances the actual wage rate must fall below the subsistence rate, resulting in a fall in population until the level is such as to permit subsistence wages to be paid. This example represents Smith's 'declining' state, the cases cited being Bengal and certain East Indian colonies; areas where the decline in the wages fund had led to want, 'famine and mortality', until 'the number of inhabitants ... was reduced to what could easily be maintained by the revenue and stock which remained' (WN, I. viii. 26).

In the 'advancing state' an increase, or series of (annual) increases, in the size of the wages fund causes rates in excess of the subsistence level to be paid at least for as long as it takes to increase the level of population; an increase which would inevitably follow from the higher standard of living involved (WN, I. viii. 40). Smith also pointed out that the feature of the 'advancing state' would be a continuous improvement in the demand for labour, thus making it possible for high wage rates to be paid over a number of years, and at least for as long as the *rate* of increase in the demand for labour exceeded the rate of increase in supply. Smith considered the case of North America to be a good example of the trend, but also that many European countries, including Great Britain, showed the same tendency, albeit to a lesser degree (WN, I. viii. 22). All three cases illustrate the same basic principle; namely, that the demand for men, 'like that for any other commodity, necessarily regulates the production of men' (WN, I. viii. 40).

Profit was not considered by Smith to be the reward payable for undertaking the managerial function of 'inspection and direction' but rather as the compensation for the trouble taken, and the risks incurred, in combining the factors of production (WN, I. vi. 5). The profits which accrue to individual producers will be affected by the selling price of the commodity and its cost of production. Profits are thus likely to be particularly sensitive to changes in the direction of demand, together with the 'good or bad fortune' of rivals and customers; facts which make it difficult to speak of an 'ordinary or average' rate of return (WN, I. ix. 3). However, Smith did suggest that the rate of *interest* would provide a reasonably accurate index of profit levels at any one time and over time, basically on the ground that the rate payable for borrowed funds would reflect the profits to be gained from their use: 'It may be laid down as a maxim, that wherever a great deal can be made by the use of money, a great deal will commonly be given for the use of it; and that wherever little can be made by it, less will commonly be given for it' (WN, I. ix. 4).

At least as a broad generalization, Smith felt able to suggest that the rate of profit accruing at any one point in time (other things remaining equal, and with wage rates given) would be determined by the quantity of stock (capital) available, taken in conjunction with the volume of business to be transacted by it, or the extent of the outlets for profitable investment. It thus followed that over time the rate of profit will tend to fall, partly in consequence of the gradual increase of stock, and partly because of the increasing difficulty of finding 'a profitable method of employing any new capital'. The 'diminution of profit is the natural effect of ... prosperity' (WN, I. ix. 10), although, as Smith pointed out, in advancing states the tendency for profits to fall might be reversed or halted, due to the acquisition of new investment outlets or of new territories (WN, I. ix. 12).

The basic points are clear: in the long term the tendency is for profits (like wages) to fall. At any one point in time (say, a single year), the 'ordinary or average' rate of profit prevailing must be a function of the quantity of stock and the 'proportion of business' to which it can be applied. Smith made an important qualification to the latter point when he indicated that even where the quantity of stock remains the same (say, in two different time periods), other things remaining equal, the rate of profit will also be related to the prevailing wage rate. If labour is relatively abundant in relation to a given capital stock (that is, the wages fund), the rate of profit will be higher, and wage rates lower, than they would be where labour was relatively scarce.

In the following chapter Smith added a further important dimension to his treatment of wages and profits. The point follows directly from his recognition (following Hutcheson) of the fact that employments differ qualitatively. As Smith put it, 'certain circumstances in the employments themselves ... either really, or at least in the imaginations of men, make up for a small pecuniary gain in some, and counter-balance a great one in others' (WN, I. x. a. 2). He noted, for example, that wage rates would tend to vary between different types of employment according to the difficulty of learning the trade, the constancy of employment and the degree of trust involved. Similarly, he observed that both wages and profits would vary with differences in the agreeableness of the work, and with the probability of success in particular fields. He concluded that in a competitive environment, 'The whole of the advantages and disadvantages of the different employments of labour and stock must, in the same neighbourhood, be either perfectly equal or continually tending to equality' (WN, I. x. 1).

Rent is defined as the 'price paid for the use of land' (WN, I. xi. a. 1), a price paid because land is of itself productive, part of the property of individuals and (presumably) scarce. Smith argued that rent constitutes a pure surplus; the proprietors of land emerge as 'the only one of the three orders whose revenue costs them neither labour nor care, but comes to them, as it were, of its own accord' (WN, I. xi. p. 8). Moreover, Smith suggested that rent payments are somewhat akin to a 'monopoly price' at least in the broad sense that they are generally the highest which can be got in the 'actual circumstances of the land' (WN, I. xi. a. 1). Smith recognized that rent payments would vary with both the fertility and the situation of the land involved.

Smith generally took the view that land used for the production of human food would always yield a rent, and indeed computed that rent would be of the order of one-third of the gross produce. Moreover, he suggested that in the long term, rent payments would tend to increase, at least absolutely, due to the increased use of the available stock (of land) which the growth of population inevitably involves. 'The extension of improvement and cultivation tends to raise it directly. The landlord's share of the produce necessarily increases with the increase of the produce' (WN, I. xi. p. 2). He added that the real value of the landlord's receipts would also tend to increase over time, since all 'those improvements in the productive powers of labour, which tend directly to reduce the real price of manufactures, tend indirectly to raise the real rent of land' (WN, I. xi. p. 4).

Two aspects of Smith's argument are of particular importance in the present context. First, the analysis serves to suggest that at any point in time, or during any given annual period, rent payments will be a function of the proportion (of the fixed stock of land) used, where the latter is in turn a function of the level of population. Secondly, Smith's argument indicates that during any given annual period rent payments will be related not only to the fertility of the soil but also to the prevailing rates of wages and profit (WN, I. xi. a. 8).

A MACROECONOMIC MODEL

It is apparent that there is a 'static' element in Smith's treatment of distribution, linking it to the theory of price. There is also a dynamic element, in the sense that Smith was partly concerned with long-run trends in rates of return, treating factors as flows rather than stocks.

The first theme was to be continued in terms of Smith's treatment of period analysis in the physiocratic manner; the second is relevant in the context of the discussion of growth.

Period analysis. Smith's analysis of the 'circular flow' may be seen as a direct development of results already stated in connection with the theory of price. Costs of production are incurred by those who create commodities, thus providing individuals with the means of exchange. It follows that if the price of each good (in a position of equilibrium) comprehends payments made for rent, wages and profit, according to their natural rates, then 'it must be so with regard to all the commodities which compose the whole annual produce of the land and labour of every country, taken complexly' (WN, II. ii. 2). Smith concluded: 'The whole price or exchangeable value of that annual produce, must resolve itself into the same three parts, and be parcelled out among the different inhabitants' (ibid.). Smith thus established that there must be a relationship between aggregate output and aggregate income: 'The gross revenue of all the inhabitants of a great country, comprehends the whole annual produce of their land and labour' (WN, II. ii. 5).

The three major socio-economic groups have distinctive and particular roles. The properties of land are typically associated with habits of expense and conspicuous consumption, while wage labour as a group faces the problem of meeting more basic levels of need. It is the 'undertakers' who are normally linked with the 'principle which prompts to save' (WN, II. iii. 28) and with a willingness to invest in both fixed and circulating capital; categories which are reminiscent of physiocratic teaching.

Fixed capital is defined as that portion of savings used to purchase 'useful machines' or to improve, for example, the productive powers of land, the characteristic feature being that goods are created, and profits ultimately acquired, by using and *retaining* possession of the investment goods involved. *Circulating capital* is that portion of savings used to purchase investment goods other than 'fixed' implements, such as labour power or raw materials, the characteristic feature being that goods are produced through temporarily 'parting with' the funds so used. Smith also noted that different trades would use different proportions of fixed and circulating capital, and that no fixed capital 'can yield any revenue but by means of a circulating capital' (WN, II, i. 25).

The system which Smith described featured the production and use of both investment and consumption goods, but also a demand for *services* which do not *directly* contribute to the (annual) output of commodities (in physical terms) and which thus cannot be said to contribute to that level of income associated with it. Smith formally described such labour as 'unproductive', but did not deny that services of this kind were useful. He pointed out that the services of 'players, buffoons, opera singers, and musicians' have a certain *value* because they represent sources of satisfaction to those who pay for them. He also observed that the services provided by governments, such as justice and defence, which are paid for out of taxes, have a value, the reason being that society could not subsist without them. However, all such services are by definition unproductive:

> The sovereign ... with all the officers both of justice and war who serve under him, the whole army and navy, are unproductive labourers. They are the servants of the publick, and are maintained by a part of the annual produce of the industry of other people (WN, II. iii. 2).

Smith then proceeded to develop a model of the 'circular flow' which owed much to physiocratic analysis, while giving his account a distinctive style by dividing the stock of *society* into a number of components. These are, first, that part of total stock which is reserved for immediate consumption, and which is held by *all* consumers (undertakers, labour and proprietors). The characteristic feature of this part of the total stock is that it affords no revenue to its possessors since it consists in 'the stock of food, cloathes, household furniture, etc. which have been purchased by their proper consumers, but which are not yet entirely consumed' (WN, II. i. 12).

Secondly, there is that part of the total stock which may be described as 'fixed capital' and which will again be distributed between the various groups in society. This part of the stock, Smith suggested, is composed of the 'useful machines' purchased in preceding periods and held by the undertakers engaged in manufacture, and the quantity of useful buildings and of 'improved land' in the possession of the 'capitalist' farmers and the proprietors, together with the 'acquired and useful abilities' of all the inhabitants (WN, i. 13–17), that is, human capital.

Thirdly, there is that part of the total stock which may be described as 'circulating capital' and which again has several components. These include the quantity of money necessary to carry on the process of circulation (WN, II. iii. 23); the stock of provisions and other agricultural products which are available for sale during the current period, but which are still in the hands of either the farmers or merchants; the stock of raw materials and work in process, which is held by merchants, undertakers or those capitalists (i.e. undertakers) engaged in the agricultural sector (including mining etc.). Finally, there is the stock of manufactured goods (consumption and investment) created during a previous period, but which remain in the hand of undertakers and merchants at the beginning of the period examined (WN, II. i. 19–22).

The logic of the process can best be represented by distinguishing between the activities involved. Suppose, at the beginning of the time period in question, that the major capitalist groups possess the total net receipts earned from the sale of products in the previous period, and that the undertakers engaged in agriculture operate by transmitting the total rent due to the proprietors of land, for the use of that factor. The income thus provided enables the proprietors to make necessary purchases of consumption goods in the current period, thus contributing to reduce the stocks of such goods available for sale. The undertakers (capitalists) engaged in both sectors, together with the merchant groups, transmit to wage labour the content of the wages fund, thus providing this socio-economic class with an income which can be used in the current period. The undertakers (or entrepreneurs) engaged in agriculture and manufactures purchase consumption and investment goods from each other (through the medium of retail and wholesale merchants), thus generating a series of expenditures which *link* the two sectors. The process of circulation may be seen to be completed by the purchases made by individual undertakers *within* their own sectors. These purchases will include consumption and investment goods, thus contributing still further to reduce the stocks of commodities which formed part of the circulating capital of the society at the beginning of the period (i.e. year).

Given these points, the working of the system can be represented in terms of a series of *flows* whereby money (accruing in the form of rent, wages and profit) is exchanged for commodities. The consumption goods withdrawn from the existing stock may be entirely exhausted during the current period, used to *increase* the stock 'reserved for immediate consumption', or to replace more durable goods which had reached the end of their lives in the course of the same period. Similarly, undertakers may *add* to their stocks of raw materials and of fixed capital, or *replace* machines which had finally worn out in the current period, together with the materials which had been exhausted. Looked at in this way, the 'circular flow' may be seen to involve purchases which *withdraw* goods from the circulating capital of *society*, a process which is matched by a simultaneous process of *replacement* by virtue of current production of materials and other commodities.

Two additional matters should be noted before going further. In discussing the working of the 'flow', Smith had in effect introduced a treatment 'Of the Different Employment of Capital'. As he noted, in a passage reminiscent of Turgot's *Reflections* (sect. LXXXIII), capitals may be employed in agriculture, manufacture or in the wholesale and retail trades: 'Each of those four methods of employing a capital is essentially necessary either to the existence or extension of the other three, or to the general conveniency of the society' (WN, II. v. 3).

Secondly, he noted that profit levels in each area must be seen to be interrelated, with due allowance made for the advantages and disadvantages which attend the different employments of capital (WN, III. i. 3; cf. I. x. a). Smith also pointed out that profits in the different employments of stock would tend to equality as a result of the movement of resources between fields. In a passage which recalls the earlier treatment of allocation, Smith noted that 'The consideration of his own private profit, is the sole motive which determines the owner of any capital to employ it either in agriculture, in manufactures, or in some particular branch of the wholesale or retail trade' (WN, II. v. 37).

Dynamics. In choosing to examine the working of the economy during a given time period such as a year, Smith gave his model a broadly short-run character, albeit one which *includes* a time dimension. But he did not seek to formulate *equilibrium* conditions for the model as Quesnay had done in the *Analyse*, at least in the sense that he did not try to develop an argument which used specific assumptions of a quantitative kind. Smith's lack of concern with 'macro-static' *equilibrium* was to some extent announced by the fact that he made allowance for the problem of the different *rates* at which goods may be used up.

Nor did Smith suggest that the level of output attained during any given period would be exactly sufficient to replace the goods which had been exhausted during its course. On the contrary, he argued that levels of output attained in any time period could well *exceed* previous values. Smith's main concern was with the economic growth:

> The annual produce of the land and labour of any nation can be increased in its value by no other means, but by increasing either the number of its productive labourers, or the productive power of those labourers who had before been employed (WN, II. iii. 32).

Both sources of increased output required 'additional capital' devoted either to increasing the size of the wages fund or to the purchase of 'machines and instruments which facilitate and abridge labour' (ibid.). *Net savings* are the key to the process:

> Parsimony, by increasing the fund which is destined for the maintenance of productive hands, tends to increase the number of those hands whose labour adds to the value of the subject upon which it is bestowed. It tends therefore to increase the exchangeable value of the annual produce of the land and labour of the country. It puts into motion an additional quantity of industry, which gives an additional value to the annual produce (WN, II. iii. 17).

Net savings, where used for 'productive' purposes, are likely to generate an increase in the level of output and income in subsequent periods. Where there are opportunities for investment, the process of capital accumulation and economic growth can be seen to be self-generating, indicating that Smith's version of the 'flow' is to be regarded not as a 'circle' but as a spiral of constantly expanding dimensions. It was in this connection that Smith advanced a proposition that was to figure prominently in the formulation of the classical system later to be associated with J.B. Say and James Mill; namely, that what is 'annually saved is as regularly consumed as what is annually spent, and nearly in the same time too; but it is consumed by a different set of people' (WN, II. iii. 18). This echoes an earlier statement: 'A man must be perfectly crazy who, where there is tolerable security does not employ all the stock which he commands' (WN, II. i. 30).

The treatment of growth was further supported by reference to the division of labour, which suggested that technical change was endogenous and continuous (see above, *Division of Labour*, p. 15). While Smith in effect made the point that the economic process is likely to be subject to increasing returns, it is doubtful if he fully appreciated the rate of technical change currently taking place. But he also expressed interest in other elements which could affect the *rate* of growth, all of which relate to the argument so far.

Smith noted the importance of the level of resources needed to maintain a fixed capital (WN, II. ii. 7) and drew attention to the effect of commercial failure, which always tends 'to diminish the funds destined for the maintenance of productive labour' (WN, II. iii. 26). The size of the government sector was also important, since the 'whole, or almost the whole publick revenue, is in most countries employed in maintaining unproductive hands' (II. iii. 30).

In the same vein, he drew attention to the significance of 'the enormous debts which at present oppress, and will in the long run probably ruin, all the great nations of Europe' (WN, V. iii. 10). Smith noted that the debt in Britain had reached £130 million by 1775 and that some £124 million of the total was funded (WN, V. iii. 46). Quite apart from the associated problem of taxation, Smith was concerned to point out that the practice of funding in effect meant that 'a certain portion of the annual produce' was 'turned away from serving in the function of a capital, to serve in that of a revenue' (WN, V. iii, 47). The point was a variant on Smith's basic thesis that the rate of growth must be determined by the extent to which resources are used to support productive as distinct from unproductive labour (WN, II. iii. 3).

Smith further elaborated on the basic point at issue in contending that the rate of growth would be affected by the area of investment to which specific injections of capital were applied. He contended that the main fields of investment which were mentioned in the account of the 'flow' would support, directly or indirectly, different quantities of productive labour. The *retailer* replaces the stock of the merchant from whom he purchases goods, thus supporting a certain quantity of labour even though the retailer himself is the only productive labourer directly employed. The *wholesaler* replaces the capitals of the farmers and merchants with whom he deals and from 'whom he purchases the rude and manufactured produce which he deals in, and thereby enables them to continue their respective trades' (WN, II. v. 10). Both indirectly and directly the merchant supports a larger number of productive hands than the retailer. If the wholesale trade was preferred to the retail, *manufactures* emerge as still more important, since investment in this area would indirectly support a relatively large amount of productive labour by replacing the capitals of those who supply machinery and materials, while at the same time tending directly to employ a relatively significant number of people. But undoubtedly Smith's preference was for agriculture, a point already established in LJ: 'No equal capital puts into motion a greater quantity of productive labour than that of the farmer' – leading to the conclusion that 'Of all the ways in which a capital can be employed, it is by far the most advantageous to the society' (WN, II. v. 12).

Smith advanced two additional propositions which *seem* to follow from the argument just stated. First, he asserted that where the total stock available in insufficient for the purpose of agriculture, manufacture and trade, the rate of growth will be maximized by first concentrating on the former. He believed as a matter of fact that the rate of growth in Europe was lower than it might be and that 'agriculture ... is almost every where capable of absorbing a much greater capital than has ever yet been employed in it' (WN, II. v. 37). Secondly, he argued that there is a natural *sequence* of investment: 'According to the natural course of things ... the greater part of the capital of every growing society is, first, directed to agriculture, afterwards to manufactures, and last of all to foreign commerce' (WN, III. i. 8).

Smith's theory of accumulation is the dominant theme of the second book and helps to complete the logic of the earlier exposition by clarifying the source of long-run trends in factor payments. Smith's preoccupation with the long run also helps to explain the focus of WN, I. v., where he was chiefly concerned to establish a measure of value in the context of the discussion of economic welfare. The argument was intended to illustrate the point that the real value of income can only be measured in terms of the quantity of goods or the quantity of labour (labour *embodied*) which it enables the individual 'to purchase or command' (WN, I. v. 1). Smith also sought to provide a means of measuring the extent to which individuals were better (or worse) off over long periods of time, associating improvements in welfare with 'a reduction in the sacrifices required to obtain a slab of real income' (Blaug, 1962, p. 49).

Yet 'complete' as it is, there are a number of areas of 'tension' in the work, three of which may be mentioned here. Having advanced the thesis regarding the 'natural progress of opulence', Smith went on to assert that 'this natural order of things' has:

> in all the modern states of Europe, been, in many respects, entirely inverted. The foreign commerce of some of their cities has introduced all their finer manufactures ... and manufactures and foreign commerce, together, have given birth to the principal improvements of agriculture (WN, III. i. 9).

These passages preface the analysis of Book III, which traces the emergence of the stage of commerce and have the remarkable effect of presenting the historical *record* which had been featured in LJ as being in some sense *un*natural.

Similar difficulties surround Smith's ranking of areas of investment in Book II, a ranking which is employed in the analysis of the relationship with America in order to 'demonstrate' that the rate of growth would diverge from that of the mother country. The nature of the relationship with America, Smith contended, had the effect of confining the colonists to the development of primary products (WN, IV. vii. c. 51), while in contrast, the colonial trade of Great Britain had drawn capital from a near market (Europe) and diverted it to a distant market, while forcing a certain amount of capital from a direct to an indirect foreign trade – all with consequent effects on the rate of return, the employment of productive labour and therefore on the rate of economic growth.

Governor Pownall was the first to observe that Smith had not led *empirical* evidence in support of his case (1776, Corr., 369). In recognizing Smith's reliance on the different productivities of investment, Pownall also noted that 'propositions' which had been advanced in Book II were used 'in the second part of your work [Book IV] as data; whence you endeavour to prove, that the monopoly of the colony trade is a disadvantageous commercial institution' (Corr., 354). Smith acknowledged Pownall's perceptive analysis (letter 182, dated London, 1777) and later wrote to Andreas Holt (Corr., letter 208, dated October 1780) that he had met the Governor's objections in the second edition of WN. Far from so doing, Smith added a passage to the third edition of 1783, the year of peace with America, which suggests that it is unnecessary to 'say any thing further, in order to expose the folly of a system, which fatal experience has now sufficiently exposed' (WN, IV. viii. 15).

A third area of criticism is revealed in David Ricardo's *Principles of Political Economy and Taxation* (1817). Ricardo sought to generalize the labour *embodied* theory of value, which Smith had confined to the primitive state where labour is the only factor of production (WN, I. vi. 7), combining this with a clear statement of a theory of differential rent, which effectively removed the ambiguities in Smith's treatment. It is now well known that he also deployed these areas of analysis together with Smith's population mechanism in producing a formal account of the progression from the 'advancing' to the 'stationary' state, at which Smith had also hinted.

POLICY

Smith's analytical apparatus, allied to his judgement with respect to the probable trends of the economy, led him to advance the claims of economic liberty; claims which had already featured in LJ and which date back to his days in Edinburgh (Stewart, IV. 25). The argument is repeated in WN, where Smith called upon the sovereign to discharge himself from a duty:

> in the attempting to perform which he must always be exposed to innumerable delusions, and for the proper performance of which no human wisdom or knowledge could ever be sufficient; the duty of superintending the industry of private people, and of directing it towards the employments most suitable to the interests of the society (WN, IV. ix. 51).

The statement is familiar, yet conceals a point of great significance; namely, that while the institutions of the exchange economy are consistent with the emergence of personal freedom (for example, under the law), they are not of themselves sufficient to establish what Smith described as the 'system of natural liberty' (ibid.). In fact, one of the most important functions of government is that of *identifying* and *removing* impediments to the effective working of the economy. Smith drew attention, for example, to the adverse effects of the statute of apprenticeship, and of corporate privileges. Regulations of this kind were criticized on the ground that they were both impolitic and unjust: unjust in that controls over qualification for entry to a trade were a violation 'of this most sacred property which every man has in his own labour' (WN, I. x. c. 12) and impolitic in that such regulations are not of themselves sufficient to guarantee competence. But Smith particularly emphasized that the regulations in question would adversely affect the working of the market mechanism. The 'statute of apprenticeship obstructs the free circulation of labour from one employment to another, even in the same place. The exclusive privileges of corporations obstruct it from one place to another, even in the same employment' (WN, I. x. c. 42). He also commented on the problems presented by the Poor Laws and the Laws of Settlement (WN, IV. ii. 42), which further restricted the free movement of labour from one geographical location to another.

Smith objected to positions of privilege, such as monopoly power, which he regarded as creations of the civil law. The institution was again represented as impolitic and unjust: unjust in that a monopoly position is one of privilege and advantage, and therefore 'contrary to that justice and equality of treatment which the sovereign owes to all the different orders of his subjects'; impolitic in that the prices at which goods so controlled are sold are 'upon every occasion the highest that can be got' (WN, I. vii. 27). He added that monopoly is 'a great enemy to good management' (WN, I. xi. b. 5) and that the institution had the additional defect of restricting the flow of capital to the trades affected as a result of the legal barriers to entry which were involved.

It is useful to distinguish Smith's objection to monopoly from his criticism of one expression of it; namely, the mercantile system of regulation which he described as the 'modern system' of policy, best understood 'in our own country and in our own times' (WN, IV. 2). Smith asserted that mercantile policy aimed to secure a positive balance of trade through the control of exports and imports, a policy whose 'logic' was best expressed in terms of the Regulating Acts of Trade and Navigation, which currently determined the pattern of trade between Great Britain and her colonies and which were designed to create in effect a self-sufficient Atlantic Economic Community.

Smith objected to current policies of the type described on the ground that they artificially restricted the market and thus damaged opportunities for economic growth. It was Smith's contention that such policies were liable to that general objection which may be made to all the different expedients of the mercantile system, 'the objection of forcing some part of the industry of the country into a channel less advantageous than that in which it would run of its own accord' (WN, IV. v. a. 24). In WN Smith placed more emphasis on interference with the allocative mechanism than he had done in LJ, where greater attention had been given to the inconsistency which was involved in seeking a positive balance of trade, an argument which relied heavily on Hume's analysis of the Specie Flow.

While it is difficult to judge the extent to which the claim for economic liberty explains the contemporary reception of WN, it may have been a major factor, at least in Britain (Schumpeter, 1954, p. 185). There can be no doubt that later generations found Smith's argument (and rhetoric) attractive. The celebrations to mark the fiftieth anniversary of the book showed a wide and continuing acceptance of the doctrines of free trade. In 1876, at a dinner held by the Political Economy Club to mark the centenary of WN, one speaker identified free trade as the most important consequence of the work done by 'this simple Glasgow professor', and predicted that 'there will be what may be called a large negative development of Political Economy tending to produce an important beneficial effect; and that is, such a development of Political Economy as will reduce the functions of government within a smaller and smaller compass' (Black, 1976, p. 51).

This view still commands wide contemporary support.

There can be no argument with Jacob Viner's contention that 'Smith in general believed that there was, to say the least, a strong presumption against government activity' (Viner, 1928, p. 140). But as Viner also reminded his auditors during the course of the Chicago conference which celebrated the 150th anniversary of the publication of WN, 'Adam Smith was not a doctrinaire advocate of laissez-faire. He saw a wide and elastic range of activity for government' (pp. 153–4). A number of examples, all identified by Viner in a classic article, may briefly be reviewed here.

First, Smith was prepared to justify specific policies to meet particular needs as these arose; the principle of intervention *ad hoc*. He defended the use of stamps on plate and linen as the most effectual guarantee of quality (WN, I. x. c. 13), the compulsory regulation of mortgages (WN, V. ii. h. 17), the legal enforcement of contracts (WN, I. ix. 16) and government control of the coinage. In addition, he supported the granting of temporary monopolies to mercantile groups, to the inventors of new machines and, not surprisingly, to the authors of new books (WN, V. i. e. 30). He further advised governments that where they were faced with taxes imposed by their competitors, retaliation could be in order, especially if such action had the effect of ensuring the 'repeal of the high duties or prohibitions complained of. The recovery of a great foreign market will generally more than compensate the transitory inconveniency of paying dearer during a short time for some sorts of goods' (WN, IV. ii. 39).

Secondly, Smith advocated the use of taxation, not as a means of raising revenue but as a source of social reform, and as a means of compensating for what would now be described as a defective telescopic faculty. In the name of the *public* interest, Smith supported taxes on the retail sale of liquor in order to discourage the multiplication of alehouses (WN, V. ii. g. 4) and differential rates on ale and spirits in order to reduce the sale of the latter (WN, V. ii. k. 50). He advocated taxes on those proprietors of land who demanded rents in kind, and on those leases which prescribed a certain form of cultivation. In the same way, Smith argued that the practice of selling a future, for the sake of present, revenue should be discouraged on the ground that it reduced the working capital of the tenant and at the same time transferred a capital sum to those who would use it for the purposes of consumption (WN, V. ii. c. 12) rather than investment which would directly support productive labour.

Smith was well aware, to take a third example, that the modern version of the 'circular flow' depended on paper money and on credit; in effect, a system of 'dual circulation' involving a complex of transactions linking producers and merchants, and dealers and consumers (WN, II. ii. 88). It is in this context that he advocated control over the rate of interest, to be set in such a way as to ensure that 'sober people are universally preferred, as borrowers, to prodigals and projectors' (WN, II. iv. 15). He was also willing to regulate the small note issue in the interests of a stable banking system. To those who objected to such a proposal Smith replied that the interests of the community required it, and concluded that 'the obligation of building party walls, in order to prevent the communication of fire, is a violation of natural liberty, exactly of the same kind [as] as the regulations of the banking trade which are here proposed' (WN, II. ii. 94). Although Smith's monetary analysis is not regarded as amongst the strongest of his contributions, it should be remembered that as a witness of the collapse of the Ayr Bank, he was acutely aware of the problems generated by a sophisticated credit structure, and that it was in this context that he articulated a very general principle; namely, that 'those exertions of the natural liberty of a few individuals, which might endanger the security of the whole society, are, and ought to be, restrained by the laws of all governments; of the most free, as well as of the most despotical' (WN, II. ii. 94).

Fourthly, emphasis should be given to Smith's contention that a major responsibility of government must be the provision of certain public works and institutions for facilitating the commerce of the society which were 'of such a nature, that the profit could never repay the expense to any individual or small number of individuals, and which it, therefore, cannot be expected that any individual or small number of individuals should erect or maintain' (WN, V. i. c. 1). The examples of public works which he provided include roads, bridges, canals and harbours – all thoroughly in keeping with the conditions of the time and with Smith's emphasis on the importance of transport as a contribution to the effective operation of the market and to the process of economic growth. But although the list is short by modern standards, the discussion is of interest for two main reasons. First, Smith contended that public works or services should only be provided where market forces have failed to do so; secondly, he insisted that attention should be given to the requirements of efficiency and equity.

As Nathan Rosenberg (1960) has pointed out in an important article, Smith did not argue that governments should *directly* provide relevant services; rather, they should establish institutional arrangements so structured as to engage the motives and interests of those concerned. Smith tirelessly emphasized the point that in every trade and profession 'the exertion of the greater part of those who exercise it, is always in proportion to the necessity they are under of making that exertion' (WN, V. i. f. 4); teachers, judges, professors, civil servants and administrators alike.

With regard to equity, Smith argued that public works such as highways, bridges and canals should be paid for by those who use them and in proportion to the wear and tear occasioned – an expression of the general principle that the beneficiary should pay. He also defended direct payment on the ground of efficiency since only by this means would it be possible to ensure that necessary services would be provided where there was an identifiable need (WN, V. i. d. 6).

Yet Smith recognized that it would not always be possible to fund or to maintain public services without recourse to general taxation. In this case he argued that 'local or provincial expenses of which the benefit is local or provincial' ought to be no burden on general taxation since 'It is unjust that the whole society should contribute towards an expense of which the benefit is confined to a part of society' (WN, V. i. i. 3). However, he did agree that a general contribution would be appropriate in cases where public works benefit the whole society and cannot be maintained by the contribution 'of such particular members of the society as are most immediately benefited by them' (WN, V. i. i. 6).

But here again, the main features of the system of liberty are relevant in that they affect the way in which taxation should be imposed. Smith pointed out on welfare grounds that taxes should be levied in accordance with the canons of equality, certainty, convenience and economy (WN, V. ii. b), and insisted that they should not be raised in ways which infringed the liberty of the subject – for example, through the odious visits and examinations of the tax-gatherer. Similarly, he argued that taxes ought not to interfere with the allocative mechanism (as, for example, taxes on necessities or particular employments) or constitute important disincentives to the individual effort on which the effective operation of the whole system depended (for example, taxes on profits or on the produce of land).

ETHICS AND HISTORY

The policy views which have just been considered are closely related to Smith's economic analysis. Others are only to be fully appreciated when seen against the background of his work on ethics and jurisprudence.

It will be recalled that for Smith moral judgement depends on a capacity for acts of imaginative sympathy, and that such acts can only take place within the context of some social group (TMS, III. i. 3). However, Smith also observed that the mechanism of the impartial spectator might well break down in the context of the modern economy, due in part to the size of the manufacturing units and of the cities which housed them.

Smith observed that in the actual circumstances of modern society, the poor man could find himself in a situation where the 'mirror' of society (TMS, III. i. 3) was ineffective. The 'man of rank and fortune is by his station the distinguished member of a great society, who attend to every part of his conduct, and who thereby oblige him to attend to every part of it himself'. But the 'man of low condition', while 'his conduct may be attended to' so long as he is a member of a country village, 'as soon as he comes into a great city, he is sunk in obscurity and darkness. His conduct is observed and attended to by nobody, and he is therefore very likely to neglect it himself, and to abandon himself to every sort of low profligacy and vice' (WN, V. i. g. 12).

In the modern context, Smith suggests that the individual thus placed would naturally seek some kind of compensation, often finding it not merely in religion but in religious *sects*; that is, small social groups within which he can acqure 'a degree of consideration which he never had before' (WN, V. i. g. 12). Smith noted that the morals of such sects were often disagreeably 'rigorous and unsocial', recommending two policies to offset this.

The first of these is learning, on the ground that science is 'the great antidote to the poison of enthusiasm and superstition'. Smith suggested that government should institute 'some sort of probation, even in the higher and more difficult sciences, to be undergone by every person before he was permitted to exercise any liberal profession, or before he could be received as a candidate for any honourable office of trust or profit' (WN, V. i. g. 14). The second remedy was through the encouragement given to those who might expose or dissipate the folly of sectarian bitterness by encouraging an interest in painting, music, dancing, drame – and satire (WN, V. i. g. 15).

If the problems of solitude and isolation consequent on the growth of cities explain Smith's first group of points, a related trend in the shape of the division of labour helps to account for the second. In the earlier part of the argument, Smith had emphasized the gain to society at large which arose from improved productivity. But he noted later that this important source of economic benefit could also involve social costs:

> In the progress of the division of labour, the employment of the far greater part of those who live by labour, that is, of the great body of the people, comes to be confined to a few very simple operations; frequently to one or two. But the understandings of the greater part of men are necessarily formed by their ordinary employments. The man whose life is spent in performing a few simple operations, of which the effects too are, perhaps, always the same, or very nearly the same, has no occasion to exert his understanding, or to exercise his invention in finding out expedients for removing difficulties which never occur (WN, V. i. f. 50).

Smith went on to point out that despite a dramatic increase in the level of *real income*, the modern worker could be relatively worse off than the poor savage, since in such primitive societies the varied occupations of all men – economic, political and military – preserve their minds from that 'drowsy stupidity, which, in a civilized society, seems to benumb the understanding of almost all the inferior ranks of people' (WN, V. i. f. 51). It is the fact that the 'labouring poor, that is the great body of the people' will fall into the state outlined that makes it necessary for government to intervene.

Smith's justification for intervention is, as before, market failure, in that the labouring poor, unlike those of rank and fortune, lack the leisure, means or (by virtue of their occupation) the inclination to provide education for their children (WN, V. i. f. 53). In view of the nature of the problem, Smith's programme seems rather limited, based as it is on the premise that 'the common people cannot, in any civilized society, be so well instructed as people of some rank and fortune' (WN, V. i. f. 54). However, he did argue that they could all be taught 'the most essential parts of education ... to read, write, and account' together with the 'elementary parts of geometry and mechanicks' (WN, V. i. f. 54, 55). Smith added:

The publick can *impose* upon almost the whole body of the people the necessity of acquiring those most essential parts of education, by obliging every man to undergo an examination or probation in them before he can obtain the freedom in any corporation, or be allowed to set up any trade either in a village or town corporate (WN, V. i. f. 57; italics supplied).

Distinct from the above, although connected with it, is Smith's concern with the decline of martial spirit, which is the consequence of the nature of the fourth, or commercial, stage. He concluded that:

Even though the martial spirit of the people were of no use towards the defence of the society, yet to prevent that sort of mental mutilation, deformity and wretchedness, which cowardice necessarily involves in it, from spreading themselves through the great body of the people would still deserve the most serious attention of government (WN, V. i. f. 60).

Smith went on to liken the control of cowardice to the prevention of 'a leprosy or any other loathsome and offensive disease' – thus moving Jacob Viner to add public health to Smith's already lengthy list of governmental functions (Viner, 1928, p. 150). Such concerns have enabled Winch (1978) to find in Smith evidence of the *language* of an older, classical, concern with the problem of citizenship. Others (e.g. see contributions in Hont and Ignatieff, 1983) have located Smith more firmly in the tradition of civic humanism.

The historical dimension of Smith's work also affects the treatment of policy, noting as he did that in every society subject to a process of transition, 'Laws frequently continue in force long after the circumstances, which first gave occasion to them, and which could also render them reasonable, are no more' (WN, III. ii. 4). In such cases Smith suggested that arrangements which were once appropriate but are now no longer so should be removed, citing as examples the laws of succession and entail; laws which had been appropriate in the feudal period but which now had the effect of limiting the sale and improvement of land. The continuous scrutiny of the *relevance* of particular laws is an important function of the 'legislator' (Haakonssen, 1981).

In a similar way, the treatment of justice and defence, both central services to be organized by the government, are clearly related to the discussion of the stages of history, an important part of the argument in the latter case being that a gradual change in the economic and social structure had necessitated the formal provision of an army (WN, V. i. a, b).

But perhaps the most striking and interesting features emerge when it is recalled that for Smith the fourth economic stage could be seen to be associated with a particular form of social and political structure which determines the *outline of government* and the context within which it must function. It may be recalled in this connection that Smith associated the fourth economic stage with the elimination of the relation of direct dependence which had been a characteristic of the feudal agrarian period. Politically, the significant and associated development appeared to be the diffusion of power consequent on the emergence of new forms of wealth which, *at least in the peculiar circumstances of England,* had been reflected in the increased significance of the House of Commons.

Smith recognized that in this context government was a complex instrument, that the pursuit of office was itself a 'dazzling object of ambition' – a competitive game with its object the attainment of 'the great prizes which sometimes come from the wheel of the great state lottery of British politicks' (WN, IV. vii. c. 75).

Yet for Smith the most important point was that the same economic forces which had served to elevate the House of Commons to a superior degree of influence had also served to make it an important focal point for sectional interests – a development which could seriously affect the legislation which was passed and thus affect that extensive view of the common good which ought ideally to direct the activities of Parliament.

It is recognized in the *Wealth of Nations* that the landed, moneyed, manufacturing and mercantile groups all constitute special interests which could impinge on the working of government. Smith referred frequently to their 'clamourous importunity', and went so far as to suggest that the power possessed by employers generally could seriously disadvantage other classes in the society (WN, I. x. c. 61; cf. I. viii. 12, 13).

Smith insisted that any legislative proposals emanating from this class:

ought always to be listened to with great precaution, and ought never to be adopted till after having been long and carefully examined, not only with the most scrupulous, but with the most suspicious attention. It comes from an order of men, whose interest is never exactly the same with that of the publick, who have generally an interest to deceive and even to oppress the publick, and who accordingly have, upon many occasions, both deceived and oppressed it (WN, I. xi. p. 10).

He was also aware of the dangers of manipulation arising from deployment of the civil list (LJ, (A), iv. 175–6).

It is equally interesting to note how often Smith referred to the constraints presented by the 'confirmed habits and prejudices' of the people, and to the necessity of adjusting legislation to what 'the interests prejudices, and temper of the times would admit of' (WN, IV. v. b. 40, 53, and V. i. g. 8; cf. TMS, VI. ii. 2. 16). Such passages add further meaning to the discussion of education. An educated people, Smith argued, would be more likely to see through the interested complaints of faction and sedition. He added a warning and a promise in remarking that:

In free countries, where the safety of government depends very much on the favourable judgment which the people may form of its conduct, it must surely be of the highest importance that they should not be disposed to judge rashly or capriciously concerning it (WN, V. i. f. 61).

THE LITERATURE OF SCIENCE

In contrast to the modern reader, students of Smith's course in Glasgow would more readily perceive that the different parts into which it fell were important of themselves, and also that they display a certain pattern of interdependence. The ethical argument clearly indicates the manner in which general rules of conduct, including those of *justice*, emerge and postulates the need for some system of government or magistracy. The treatment of jurisprudence shows the manner in which government emerged and developed through time, while throwing some light on the actual content of the rules of behaviour which were manifested in different societies.

It would also be evident to Smith's students that the treatment of economics was based upon psychological judgements (such as the desire for status) which are only explained in the ethics, and that this branch of Smith's argument takes as given that particular socio-economic structure which is appropriate to the fourth economic stage, that of commerce. This kind of perspective can only be attained by examining the logical progression of ideas as outlined in the lectures on ethics, jurisprudence and economics as they unfolded in the order in which they are now known to have been delivered. Equally, the treatment of public policy in WN is transformed in its meaning when seen not merely as a development of the earlier treatment of economics but also in terms of the appropriate ethical and jurisprudential setting.

But it should also be recalled that each separate component of the system represents scientific work in the style of Newton, contributing to a greater whole which was conceived in the same image. Smith's scientific aspirations were real, as was his consciousness of the methodological tensions which may arise in the course of such work. Such facts make it appropriate to conclude this account by reference to Smith's awareness, and treatment, of the literature of science.

Smith's interest in mathematics dates from his time as a student in Glasgow (Stewart, I. 7). He also appears to have maintained a general interest in the natural and biological sciences, facts which are attested by his purchases for the University Library (Scott, 1937. p. 182) and for his own collection (Mizuta, 1967). Smith's 'Letter to the Authors of the *Edinburgh Review*' (1756), where he warned against any undue preoccupation with Scottish literature, affords evidence of wide reading in the physical sciences, and also contains references to contemporary work in the French *Encyclopédie* as well as to the productions of Buffon, Daubenton and Reaumur. D.D. Raphael has argued that the Letter owes much to Hume (TMS, 10, 11; cf. Bryce, EPS, 248, n. 13).

The essay on astronomy, which dates from the same period (it is known to have been written before 1758), indicates that Smith was familiar with classical as well as with more modern sources, such as Galileo, Kepler and Tycho Brahe, a salutary reminder that an 18th-century philosopher could work close to the frontiers of knowledge in a number of fields.

But Smith was also interested in science as a form of communication, arguing in the LRBL that the way in which this type of discourse is organized should reflect its purpose as well as a judgement as to the psychological characteristics of the audience to be addressed.

In a lecture delivered on 24 January 1763 Smith noted that didactic or scientific writing could have one of two aims: either to 'lay down a proposition and prove this, by the different arguments that lead to that conclusion' or to deliver a system in any science. In the latter case Smith advocated what he called the Newtonian method, whereby we 'lay down certain principles known or proved in the beginning, from whence we account for the several phenomena, connecting all together by the same Chain' (LRBL, ii. 133). Two points are to be noted. First, Smith makes it clear that Descartes rather than Newton was the first to use this method of *exposition*, even although the former was now perceived to be the author of 'one of the most entertaining Romances that have ever been wrote' (LRBL, ii. 134; cf. Letter 5). Secondly, his reference to the pleasure to be derived from the 'Newtonian method' (LRBL, ii. 134) draws attention to the problem of scientific *motivation*, a theme which was to be developed in the 'Astronomy', where Smith considered those principles 'which lead and direct philosophical enquiry'.

The 'Astronomy' takes as given certain results which had already been established in the lectures on language and in the *Considerations*; namely, that men have a capacity for acts of 'arrangement or classing, of comparison, and of abstraction' (LRBL, ii. 207; cf. Corr., letter 69, dated 7 February 1763).

But the essay on astronomy approaches the matter in hand in a different way by arguing that a mind thus equipped derives a certain pleasure from the contemplation of relation, similarity or order – or as Hume would have put it, from a certain association of ideas. Smith struck a more original note in arguing that when the mind confronts a new phenomenon which does not fit into an already established classification, or where we confront an unexpected association of ideas, we feel the sentiment of surprise, and then that of wonder (Astronomy, II. 9). This is typically followed by an attempt at explanation with a view to returning the 'imagination' to a state of tranquillity (Astronomy, II. 6).

Looked at in this way, the task of explanation is related to a perceived need, which can only be met if the account offered is coherent and conducted in terms which are capable of accounting for observed appearances in terms of 'familiar' principles. It was Smith's contention that the philosopher or scientist would react in the same way as the casual observer, and that nature as a whole 'seems to abound with events which appear solitary and incoherent', thus disturbing 'the easy movement of the imagination' (Astronomy, II. 12). But he also observed that philosophers pursue scientific study 'for its own sake, as an original pleasure or good in itself' (Astronomy, III. 3).

The bulk of the essay is concerned to illustrate the extent to which the four great systems of thought which he identified were actually able to 'soothe the imagination', these being the systems of Concentric and Eccentric Spheres, together with the theories of Copernicus and Newton. But Smith added a further dimension to the argument by seeking to expose the dynamics of the process; arguing that each thought-system was subject to a process of modification as new observations were made. Smith suggested that each system was subjected to a process of development which eventually resulted in unacceptable degrees of complexity, thus paving the way for the generation of an alternative explanation of the same phenomena, but one which was better suited to meet the needs of the imagination by offering a simpler account (Astronomy, IV. 18, 28). In Smith's eyes, the work of Sir Isaac Newton thus marked the apparent culmination of a long historical process (Astronomy, IV. 76).

The argument as a whole also contains some radical conclusions. There is nothing in the analysis which suggests that the Netownian (or Smithian) system embodies some final truth. At the same time, Smith seems to have given emphasis to what is now known as the problem of 'subjectivity' in science in arguing that scientific thought often represents a reaction to a perceived psychological need. He also likened the pleasure to be derived from great productions of the scientific intellect to that acquired when listening to a 'well composed concerto of instrumental music' (Imitative Arts, II. 30). Elsewhere he referred to a propensity, natural to all men, 'to account for all appearances from as few principles as possible' (TMS, VII. ii. 2. 14) and commented further on the ease with which the 'learned give up the evidence of their senses to preserve the coherence of the ideas of their imagination' (Astronomy, IV. 35). Smith also emphasized the role of the prejudices of sense and education in discussing the reception of new ideas (Astronomy, IV. 35).

He drew attention to the importance of analogy in suggesting that philosophers often attempt to explain the unusual by reference to knowledge gained in unrelated fields, noting that in some cases the analogy chosen could become not just a source of 'ingenious similitude' but 'the great hinge upon which everything turned' (Astronomy, II. 12).

Smith made extensive use of mechanistic analogies, derived from Newton, seeing in the universe 'a great machine' wherein we may observe 'means adjusted with the nicest artifice to the ends which they are intended to produce' (TMS, II. ii. 3. 5). In the same way he noted that 'Human society, when we contemplate it in a certain abstract and philosophical light, appears like a great, an immense machine' (TMS, VII. ii. 1. 2), a position which leads quite naturally to a distinction between efficient and final causes (TMS, II. ii. 3. 5), which is not inconsistent with the form of Deism associated with Newton himself. It is also striking that so systematic a thinker as Smith should have extended the mechanistic analogy to systems of thought:

Systems in many respects resemble machines. A machine is a little system, created to perform, as well as to connect together, in reality, those different movements and effects which the artist has occasion for. A system is an imaginary machine invented to connect together in the fancy those different movements and effects which are already in reality performed (Astronomy, IV. 19).

Each part of Smith's contribution is in effect an 'imaginary' machine which conforms closely to his own stated rules for the organization of scientific discourse. All disclose Smith's perception of the 'beauty of a systematical arrangement of different observations connected by a few common principles' (WN, V. i. f. 25). The whole reveals much as to Smith's drives as a thinker, and throws an important light on his own marked (subjective) preference for system, coherence and order.

SELECTED WORKS

Editions and Abbreviations. An excellent edition of the *Lectures on Jurisprudence* was brought out by Edwin Cannan in 1896. Cannan also prepared a valuable edition of the *Wealth of Nations* in 1904. J.M. Lothian edited the *Lectures on Rhetoric* in 1963.

Subsequent references are to the Glasgow edition of the *Works and Correspondence of Adam Smith* (Oxford: Clarendon Press, 1976–83) and follow the usages of that edition. The edition consists of:

I   *The Theory of Moral Sentiments* (TMS). Ed. by D.D. Raphael and A.L. Macfie (1976).

II   *An Inquiry into the Nature and Causes of the Wealth of Nations* (WN). Ed. R.H. Campbell, A.S. Skinner and W.B. Todd (1976).

III   *Essays on Philosophical Subjects* (EPS). Ed. D.D. Raphael and A.S. Skinner (1980). This volume includes;

- (i)   'The History of the Ancient Logics and Metaphysics' (Ancient Logics)
- (ii)   'The History of the Ancient Physics' (Ancient Physics)
- (iii)   'The History of Astronomy' (Astronomy)
- (iv)   'Of the Affinity between Certain English and Italian Verses' (English and Italian Verses)
- (v)   'Of the External Senses' (External Senses)
- (vi)   'Of the Nature of the Imitation which takes place in what are called the Imitative Arts' (Imitative Arts)
- (vii)   'Of the Affinity between Music, Dancing and Poetry'.

Items (i) to (vii), above, were prepared by W.P.D. Wightman.

- (viii)   'Of the Affinity between Certain English and Italian Verses'
- (ix)   Contributions to the *Edinburgh Review* (1755–6):
  - (a)   Review of Johnson's Dictionary
  - (b)   A Letter to the Authors of the *Edinburgh Review* (Letter).
- (x)   Preface to William Hamilton's *Poems on General Occasions*.

Items (viii) to (x), above, were prepared by J.C. Bryce.

- (xi)   Dugald Stewart, 'Account of the Life and Writings of Adam Smith LL.D.' (Stewart)

Edited by I.S. Ross.

IV   *Lectures on Rhetoric and Belles Lettres* (LRBL) Edited by J.C. Bryce; general editor, A.S. Skinner (1983).

This volume includes:

'Considerations Concerning the First Formation of Languages' (Considerations)

V   *Lectures on Jurisprudence* (LJ)

Edited by R.L. Meek, P.G. Stein and D.D. Raphael (1978). This volume includes:

- (i)   Student notes for the session 1762–3 (LJA)
- (ii)   Student notes for the session 1763–4 but dated 1766 (LJB)
- (iii)   The 'Early Draft' of the *Wealth of Nations* (ED)
- (iv)   Two Fragments on the Division of Labour (FA) and (FB)

VI   *Correspondence of Adam Smith* (Corr.). Edited by E.C. Mossner and I.S. Ross (1977). This volume includes:

- (i)   'A Letter from Governor Pownall to Adam Smith (1776)'
- (ii)   'Smith's Thoughts on the State of the Contest with America, February 1778'. Edited by D. Stevens.
- (iii)   Jeremy Bentham's 'Letters' to Adam Smith (1787, 1790).

Associated volume

Essays on Adam Smith (EAS). Edited by A.S. Skinner and T. Wilson (1975).

References to Corr. give letter number and date. References to LJ and LRBL give volume and page number from the MS. All other references provide section, chapter and paragraph number in order to facilitate the use of different editions. For example: Astronomy, II. 4 = 'History of Astronomy', section II, para. 4, Stewart, I. 12 = Dugald Stewart, 'Account', section I, para. 12, TMS, I. i. 5. 5 = TMS, Part I, section i, chapter 5, para. 5, WN, V. i. f. 26 = WN, Book V, chapter i, section 6, para. 26.

BIBLIOGRAPHY

Bagolini, L. 1975. The topicality of Adam Smith's notion of sympathy and judicial evaluation. In *Essays on Adam Smith*, ed. T. Wilson and A.S. Skinner, Oxford: Clarendon Press, 100–13.

Black, R.D.C. 1976. Smith's contribution in historical perspective. In *Essays on Adam Smith*, ed. T. Wilson and A.S. Skinner, Oxford: Clarendon Press, 42–63.

Blaug, M. 1962. *Economic Theory in Retrospect*. London: Heinemann; Homewood, Ill.: R.D. Irwin.

Campbell, R.H. and Skinner, A.S. 1982. *Adam Smith*. London: Croom Helm; New York: St. Martin's Press.

Campbell, T.D. 1971. *Adam Smith's Science of Morals*. London: Allen & Unwin.

Haakonssen, K. 1981. *The Science of a Legislator: The Natural Jurisprudence of David Hume and Adam Smith*. Cambridge: Cambridge University Press.

Hollander, S. 1973. *The Economics of Adam Smith*. Toronto: University of Toronto Press.

Hont, I. and Ignatieff, M. 1983. *Wealth and Virtue: The Shaping of Political Economy in the Scottish Enlightenment*. Cambridge: Cambridge University Press.

Howell, W.S. 1975. Adam Smith's lectures on rhetoric: an historical assessment. EAS, 11–43.

Koebner, R. 1961. *Empire*. Cambridge: Cambridge University Press; New York: Grosset and Dunlap, 1965.

Lindgren, J.R. 1973. *The Social Philosophy of Adam Smith*. The Hague: Martinus Nijhoff.

Macfie, A.L. 1967. *The Individual in Society: Papers on Adam Smith*. London: Allen & Unwin.

Meek, R.L. 1962. *The Economics of Physiocracy: Essays and Translations*. London: Allen & Unwin.

Meek, R.L. 1973. *Turgot on Progress, Sociology and Economics*. Cambridge: Cambridge University Press.

Meek, R.L. 1976. *Social Science and the Ignoble Savage*. Cambridge: Cambridge University Press; New York: Cambridge University Press.

Mizuta, H. 1967. *Adam Smith's Library*. Cambridge: Cambridge University Press.

O'Brien, D.P. 1975. *The Classical Economists*. Oxford: Oxford University Press.

Rae, J. 1895. *Life of Adam Smith*. London: Macmillan; New York: A.M. Kelley, 1965.

Raphael, D.D. 1985. *Adam Smith*. Oxford: Oxford University Press.

Rosenberg, N. 1960. Some institutional aspects of the *Wealth of Nations*. *Journal of Political Economy* 68, 557–70.

Schumpeter, J.A. 1954. *History of Economic Analysis*. London: Allen & Unwin.

Scott, W.R. 1900. *Francis Hutcheson*. Cambridge: Cambridge University Press.

Scott, W.R. 1937. *Adam Smith as Student and Professor*. Glasgow: Jackson.

Skinner, A.S. 1979. *A System of Social Science: Papers Relating to Adam Smith*. Oxford: Oxford University Press; New York: Oxford University Press.

Taylor, W.L. 1965. *Francis Hutcheson and David Hume as Predecessors of Adam Smith*. Durham, North Carolina: Duke University Press.

Anarchism

GEORGE WOODCOCK

A doctrine whose nature is suggested by its name, derived from the Greek *an archos*, meaning 'no government'. The term *anarchist* appears to have been first used in a pejorative sense during the English Civil War, against the Levellers, one of whose enemies called them 'Switzerizing anarchists', and during the French Revolution by most parties in deriding those who stood to the left of them in the political spectrum. It was first used positively by the French writer Pierre-Joseph Proudhon in 1840 when, in his *Qu'est-ce-que la propriété?*, a controversial essay on the economic bases of society, he defined his own political position by declaring, perhaps to shock his readers into attention, 'I am an anarchist.' Proudhon then explained his view that the real laws by which society operates have nothing to do with authority but are inherent in the very nature of society; he looked forward to the dissolution of authority and the liberation of the natural social order which it submerged. He went on, in his rather paradoxical manner, to declare: 'As man seeks justice in equality, so society seeks order in anarchy. Anarchy – the absence of a sovereign – such is the form of government to which we are every day approximating.'

Proudhon's attitude was typical of the anarchists in all periods. They have argued that man is a naturally social being, who through mutual aid evolves voluntary social institutions that can work effectively without the need for government, which in fact inhibits and distorts them. The important transformation of society, anarchists argue, will not be the political one of a change of rulers or a change of constitution, since political organization must be discarded; it must be replaced by the economic organization of the resources of a society without government. Thus, while they differ from socialists and communists in denying the state and any form of state control or initiative, anarchists agree with them in being opposed to capitalism, in seeking to abolish what one of their earliest thinkers, William Godwin, called 'accumulated property' and to replace it with some kind of common ownership of the means of production. Only a few extreme individualists have stood outside this pattern, as Max Stirner did.

The basic ideas of anarchism predate the use of the title *anarchist*. Some historians have found their origin in early religious movements that stood outside ordinary society, refused to obey its laws and attempted in some way to own their goods in common, like the Essenes, the Anabaptists and the Doukhobors. But in these cases the search seems to have been for spiritual salvation through a progressive retreat from involvement in the material world, and they have little in common with anarchism as a secular doctrine directed towards social transformation.

However, there are at least two social thinkers anterior to Proudhon who seem to fit the necessary criteria to be regarded as anarchists, since (a) they present a fundamental criticism of the existing governmental structure of society; (b) they present an alternative libertarian vision of a society based on cooperation rather than on coercion; and (c) they propose a method or methods of proceeding from one to the other.

The first is Gerrard Winstanley, the leader of the Diggers, a small communitarian group who emerged in England during the Commonwealth. In his 1649 pamphlet, *Truth Lifting Up its Head Above Scandals*, which departed entirely from religious orthodoxy by equating God with Reason, Winstanley laid down what afterwards became basic propositions among the anarchists: that power corrupts, that property and freedom are incompatible, and that authority and property between them are the main causes of crime; that only in a rulerless society where work and products are shared will men be both free and happy, because they will be acting according to their own judgements and not according to laws imposed from above. Winstanley went beyond theory to direct action when he declared that only by their own action could the people change their lot, and he led his own followers in an occupation of English common lands, where they sought to set up an agrarian community in which all goods were shared. Despite the passive resistance they offered, the Diggers were finally forced off their land and Winstanley vanished into obscurity.

His ideas lingered in the dissenting sects of the 18th century, where they were picked up by William Godwin. In 1793 he published a massive treatise on the nature of government, *Political Justice*, which has often been described as the most thorough exposition of anarchist theory, though Godwin never called himself an anarchist. *Political Justice* does in fact admirably present the classic anarchist arguments that authority is against nature and that social evil exists because men are not free to act according to reason; 'accumulated property' is to be condemned because it is a source of power over other men.

Godwin anticipated the general anarchist emphasis on decentralization by sketching out a social organization in which the small autonomous community, or parish, would be the basic unit. He envisaged a loose economic system in which he anticipated Marx's slogan, 'From each according to his abilities, to each according to his needs', by proposing that – capital in the form of 'accumulated property' having been dissolved – men would freely transfer goods to each other according to need, and all would share in production. Though he seems to have imagined fairly accurately the labour-saving powers of machinery, since he prophesied a drastic reduction of the work day, he does not appear to have taken into account the more complex work relationships that the industrial revolution and factory production were already beginning to create. In the political organization of his parishes he anticipated later anarchists by rejecting such standard democratic procedures as voting, since he regarded the rule of the majority as a form of tyranny. He not only envisaged society moving to a practice of consensus after its liberation from government, but also hoped that such a liberation would come into being through education and peaceful discussion. His anarchism was evolutionary rather than revolutionary.

The distinction between evolution and revolution is important since, apart from variations in their proposals for the economic organization of society, the main differences between the anarchists who began to appear with Proudhon were in their views of the necessary strategies for achieving the aim they all held in common – the abolition of the state and all forms of government, and their replacement by voluntary and cooperative forms of administration.

Some, like Leo Tolstoy, Henry David Thoreau and the Dutch anarchist leader, Domela Nieuwenhuis, were pacifists, aiming to change society by the practice of civil disobedience. Mohandas K. Gandhi, who more than once termed himself an anarchist and who envisaged a decentralized society of village communes, was perhaps the most important of their company.

Proudhon was nearer to the pacifists in his view of the tactics of social change than he was to the later leaders of organized European anarchism. Though he often spoke of revolution, he hoped that peaceful change might come about through the creation of workers' economic organizations. Proudhon's mutualism, as he called it, was a mixture of peasant individualism and cooperativism aimed at the reorganization of society on an egalitarian basis. He set out to shock his readers by declaring that 'property is theft', but by this he really meant the use of property to exploit the labour of others. 'Possession' – the right of an individual worker or group of workers to control the land or machines necessary for production – he regarded as necessary for liberty. In the book that may be his masterpiece, *The General Idea of the Revolution in the Nineteenth Century*, written in prison because of his criticisms of Napoleon III, he sketched out the picture of a society of independent peasants and artisans with their small farms and workshops, and of factories and utilities like railways run by associations of workers, linked together by a system of mutual credit based on productivity and administered by people's banks like that which he attempted to establish during the revolution of 1848. Instead of the centralized state, he suggested a federal system of autonomous local communities and industrial associations, bound by contract and mutual interest rather than by laws, with arbitration replacing courts of justice, workers' management replacing bureaucracy, and integrated education replacing academic education. Out of such a pattern, Proudhon believed, would emerge the natural social unity which he equated with anarchy and in comparison with which, he believed, the existing order would appear as 'nothing but chaos, serving as a basis for endless tyranny'.

Proudhon was the real founder of the organized anarchist movement. He laid down its theoretical foundations in a continental European context where Godwin was virtually unknown, so that Mikhail Bakunin, possibly the best-known and most influential of anarchists, once admitted: 'Proudhon is the master of us all.' Proudhon's followers, who called themselves mutualists, were active in the foundation of the International Working Men's Association, the so-called First International, which provided the first of many battlegrounds between the authoritarian socialism of the Marxists and the libertarian socialism of the anarchists.

In the early days of the International the struggle was between Marx and his followers and the disciples of Proudhon, who had died in 1864, the year the International was founded. Later the struggle took a new form, since Proudhon's disciples were replaced in opposing Marx by the followers of Bakunin, a Russian aristocrat turned conspirator, and the conflict between them eventually destroyed the organization. It was basically the conflict between Marx's idea of the workers seizing control of the state to carry out the revolution, and Bakunin's idea of the workers carrying out the revolution in order to destroy the state and all the other manifestations of political power.

Bakunin accepted Proudhon's federalism and the argument in favour of working-class direct action, which the latter had developed in his final posthumously published work, *De la capacité politique des classes ouvrières* (The political capability of the working classes). But he argued that the modified property rights (the rights of 'possession') which Proudhon contemplated for individual peasants and artisans were impractical, and instead he proposed that the means of production should be owned collectively (hence his followers were called 'collectivists'). However, he still held like Proudhon that each man should be remunerated only according to the amount of work he actually performed; in other words, though in a slightly different form, the wages system would continue.

The second important difference lay in views of revolutionary method. Proudhon believed that one could create within existing society the mutualist associations that would replace it, and for this reason he came to oppose violent revolutionary action which aimed at an abrupt transition. Bakunin did not believe that such a piecemeal method could work. As a romantic revolutionary, he argued that 'the passion for destruction is also a creative passion', and taught that a violent uprising was the necessary prelude to the construction of a free and peaceful society.

The individualism and non-violence implicit in Proudhon's vision were thrust into the side currents of anarchism; Tolstoy, who had known Proudhon, largely incorporated them in his teachings of a radical Christian anarchism. But down to the destruction of anarchism as a mass movement at the end of the Spanish Civil War in 1939, Bakunin's stress on violence and on a collectivized economic system remained dominant among anarchists in most countries.

The tactics of violent action varied, though they tended to be conditioned by the doctrine of propaganda by deed, which emerged during the 1870s among the Italian anarchists and was particularly propagated by Errico Malatesta. Individual assassinations, largely justified by this doctrine, became numerous around the turn of the century; a President of France and a President of the United States were among the victims. There were anarchist-inspired mass insurrections in Spain and Italy and, during the Russian Civil War, in the Ukraine, where for several years the anarchist leader Nestor Makhno established libertarian institutions over a wide area and protected them by a numerous Insurrectionary Army.

There were also variations in the concepts of collectivism which the anarchists pursued, exemplified particularly in anarchist communism and anarcho-syndicalism.

Anarchist communism was mainly developed by Peter Kropotkin, a Russian prince and a distinguished geographer who abandoned his privileges for the revolutionary cause, though the idea may have been developed first by the French geographer Elisée Reclus. Kropotkin wrote a number of the seminal works of anarchism, including *Mutual Aid: A Factor in Evolution*, in which he traced the development of cooperation among animals and men, and *Fields, Factories and Workshops*, in which he argued for the decentralization of industry that he considered an essential accompaniment to a non-governmental society.

The work in which Kropotkin most developed the idea of anarchist communism was *La Conquête du pain* (The conquest of bread), a kind of non-fictional utopia sketching out the vision of a revolutionary society organized as a federation of free communist groups. Kropotkin moved beyond Bakunin's collectivism, which envisaged common ownership of the means of production, to a complete communism in terms of distribution, which meant that need rather than merit would be the reason why a man should receive the means of life. Kropotkin argued that any payment according to the value of the work was a variant on the wages system, and that the wages system condemned man to economic slavery by regulating his patterns of work. Just as Kropotkin's anarchism was based on the idea (developed in *Mutual Aid*) that man was naturally social, so his idea of free communism was based on the notion that man was naturally responsible, and in a free society would neither shirk on his work nor take more than he needed from the common store.

Anarcho-syndicalism arose out of the involvement of anarchist activists in the French trade union movement, which revived during the 1880s after the proscriptions of working-class organizations that followed the Paris Commune of 1870. Industrial militancy seemed to offer a broad field for the direct action which the anarchists already advocated, and the anarcho-syndicalists tended to oppose to the gradualist tendencies of orthodox unionists, who sought the best possible deal with existing society, the intent to change that society by proceeding directly to the assumption of industrial control by the workers. Thus their unions, while not neglecting to fight for better conditions, were ultimately revolutionary in their intent, and a philosophy of incessant struggle developed among them. This concept was adapted by writers like Georges Sorel, who in *Réflexions sur la violence* suggested that the important aspect of revolutionary syndicalism was the myth of struggle and the cult of violence, which he believed had a regenerating effect on society. However, the working-class anarcho-syndicalist spokesmen, like Fernand Pelloutier, Emile Pouget and Paul Delesalle, rejected Sorel's theories, and believed that relentless industrial struggle, by violent and peaceful means, culminating in general strikes, could in fact destroy the capitalist system and the state at the same time. When that happened, the syndicates would be transformed from organs of struggle into the organizational bodies of the new society, taking over places of production and organizing transport and distribution. In this way they were developing Proudhon's concept of mutualist institutions evolving within the society they would eventually replace. Anarchist purists, notably Errico Malatesta, distrusted the anarcho-syndicalists, fearing that a trade union movement that controlled all industry might itself be corrupted by power.

For many years before World War I, the anarcho-syndicalists controlled the leading French trade union organization, the CGT (Confédération Générale du Travail); after the war it was taken over by the communists, who had gained added prestige among the workers through the success of the Russian Revolution.

Anarcho-syndicalism, however, spread from France to Spain, where it became a powerful working class movement. The anarchist federation of unions (Confederación Nacional del Trabajo) was the largest labour organization in Spain, at times reaching more than two million members. It was a model of anarchist decentralization, employing only one paid secretary in its federal office, the actual tasks of organization being carried out in their spare time by workers chosen by their fellows. The CNT was strong among the peasants of Andalusia as well as in the factories of Catalonia. The civil war in 1936–39 brought Spanish anarchism to its apogee, which was followed quickly by its downfall. The experience of decades of street fighting enabled anarchist workers in the eastern cities of Spain to defeat the generals in the early days of Franco's military uprising. Later they sent their militia columns to the various fronts. At the same time they tried to bring about their anarchist millenium behind the lines by expropriating the factories and the large estates. Reports suggest that many of the factories were well run by the workers and that the collectivization of the land induced the peasants to work with pride and devotion. But the experiments were too brief for valuable conclusions to be drawn from them, since the anarchists' hatred of authority made them as inefficient in creating armies as they seem to have been efficient in organizing collective work, and their experimental communes were suppressed at the time of Franco's victory.

The outcome of the Spanish civil war led to a general decline of anarchism during the 1940s and 1950s. However, in the generally radical atmosphere of the 1960s it underwent a revival; anarchist groups appeared once again in Europe and North America, the movement's history was written by scholars, and the works of the great anarchist theoreticians appeared again in print. Anarchism has not become again a mass movement of the kind that once flourished in Spain and to a lesser degree in France, Italy and briefly in the Ukraine. But it is a visible movement once more. Anarchist ideas of decentralization have spread widely and have merged with those of the environmental movement. It now survives more as an intellectual trend, encouraging a critical view of the institutions and practices of authority, than as a quasi-apocalyptic movement which envisaged the end of government as a possible and not distant goal.

BIBLIOGRAPHY

Joll, J. 1964. *The Anarchists*. London: Eyre & Spottiswoode; New York: Grosset and Dunlap, 1966.

Marshall, P.H. 1984. *William Godwin*. New Haven: Yale University Press.

Masters, A. 1974. *Bakunin, The Father of Anarchism*. New York: Saturday Review Press.

Read, H. 1954. *Anarchy and Order: Essays in Politics*. London: Faber & Faber.

Rocker, R. 1938. *Anarcho-Syndicalism*. London: Secker & Warburg.

Woodcock, G. 1956. *Pierre-Joseph Proudhon: A Biography*. London: Routledge & Kegan Paul.

Woodcock, G. 1962. *Anarchism: A History of Libertarian Ideas and Movements*. Cleveland: Meridian Books.

Woodcock, G. and Avakumovic, I. 1950. *The Anarchist Prince: A biographical study of Peter Kropotkin*. London: T.V. Boardman & Co.

Claude Frédéric Bastiat

R.F. HÉBERT

French economist and publicist, Bastiat was born at Bayonne on 30 June 1801, the son of a merchant in the Spanish trade, and died in Rome on 24 December 1850. Orphaned at the age of nine, he nevertheless received an encyclopedic education before entering his uncle's business firm in 1818. By 1824 he was expressing dissatisfaction with his employment. Upon inheriting his grandfather's estate in 1825, he left business and became a gentleman farmer at Mugron, but showed no more aptitude for agriculture than he had for commerce. So he became a provincial scholar, establishing a discussion group in his village and reading voraciously. His later writings show familiarity with the works of French, British, American and Italian authors, among them Say, Smith, Quesnay, Turgot, Ricardo, Mill, Bentham, Senior, Franklin, H.C. Carey, Custodi, Donato and Scialoja.

Bastiat left France in 1840 to study in Spain and in Portugal, where he tried unsuccessfully to establish an insurance company. Returning to Mugron, he learned (in the course of seeking information for his study club) of Cobden's Anti-Corn Law League and became an ardent free-trader (the 'French Cobden'). As a complete unknown in economics, he submitted a stirring article to the *Journal des économistes* in 1844, dealing with the influence of protectionism on France and England. It created an immediate sensation and raised a clamour for more from the editors. This response encouraged Bastiat's *Economic Sophisms*, which quickly sold out upon its publication in 1845, and was soon thereafter translated into English and Italian. In 1846 Bastiat moved to Paris, where he established the Association for Free Trade and quickened his literary activity, endangering his frail health in the process. A torrent of articles, pamphlets and books now flowed from his talented pen, undoubtedly made possible in such short order by the preceding twenty years of practically uninterrupted reflection. Some scholars say the frenzy produced more heat than light, yet on the whole, economics is better off for Bastiat's herculean efforts.

Bastiat was one of several writers (Quesnay, Smith, Say and Carey were the others) who formed the doctrine of Harmonism, or the optimistic idea that class interests naturally and inevitably coincide so as to promote economic development. The major challenge to this view came from Ricardo and Malthus, whose theories cast a sinister shadow over the prospect of economic progress. As against Ricardo's system, Bastiat erected a theory of value based on the idea of service. He distinguished between utility and service, identifying the former as insufficient, of itself, to establish value, because certain free goods (sun, air, water) have utility. Bastiat considered all commercial transactions as exchanges of service, with value measured in terms of the trouble a buyer saves by making the purchase.

J.E. Cairnes complained that this merely confounded what Ricardo had sought to delineate, namely those cases in which value is proportioned to effort and sacrifice from those in which it is not. A more fundamental criticism is that Bastiat's theory, notwithstanding denials to the contrary, is simply a labour theory in different guise. It is noteworthy, however, that Bastiat's idea bears a close resemblance to the notion of 'public utility' which Dupuit applied so successfully to the measure of gain from transport improvements, and in which reduction of costs effected by the improved service became the central issue. Yet any connection between the two, tenuous as it may be, must be considered to run from Dupuit to Bastiat rather than the reverse, since Dupuit published his famous article on public works and marginal utility before Bastiat abandoned his earlier polemics in favour of more 'constructive' attempts at theory. Bastiat's theory of rent, also clearly aimed against Ricardo, denied the notion of unearned income, again advancing the view that the value of land (always in the absence of government interference) derives entirely from the services it renders.

Generally, judgement on Bastiat has been that he made no original contributions to economic analysis. Cairnes, Sidgwick and Böhm-Bawerk discounted his pure economics completely. Marshall said that he understood economics hardly better than the socialists against whom he declaimed. And Schumpeter declared that Bastiat was not a *bad* theorist, he was simply no theorist at all.

Schumpeter also described Bastiat as 'the most brilliant economic journalist who ever lived', and so weighty a thinker as Edgeworth praised Bastiat's genius for popularizing, in the best sense of the term, the economic discoveries of his predecessors. Almost all commentators agree that Bastiat was unrivalled at exposing economic fallacies wherever he found them, and he found them everywhere. He was quite simply a genius of wit and satire, frequently described as a combination of Voltaire and Franklin. He had the habit of exposing even the most complex economic principles in amusing parables that both charmed and educated his readers. His writings retain their currency, even today. And as Hayek has reminded us in his introduction to Bastiat's *Selected Essays*, his central idea continues to command attention: the notion that if we judge economic policy solely by its immediate and superficial effects, we shall not only not achieve the good results intended, but certainly and progressively undermine liberty, thereby preventing more good than we can ever hope to achieve through conscious design. This principle is exceedingly difficult to elaborate in all of its profundity, but it is one which has galvanized the thought of contemporary economists, such as Hayek and Friedman.

Over the long haul, Bastiat's influence has waxed and waned. In his own day he received the ready support of Dunoyer, Blanqui, Chevalier and Garnier. Francis A. Walker introduced his doctrines into America at about the time of the Civil War. Pre-World War I French liberals such as Leroy-Beaulieu, Molinari and Guyot relied on his authority. Bastiat's ideas subsequently went into a long decline, only to become resurgent in the late 20th century among libertarian economists dissatisfied with Keynesian orthodoxy and Marxist alternatives. Ironically, Bastiat's originality is exhibited most in his contribution to political theory, which has drawn surprisingly little attention to this day.

SELECTED WORKS

1844. De l'influence des tarifs français et anglais sur l'avenir des deux peuples. *Journal des économistes* 9, 244–71.
1964. *Economic Sophisms*. Trans. A. Goddard, Princeton: D. Van Nostrand.
1964. *Selected Essays on Political Economy*. Trans. S. Caine, Princeton: D. Van Nostrand.
1964. *Economic Harmonies*. Trans. W.H. Boyers, Princeton: D. Van Nostrand.

BIBLIOGRAPHY

Baudin, L. 1962. *Frédéric Bastiat*. Paris: Dalloz.
Hayek, F.A. 1964. Introduction to F. Bastiat. In *Selected Essays on Political Economy*. Princeton: D. Van Nostrand.
Russell, D. 1963. *Frédéric Bastiat: Ideas and Influence*. Irvington-on-Hudson, New York: Foundation for Economic Education.

Jeremy Bentham

ROSS HARRISON

Bentham was born in London on 15 February 1748, the son and grandson of a lawyer; he died in London on 6 June 1832. Destined by his father to be a lawyer, the law formed the centre of his long life. However, he turned at an early age from the idea of making money by the practice of law as it is and instead concentrated on the study of law as it ought to be. Bentham spent most of his life writing, accumulating piles of manuscript material on the theory of law and all associated subjects. At first these manuscripts were turned by him into books, but for most of his life he depended upon disciples to do the editing for him. Hence much of the important work which appeared in his lifetime appeared in French, edited by his Genevan disciple, Etienne Dumont, and other important material has only been published in this century. As well as the general theoretical work, Bentham wrote a mass of material designed to press particular schemes of improvement on the government, such as the design of prisons and poorhouses, new systems of taxation and a plan for interest-bearing currency. His economic work is contained in some of these occasional writings, largely unpublished in his lifetime, an early tract entitled *Defence of Usury* (1787), which was quite successful in its day, and some more theoretical treatises which also only existed in manuscript until edited by Werner Stark in 1952–4. Stark's edition, in three volumes, contains all the relevant material.

Whether engaged in writing, polemic or practical projects, Bentham spent most of his life in England, indeed in London. However, he travelled as far as Russia when relatively young, spending a couple of years on the new estates being opened up by Prince Potemkin. His *Defence of Usury*, just as his famous prison proposals, the *Panopticon* (1791), was written as a series of letters from 'Crichoff', in White Russia'. Bentham also actively bombarded the new revolutionaries in France with proposals and was elected by them as an honary citizen of the new French Republic. He developed a worldwide active discussion with promoters of reform and new legislation and became, appropriately enough for the inventor of the word 'international', an international figure.

Bentham's work in economics, as in most other particular areas of enquiry, is best seen as auxiliary to his central, overall project, the production of a complete, rational code of law. After asking himself at an early age how, by his own thought and invention, he might best aid humanity, Bentham, in typical 18th-century fashion, decided that this should be by the construction of legislation. The aim of such legislation was to be happiness; by making good laws, men would be made good; that is, seekers of their own and others' happiness. Right at the start of Bentham's first published work, the *Fragment on Government*, appears the famous formula, stating that the 'fundamental axiom' is that 'it is the greatest happiness of the greatest number that is the measure of right and wrong' ([1776] 1977, p. 393). This principle, variously called by him 'the greatest happiness principle' or 'the principle of utility' neither was, nor was claimed by Bentham to be, original. He took it as an obvious goal, and found not only its spirit but also the form of words in such predecessors as Helvetius and Beccaria (the famous formula occurs, for example, in the 1767 English translation of Beccaria, p. 2). The idea of attaining such an end by legislation is also something which he naturally took over from the same predecessors.

The central idea of Bentham's work, therefore, was to invent laws so that people would act so as to bring about the greatest happiness. Men, that is, acting naturally, would be placed in such a system of regulation and sanctions that, following these natural courses, they would not only satisfy themselves but also produce the greatest happiness. The legislator, therefore, needs two principles to guide him in his work, one about what ought to happen, which sets his aim, and one about that naturally happens to human beings under various conditions, which tells him the nature of his raw material. The first is provided by the greatest happiness principle. The second is provided by a principle of psychological hedonism (also prevalent in Beccaria and Helvetius) declaring that people act so as to maximize their apparent interest. The legislator can hence plan rewards and punishments designed to get such self-interested individuals to do as they ought. Acts contrary to the general happiness will be crimes, and crimes will be controlled because they will not pay: the certainty and amount of punishment will render them a bad bargain. Bentham's economics, like his psychology, is therefore an amplification of this natural principle of self-interest: it is shown what the effects of various legislative acts would be, and hence provides information of use to the legislator.

It is worth stressing that there are two principles at work in Bentham (or that, in more modern language, he is engaged in normative as well as descriptive welfare economics), because it is sometimes thought that there is just one principle at work, or that the normative one is meant to follow directly in some simple way from the descriptive one (persons making this mistake may be thinking of J.S. Mill's work *Utilitarianism* [1861], and its subsequent criticism, not of Bentham). Yet the famous declamatory start of Bentham's main theoretical work, the *Introduction to the Principles of Morals and Legislation*, which declares that 'Nature has placed mankind under the governance of two sovereign masters, *pain* and *pleasure*' ([1789] 1970, p. 11), goes on immediately to declare that these masters (which are for Bentham the elements of happiness) create both the standard of right and wrong and also the 'chain of causes and effects' (i.e. both what ought to happen and also what does happen). Similarly, to take the great work of the end of Bentham's life, the *Constitutional Code*, Bentham starts from two 'first principles': 'the greatest happiness principle and the self-preference principle' (1830b, vol. IX, p. 8). Analogously, it is a mistake to think that Bentham espouses the idea of a natural harmony of interests so that all men acting in a self-interested way will be kept by some hidden hand on course for universal happiness. On the contrary, Bentham is clear that legislative interference, that is, the threat of punishment to make some otherwise undesired conduct in someone's interest, is essential. Similarly, there is no conflict, as Elie Halévy supposed, between a Benthamite economics which supposes a natural identity of interests, and a legislative project which requires an artificial identification of interests (Halévy, 1928, pp. 17, 33). The economics merely provides natural facts about how men behave to be used by the legislator in his planning; knowing these facts, he knows when to interfere and when not; however, there can be no *a priori* supposition that the general happiness will come about anyway even if he does not interfere. As Bentham puts it in the *Manual of Political Economy*, 'the great object ... is to know what ought and what ought not to be done by government. It is in this view and in this view only that the knowledge of what is done and takes place without the interference of government can be of any practical use' (Bentham [1787], 1952, vol. I, p. 224).

Bentham spent much of his life constructing plans for institutions, whether they were very large institutions like nation states or much smaller ones like prisons, workhouses or banking systems. Following from the task set by his two leading principles, the leading idea of any such design could be set by the target enunciated in another specially named principle, the '*Duty and Interest* junction principle', which is 'to make it each man's *interest* to observe on every occasion that conduct which it is his *duty* to observe' (Bentham, 1798, vol. VIII, p. 380). In prisons and workhouses, this meant that he advocated contract management; with regard to state offices, their sale to the highest bidder; in general, an opposition to salaried officials. Here he is clearly influenced by Smith, who noted that in a University where a professor is salaried, 'his interest is ... set as directly in opposition to his duty as it is possible to set it' (Smith [1776], 1976, vol. II, p. 284); Bentham similarly talks of the salaries of professors in his *Rationale of Reward* (1825, p. 154). His concern for the management of institutions and his love of detailed planning is also shown by the work he did developing new systems of accounting for use in them (described in Goldberg, 1957).

The general principle of value from which such recommendations follow – namely that the greatest happiness of the greatest number should be promoted – may look as if it prescribes maximization in two different dimensions and hence has no solution. However, Bentham was quite clear that 'the greatest number' in the formula is just an auxiliary description; what the formula invokes is the greatest happiness, quite independently of how it is distributed. What is meant by 'happiness' is the occurrence of pleasure and the absence of pain, these two being supposed to be directly comparable with each other and it being supposed that all other elements of value or disvalue may be reduced to one or the other. Utility, the source of value for Bentham, is hence taken to be 'that property in any object, whereby it tends to produce benefit, advantage, pleasure, good or happiness, (all this in the present case comes to the same thing) or (what comes again to the same thing) to prevent the happening of mischief, pain, evil, or unhappiness' ([1789] 1970, p. 12).

Such happiness, or such quantity of pleasure and pain, is supposed by Bentham to be calculable or measurable, and he takes it that empirical observation reveals that several factors have an influence on it. In chapter 4 of the *Introduction*, which is entitled 'Value of a lot of pleasure or pain: how to be measured' ([1789] 1970, p. 38), Bentham lists seven such factors: intensity, duration, certainty, propinquity, fecundity, purity and extent. Earlier manuscripts show a rough attempt to reduce these to numerical scales, and in this chapter he cites it as universally understood that the value of an article varies as its certainty of possession and the 'nearness or remoteness of the time at which, if at all, it is to come into possession' (p. 41). Bentham, that is, just takes it as an empirical fact that people exhibit time preference; and, taking this as a measure of the pleasure or pain which people find in things, hence discovers it to be a factor of their value. By 'fecundity' and 'purity' Bentham means the further pleasures or pains to which a particular one leads; given that he is summing up all the pleasures anyway, Bentham did not in fact need to list these as separate factors. Similarly, by the 'extent' of a pleasure he means the number of persons affected by it; again, since he can count all these separate pleasures separately, he did not need to ist this as an additional factor of any one of them.

In accord with his view that utility was the single source of value, Bentham criticized Smith for distinguishing between value in use and value in exchange. He explains away the water and diamonds paradox (that useless diamonds are held to be more valuable than useful water), which Smith thought required this distinction by taking the value of an abundant commodity like water as its value at the margin. 'If the whole quantity required is available', as Bentham puts it, 'the surplus has no kind of value'; that is, it is of no use except, as he notes, in cases of scarcity. Then water 'has a value in exchange superior to that of wine' (Bentham, 1954, vol. III, pp. 87, 88). The value of diamonds is also value in use for Bentham; giving pleasure, they possess utility.

Bentham's attempts at actual measurement were as sketchy as his conviction that measurement was possible was unshakeable. In early manuscripts he does talk of money as 'the instrument for measuring the quantity of pain or pleasure', and works with an example in which someone is indifferent between having a particular pleasure and having a particular sum of money. However, in the published work, money is not used as a measure; no doubt with good reason, because Bentham clearly held that equal increments of something which provided utility did not provide equal increments of utility. This follows from something which Bentham did produce and work out in a little detail: a set of psychological principles ('axioms of mental pathology', as he called them) which describe how happiness varies with variations of something which produces it. The key assumption, or axiom, here is that, although for unequal fortunes 'he who has the most wealth has the most happiness', 'the excess in happiness of the richer will not be so great as the excess of his wealth' (Bentham, 1802, vol. II, p. 20; 1864, p. 103). In other words, money (or any other producer of utility) has diminishing marginal utility, and Bentham clearly spells out the consequences of this, in particular for equality. He frequently lists four subsidiary goals as means to the overall goal of general happiness: subsistence, security, abundance and equality. It follows from these axioms of mental pathology that, as long as the other subsidiary ends are not interfered with, greater happiness will be produced by promoting greater equality.

These subsidiary ends show that considerable interference by government is licensed by Bentham. Both security and subsistence demand action by the state; and the state should also do what it can to promote abundance and equality. Bentham indeed thinks that security, and the rights which make it up, such as rights to life or property, are produced by the state and do not exist antecedently to the state. Hence any tax proposals or measures of redistribution designed to produce poor relief or subsistence cannot be objected to because they are supposed to interfere with people's natural liberties or natural rights to property. For Bentham such things are complete chimeras, total fictions, nonsense. So, in a late pamphlet, the *Defence of a Maximum*, he can argue in favour of the state interference with the price of bread, saying that he will 'leave it to Adam Smith, and the champions of the rights of man ... to talk of invasions of natural liberty' (1954, vol. III, p. 258; he is presumably thinking of Smith [1776], 1976, vol. II, p. 208); for Bentham, there is no such thing to be interfered with. So as well as defence, justice and the public works permitted by Smith, Bentham also thought that the state should promote institutes for the propagation of knowledge, take control of health, insurance and possibly some communications – he notices that the benefits of a canal accrue 'in portions altogether unassignable, among individuals more clearly unassignable' in the *Institute of Political Economy* (1954, vol. III, p. 338); in other words, it is a public good. Bentham also produced a series of detailed proposals for state control of banking and the issue of paper currency.

Bentham was therefore not resistant to the idea of state activity, and he draws up several lists of 'agenda'; that is, areas where it is appropriate for the state to act. However, in spite of the specific criticisms, he does carry over the chief lines of Smithian economics so far as to hold that, in general, more happiness is produced if the state does not attempt to exercise control. The 'general rule' with respect to 'agenda' makes '*Be quiet* ... the motto, or watch word, of government' (1954, vol. III, p. 333). While considering any state intervention, it must be shown that it produces more good than the mischief of the most onerous current tax. It is assumed that, in general, once security and subsistence have been provided, more value (i.e. more pleasure) will be produced if people, who are supposed normally to know their own interests better than anyone else, are left free to pursue their own pleasures. Bentham's early pamphlet the *Defence of Usury* was indeed an attempt to out-Smith Smith by arguing that the rate of interest on money should be outside government control; and its last letter is a defence of 'projectors' against Smith. Indeed, Bentham not only defended projectors but was himself one to the extent that he hoped to make money out of his own project, the panopticon prison. He intended to be its first contract manager, having control of the criminals of England and setting them to work for profit.

Given Bentham's perspective as a legislator, political economy and the role of the state necessarily form a large part of any account of his work. However, having a theoretical mind, Bentham tended to become involved in issues for their own sake even if he had originally only considered them as means to an end. Hence his proposals for a new form of interest-bearing circulating currency led to a year's study of the effects of paper money and inflation, partly empirical and partly theoretical. The resulting work, the *Circulating Annuities* (1801), therefore not only consists of such typically Benthamite features as an engraving of the proposed new currency but also an analysis of the effects of the introduction of new paper money; and such analysis also occurs in the later occasional pamphlet *The True Alarm*. In his early work Bentham had thought that one reason why the scope for state interference was limited was that trade was always limited by capital; the government, not being able to increase capital, could hence do little for trade. Such is a predominant theme of the early *Manual of Political Economy*. However, when he reconsidered the matter, Bentham realized that, when there was unemployment, a monetary change might have a real effect by drawing new labour into the workforce. Hence money 'with regard to labour which as yet has not been brought into action, adds to the real quantity of wealth (according to the application made of the labour), and does not add to the nominal price of goods' (1952, vol. II, pp. 310–11). Discovering that monetary changes may lead to 'an increase of real wealth' (p. 313) leads Bentham into occasional criticism of Smith; leads him to say things like that, in one way, 'money, it would seem, is the cause, and the cause *sine qua non*, of labour and general wealth' (p. 324); means that he departs from his masters by extolling luxury expenditure and talking of forced saving; and by holding that new money may move wealth from the unproductive to the productive classes.

Although such remarks only form a passing part of an occasional work designed to encourage the government in a particular project, here, as elsewhere, Bentham throws out hints and insights which have only properly been developed later by others. The general tenor of his *True Alarm* pamphlet, and in particular his account of these monetary effects, meant that he was sufficiently out of tune with orthodox opinion for his followers to think that it was not worth editing and publishing: Dumont consulted James Mill and Ricardo, and they advised against it (Ricardo's critical running commentary can be found in Ricardo, 1951). However, such Benthamite remarks are only occasional. The more persistent work is the account of how far the state should interfere in the running of the economy; which in turn is but part of the overall project of deciding the complete code of law for a state engaged in promoting the general happiness.

SELECTED WORKS

1776. *A Fragment on Government*. London: T. Payne. Revised and edited by J.H. Burns and H.L.A. Hart, London: Athlone Press, 1977.

1787. *Defence of Usury*. London: T. Payne & Son. In Bentham (1952), vol. I.

1789. *An Introduction to the Principles of Morals and Legislation*. London: T. Payne & Son. Reissued, ed. J.H. Burns and H.L.A. Hart, London: Athlone Press, 1970.

1791. *Panopticon*. Dublin: Thomas Byrne. In Bentham (1843), vol. IV.

1793. *Escheat vice Taxation*. In Bentham (1952), vol. I.

1798. *Pauper Management Improved*. In Bentham (1843), vol. VIII.

1801. *Circulating Annuities*. London. In Bentham (1952), vol. II.

1802. *Traités de législation civile et pénale*. Ed. E. Dumont, 3 vols, Paris.

1808. *Scotch Reform*. London: J. Ridgway. In Bentham (1843), vol. V.

1811. *Théorie des peines et des récompenses*. Ed. E. Dumont. London.

1815. *A Table of the Springs of Action*. London: R. & A. Taylor. In Bentham (1843), vol. I.

1824. *The Book of Fallacies*. Ed. J.S. Mill, F. Place and P. Bingham, London: J. & H.L. Hunt.

1825. *The Rationale of Reward*. Trans. and ed. R. Smith, London: J. & H.L. Hunt.

1827. *Rationale of Judicial Evidence*. Ed. J.S. Mill, London: Hunt and Clarke.

1830a. *The Rationale of Punishment*. Trans. and ed. R. Smith, London: Robert Heward.

1830b. *Constitutional Code*. In Bentham (1843), vol. IX.

1843. *The Works of Jeremy Bentham*. 11 vols. Ed. J. Bowring, Edinburgh: William Tait, 1838–43.

1864. *The Theory of Legislation*. Trans. Richard Hildreth from Bentham (1802), ed. C.K. Ogden, London: Kegan Paul & Co., 1931.

1952–4. *Jeremy Bentham's Economic Writings*. 3 vols, ed. W. Stark, London: George Allen & Unwin. Vol. I includes Bentham (1787), (1793) and the *Manual of Political Economy*; vol. II contains *Circulating Annuities*; vol. III contains *Defence of a Maximum, The True Alarm* and the *Institute of Political Economy*.

1970. *Of Laws in General*. Ed. H.L.A. Hart, London: Athlone Press.

1977. *A Comment on the Commentaries*. Ed. J.H. Burns and H.L.A. Hart, London: Athlone Press.

1983. *Deontology*. Ed. John Bowring, 2 vols, London: Longman & Co.; Edinburgh: William Tait, 1834; reissued, edited by Amnon Goldworth, Oxford: Clarendon Press.

BIBLIOGRAPHY

Goldberg, L. 1957. Jeremy Bentham: critic of accounting method. *Accounting Research*, July, 218–45.

Halévy, E. 1928. *The Growth of Philosophic Radicalism*. Trans. Mary Morris, London: Faber.

Harrison, R. 1983. *Bentham*. London: Routledge & Kegan Paul.

Hart, H.L.A. 1982. *Essays on Bentham*. Oxford: Oxford University Press.

Hume, L.J. 1981. *Bentham and Bureaucracy*. Cambridge: Cambridge University Press.

Hutchison, T.W. 1956. Bentham as an economist. *Economic Journal* 66, June, 288–306.

Mack, P. 1962. *Jeremy Bentham: An Odyssey of Ideas*. London: Heinemann.

Mill, J.S. 1832. Bentham. *London and Westminster Review*. In *Collected Works of John Stuary Mill*, ed. J.M. Robson, London and Toronto: Routledge & Kegan Paul and University of Toronto Press, 1969, vol. X.

Mill, J.S. 1861. *Utilitarianism*. In *Collected Works of John Stuart Mill*, ed. J.M. Robson, London and Toronto: Routledge & Kegan Paul and University of Toronto Press, 1969, vol. X.

Petrella, F. 1977. Benthamism and the demise of classical economic Ordnungspolitik. *History of Political Economy* 92, Summer, 215–36.

Ricardo, D. 1951–73. *The Works and Correspondence of David Ricardo.* Ed. P. Sraffa, Cambridge: Cambridge University Press, Vol. III; New York: Cambridge University Press, 1973.

Robbins, L. 1952. *The Theory of Economic Policy in English Classical Political Economy.* London: Macmillan.

Robbins, L. 1970. *The Evolution of Modern Economic Theory.* London: Macmillan.

Smith, A. 1776. *An Inquiry into the Nature and Causes of the Wealth of Nations.* Ed. Edwin Cannan, Chicago: University of Chicago Press, 1976.

Stark, W. 1941. Liberty and equality, or Jeremy Bentham as an economist: I. Bentham's doctrine. *Economic Journal* 51, April, 56–79.

Stark, W. 1946. Liberty and equality, or Jeremy Bentham as an economist: II. Bentham's influence. *Economic Journal* 56, December, 583–608.

Taylor, W.L. 1955. Bentham as economist: a review article. *South African Journal of Economics* 23, March, 66–74.

Collective Action

MANCUR OLSON

For a long while, economists, like specialists in other fields, often took it for granted that groups of individuals with common interests tended to act to further those common interests, much as individuals might be expected to further their own interests. If a group of rational and self-interested individuals realized that they would gain from political action of a particular kind, they could be expected to engage in such action; if a group of workers would gain from collective bargaining, they could be expected to organize a trade union; if a group of firms in an industry would profit by colluding to achieve a monopoly price, they would tend to do so; if the middle class or any other class in a country had the power to dominate, that class would strive to control the government and run the country in its own interest. The idea that there was some tendency for groups to act in their common interests was often merely taken for granted, but in some cases it played a central conceptual role, as in some early American theories of labour unions, in the 'group theory' of the 'pluralists' in political science, in J.K. Galbraith's concept of 'countervailing power', and in the Marxian theory of class conflict.

More recently, the explicit analysis of the logic of individual optimization in groups with common interests has led to a dramatically different view of collective action. If the individuals in some group really do share a common interest, the furtherance of that common interest will automatically benefit each individual in the group, whether or not he has borne any of the costs of collective action to further the common interest. Thus the existence of a common interest need not provide any incentive for individual action in the group interest. If the farmers who grow a given crop have a common interest in a tariff that limits the imports and raises the price of that commodity, it does not follow that it is rational for an individual farmer to pay dues to a farm organization working for such a tariff, for the farmer would get the benefit of such a tariff whether he had paid dues to the farm organization or not, and his dues alone would be most unlikely to determine whether or not the tariff passed. The higher price or wage that results from collective action to restrict the supply in a market is similarly available to any firm or worker that remains in that market, whether or not that firm or worker participated in the output restriction or other sacrifices that obtained the higher price or wage. Similarly, any gains to the capitalist class or to the working class from a government that runs a country in the interests of that class, will accrue to an individual in the class in question whether or not that individual has borne the costs of any collective action. This, in combination with the extreme improbability that a given individual's actions will determine whether his group or class wins or loses, entails that a typical individual, if rational and self-interested, would not engage in collective action in the interest of any large group or class.

Analytically speaking, the benefits of collective action in the interest of a group with a common interest are a public or collective good to that group; they are like the public goods of law and order, defence, and pollution abatement in that voluntary and spontaneous market mechanisms will not provide them. The fundamental reality that unifies the theory of public goods with the more general logic of collective action is that ordinary market or voluntary action fails to obtain the objective in question. It fails because the benefits of collective or public goods, whether provided by governments or non-governmental associations, are not subject to exclusion; if they are received by one individual in some group, they automatically also go to the others in that group (Olson, 1965).

Since many groups with common interests obviously do not have the power to tax or any comparable resource, the foregoing logic leads to the prediction that many groups that would gain from collective action will not in fact be organized to act in their common interests. This prediction is widely supported. Consumers have a common interest in opposing the legislation that gives various producer groups supra-competitive prices, and they would sometimes also have a common interest in buyers' coalitions that would countervail producer monopolies, but there is no major country where most consumers are members of any organization that works predominantly in the interest of consumers. The unemployed similarly share a common interest, but they are nowhere organized for collective action. Neither do most taxpayers, nor most of the poor, belong to organizations that act in their common interest (Austen-Smith, 1981; Brock and Magee, 1978; Chubb, 1983; Hardin, 1982; Moe, 1980; Olson, 1965).

Though some groups can never act collectively in their common interest, certain other groups can, if they have ingenious leadership, overcome the difficulties of collective action, though this usually takes quite some time. There are two conditions either of which is ultimately sufficient to make collective action possible. One condition is that the number of individuals or firms that would need to act collectively to further the common interest is sufficiently small; the other is that the groups should have access to 'selective incentives'.

The way that small numbers can make collective action possible at times is most easily evident on the assumption that the individuals in a group with a common interest are identical. Suppose there are only two large firms in an industry and that each of these firms will gain equally from any government subsidy or tax loophole for the industry, or from any supra-competitive price for its output. Clearly each firm will tend to get half of the benefit of any lobbying it does on behalf of the industry, and this can provide an incentive for some unilateral action on behalf of the industry. Since each firm's action will have an obvious impact on the profits of the other, the firms will have an incentive to interact strategically with and bargain with one another. There would be an incentive to continue this strategic interaction or bargaining until a joint maximization or 'group optimal' outcome had been achieved. This same logic obviously also applieds to collective action in the form of collusion to obtain a supra-competitive price, and thus we obtain the well-known incentive for oligopolistic collusion in concentrated industries whenever there are significant obstacles to or costs of entry. As the number in a group increases, however, the incentive to act collectively diminishes; if there are ten identical members of a group with a common interest, each gets a tenth of the benefit of unilateral action in the common interest of the group, and if there are a million, each gets one millionth. In this last case, even if there were some incentive to act in the common interest, that incentive would cease long before a group-optimal amount of collective action had taken place. Strategic interaction or voluntary bargaining will not occur since no two individuals have an incentive to interact strategically or to bargain with one another. This is because the failure of one individual to support collective action will not then have any perceptible effect on the incentive any other individual faces, so there is no incentive for strategic interaction or rational bargaining. Thus we obtain the result that, in time, sufficiently small groups can act collectively, but that this incentive for collective action decreases monotonically as the group gets larger and disappears entirely in sufficiently large or 'latent' groups.

When the parties that would profit from collective action have very different demand curves, the party with the highest absolute demand for collective action will have an incentive to engage in some amount of collective action when no other member of the group has such an interest. This leads to a paradoxical 'exploitation of the great by the small'. This is true to a greater degree and is evident much more simply if income effects are ignored, as in the demand curves for a collective good depicted in Figure 1. When the party with the highest demand curve for the collective good, D_h, has obtained the amount of the collective good, Q_1, that is in its interest unilaterally to provide, any and all parties with

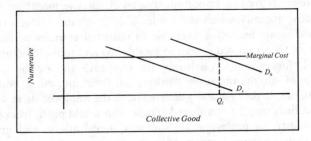

Figure 1

a lower demand curve, such as D_s, will automatically receive this same amount, and thus have no incentive to provide any amount at all! (Olson, 1965). When income effects and certain 'private good' aspects of some collective goods are taken into account the results are less extreme, but a distribution of burdens disproportionally unfavourable to the parties with the absolutely larger demands tends to remain. This disproportion has been evident, for example, in various military alliances and international organizations, in cartels, and in metropolitan areas in which metropolis-wide collective goods are provided by independent municipalities of greatly different size (Olson and Zeckhauser, 1966; Sandler, 1980).

The other condition, besides small numbers, that can make collective action possible, is 'selective incentives'. Those large groups that have been organized for collective action for any substantial period of time are regularly found to have worked out special devices, or selective incentives, that are functionally equivalent to the taxes that enable governments to provide public goods (Olson, 1965; Hardin, 1982). These selective incentives either punish or reward individuals depending on whether or not they have borne a share of the costs of collective action, and thus give the individual an incentive to contribute to collective action that no good that is or would be available to all could provide. The most obvious devices of this kind are the 'closed shop' and picket line arrangements of labour unions, which often make union membership a condition of employment and control the supply of labour during strikes (see, for example, McDonald, 1969; Gamson, 1975). Upon investigation it becomes clear that labour unions are not in this respect fundamentally different from other large organizations for collective action, which regularly have selective incentives that, though usually less conspicuous than the closed shop or the picket line, serve the same function.

Farm organizations in several countries, and quite notably in the United States, obtain most of their membership by deducting the dues in farm organizations from the 'patronage dividends' or rebates of farm cooperatives and insurance companies that are associated with the farm organizations. The professional associations representing such groups as physicians and lawyers characteristically have either relatively discreet forms of compulsion (such as the 'closed bar') or subtle individual rewards to association members, such as access to professional publications, certification, referrals, and insurance. In small groups, and sometimes in large 'federal' groups that are composed of many small groups, social pressure and social rewards are also important sources of selective incentives.

The selective incentives that are needed if large groups are to organize for collective action are less often available to potential entrants or those at the lower levels of the social order than to established and well-placed groups. The unemployed, for example, obviously do not have the option of making membership of an organization working in their interest a condition of employment, nor do they naturally congregate as the employed do at workplaces where picket lines may be established. Those who would profit from entering a cartelized industry or profession are similarly almost always without selective incentives. Experience in a variety of countries also confirms that those with higher levels of education and skill have better access to selective incentives than lower income workers; highly trained professionals such as physicians and attorneys usually come to be well organized before labour unions emerge, and the unions of skilled workers normally emerge before unions representing less skilled workers. The correlation between income and established status and access to selective incentives works in the same direction as the lesser difficulty of collective action of small groups of large firms in relatively concentrated industries explained above. Together these two factors generate a tendency for collective action to have, in the aggregate though not in all cases, a strong anti-egalitarian and pro-establishment impact (Olson, 1984).

The study of collective action goes back to the beginnings of economics, but then came to be strangely neglected during most of the rest of the history of the subject. Though this is not generally realized, the study of collective action, admittedly only in an inductive and intuitive way, was a crucial part of Adam Smith's analysis of the inefficiencies and inequities in the economies he observed (Smith, 1776). Smith even noted that the main beneficiaries of collective action in his time were by no means the poor or those of average means. He also emphasized the tendency for urban interests to profit from collective action at the expense of rural people, because the geographical dispersion of agricultural interests made it more difficult for them to combine to exert political influence or to fix prices; this emphasis presumably owed something to the poor transportation and communication systems in his day, which presumably obstructed the organization of rural interests more in his time than it does in developed countries now.

The label that Adam Smith gave to the set of public policies, monopolistic combinations, and ideas that he attacked was, after all, 'mercantilism', because the single most important source of the evils was the collective action of merchants, or merchants and 'masters', especially those organized into guilds or 'corporations'. In his discussion of the 'Inequalities Occasioned by the Policy of Europe' and of 'The Rent of Land' (Bk. I, ch. 10, pt. ii and ch. 11), Smith emphasized that 'whenever the legislature attempts to regulate the differences between masters and their workmen, its counsellors are always the Masters'. Similarly,

> it is everywhere much easier for a rich merchant to obtain the privilege of trading in a town corporate, than for a poor artificer to obtain that of working in it.... Though the interest of the labourer is strictly connected with that of the society... his voice is little heard and less regarded.

The rural interests are similarly at a disadvantage, according to Smith, especially as compared with those in 'trade and manufactures':

> The inhabitants of a town, being collected into one place, can easily combine together. The most insignificant trades carried on in towns have accordingly, in some place or another, been incorporated, and even where they have never been incorporated... voluntary associations and agreements prevent that free

competition which they cannot prohibit... The trades which employ but a small number of hands run most easily into such combinations... People of the same trade seldom meet together, even for merriment and diversion, but the conversation ends in a conspiracy against the public, or in some contrivance to raise prices.

By contrast, 'the inhabitants of the country, dispersed in distant places, cannot easily combine together'.

These passages, though not in the order they appear in Smith, nonetheless correctly convey his altertness to collective action. Though the handicap that rural interests face in organizing for collective action is far less in developed countries today than it was in Smith's time, even this part of his argument still generally holds true in the developing countries, where transportation and communication in the rural areas are poor, peasants are generally unrepresented, and agricultural commodities normally underpriced (Anderson and Hayami, 1986; Schultz, 1978; Olson, 1985).

Adam Smith's insights into collective action and its consequences were ignored until recent times. Presumably one reason is that most economists in the 19th and early 20th centuries were mainly interested in the logic of the case for competitive markets. The logic of collective action, by contrast, is really a general statement of the logic of market failure; it embodies the central insight of the theories of public goods and externalities, that markets and voluntary market-type arrangements do not generally work in those cases where the beneficiaries of any collective good or benefit cannot be excluded because they have not paid any purchase price or dues (Baumol, 1952). It was not until Knut Wicksell's 'New Principle of Just Taxation' was published in German in 1896 (Musgrave and Peacock, 1967) that any economist revealed a clear understanding of the nature of public goods, and only with the publication of Samuelson's articles in the 1950s (Samuelson, 1955) that this idea came to be generally understood in the English-speaking world.

A second obstacle to the development of the logic of collective action was that collective action by governments was normally taken for granted. Notwithstanding the difficulties of collective action, anarchy is relatively rare because a government that provides some sort of law and order quickly takes over. This in turn is due to conquerors and the gains they obtain in increased tax revenues from establishing some system of law and order and property rights. In the absence of the provision of these most elemental collective goods, there is not much for a conqueror to take, so the historic first movement of the invisible hand is evident in the incentive conquerors have to establish law and order. Those who lead the governments that succeed conquerors obviously must maintain a system of law and order if they are to continue collecting significant tax revenues. Since governments providing basic collective goods have been ubiquitous, the classic writers on public goods like Wicksell and Samuelson did not even ask how collective goods emerged in the first place. They focused instead on how to determine what was an appropriate sharing of the tax burdens and on the difficulty of determining what level of provision of public goods was Pareto-optimal. This in turn naturally led to Wicksell's recommendation that only those public expenditures that could, with an appropriate allocation of the tax burdens, command approximate unanimity, should normally be permitted, and to Samuelson's and Musgrave's (1959) concern for the non-revelation of preferences for public goods. The difficulties of collective action and public good provision on a voluntary basis therefore naturally did not gain any theoretical attention.

When, as in the new political economy or public choice, the focus is also on the efforts of extra-governmental groups to obtain the gains from lobbying, cartelization, and collusion, and on private action to obtain collective benefits of other kinds, a more general conception becomes natural (Barry and Hardin, 1982; Olson, 1965; Taylor, 1976). It then becomes clear that the likelihood of voluntary collective action depends dramatically on the size of the group that would gain from collective action. When a group is sufficiently small and there is time for the needed bargaining, the desired collective goods will normally be obtained through voluntary cooperation (Frohlich, Oppenheimer, and Young, 1971). If there are substantial differences in the demands for the collective good at issue, there will be the aforementioned paradoxical 'exploitation of the great by the small'. When the number of beneficiaries of collective action is very large, voluntary and straightforward collection action is out of the question, and taxes or other selective incentives are indispensable. Selective incentives are available only to a subset of those extragovernmental groups that would gain from collective action. Even those extra-governmental groups that do have the potential of organizing through selective incentives will usually have great difficulty in working out these (often subtle) devices, and will normally succeed in overcoming the great difficulties of collective action only when they have relatively ingenious leadership and favourable circumstances.

It follows that it is only in long-stable societies that many extra-governmental organizations for collective action will exist. In societies where totalitarian repression, revolutionary upheavals, or unconditional defeat have lately destroyed organizations for collective action, few groups will have been able in the time available to have overcome the formidable difficulties of collective action. It has been shown elsewhere (Mueller, 1983; Olson, 1982), that (unless they are very 'encompassing') organizations for collective action have extraordinarily anti-social incentives; they engaged in distributional struggles, even when the excess burden on such struggles is very great, rather than in production. They also will tend to make decisions slowly and thereby retard technological advance and adaptations to macroeconomic and monetary shocks. It follows that societies that have been through catastrophes that have destroyed organizations for collective action, such as Germany, Japan, and Italy, can be expected to enjoy 'economic miracles'. An understanding of collective action also makes it possible to understand how Great Britain, the country that with the industrial revolution discovered modern economic growth and had for nearly a century the world's fastest rate of economic growth, could by now have fallen victim to the 'British disease'. The logic of collective action, in combination with other theories, also

67

makes it possible to understand many of the other most notable examples of economic growth and stagnation since the Middle Ages, and also certain features of macroeconomic experience that contradict Keynesian, monetarist, and new classical macroeconomic theories (Balassa and Giersch, 1986).

BIBLIOGRAPHY

Anderson, K. and Hayami, Y. 1986. *The Political Economy of Protection.* Sydney: George Allen & Unwin.

Austen-Smith, D. 1981. Voluntary pressure groups. *Economica* 48, May, 143–53.

Balassa, B. and Giersch, H. (eds) 1986. *Economic Incentives* Proceedings of the International Economic Association, London: Macmillan.

Barry, B. and Hardin, R. (eds) 1982. *Rational Man and Irrational Society.* Beverly Hills: Sage.

Baumol, W.J. 1952. *Welfare Economics and the Theory of the State.* Cambridge, Mass.: Harvard University Press.

Brock, W. and Magee, S. 1978. The economics of special interest groups: the case of the tariff. *American Economic Review* 68(2), May, 246–50.

Chubb, J. 1983. *Interest Groups and Bureaucracy.* Stanford: Stanford University Press.

Frohlich, N., Oppenheimer, J. and Young, O. 1971. *Political Leadership and Collective Boards.* Princeton: Princeton University Press.

Gamson, W.A. 1975. *The Strategy of Social Protest.* Homewood, Ill.: Dorsey.

Hardin, R. 1982. *Collective Action.* Baltimore: Johns Hopkins University Press for Resources for the Future.

McDonald, D.J. 1969. *Union Man.* New York: Dutton.

Moe, T.M. 1980. *The Organization of Interests.* Chicago: University of Chicago Press.

Mueller, D.C. (ed.) 1983. *The Political Economy of Growth.* New Haven: Yale University Press.

Musgrave, R.A. 1959. *The Theory of Public Finance.* New York: McGraw-Hill.

Musgrave, R.A. and Peacock, A.T. (eds) 1967. *Classics in the Theory of Public Finance.* 2nd edn, New York: McGraw-Hill.

Olson, M.L. 1965. *The Logic of Collective Action.* Cambridge, Mass.: Harvard University Press.

Olson, M.L. 1982. *The Rise and Decline of Nations.* New Haven: Yale University Press.

Olson, M.L. 1984. Ideology and growth. In *The Legacy of Reaganomics*, ed. C.R. Hulten and I.V. Sawhill, Washington: Urban Institute Press, DC.

Olson, M.L. 1985. Space, organization, and agriculture. *American Journal of Agricultural Economics* 67, December, 928–37.

Olson, M.L. and Zeckhauser, R. 1966. An economic theory of alliances. *Review of Economics and Statistics* 48, August, 266–79.

Samuelson, P.A. 1955. Diagrammatic exposition of a theory of public expenditure. *Review of Economics and Statistics* 37, November, 350–56.

Sandler, T. (ed.) 1980. *The Theory and Structure of International Political Economy.* Boulder, Colorado: Westview.

Schultz, T.W. 1978. *Distortion of Agricultural Incentives.* Bloomington: Indiana University Press.

Smith, A. 1776. *An Inquiry into the Nature and Causes of the Wealth of Nations.* London: J.M. Dent, 1910; New York: Modern Library, 1937.

Taylor, M. 1976. *Anarchy and Cooperation*. London: John Wiley; New York: John Wiley & Sons Inc.

Wicksell, K. 1896. A new principle of just taxation. Trans. from the German by J.A. Buchanan, in Musgrave and Peacock (1967).

Common Law

P.S. ATIYAH

Common law is a system of law and legal processes which originated in England shortly after the Norman Conquest and after several centuries of continuous development was exported to the English colonies, and so came to be the basis of the law of the greater part of the United States, as well as of Australia, New Zealand, most of Canada and (to a lesser degree) also of India, Pakistan, Bangladesh and many parts of Africa. The chief characteristic of the common law has always been that its development has lain largely in the hands of the judges, and that it has therefore grown and changed incrementally, case by case, in the course of actual litigation.

In modern times the term 'common law' is used in a variety of senses. In the broadest sense, it continues to be used to refer to the entire system of law originating in England which now forms the basis of the law in the greater part of the former British Empire, often nowadays called the 'commmon law world'. In this sense the common law is often contrasted with the 'civil law' which derives from the law of ancient Rome, and today operates in most of Western Europe, as well as in a number of other countries (such as Japan and Egypt) which have borrowed their law from European countries. One of the chief characteristics of the modern civil law is that it derives its authority from one or more basic Codes of law; and it remains a principal distinction between common law and civil law countries that the former have not generally codified their law. And even in common law jurisdictions (such as California, for example) where there does today exist a kind of common law Code, it differs fundamentally in nature from the civil law Codes; in particular the system of precedent, and the authority of the judges to interpret and develop such common law Codes are quite different from those recognised in civil law countries.

The term 'common law' is also often used in various narrower senses. In the most important of these narrower senses, the common law is often contrasted with legislation, so that the lawyer in a common-law country still thinks of legislation as a type of law different from the 'common law', which is basically

70

judge-made law. The term 'common law' is sometimes used in yet a third relevant sense in which it is distinguished from a body of law, known technically as 'Equity' which was originally supplementary to the common law, and was developed in the separate Court of Chancery. Today common law (in this narrow sense) and 'Equity' are almost everywhere merged and administered by a single set of courts.

The common law (in the first two senses identified above) has traditionally been associated with the economics of the free market in at least two different ways. First, there is a strain of thought, represented in particular by Hayek (1973), which seems to suggest that a system of law, like the common law, which is largely judge-made, is inherently more likely to favour and protect individual freedoms, and among them (or especially) economic freedoms. But this is an implausible and indeed eccentric claim, which seems to involve confusion of the first two senses of the term of 'common law' referred to above. Because most redistribution is accomplished in modern democracies by legislative measures, it is easy to assume that a legal system which owes little to legislation will be more likely to recognize and protect the freedom of the market, but the amount of redistribution which occurs in a legal system does not necessarily depend upon whether that society is part of the common law world. There is no *a priori* reason to suppose that judges left to themselves by a legislature will necessarily favour the economics of the market. In the last analysis, the policies favoured by judges will depend upon their own preferences, their culture and traditions.

But there is a second way in which the common law has traditionally been associated with the freedom of the market, and this association rests upon the historical facts of the last three centuries. The concept of the Rule of Law which came to be recognized and defended in England after the revolution of 1688 has been seen by many as having favoured the development of a free market economy in England prior to and during the early years of the industrial revolution. Because of this historical fact it was for a long time almost an article of faith among English writers that the common law and the freedom of the market were closely associated. This view is today less strongly held in England, as a result no doubt of the fact that, while Englishmen still like to believe in the Rule of Law (despite grave doubts in some quarters as to whether this concept has much meaning), they are by no means so wedded to the free market as they were. In America, where the Constitution of 1788 substantially embodied the English traditions as to the Rule of Law, as well as the then accepted ideology of the free market, the association between the two has survived rather more strongly.

The reasons for the traditional belief in the close association between the common law and the freedom of the market must therefore be sought in history, and in particular in English history during the period from approximately 1770 to 1870, when the free market economy was largely in process of being established. And of all parts of the common law, none was more important for this purpose than the law of contract, because this was the part of the law most intimately related to the economic system. Indeed, the story of English law between 1770 and 1870 was to a large degree the story of how the law of contract was converted into the law of the free market, and of how the ideology of freedom of contract became one of the great intellectual movements of history (Atiyah, 1979).

The first three-quarters of the 18th century was a period of transition in England, during which many older ideas about contract and the market were being displaced by the newer ideas which gradually became dominant towards the end of the century. Among the older ideas at least three can be identified as particularly hostile to the laws needed to serve the emerging free market economy. First, there was a regulatory element in the law and the economy dating back to Tudor times, represented for instance by statutory controls of wages and prices of many commodities, and by the apprenticeship laws which controlled entry to many trades with outdated and largely unnecessary restrictions. Secondly, there was a paternalistic element in much contract law at this time, with the courts still being willing to relieve various classes of persons from the consequences of bad bargains which they had made. This paternalism was particularly pronounced under various doctrines of Equity, such as rules for the relief of mortgagors, rules against the enforcement of contractual penalties and forfeitures, rules for the protection of seamen and 'expectant heirs', and so forth. Thus, in the third sense of the term the 'common law' identified above, it can be said that the common law was always more market-oriented than Equity. Thirdly, there was a traditional moralistic element in the contract law of the 18th century, and this also took different forms, such as the general hostility to usury (as to which see Simpson, 1975, pp. 510–18), and the attempts to regulate the way in which essential foods and drinks were sold by use of the traditional marketing offences. The 'moral' roots of older law were also related to ideas about 'just prices' which, though rarely openly recognized in the common law, seem to have been influential at least in some of the cases in Equity, where there are signs that the Chancellors did have some vague sense of unease if they were asked to enforce contracts at prices which seemed to them very unfair, or on terms which were (in the language of the law) 'unconscionable'.

In addition to these specific instances of interference with the binding force of private contracts, there were important respects in which the whole concept of a general contract law remained relatively undeveloped at this time. Thus, while the law recognized and enforced specific types of contracts, such as contracts for the sale of land, contracts of insurance and so forth, there was, as yet, little sign of a general law of contract, governing all types of transaction. Then also, it remains unclear how far the contract law of this period actually recognized and enforced wholly executory contracts, in the sense of awarding damages for breach of a contract prior to any acts of performance or detrimental reliance by any of the parties. And finally, it is clear that, from the standpoint of today, the law of contract in the 18th century had not yet freed itself from dependence on the law of property. Of course, in one sense contract law can never be free from a dependence on property entitlements, because contract law is the mechanism by which entitlements are exchanged; but there are clear signs in the 18th century that contract law was still closely tied to property law in another sense, in the sense (for instance) that the proprietary aspects of many transactions were still regarded as more important that the promissory or contractual aspects. So, for instance, the right of a mortgagor to redeem the mortgaged property was protected by the courts, even when by the terms of the mortgage documents he had forfeited that right by delay in repaying the loan. It was assumed that if the mortgagee received back his money, with interest and costs, he was adequately protected by the law, even though the contract itself would have given him more extensive rights.

During the century beginning around 1770 these older ideas and traditions gradually gave way before the ideology of freedom of contract; but it would be wrong to think that this ideology did not have long roots and antecedents in still earlier periods. There are, even in the 16th and 17th centuries, many signs of incipient economic liberalism among the lawyers such as Coke, who bequeathed to the common law a hatred of monopolies as well as a passion for individual liberties (Wagner, 1935). And Thomas Hobbes, in a well-known passage in *Leviathan*, had swept away all the medieval learning about 'just prices' and declared that '[t]he value of all things contracted for, is measured by the Appetite of the Contractors; and therefore the just value, is that which they be contended to give' (Hobbes [1651] 1968, p. 208). So the ideology of freedom of contract certainly had origins going back well beyond the 18th century. Nevertheless, it does seem (though the matter remains controversail) that major changes in the law began during the course of that century which gathered pace as the century progressed.

Certainly, a great deal occurred to change the character of contract law from the last quarter of the 18th century until well into the 19th century, and there is much evidence that many of these changes in the law were profoundly influenced by classical economic theory, and perhaps still more by popular versions of classical economic theory. First, the relics of the Tudor regulatory economy gradually disappeared. Wage regulation had become increasingly obsolete in practice during the 18th century, and a major challenge to the older laws in the name of freedom of contract had taken place in the celebrated case of the Gloucestershire Weavers (1756–7), (Atiyah, 1979, pp. 73–4). By the early 19th century most of the legislation authorizing the fixing of wages had been repealed. So too was the Statute of Apprentices, after many years during which its operation had been gradually whittled down by the judges. Secondly, the signs of paternalism which are still found in 18th-century Equity seem to have disappeared gradually as the judges hardened their hearts and toughened their minds. For example, signs of an attempt to introduce implied warranties on the sale of goods for the protection of buyers, which can be detected in the 18th century, were largely scotched, and the principle of *caveat emptor* reasserted with full vigour. The equitable doctrines allowing the courts to relieve various unfortunates from the effects of hard bargains were gradually whittled down, although they never disappeared altogether. Third, the moralistic elements in the law were also gradually whittled down. The law of contract came increasingly to be seen to be neutrally enforcing agreements which must be presumed to be beneficial to both parties. The only moral component left in the law of contract during the 19th century seemed to derive from the binding nature of promises.

The subjective theory of value also seems to have been largely accepted by the judges even before it had been wholly accepted by economists. Although the common law had always insisted that a promise be supported by some 'consideration', some reason, before it would be enforced (and to that extent at least contained a paternalist element), the growing acceptance of the subjective theory of value meant that the doctrine of consideration became much less important during the 19th century. So for instance, in *Haigh* v. *Brooks* (1840, 113 English Reports 124) the judges enforced a promise to pay £9000 in return for the giving up of a guarantee previously given by the promisor, even though it now appeared that the guarantee might be unenforceable and legally worthless. The promisor had valued it at £9000, said the judges; it was not for them to say that the document was worthless. For similar reasons, the prejudice against usury had gradually been overcome, and the usury laws were totally repealed in England in 1854.

In these ways, then, the principle that contracts are binding and must be strictly enforced had been greatly strengthened, and exceptional cases had been whittled down by the middle of the 19th century. In addition, other changes had occurred in the general nature of contract law, which were closely related to the growing trend to see contract law as the law of the free market. First, it was during this period that a general law of contract came into existence for the first time in the common law world. And the process of generalization was important to the ideology of the law in a number of respects. In particular, the generalizing of contractual ideas meant that the law had to become more abstract, more broadly principled. Principles had to be developed which could be applied equally to (say) commercial contracts for the sale of wheat, to contracts of employment, and (for instance) to personal contracts such as the contract to marry. This abstraction may have helped the law become more neutral, less inclined to pursue any redistributive tendencies, such as may exist where (say) there is a separate body of legal doctrine dealing with contracts of employment, or with residential leases, or with loan transactions.

Next, it seems clear that another major development during this period was the gradual shift in emphasis in contract law away from treating contracts as present, or partly performed exchanges, and towards treating them as private planning devices, made in advance to allocate risks. The wholly executory contract became clearly recognized by the law, so that it now became possible for a person to sue for damages for breach of a pure promise, even where no performance or detrimental reliance had taken place. The justification for requiring damages to be paid in such circumstances was never clearly enunciated, and indeed, specific justification was rarely seen to be necessary. It was widely assumed that the broad principle of freedom of contract required, not only that parties be left free to make their own exchanges, but that the law should be available in aid of a party to enforce his claim to damages where the other failed to perform. John Stuart Mill was the first economist to point out that a policy of *laissez-faire* could not be used to justify the enforcement of executory contracts (Mill, 1848, vol. 2, p. 386), but even modern economists do not generally pursue this line of thought, though some libertarians have done so.

And finally, 19th-century contract law increasingly freed itself from its dependence on property law. Although obviously entitlements still remain the subject matter of all contracts, contract law has become much less concerned with specific items of property, and is more concerned with wealth as a kind of fungible property. The reason for this was basically that 19th-century contract law was dominated by the needs of merchants and traders, to whom all property is in principle replaceable with money. A merchant can be assumed to be indifferent between a piece of property, and the value of that property. Similarly, as contracts came to be increasingly seen as fundamentally risk-allocation devices, the particular entitlements or property to which the risks attached became less important.

By the last quarter of the 19th century, the process of developing a mature body of general contract law had largely been completed in England, and although a similar process took place in America (Horwitz, 1977), there is ground for believing that that was not completed for another fifty years or so. Freedom of contract had, apparently, reached its highest point. But although this was true of the ideology of freedom of contract among lawyers and judges, it was not really true of the views of economists or of the politicians, or of the public. By the late 19th century, neoclassical economists were already beginning to write sceptically about the sweeping effects of freedom of contract which had been attributed to the classical economists, and were pointing out the many possible causes of market failure such as information difficulties, externalities and monopoly. And although most of the older regulatory legislation had been repealed in the first half of the 19th century, Parliament had at the same time been gradually building up a completely new body of regulatory enactments dealing with new industrial problems – factories, coal mines, safety at sea for seamen and emigrant passengers, public health, the adulteration of food and drink, regulation of the weights and measures used for sales, and so on. Much of this new legislation had been a pragmatic response to perceived evils, and though some of it could have been justified economically by arguments concerning misinformation or externalities, much of it would have been difficult to justify except on the assumption of paternalistic or redistributive motives. Some of it may have been inspired by sheer impatience, an unwillingness to give the market time to work, or a belief that the short-term costs of market failures were so severe that legislative correction was necessary without regard to the long term distortions this might produce.

What is quite clear is that by the time the English commmon law and common lawyers had accepted the teachings (as they were thought to be) of the classical economists on freedom of contract, these teachings were already somewhat out of date. The result was that the mature common law of contract was seriously deficient in a number of respects. It was first of all deficient in its almost total neglect of the problem of externalities. Contracting parties were entitled to pursue their own interests, regardless of the effect of their contract on third parties, or the public. Only in the most extreme cases of actual illegality would the courts generally refuse to uphold a contract. Secondly (although this certainly could not be laid at the door of the classical economists), there had been, during the 19th century, a serious neglect by common lawyers of the problem of monopoly. This may well have been largely due to the fact that for the greater part of this period the British economy was itself highly competitive, and in little danger from monopolies. But the complacent assumption that cartels were unstable and were always vulnerable to internal or external competition was in England (though not in America) carried over by lawyers and courts into new conditions towards the end of the 19th century, and well into the present century, when it was utterly out of date. A second result of this failure of the common law to keep pace with economic theory and political reality, was the growing gulf between the common law and legislation. Once again, extensive legislative intervention with freedom of contract began to become commonplace, and much of it was increasingly redistributive in character.

During the course of the present century this process continued at an increasing pace until 1980 or thereabouts, since when there are signs that history has virtually reversed itself. Disillusion with the free market, particularly in England, increased during the great depression in the 1930s until, by the end of World War II, a Labour Government was elected to power with a massive majority and with a mandate to lay the foundations for a socialist state and a socialist economic system. Since then England has increasingly learned to live with a 'mixed economy', to a large part of which the traditional law of contract seems irrelevant because the public sector is often controlled by public laws rather than by contract law. But even in areas where private law continues to operate, the common law of contract has become increasingly affected by legislative intervention. Virtually all types of consumer transactions are today controlled or affected to some degree by legislation, including consumer credit contracts, contracts of employment, residential leases, and insurance contracts. Unconscionable, or unfair contracts are increasingly subjected to judicial control. Many areas of law which were formerly controlled largely by contract, such as family law, are now subject to extensive judicial discretionary control. Even business and commercial contracts are subject to vast bodies of legislative and regulatory laws, some, such as the modern monopoly or anti-trust laws, being designed to preserve the operation of a competitive market, but much of it still being designed to restrict competition or the operation of the free market.

America has not gone so far down this road as Britain and other common-law countries, and indeed, for a long time, in the late 19th and early 20th centuries, constitutional decisions of the United States Supreme Court in the name of freedom of contract, actually prevented similar developments. Much legislative intervention with freedom of contract was, during this period, declared unconstitutional, frequently over the dissent of Justice Holmes. By the late 1930s, however, the majority of the court had largely accepted Holmes's view, and since then, legislative intervention with freedom of contract has not been regarded as per se unconstitutional. This shift in the court opened the door to the same kind of regulation and intervention which had already been taking place in Britain, and although America has not, like Britain, brought large-scale industries within the public sector and therefore partially outside the control of contract law, most of the other legislative developments of the British type certainly have their parallel in America. No doubt some contracts are more regulated in Britain, but conversely there are plenty of examples of legislative interference with freedom of contract in America which are not to be found in Britain.

These vast changes in the operation of the common law have accompanied or brought with them a change in ideology once again. Paternalism and redistribution were, at least until around 1980, increasingly favoured by many writers and teachers of contract law, as well as large sectors of the electorate. Even the judges became much more sympathetic to arguments based on concepts like unconscionability and inequality of bargaining power. In America, unconscionability was given express legitimacy as a device for overturning unfair contracts by the Uniform Commercial Code, and was increasingly used by the judges as a matter of common law as well. Many relationships of a contractual character (for instance, that of physician and patient) and others of a virtually contractual character (for instance, that between manufacturers of products and ultimate purchasers and consumers) are, both in American and Britain, increasingly regulated by tort law rather than contract law, at least where things go badly wrong and legal actions for damages are brought based on negligent conduct, or on defects in the goods. In such malpractice or products liability actions the appropriate standards of care or quality are set by judges and juries and not by the contracting parties, and contractual exculpatory clauses are often denied legal validity.

Since about 1980 there have been increasing signs that the tide has turned yet again, both in Britain and America. Obviously, and visibly, British and American governments have since then been trying to reassert the virtues of the free market and roll back the frontiers of regulation, and in this they are being vigorously supported by some lawyers and law teachers in America, though not to any real extent in Britain. It is not yet clear what the impact of this is going to be on the future of the common law of contract. One possible scenario is that, as in the late 19th century, the courts will be behind the times, but that on this occasion they will be hostile to the reasserted belief in the free market and will continue to defend paternalist and redistributive intervention in free contracts, particularly where one of the parties to the contract is a consumer or 'small man' thought to be weak in bargaining power. But another possible scenario is that the new enthusiasm for the free market will prove but a short-lived hiccup in the long-term trend towards paternalist and redistributive policies. In either event it seems unlikely that for many years to come British of American courts will be enforcing contracts according to the full rigour of the common law.

BIBLIOGRAPHY

Atiyah, P.S. 1979. *The Rise and Fall of Freedom of Contract.* Oxford: Oxford University Press.

Hayek, F.A. 1973. *Law, Legislation and Liberty,* Vol. 1, *Rules and Orders.* London: Routledge & Kegan Paul; 3 vols, Chicago: University of Chicago, 1979.

Constitutional Economics

JAMES M. BUCHANAN

The term *Constitutional Economics* (Constitutional Political Economy) was introduced to define and to classify a distinct strand of research inquiry and related policy discourse in the 1970s and beyond. The subject matter is not new or novel, and it may be argued that 'constitutional economics' is more closely related to the work of Adam Smith and the classical economists than its modern 'non-constitutional' counterpart. Both areas of inquiry involve positive analysis that is ultimately aimed at contributing to the discussion of policy questions. The difference lies in the level of or setting for analysis which, in turn, implies communication with different audiences.

Orthodox economic analysis, whether this be interpreted in Marshallian or Walrasian terms, attempts to explain the choices of economic agents, their interactions one with another, and the results of these interactions, within the existing legal–institutional–constitutional structure of the polity. Normative considerations enter through the efficiency criteria of theoretical welfare economics, and policy options are evaluated in terms of these criteria. The policy analyst, building on the analysis, presents his results, whether explicitly or implicitly, to the political decision-makers, who then make some ultimate determination from among the available set. In this role the policy analyst directly, and the theorist indirectly, are necessarily advising governmental decision-makers, whoever these may be.

By both contrast and comparison, constitutional economic analysis attempts to explain the working properties of alternative sets of legal–institutional–constitutional rules that constrain the choices and activities of economic and political agents, the rules that define the framework within which the ordinary choices of economic and political agents are made. In this sense, constitutional economics involves a 'higher' level of inquiry than orthodox economics; it must incorporate the results of the latter along with many less sophisticated subdisciplines. Normative considerations enter the analysis in a much more complex manner than through the artificially straightforward efficiency criteria.

Alternative sets of rules must be evaluated in some sense analogously to ranking of policy options within a specified institutional structure, but the epistemological content of the 'efficiency' criteria becomes more exposed.

The constitutional economist, precisely because the subject matter is the analysis of alternate sets of rules, has nothing to offer by way of policy advice to political agents who act within defined rules. In this sense, constitutional economics is not appropriately included within 'policy science' at all. At another level, however, the whole exercise is aimed at offering guidance to those who participate in the discussion of constitutional change. In other words, constitutional economics offers a potential for normative advice to the member of the continuing constitutional convention, whereas orthodox economics offers a potential for advice to the practising politician. In a real sense, constitutional economics examines the *choice of constraints* as opposed to the *choice within constraints*, and as this terminology suggests, the disciplinary attention of economists has almost exclusively been placed on the second of these two problems.

A preliminary illustration of the distinction may be drawn from the economics of monetary policy. The constitutional economist is not directly concerned with determining whether monetary ease or monetary restrictiveness is required for furthering stabilization objectives in a particular setting. On the other hand, he is directly concerned with evaluating the properties of alternative momentary regimes (e.g. rule-directed versus discretionary, fiat versus commodity standards). The ultimate objective of analysis is the choice among the institutions within which political agents act. The predicted behaviour of these agents is incorporated in the analysis of alternative sets of constraints.

I CONSTITUTIONAL ECONOMICS AND CLASSICAL POLITICAL ECONOMY. As suggested, Constitutional Economics is related to classical political economy and it may be considered to be an important component of a more general revival of the classical emphasis, and particularly as represented in the works of Adam Smith. (The closely related complementary components are discussed briefly in section III.) One obvious aim of the classical political economists was to offer an explanation and an understanding of how markets operate without detailed political direction. In this respect, orthodox neoclassical economics follows directly in the classical tradition. But the basic classical analysis of the working of markets was only a necessary step toward the more comprehensive purpose of the whole exercise, which was that of demonstrating that, precisely because markets function with tolerable efficiency independently of political direction, a powerful normative argument for constitutional structure exists. That is to say, Adam Smith was engaged directly in comparing alternative institutional structures, alternative sets of constraints within which economic agents make choices. In this comparative analysis, he found it essential to model the working properties of a non-politicized economy, which did not exist in reality, as well as the working properties of a highly politicized mercantilist economy, which could be directly observed.

There is no need here to enter the lists on either side of the 'ideas have consequences' debate. We know that the economy of Great Britain was effectively de-politicized in the late 18th and early 19th centuries, and from the analysis of Smith and his classical fellow travellers there emerged both positive understanding of economic process and philosophical argument for a particular regime. The normative argument for laissez faire was, perhaps inevitably, intermingled with the positive analysis of interaction within a particular structure of constraints, essentially those that describe the minimal, protective, or night-watchman state. Economics, as a social science, emerged, but in the process attention was diverted from the institutional structure. Even the predicted normative reaction against the overly zealous extension of the laissez faire argument was couched in 'market failure' terms, rather than in the Smithian context of institutional comparison. The early socialist critique of market order, both in its Marxist and non-Marxist variants, was almost exclusively negative in that it elaborated putative failures of markets within an unexamined set of legal-political rules while it neglected analysis of the alternative rules that any correction of the alleged failures might require. Only with the debates on socialist calculation in the decades prior to World War II did the issues of comparative structure come to be examined.

It was only in the half-century after these debates that political economy, inclusively defined, returned, in fits and starts, to its classical tradition. Given the legal order of the protective state (the protection of property and the enforcement of contracts), we now know that under some conditions 'markets fail' when evaluated against idealized criteria, whether these be 'efficiency', 'justice' or other abstract norms. We also know that 'politics fails' when evaluated by the same criteria. Any positive analysis that purports to be of use in an ultimate normative judgement must reflect an informed comparison of the working properties of alternative sets of rules or constraints. This analysis is the domain of Constitutional Economics.

II CONSTITUTIONAL ECONOMICS AND SOCIAL PHILOSOPHY. Classical political economy emerged from moral philosophy, and its propounders considered their efforts to fall naturally within the limits of philosophical discourse. As a modern embodiment, Constitutional Economics is similarly located, regardless of disciplinary fragmentation. How can persons live together in liberty, peace and prosperity? This central question of social philosophy requires continuing contributions from many specialists in inquiry, surely including those of the constitutional economists. By their focus directly on the ultimate selection of a set of constraining rules within which ordinary social interaction takes place, constitutional economists remove themselves at least one stage further from the false position of 'social engineer' than their counterparts in orthodox economics. Precisely because there is no apparently simple evaluative criterion analogous to 'allocative efficiency' at hand, the constitutional economist is less tempted to array alternatives as if an unexamined criterion commands universal assent. The artificial abstraction of 'social utility' is likely to be less appealing to those who concentrate on choices among constraints than to those who examine choices within constraints.

If, however, there is no maximand, how can ultimate normative consequence emerge? In this respect, one contribution lies at the level of positive analysis rather than in a too-hasty leap into normative evaluation. Classical political economy contains the important principle of spontaneous coordination, the great discovery of the 18th century. This principle states that, within the legal umbrella of the minimal state and given certain conditions, the market 'works'. Even if in the principle's modern embellishment we must add 'warts and all', we still have come a long way toward a more comprehensive understanding of the alternatives for social order. To the extent that his efforts expand the public understanding of this principle, in application to all institutional settings, the constitutional economist remains under less apparent compulsion to advance his own privately preferred 'solutions' to the ultimate choice among regimes.

III THE NEW POLITICAL ECONOMY. Care should be taken not to claim too much for Constitutional Economics, especially if a narrow definition is used. As noted earlier, this research programme, by designation, emerged in the 1970s to describe efforts at analysing the effects of alternative sets of rules, as opposed to analyses of choices made within existing and unexamined structures. In a more comprehensive overview of developments after World War II, Constitutional Economics takes its place among an intersecting set of several research programmes, all of which have roots in classical political economy. Critical emphases differ as among the separate programmes, but each reflects efforts to move beyond the relatively narrow confines of orthodox neoclassical economics.

In continental Europe, the whole set of subdisciplines is included under the rubric 'The New Political Economy'. Within this set we can place (1) Public Choice, from which Constitutional Economics emerged; (2) Economics of Property Rights; (3) Law and Economics or Economic Analysis of Law; (4) Political Economy of Regulation; (5) the New Institutional Economics, and (6) the new Economic History. Defined imperialistically, Constitutional Economics would parallel the inclusive term and embrace all of these programmes, since some attention is drawn in each case to the legal–political constraints within which economic and political agents choose. Differences can be identified, however, and it may be useful to summarize some of these here, even if detailed discussion of the other research programmes cannot be attempted.

Public Choice, in its non-constitutional aspects of inquiry, concentrates attention on analyses of alternative political choice structures and on behaviour within those structures. Its focus is on predictive models of political interactions, and is a preliminary but necessary stage in the more general constitutional inquiry. The economics of property rights, law and economics, and the political economy of regulation remain somewhat closer to orthodox economic theory than Constitutional Economics or Public Choice. The standard efficiency norm remains central to these subdisciplines, both as an explanatory benchmark and as a normative ideal. The new institutional economics is directed more toward the interactions within particular institutional forms rather than toward the comprehensive structure of political rules (Furubotn and Richter, 1980; Frey,

1984). Some elements of the new economic history closely parallel Constitutional Economics, with, of course, an historical rather than a comparative emphasis (North and Thomas, 1973).

IV PRESUPPOSITIONS. Constitutional Economics, along with the related research programmes mentioned above, shares a central methodological presupposition with both its precursor, classical political economy, and its counterpart in modern neoclassical microeconomics. Only individuals choose and act. Collectivities, as such, neither choose nor act and analysis that proceeds as if they do is not within the accepted scientific canon. Social aggregates are considered only as the results of choices made and actions taken by individuals. The emphasis on explaining non-intended aggregative results of interaction has carried through since the early insights of the Scottish moral philosophers. An aggregative result that is observed but which cannot, somehow, be factored down and explained by the choices of individuals stands as a challenge to the scholar rather than as some demonstration of non-individualistic organic unity.

Methodological individualism, as summarized above, is almost universally accepted by economists who work within mainstream, or non-Marxian, traditions. A philosophical complement of this position that assumes a central role in Constitutional Economics is much less widely accepted and is often explicitly rejected. A distinction must be drawn between the methodological individualism that builds on individual choice as the basic unit of analysis and a second presupposition that locates the ultimate sources of value exclusively in individuals.

The first of these presuppositions without the second leaves relatively little scope of the derivation of constitutional structures from individual preferences. There is no conceptual normative bridge between those interests and values that individuals might want to promote and those non-individualistic values that are presumed to serve as ultimate normative criteria. The whole constitutional exercise loses most if not all of its *raison d'être* in such a setting. If the ultimate values which are to be called upon to inform the choices among institutions are non-individualistic, then there is, at best, only an instrumental argument for using individually expressed preferences in the process of discovering those values.

On the other hand, if the second presupposition concerning the location of the ultimate sources of value is accepted, there is no *other* means of deriving a 'logic of rules' than that of utilizing individually expressed interests. At base, the second presupposition implies democracy in governance, along with the accompanying precept that this structure of decision-making only takes on normative legitimacy with the prefix 'constitutional' appended to it.

V WICKSELL AS PRECURSOR. The single most important precursor to Constitutional Economics in its modern variant is Knut Wicksell, who was individualist in both of the senses discussed above. In his basic work on fiscal theory (*Finanztheoretische Untersuchungen*, 1896), Wicksell called attention to the significance of the rules within which choices are made by political agents, and he recognized that efforts at reform must be directed toward changes in the rules for making decisions rather than toward modifying expected results through influence on the behaviour of the actors.

In order to take these steps, Wicksell needed some criterion by which the possible efficacy of a proposed change in rules could be judged. He introduced the now-familiar unanimity or consensus test, which is carried over into Constitutional Economics and also allows the whole research programme to be related closely to the contractarian tradition in political philosophy. The relationship between the Wicksellian and the Paretian criteria is also worthy of note. If only individual evaluations are to count, and if the only source of information about such evaluations is the revealed choice behaviour of individuals themselves, then no change could be assessed to be 'efficient' until and unless some means could be worked out so as to bring all persons (and groups) into agreement. If no such scheme can be arranged, the observing political economist remains silent. The Wicksellian contribution allowed the modern economist to bring the comparative analysis of rules or institutions within a methodological framework that utilizes and builds on the efficiency criterion, which, when interpreted as indicated, does not require departure from either of the individualistic presuppositions previously discussed.

VI *Homo Economicus* IN CONSTITUTIONAL CHOICE. Constitutional Economics, as distinct from the complementary research programme on political constitutions that are within the boundaries of law, political science, sociology and other disciplines, goes beyond the logical presuppositions of individualism to incorporate non-tautological models of individual utility maximization. *Homo economicus* takes a central role in comparative institutional inquiry. Individuals are assumed to seek their own interests, which are defined so as to retain operational content.

Two quite different arguments can be made in support of this postulate in Constitutional Economics. The first is based simply on methodological consistency. To the extent that individuals are modelled as utility maximizers as they participate in market relationships, there would seem to be no basis for postulating a shift in motivation as they behave within non-market constraints. There is at least a strong presumption that individuals do not undergo character transformation when they shift from roles as buyers or sellers in the market-place to roles as voters, taxpayers, beneficiaries, politicians or bureaucrats in the political process. A more sophisticated reason for postulating consistency in behaviour lies in the usefulness of the model for the whole exercise of institutional comparison. If the purpose is to compare the effects of alternative sets of constraints, some presumption of behavioural consistency over the alternatives is necessary in order to identify those differences in results that are attributable to the differences in constraints.

A second argument for introducing *homo economicus* in Constitutional Economics is both more complex and more important. It is also the source of confusion because it is necessary to distinguish carefully between the use of *homo economicus* in predictive social science, specifically in positive Public Choice and in neoclassical economics, and in Constitutional Economics. There is an argument for using the construction in the latter, even if there are demonstrated empirical limits on the explanatory power of the model in the former.

The argument is implicit in the work of the classical economists. It was stated as a methodological principle by both David Hume and J.S. Mill:

> In constraining any system of government, and fixing the several checks and controls of the constitution, each man ought to be supposed a knave, and to have no other end, in all his actions, than private interest (Hume [1741], 1963, pp. 117–18).

> The very principle of constitutional government requires it to be assumed that political power will be abused to promote the particular purposes of the holder; not because it is always so, but because such is the natural tendency of things, to guard against which is the special use of free institutions (Mill [1861], 1977, p. 505).

The ultimate purpose of analysing alternative sets of rules is to inform the choice among these sets. The predicted operating properties of each alternative must be examined, and these properties will reflect the embodied models of individual behaviour within the defined constraints. Behavioural departures from the presumptive models used in deriving the operating properties will, of course, be expected. But the costs of errors may not be symmetrically distributed around the single best predictive model. The predicted differential loss from behavioural departures from a model that involves 'optimistic' motivational assumptions may be much larger than the predicted differential gain if the model is shown to be an accurate predictor. Hence, comparative evaluation of an institution based on an altruistic model of behaviour should take into account the possible non-linearity in the loss function that describes departures from the best estimates. (In legal practice, formal contracts include protections gainst worst-case behaviour patterns.) In constitutional choice, therefore, there is an argument for incorporating models of individual behaviour that presume more narrowly defined self-interest than any empirical record may warrant (Brennan and Buchanan, 1985).

VII APPLICATIONS. Applications of Constitutional Economics, as a research programme, have emerged in several settings. First, consider taxation. Post-Marshallian economic theory, either in its partial or general equilibrium model, was often applied to tax incidence. Analysis was directed toward predicting the effects of an exogenously imposed tax on the private economizing behaviour of persons in their varying capacities as demanders and suppliers of goods and services in the market-place. Building on this base of positive analysis, normative welfare economics allows a ranking among alternative equi-revenue tax instruments in terms of the Paretian standard. In both the positive and normative aspects, neoclassical tax theory embodies the presumption that taxes, as such, are exogenous to the choice process.

The major contribution of modern Public Choice, as a subdiscipline in its own right, has been that of endogenizing political decision-making. In its direct emphasis, public choice theory examines the political decision rules that exist with a view toward making some predictions about just what sort of tax institutions or tax instruments will emerge. Constitutional Economics, as an extended research programme that emerges from Public Choice, goes a step further and uses the inputs from both neoclassical economics and public choice theory to analyse how alternative political rules might generate differing tax rules.

The relevant constitutional choice may be that of granting government authority to levy taxes on Tax Base A or Tax Base B. Suppose that under the neoclassical equi-revenue assumption, analysis demonstrates that the taxing of A generates a lower excess burden than the taxing of B. Analysis of the political choice process may demonstrate, however, that government, if given the authority to tax A, will tend to levy a tax that will generate *more* revenue than would be forthcoming under an authority to tax B. The equi-revenue alternatives may not be effective political alternatives under any plausibly acceptable modelling of the behaviour of political agents. Once this simple point is recognized, the normative significance of the neoclassical ranking of tax instruments is reduced. Discussion shifts necessarily to the level of interaction between political decision structures and fiscal institutions.

A second application of Constitutional Economics is found in the post-Keynesian discussion of budgetary policy. The Keynesian advocacy of the use of governmental budgets to accomplish macroeconomic objectives was based on a neglect of the political decision structure. The proclivity of democratic governments to prefer spending over taxing, and hence to bias budgets toward deficit, is readily explained in elementary public choice theory (Buchanan and Wagner, 1977). This essential step in public choice reasoning leads naturally to inquiry into the relationships between the constraints that may be placed on political choice and predicted patterns of budgetary outcomes. Out of this intensely practical, and important, application of Constitutional Economics emerged the intellectual bases for the normative argument that, in the post-Keynesian era when moral constraints on political agents have lost much of their previous effectiveness, formal rules limiting deficit financing may be required to insure responsible fiscal decisions. In the modern setting, such rules would limit spending rates. But it is perhaps worth noting that, in the political environment of Sweden in the 1890s, Wicksell advanced analytically similar proposals for reform in the expectation that, if the suggested reforms should be implemented, public sector outlay would increase.

The analysis of alternative rules for 'the transfer constitution' represents a third application of constitutional economics. With the 1971 publication of John Rawls's *A Theory of Justice*, renewed attention came to be placed on principles of distributive justice. Although explicitly pre-constitutional, Rawls's work has a close relationship with the efforts to derive criteria for political and economic rules of social interaction. Economists, as well as other social scientists and social philosophers, have come increasingly to recognize that the untrammelled interplay of interest-group politics is unlikely to further objectives for distributive justice. Analysis of how this politics operates in the making of fiscal transfers suggests that principled adjustments in the post-tax, post-transfer distribution of values is only likely to be achieved if the institutional rules severely restrict the profitability of investment in attempts to subvert the transfer process.

Further applications include the regulatory constitutions, along with the organization of public enterprises. In its inclusive definition, Constitutional Economics becomes the analytical route through which institutional relevance is reintroduced into a sometimes sterile social science. In its less inclusive definition, Constitutional Economics, along with its related and complementary research programmes, restores 'political' to 'economy', thereby bringing a coherence that was absent during the long hiatus during which 'economics' made putative claims to independent status.

BIBLIOGRAPHY

Brennan, G. and Buchanan, J.M. 1980. *The Power to Tax: Analytical Foundations of the Fiscal Constitution.* Cambridge: Cambridge University Press.

Brennan, G. and Buchanan, J.M. 1985. *The Reason of Rules: Constitutional Political Economy.* Cambridge: Cambridge University Press.

Buchanan, J.M. 1974. *The Limits of Liberty: Between Anarchy and Leviathan.* Chicago: University of Chicago Press.

Buchanan, J.M. and Tullock, G. 1962. *The Calculus of Consent: Logical Foundations of Constitutional Democracy.* Ann Arbor: University of Michigan Press.

Buchanan, J.M. and Wagner, R.E. 1977. *Democracy in Deficit: The Political Legacy of Lord Keynes.* New York: Academic Press.

Frey, B. 1984. A new view of economics: comparative analysis of institutions. *Scelte Pubbliche* 1, 17–28.

Furubotn, E.G. and Richter, R. (eds) 1980. The New Institutional Economics – a symposium. *Zeitschrift für die gesamte Staatswissenschaft,* 140.

Hayek, F.A. 1973–9. *Law, Legislation, and Liberty.* 3 vols, Chicago: University of Chicago Press.

Hume, David. 1741. On the interdependency of Parliament. In *Essays, Moral, Political and Literary,* London: Oxford University Press, 1963.

McKenzie, R. 1982. *Bound to Be Free.* Palo Alto: Hoover Press.

McKenzie, R. (ed.) 1984. *Constitutional Economics.* Lexington, Mass.: Lexington Books.

Mill, J.S. 1861. Considerations on representative government. In *Essays on Politics and Society,* Vol. XIX of *Collected Works of J.S. Mill,* Toronto: University of Toronto Press, 1977.

North, D.C. and Thomas, R.P. 1973. *The Rise of the Western World: A New Economic History.* Cambridge: Cambridge University Press.

Rawls, J. 1971. *A Theory of Justice.* Cambridge, Mass.: Harvard University Press.

Wicksell, K. 1896. *Finanztheoretische Untersuchungen.* Jena: Gustav Fischer. Central portions of this work were published in English translation as 'A new principle of just taxation' in *Classics in the Theory of Public Finance,* ed. R.A. Musgrave and A.T. Peacock, London: Macmillan, 1959.

Economic Freedom

ALAN PEACOCK

Economic freedom describes a particular condition in which the individual finds himself as a result of certain characteristics in his economic environment. Taking a simple formulation of decision-making in which it is assumed that the individual maximizes his satisfaction both as a consumer of private and government goods and services and as a supplier of factor services, his position may be depicted as follows:

$$\text{Max } U^i = U^i(x^i, q_k, a^i) \tag{1}$$

Subject to

$$p_k^c \cdot x^i + T_k^i = Y^i = \varphi(a^i) = p_k^a \cdot a^i \tag{2}$$

where x^i is a vector of 'private goods', q_k is a vector of goods supplied by government, a^i is a vector of factor inputs, p_k^c is a vector of product prices for private goods, p_k^a is a vector of factor prices, T_k^i is net tax liability of individual i (tax obligation *less* transfers), Y^i is personal income before tax of individual i and subscript k denotes an exogenously determined variable.

Assuming the budget constraint (2) is exactly satisfied, the individual maximizes his satisfaction solving for the vector of private-goods consumption in terms of their prices, disposable income and predetermined levels of public goods available for consumption, where goods prices and factor prices, quantities of factor inputs and tax liabilities are either known or predicted by the individual.

Economic freedom requires that the various terms in the budget constraint reflect the absence of 'preference or restraint' (Adam Smith) on the individual. Therefore p_k^c is a vector of product prices which result from the operation of competitive market forces with the individual being free to choose between alternatives. Similarly, p_k^a must be characterized by competition in the factor market with the individual being 'free to bring both his industry and capital into competition with those of any other man or order of men' (Adam Smith). There is less certainty concerning the constraints placed on T_k and q_k. Some writers

88

would argue that economic freedom requires a pre-established limit on the values of T_k and q_k either expressed or implied in a country's constitution (Nozick's 'minimal state'; see Nozick, 1974). Others would argue that within a system of democratic government it should be possible to devise voting systems through which individuals express their preferences for values of T_k and q_k which simulate if they do not replicate the competitive market in the private sector (see Buchanan, 1975). All agree, however, that economic freedom is not compatible with large values of T and q in relation to values of x^i, mainly because a large public sector increases the monopoly power of public servants both as suppliers of public goods and factor services to produce them and encourages the growth of private monopolies as a defence against public monopsony buying.

ECONOMIC FREEDOM AND LIBERTARIAN PHILOSOPHY. There are features of this attempt at a 'technical' definition which may be called in question and which must be considered later, but it will be recognizable to those economists who have elevated economic freedom to an important goal in its own right and have claimed that it is the most important means of ensuring that the economy develops at the right 'tempo'. Discussion of the usefulness of the concept of economic freedom, therefore, centres on these two libertarian propositions.

The first proposition is contained in a striking passage in Book III of his *Essays on Liberty*: J.S. Mill wrote:

> He who lets the world, or his own portion of it, choose his plan of life for him, has no need of any other faculty than the ape-like one of imitation. He who chooses to plan for himself, employs all his faculties. He must use observation to see, reasoning and judgment to foresee, activity to gain materials for decision, discrimination to decide and, when he has decided, firmness and self-control to hold to his deliberate decision... It is possible that he might be guided on some good path, and kept out of harm's way, without any of these things. But what will be his comparative worth as a human being? It really is of importance, not only what men do, but also what manner of men they are that do it (Mill, 1859).

The passage captures the essence of the libertarian view of the good society, clearly implying that it requires that individuals should accept the necessity for choosing and for recognizing their responsibility for making choices. It must simultaneously require that, to develop the capacity for choosing, individuals must have the widest possible freedom of choice in the acquisition and disposal of resources. Two further conclusions follow.

The only restriction on economic freedom experienced by the individual should be when such freedom harms others.

The individual is not accountable to society for his actions and this, together with the different and changing preferences of individuals, makes libertarians distance themselves from attempts to establish a 'social welfare function' (cf. Rowley and Peacock, 1975).

The second proposition maintains that economic freedom brings the added bonus of promoting the economic welfare of both the individual and of society.

Economic freedom encourages the individual to 'better his condition' (Smith, 1776) by exploiting opportunities for specialization and gains from trade which will be fully realized through the spontaneous emergence of markets. Not only is economic freedom regarded as the only material condition compatible with human dignity but it is also a necessary condition for the economic growth of the economy and for its adjustment to the changing preference structures of its members in response to market forces. The market is a 'discovery process' (Hayek, 1979) in which participants adjust to change, giving rise to the notion of the 'invisible hand' which coordinates human economic actions automatically without recourse to government intervention. *Pace* Hahn (1982) and others, libertarians do not attach importance to a general equilibrium solution, attained by the operation of competitive market forces (cf. Barry, 1985). Indeed, though some exceptions will be noted below, it is claimed by supporters of the doctrine of economic freedom that disturbance of the natural process of exchange by government intervention assumes knowledge of the intricacies of the economy which is vouchsafed to no one, but there is no guarantee that officials, who maximize their private interests like everyone else, would be willing to maximize some social optimum even if they knew how to do so.

It was clearly recognized, by Hume and Smith for example, that for markets to work efficiently there must be a well-defined system of property rights and that costs of contracting between individuals in order to benefit from gains-from-trade would need to be minimized. The promotion of market efficiency was therefore bound to require some government intervention. No specialization or gains-from-trade would take place in a society in which there was no machinery for settling disputes and for preserving law and order. Acceptance of coercive intervention, however, requires that the 'rule of law' prevails. The law must be prospective and never retrospective in its operation, the law must be known and, as far as possible, certain, and the law must apply with equal force to all individuals without exception or discrimination. The state could also have a role in reducing the costs of contracting both by the removal of barriers to trade and to factor mobility and by the positive encouragement to the reduction in the costs of transport. In this latter respect Adam Smith supported reduction in the 'expense of carriage' by state financing of road building and supervision of financial methods to promote road maintenance and improvement.

At no stage thereofre in the development of the doctrine of economic freedom, as understood by economists, was it regarded as synonymous with 'laissez-faire'. At the same time, the role of the state in respect of the promotion of economic freedom was and has remained strictly limited in libertarian thinking. Indeed, some modern libertarians devote much discussion to the possibilities of 'privatizing' even such traditional functions of the state as the maintenance of law and order.

SOME PROBLEMS RAISED BY THE CONCEPT OF ECONOMIC FREEDOM. The most obvious question posed to libertarians by those who are sceptical of their position is that the system of economic freedom is silent on the question of the distribution of property rights. In terms of our simple model, what principle should determine the values of $Y^1, \ldots, Y^i, \ldots, Y^n$ which, when aggregated, would describe some initial distribution of income as measured, say, by the shape of the Lorenz Curve? What reason have we for supposing that the 'optimal' distribution of income would emerge from the process of economic exchange between individuals?

The answer to this question does not find libertarians speaking with one voice. The problem is not one of principle, for the ultimate test to them is how far any government intervention represents a restriction of freedom. The problem is one of interpretation. It would be difficult today to find libertarians who would object to government intervention designed to assure protection to those who are severely deprived. Thus Hayek has argued that so long as 'a uniform minimum income is provided outside the market to all those who, for any reason, are unable to earn in the market an adequate maintenance, this need not lead to a restriction of freedom, or conflict with the Rule of Law'. This still leaves room for much disagreement among libertarians as to the precise level of the minimum and how to decide on who is entitled to receive it. Some supporters of the libertarian position, including the present author, would go much further and argue, along with J.S. Mill, that concentrations of wealth sustained over lengthy time periods can endanger economic freedom, not to speak of political freedom, by the association of such concentrations with the concentration of power of wealthy individuals over the less fortunate.

If the concept of economic freedom cannot embrace some precise guidance about the extent to which economic exchanges should be interfered with, it certainly places limits on the form of that interference. Thus libertarians, to the extent that they accept the need for a state-guaranteed minimum standard of living, prefer the use of money transfers to individuals rather than the provision of social services below or at zero cost, that is to say the economic condition of individuals in receipt of state support should be reflected in reduction in T_k^i (whose value may have to be negative) rather than an increase in q_k. Thus it is argued that individuals then retain responsibility for the purchase of goods and services designed to promote their own welfare and that the power of the state over the individual by bureaucratic dictatorship of preferences and by the lack of incentives in the public sector to economize in resource use is circumscribed.

A more severe test for the practicality of libertarian measures, designed to permit some redistribution without increasing the power of the state, arises in the case of any attack on the concentration of wealth. Clearly, a system of inheritance taxation which results in the transfer of capital from the private to the public sector would not conform to libertarian thinking, not only because this would discourage private saving but also because it would build up the power of the state. A system of taxation would have to be devised which not only did not discourage accumulation of private capital but also simultaneously encouraged legators to disseminate capital in favour of those with little capital. It is a long time since libertarians have plucked up the courage to try to develop such a system, given that eminent public finance specialists have failed in their attempts to fulfil these requirements.

The second major question arises from the persistent objection of Marxists and other Socialist writers that the system of economic freedom, as depicted by the libertarians, fails to solve the problem of 'worker alienation'. It may be that the system of economic freedom can allow employees alone or in combination with others to influence the price of factor inputs (p_k^a) and the work/leisure combination (a^i), variables which play a crucial part in individual welfare. The fact remains that the system of property rights, which libertarians support, includes the individual ownership of capital and the use of capitalistic methods of production which imply an authority relationship between employer and worker. The hierarchical order at the place of work seems at complete variance with the independence of economic action attributed to the individual by the supporters of economic freedom.

Reactions to this argument by libertarians are sometimes reminiscent of the Scots preacher who, on recognizing a theological difficulty in his sermon, recommended his congregation to look the difficulty squarely in the face and pass it by. However, even Socialist writers, notably the prominent Marxist Ota Sik (1974), have recognized that the alternative to market capitalism – collectivist production – does not solve the problem for it is not synonymous with democratization at the shop-floor level. In other words, the basis of alienation is technological and not institutional. Some libertarians, notably Mill, have made common cause with Socialists by arguing that alienation must not be taken to be an inevitable consequence of productive activity. Mill sought one solution in the encouragement of firms owned and managed by the labour force, but still subject to competition. Utopian Socialists have claimed that the only solution is to reject altogether the technology which imposes hierarchical relations in the first place. Both 'solutions' are still the subject of living debate in both the professional and political arena.

BIBLIOGRAPHY

Barry, N.P. 1985. In defense of the invisible hand. *The Cato Journal* 5(1), Spring, 133–48.
Buchanan, J.M. 1975. *The Limits of Liberty: Between Anarchy and Leviathan*. Chicago and London: University of Chicago Press.
Hahn, F. 1982. Reflections on the invisible hand. *Lloyds Bank Review* 144, April, 1–21.
Hayek, F.A. 1979. *Law, Legislation and Liberty*, Vol. 3. London: Routledge & Kegan Paul; Chicago: University of Chicago Press.
Mill, J.S. 1859. *Essay on Liberty*. Oxford: Oxford University Press, 1942; Chicago: H. Regnery, 1955.
Mill, J.S. 1871. *Principles of Political Economy*, Book IV, ch. VII. Toronto: University of Toronto Press, 1965.
Nozick, R. 1974. *Anarchy, State and Utopia*. Oxford: Basil Blackwell; New York: Basic Books.
Peacock, A. 1979. *The Economic Analysis of Government and Related Themes*. Oxford: Martin Robertson, chs 5 and 6; New York: St. Martin's Press, 1980.
Rowley, C. and Peacock, A. 1975. *Welfare Economics: A Liberal Re-Interpretation*. London: Martin Robertson.

Sik, O. 1974. The shortcomings of the Soviet economy as seen in Communist ideologies. *Government and Opposition* 9(3), 263–76.

Smith, A. 1776. *An Inquiry into the Nature and Causes of the Wealth of Nations*, Book IV, ch. 9 and Book V. Ed. R.H. Campbell, A.S. Skinner and W.B. Todd, Oxford: Clarendon Press, 1976; New York: Liberty Press, 1981.

Economic Harmony

ISRAEL M. KIRZNER

This term has been introduced frequently into economic discussion, and especially into discussions concerning the history of economic thought. Yet there seems to be a good deal of ambiguity as to what it is to mean. Moreover, there has developed considerable disagreement concerning the centrality of the 'harmony' idea to the development of economic thought, and similar disagreement concerning the extent to which the classical economists, in particular, are to be seen as harmony-theorists. We will return a little later to distinguish various different senses that have been attached to the term 'harmony' in economics. For each of these different senses, however, acceptance of the harmony thesis has been held to imply a favourable stance towards a policy of laissez-faire. It is thus not surprising that 18th-century precursors of the notion of harmony have been discovered in Cantillon and in Quesnay (Schumpeter, 1954, p. 234). And we are not surprised to find some writers emphasizing the harmony ideas they see in the classical economists, especially in Adam Smith (Halévey, 1901–4, p. 89: Heimann, 1945, p. 65), while others vehemently question the unqualified identification of these writers with harmony theories (Robbins, 1952, pp. 22–9; Samuels, 1966, pp. 6–8; Sowell, 1974, pp. 16f). It was in the middle of the 19th century that the best-known writings appeared concerning economic harmony. The term appeared in the title of two books by the American economist Henry C. Carey (Carey 1836, 1852). These works were followed by a general treatise stressing the same theme (Carey, 1858–60). The term also appeared in the title of a book by the French economic writer Frédéric Bastiat (1850). For a (muted) defence of Bastiat against widespread 19th-century charges that his work in this respect was a crude plagiarism of Carey, see Teilhac (1936, pp. 100–113), who points to the inspiration that both Carey and Bastiat received from J.B. Say. Subsequent references to harmony theories in economics generally tended to be critical, as economists began to argue (from the latter decades of the 19th century into the 20th century) for greater state intervention in market economies on perceived grounds of economic efficiency or economic justice.

During most of the 20th century economists, even when they have defended the efficiency and justice of markets, have generally not couched their arguments explicitly in terms of harmony theory. Even Ludwig von Mises who, as we shall see, was an important exception to this last generalization, relegated the notion of harmony to a distinctly subsidiary role in his system. Recent re-awakened attention to 18th-century theories of spontaneous order, especially as rediscovered and expanded in the work of Hayek, has not had the effect of reintroducing the term 'economic harmony' to current usage. We turn now to take notice of the several different (although certainly interrelated) senses in which this term has been used during the history of economics.

HARMONY AS FLOWING FROM DIVINE PROVIDENCE. A harmony 'theory' is not, in this sense, one that flows out of economic science; rather it represents an attitude of (usually religious) optimism and faith, which itself suggests and guides the course of scientific investigation.

> Just as Kepler was inspired by the doctrine of harmony in the spheres to discover the laws which govern the orbits of the planets, so the early economists were inspired by the doctrine that there is a harmony of interests in a society to formulate economic laws (Streeten, 1954, p. 208).

It was from this sense of the term that Lord Robbins vigorously dissociated the classical school. It was this optimistic doctrine that came to be referred to contemptuously by the German term 'Harmonielehre'. Archbishop Whately, who in 1832 set up a chair of political economy at Trinity College, Dublin, was an influential harmony theorist in this sense. He saw the purpose of the chair as that of combatting the irreligious implications, as he saw them, of Ricardian economics. The early Dublin professors 'were under pressure to present an optimistic or harmonius picture of how the market economy operates' and the resulting critical attitude towards Ricardian theory reflected 'these extrascientific concerns' (Moss, 1976, p. 153). A variant of this approach to the harmony doctrine was the Enlightenment view, in which Deistic philosophy perceived a natural order as responsible for 'predetermined harmony' (Mises, 1949, p. 239; Heimann, 1945, p. 49).

HARMONY THEORY AS THE DOCTRINE OF MAXIMUM SATISFACTION. When major neoclassical economists such as Marshall (1920, p. 470) and Wicksell (1901, p. 73) referred to harmony theorists, they evidently had in mind those who believed that economic theory demonstrates that free competitive markets generate maximum total satisfaction for society as a whole. 'Harmony theory' thus referred to a very specific conclusion of economic science, a conclusion central to welfare economics, but a conclusion whose validity both Marshall and Wicksell were concerned to refute. Of special concern, in this context, was the issue of whether the new marginal utility doctrines had been successfully deployed by Jevons, or by Walras, to arrive at 'harmony' conclusions similar to those that had been reached, on other grounds, by Bastiat.

Parallel to this sense of harmony was that which attributed *ethical* virtues to the distributive results of competitive markets. Thus J.B. Clark's demonstration of the justice of marginal-productivity incomes is seen as 'harmony doctrine' (Myrdal, 1932, p. 148).

HARMONY DOCTRINE AS THE DENIAL OF CLASS CONFLICT. One sense in which harmony doctrines have been understood throughout the history of economics is that in which it is sought to demonstrate the mutual compatibility of the interests of the various individuals and groups in society. In particular, such doctrines tend to dismiss the notion of inherent class conflict under capitalism. A 20th-century economist who has himself emphasized this idea of harmony of interests in the market society, put the genesis of this idea as follows:

> When the classical economists [asserted 'the theorem of the harmony of the rightly understood interests of all members of the market society' they were stressing] two points: First, that everybody is interested in the preservation of the social division of labour, the system that multiplies the productivity of human efforts. Second, that in the market society consumers' demand ultimately directs all production activities (Mises, 1949, p. 674).

Mises, indeed, saw these ideas as important results of economic science, having wide application. 'There is no conflict between the interests of the buyers and those of the sellers, between the interest of the producers and those of the consumers' (Mises, 1949, p. 357). Only in the special case of resource monopoly ownership may it happen that the 'emergence of monopoly prices... creates a discrepancy between the interests of the monopolist and those of the consumers' (Mises, 1949, p. 680).

HARMONY AND THE SPONTANEOUS ORDER TRADITION. Since the early 1940s F.A. Hayek has succeeded in drawing the attention of economists and others to a line of social analysis since the 18th century, an approach often termed the 'spontaneous order tradition'. The emphasis, in this tradition, is on the evolution of institutions and social outcomes 'which are indeed the results of human action, but not the execution of any human design' (Ferguson, 1767, p. 187, cited in Hayek, 1967, p. 96). There is no doubt that the term 'economic harmony' has often been applied as an expression of belief in the *possibility and social benignity of undesigned social outcomes*. To some extent, of course, this sense of the term overlaps those listed above, but the emphasis here is not on the denial of conflict, not on any particular welfare theorem, certainly not on any religiously based optimism, but on the counter-intuitive possibility of orderly results emerging without deliberate design from the spontaneous interplay of independently acting individuals. 'Order' in this context has come to mean 'mutually reinforcing expectations'. The following reference to this notion of harmony expresses this usage of the term:

> The great general rule governing human action at the beginning, namely that

it must conform to fair expectations, is still the scientific rule. All the forms of conduct complying with this rule are consistent with each other and become the recognized customs. The body of custom therefore tends to become a harmonious system (Carter 1907, p. 331, cited in Hayek, 1973, p. 169).

The above survey has been confined to notions of economic harmony believed to be achieved spontaneously, 'naturally', without design. For the sake of completeness it should perhaps be noted that the term 'harmony' has occasionally been used to describe the objective of *deliberate* social policy. Thus a well-known debate was initiated by E. Halévy in his claim that Bentham and the philosophical Radicals subscribed to two partly contradictory principles: the 'economic' principle of 'natural identity' (i.e. harmony) of interests, and the 'juristic' principle of the 'artificial identification of interests' (Halévy, 1901–4, pp. 15, 17, 489). Lord Robbins, in disputing Halévy concerning any contradiction in the Benthamite position, refers to the juristic principle as contending it to be 'the function of the legislator to bring about an artificial harmonization of interest' (Robbins, 1952, pp. 190f). While occasional references may be found to harmony sought to be artificially accomplished, the term has, in general, been associated almost invariably with harmony achieved undeliberately in a decentralized system.

BIBLIOGRAPHY
Bastiat, F. 1850. *Les harmonies économiques.* Paris: Guillaumin.
Carey, H.C. 1836. *The Harmony of Nature.* Philadelphia: Carey, Lea & Blanchard.
Carey, H.C. 1852. *The Harmony of Interests, Agricultural, Manufacturing, and Commercial.* 2nd edn, New York: Myron Finch.
Carey, H.C. 1858–60. *Principles of Social Science.* Philadelphia: J.B. Lippincott.
Carter, J.C. 1907. *Law, Its Origin, Growth and Function.* New York and London: G.P. Putnam's Sons.
Ferguson, A. 1767. *An Essay on the History of Civil Society.* London.
Halévy, E. 1901–4. *The Growth of Philosophic Radicalism.* Translated from the French by M. Morris, 1928, Boston: Beacon, 1955.
Hayek, F.A. 1967. *Studies in Philosophy, Politics and Economics.* Chicago: University of Chicago Press.
Hayek, F.A. 1973. *Law, Legislation and Liberty.* Vol. I: *Rules and Order*, Chicago: University of Chicago Press.
Heimann, E. 1945. *History of Economic Doctrines, An Introduction to Economic Theory.* New York: Oxford University Press.
Marshall, A. 1920. *Principles of Economics.* 8th edn, London: Macmillan, 1936; New York: Macmillan, 1948.
Mises, L. von. 1949. *Human Action: A Treatise on Economics.* 3rd edn, Chicago: Regnery, 1966.
Moss, L.S. 1976. *Mountifort Longfield: Ireland's First Professor of Political Economy.* Ottowa, Ill.: Green Hill.
Myrdal, G. 1932. *The Political Element in the Development of Economic Theory.* Translated from the German by P. Streeten, Cambridge, Mass.: Harvard University Press, 1954.
Robbins, L. 1952. *The Theory of Economic Policy in English Classical Political Economy.* London: Macmillan, 1965.

Samuels, W.J. 1966. *The Classical Theory of Economic Policy*. Cleveland and New York: World.

Schumpeter, J.A. 1954. *History of Economic Analysis*. New York: Oxford University Press.

Sowell, T. 1974. *Classical Economics Reconsidered*. Princeton: Princeton University Press.

Streeten, P. 1954. Recent controversies. Appendix to Myrdal (1932).

Teilhac, E. 1936. *Pioneers of American Economic Thought in the Nineteenth Century*. Translated from the French by E.A.J. Johnson (1936), reprinted, New York: Russell and Russell, 1967.

Wicksell, K. 1901. *Lectures on Political Economy*. Vol. I, Translated from the Swedish by E. Classen, London: Routledge and Kegan Paul, 1934; New York: A.M. Kelley, 1967.

Economic Laws

STEFANO ZAMAGNI

The social sciences, and economics in particular, separated from moral and political philosophy in the second half of the 18th century when the results of the myriad of intentional actions of people were perceived to produce regularities resembling the laws of a system. Both physiocratic thought and Smith's *Wealth of Nations* reflect this extraordinary discovery: scientific laws thought to be found only in nature could also be found in society. This extension poses several problems. A serious one refers to the tension of combining individuals' freedom of action with the scientists' desire to discover the systematic aspects of the unintended and quite often unpredictable consequences of human action, i.e. the desire to arrive at laws characterized by a certain degree of generality and permanence.

In the history of economic thought this fundamental tension has been solved in different ways. In the 18th century, the mechanistic ideal of the natural sciences, combined with the natural law idea of a harmonious order of nature, determined the way social phenomena were treated. There was a desire to discover the 'natural laws' of economic life and to formulate the natural precepts which rule human conduct. The classical economists upheld the notion that natural laws are embedded in the economic process as beneficial laws, along with the belief in the existence of rules of nature capable of being discovered. Thus the belief that things could follow the beneficial 'natural course' only in a rationally organized society which it was a duty to create according to the precepts of nature. The economic system is the mechanism by which the individual is driven to fostering the prosperity of society while pursuing his private interest. Hence the automatic operation of the economic system may be combined with freedom of individual action. This is the core of the doctrine of economic harmony. Besides being causal laws of a mechanical type, the laws of nature are providentially imposed norms of conduct. In such a setting it would have been pointless to separate means and ends, since the implementation of natural laws is both an end and a means, and even more pointless to think of a tension between 'explaining' and 'understanding' economic behaviour. Causal and teleological, positive and normative, theoretical and practical started being seen as separate categories only when the economic discourse freed itself from the philosophy of natural law and all its implications.

Post-classical economics set out to be a science of the laws regulating the economic order and of the conditions allowing these laws to operate. It became the basis of a theory that, in Jevons's own terms, proposed to construct a 'social physics'. The view of a social world ordered according to transcendent ends was abandoned in favour of an ideal of objective knowledge of economic phenomena gained through a 'positive' study of the laws that regulate market activities. In so doing, neoclassical 'positive' economics solves the aforementioned tension by extrapolating the theoretical model of natural sciences to economics: economics is to produce the laws of motion similar to those of physics, chemistry, astronomy.

But what is a scientific law and which role do laws play within the logical positivist's perspective adopted by neoclassical economics? Laws provide the foundation of a deductive scientific method of inquiry. According to the deductive–nomological conception of explanation, due to C. Hempel, laws are universal statements not requiring reference to any one particular object or spatio–temporal location. To be valid, laws are constrained neither to finite populations nor to particular times and places; they are, in effect, expressions of natural stationarities. This interpretation of the notion of law provides the so-called covering-law model of explanation with an unquestionably firm inferential foundation. Deductive logic is employed to ensure the truth status of propositions and since the deductions are (by hypothesis) predicated on true universal statements (laws), the empirical validity of these statements may be ascertained. However, what sort of constraints on economic discourse are imposed by this positivistic structure? On the one hand this structure constitutes its object; on the other hand it generates specific economic questions together with their method of solution. Following the model of natural sciences and its success in controlling a natural world made up of objects and unvarying relations among them expressed in the form of laws, the neoclassical approach arrives at a study of regularities conceived of as specifying the nature of its objects.

To capture the different interpretations of the notion of law by classical and neoclassical economists let us refer to one of the most famous of economic laws: the law of diminishing returns, also known as the law of variable proportions. Studying agricultural production, Ricardo had noted that different quantities of labour, assisted by certain quantities of other inputs (farm tools, fertilizers, etc.), could be employed on a given piece of land, i.e. it was possible to vary the proportions in which land and complex labour (labour assisted by other inputs) are employed. He accordingly arrived at the law which states that production increases resulting from equal increments in the employment of complex labour, while the quantity of land farmed remains constant, will initially be increasing and then decreasing. (To be sure, the first statement of the law is due to the physiocratic economist Turgot.)

Three points deserve attention. First, Ricardo and classical authors in general offer no formal demonstration of this law. To them, it is basically an empirical law, on which no functional association between output and variable inputs can be built. Second, the classics' use of the law refers to their theories of distribution and development: as the supply of land in the whole system is fixed, sooner or later a point will be reached at which economic growth will come to halt, notwithstanding any countervailing effects due to technical progress. Finally, the law presupposes a comparative statics framework: the pattern of the marginal products of complex labour refers to different observable equilibrium positions and not to hypothetical or virtual variations.

With the advent of the marginalist revolution, two subtle changes in the interpretation of the law took place. (a) The *de facto* elimination of the distinction between the extensive case (the case of the simultaneous cultivation of pieces of land of different fertility) and the intensive case (the application of successive doses of capital and labour to the same piece of land) with an over-evaluation of the latter. Classical economists, being interested in the explanation of rent, concentrated on the extensive case; they took also the intensive case into consideration but with many qualifications. Indeed, whereas the various levels of productivity of different qualities of land is a circumstance which may be directly observed in a given situation, the marginal productivity of a given input is related to a virtual increment in output and therefore to a virtual change in the situation. (b) The change in the method of analysis – it was preferred to reason in terms of hypothetical rather than observable changes – brought about by the shift of interest towards the intensive margin, supported the thesis of the symmetrical nature of land and other inputs. This in turn favoured the extension of the substitutability between land and complex labour from agricultural production to all kinds of production, including those in which land does not figure as a direct input. It so happened that whereas in classical economics the substitutability between land and complex labour presupposes that simple labour and equipment are strictly complementary, in neoclassical economics this substitutability is applied to all inputs indiscriminately.

However, the neoclassical interpretation of the law poses serious problems. In the first place, there is the problem of justifying, on empirical grounds, the general applicability of the substitution principle. Secondly, and more importantly, in order to allow the substitution of inputs to take place, a certain lapse of time is required during which the required modifications to the productive structure can be made. (It is certainly true that coal can replace oil to provide heating, but before this can happen it will be necessary to change the heating system.) The well-known distinction between the short-run and the long-run is a partial and indirect way to take the temporal element into consideration. In the short-run the plant is fixed by definition. It is therefore the fixed input which, in the neoclassical interpretation of the law, plays the same role as land in the classical interpretation. Now, neoclassical theory correctly states the law of diminishing returns with respect to the short-run; however, it is in the long run that the substitutability of inputs becomes actually feasible. One is therefore confronted with a dilemma: the neoclassical interpretation of the law seems to be more plausible in a long-run framework when there exists the necessary time to accommodate input adjustments; on the other hand, fixed inputs cannot, by definition, exist in the long run so that the law of variable proportions cannot be stated in such a context.

This dilemma is the price neoclassical theory has to pay for its interpretation of the law in accordance with the positivistic statute. Indeed, the power of deductive, truth-preserving rules of scientific inference is not purchased without a cost. A school of economic thought which is not prepared to sustain such a cost is the neo-Austrian. The neo-Austrian economists solve what has been called the fundamental tension by arguing economics cannot and should not provide general laws since, by its very nature, it is an idiographic and not a nomothetical discipline. The general target of economics is 'understanding' grounded in *Verstehen* doctrine: by introspection and empathy, the study of the economic process should aim at explaining individual occurrences, not abstract classes of phenomena. It follows that if by a scientific law one should mean a universal conditional statement of type 'for all x, if x is A, then x is B', statements regarding unique events cannot by definition express any regularity for the simple reason that any regularity presupposes the recurrence of what is defined as regular. In the worlds of L. von Mises, who shares with F. von Hayek the paternity of the neo-Austrian school, what assigns economics its peculiar and unique position in the orbit of pure knowledge '... is the fact that its particular theorems are not open to any verification or falsification on the ground of experience ... the ultimate yardstick of an economic theorem's correctness or incorrectness is solely reason unaided by experience' (von Mises, 1949, p. 858).

There is indeed a place for economic 'laws' in the framework of Austrian economics. The familiar 'laws' of economics (diminishing marginal utility, supply and demand, diminishing returns to factors, Say's law and so on) are seen as 'necessary truths' which explain the essential structure of the economic world but with no predictive worth. In other words, economic laws are not generalizations from experience, as it is the case within the positivistic paradigm, but are theorems which enable us to understand the economic world. It is ironic that Mises' position of radical apriorism joined to Hayek's attack on scientism and methodological monism are completely at variance with the position taken by the father of the Austrian school, Carl Menger (1883), who announced that in economic theories exact laws are defined which are just as rigorous as in fact are the laws of nature.

Between the extreme positions of neoclassical positive economics and neo-Austrian economics are those who, without denying that economics is in search for laws in the same sense in which natural sciences are and that laws perform an explanatory as well as a predictive function, underline that the explicative structure of economics, albeit nomothetical, substantially differs from that of natural sciences. This intermediate position can be traced back to Keynes's methodology which considers the conditions of truth and universality of the positivistic conception of scientific laws as far too rigid for a discipline such as economics. Two main reasons account for the different epistemological status of laws in natural sciences and in economics. First, the knowledge of economic phenomena is itself an economic variable, i.e. it changes, along with the process of its own acquisition, the economic situation to which it refers. The formulation of a new physical law does not change the course of physical processes; it does not influence the truth or falsity of the prognosis. This is not the case in economics where the prognosis, say, that in two years time there will be a boom can cause overproduction and a resulting recession. In turn, this specific aspect is strictly connected to the fact that the object of study of economics possesses an historical dimension. Economics is in time in a way that natural sciences are not. The ensuing mutability of observed regularities is well expressed by Keynes when he writes, 'As against Robbins, economics is essentially a moral science and not a natural science. This is to say it employs introspection and judgements of value' (1973, p. 297) to which he adds, 'It deals with motives, expectations, psychological uncertainties. One has to be constantly on guard against treating the material as constant and homogeneous' (p. 300).

Second, the role played by *ceteris paribus* clauses in natural sciences and in economics is substantially different. The modern economists appeal to the 'other things being equal' clause – which according to Marshall is invariably attached to any economic law – in all those cases where the classical economists were talking of 'disturbing causes'. J.S. Mill's discussion of inexact sciences is suggestive here:

> When the principles of Political Economy are to be applied to a particular case then it is necessary to take into account all the individual circumstances of that case... These circumstances have been called *disturbing causes*. This constitutes the only uncertainty of Political Economy (1836, p. 300).

Also in natural sciences we find *ceteris paribus* clauses. Indeed, a scientific theory that could dispense with them would in effect achieve perfect closure, which is a rarity. So where lies the difference? The example of the science of tides used by Mill is revealing. Physicists know the laws of the greater causes (the gravitational pull of moon) but do not know the laws of the minor causes (the configuration of the sea bottom). The 'other things' which scientists hold equal are the lesser causes. So could we conclude that just about all generalizations in both natural sciences and economics express in fact *tendency laws*, in the sense that these 'laws' truly capture only the functioning of 'greater causes' within some domain? Certainly not, since there is a world of difference between the two cases. Galileo's law of falling bodies certainly presupposes a *ceteris paribus* clause, so much so that he had to employ the idealization of a 'perfect vacuum' to get rid of the resistance of air. However, he was able to give estimates of the magnitudes of the amount of distortion that friction and the other 'accidents' would determine and which the law ignored. In other words, whereas in natural sciences the 'disturbing causes' have their own laws, this is not the case in economics where we find tendency statements with unspecified *ceteris paribus* clauses or, if specified, specified only in qualitative terms. In economics it is generally impossible to list all the conceivable inferences implied in a lawlike statement and to replace the *ceteris paribus* clause with precise conditions. So, for example, the law that 'less will be bought at a higher price' is not refuted by panic buying, nor is it confirmed by organized consumer boycotts. No test is decisive unless *ceteris* are really *paribus*.

These remarks help us to understand the role acknowledged by Keynes to laws in economic inquiry. Besides general laws, there are also rules and norms which are significant in the explanation of economic behaviour. To Keynes, it makes no sense to reduce all forms of explanation in economics to that of the covering-law model. Indeed, whereas to justify a law one has to show that it is logically derivable from some other more general statements, often called principles or postulates, the justification of rules occurs through the reference to goals and the justification of norms through the reference to values which are not general sentences, but rather intended singular patterns or even ideal entities. Since no scientific law, in the natural scientific sense, has been established in economics, on which economists can base predictions, what are used and have to be used to explain or to predict are tendencies or patterns expressed in empirical or historical generalizations of less than universal validity, restricted by local and temporal limits. Recently, Arrow has amazed orthodox economists when raising doubts about the mechanistically inspired understanding of economic processes: 'Is economics a subject like physics, true for all time or are its laws historically conditioned?' (Arrow, 1985, p. 322).

The list of generally accepted economic laws seems to be shrinking. The term itself has come to acquire a somewhat old-fashioned ring and economists now prefer to present their most cherished general statements as theorems or propositions rather than laws. This is no doubt a healthy reaction: for too long economists have been under the nomological prejudice, of positivistic origin, that the only route towards explanation and prediction is the one paved with laws, and laws as forceful as Newton's laws. Images in science are never innocent: wrong images can have disastrous effects.

BIBLIOGRAPHY

Arrow, K. 1985. Economic history: a necessary though not sufficient condition for an economist. *American Economic Review, Papers and Proceedings* 75(2), May, 320–23.

Keynes, J.M. 1973. *The General Theory and After*. Part II: *Defence and Development*. In *The Collected Writings of John Maynard Keynes*, Vol. XIV, London: Macmillan.

Menger, C. 1883. *Unterschungen über die Methode der Sozialwissenschaften*. Leipzig: Duncker & Humblot.

Mill, J.S. 1836. On the definition of political economy and the method of investigation proper to it. Reprinted in *Collected Works of John Stuart Mill, Essays on Economy and Society*, ed. J.M. Robson, Toronto: University of Toronto Press, 1967, Vol. 4.

Mises, L. von. 1949. *Human Action. A Treatise on Economics*. London: William Hodge.

Equilibrium: development of the concept

MURRAY MILGATE

From what appears to have been the first use of the term in economics by James Steuart in 1769, down to the present day, equilibrium analysis (together with its derivative, disequilibrium analysis) has been the foundation upon which economic theory has been able to build up its not inconsiderable claims to 'scientific' status. Yet despite the persistent use of the concept by economists for over two hundred years, its meaning and role have undergone some quite profound modifications over that period.

At the most elementary level, 'equilibrium' is spoken about in a number of ways. It may be regarded as a 'balance of forces', as when, for example, it is used to describe the familiar idea of a balance between the forces of demand and supply. Or it can be taken to signify a point from which there is no endogenous 'tendency to change': stationary or steady states exhibit this kind of property. However, it may also be thought of as that outcome which any given economic process might be said to be 'tending towards', as in the idea that competitive processes tend to produce determinate outcomes. It is in this last guise that the concept seems first to have been applied in economic theory. Equilibrium is, as Adam Smith might have put it (though he did not use the term), the centre of gravitation of the economic system – it is that configuration of values towards which all economic magnitudes are continually tending to conform.

There are two properties embodied in this original concept which when taken into account begin to impart to it a rather more precise meaning and a well-defined methodological status. Into this category enters the formal definition of 'equilibrium conditions' and the argument for taking these to be a useful object of analysis.

There are few better or more appropriate places to isolate the first two properties of 'equilibrium' in this original sense than in the seventh chapter of the first book of Adam Smith's *Wealth of Nations*. The argument there consists of two steps. The first is to define 'natural conditions':

> There is in every society...an ordinary or average rate of both wages and profits.... When the price of any commodity is neither more nor less than what is sufficient to pay...the wages of the labour and the profits of the stock employed...according to their natural rates, the commodity is then sold for what may be called its natural price (Smith, 1776, I.vii, p. 62).

The key point here is that 'natural conditions' are associated with a general rate of profit – that is, uniformity in the returns to capital invested in different lines of production under existing best-practice technique. In the language of the day, this property was thought to be the characteristic of the outcome of the operation of the process of 'free competition'.

The second step in the argument captures the analytical status to be assigned to 'natural conditions':

> The natural price...is, as it were, the central price, to which the prices of all commodities are continually gravitating. Different accidents may sometimes keep them suspended a good deal above it, and sometimes force them down even somewhat below it. But whatever may be the obstacles which hinder them from settling in this centre of repose and continuance, they are constantly tending towards it (I.vii, p. 65).

This particular 'tendency towards equilibrium' was held to be operative in the *actual* economic system at any given time. It is not to be confused with the familiar question concerning the stability of competitive equilibrium in modern analysis. There the question about convergence to equilibrium is posed in some *hypothetical* state of the world where none but the most purely competitive environment is held to prevail. It is also essential to observe that in defining 'natural conditions' in this fashion, nothing has yet been said (nor need it be said) about the forces which act to determine the natural rates of wages and profits, or the natural prices of commodities. It will therefore be possible to refrain from discussing the *theories* offered by various economists for the determination of these variables in most of what follows. Similarly, there will be no discussion here of existence or uniqueness of equilibrium.

'Natural conditions' so defined and conceived are the formal expression of the idea that certain systematic or persistent forces, regular in their operation, are at work in the economic system. Smith's earlier idea, that 'the co-existent parts of the universe...contribute to compose one immense and connected system' (1759, VII. ii, 1.37), is translated in this later formulation into an analytical device capable of generating conclusions with a claim to general (as opposed to a particular, or special) validity. These general conclusions were customarily referred to as 'statements of tendency', or 'laws', or 'principles' in the economic literature of the 18th and 19th centuries. It is worth emphasizing that there was no implication that these general tendencies were either swift in their operation or that they were not subject at any time to interference from other obstacles. Like sea level, 'natural conditions' had an unambiguous meaning, even if subject to innumerable cross-currents.

To put it another way, the distinction between 'general' and 'special' cases (like its counterpart, the distinction between 'equilibrium' and 'disequilibrium'), refers neither to the immediate practical relevance of these kinds of cases to actual existing market conditions, nor to the prevalence, frequency, or probability of their occurrence. In fact, as far as simple observation is concerned, it might well be that 'special' cases would be the order of the day. John Stuart Mill expressed this idea especially clearly when he held that the conclusions of economic theory are only applicable 'in the *abstract*', that is, 'they are only true under certain suppositions, in which none but general causes – causes common to the *whole class* of cases under consideration – are taken into account' (Mill, 1844, pp. 144–5'. Marshall, of course, understood their application as being subject not only to this qualification (which he spoke about in terms of 'time'), but also to the condition that 'other things are equal (1890, I.iii, p. 36). There will be cause to return to this matter below.

To unearth these regularities, one has to inquire behind the scene, so to speak, to reveal what otherwise might remain hidden. Adam Smith had set out the basis of this procedure in an early essay on 'The Principles which Lead and Direct Philosophical Enquiries':

> Nature, after the largest experience that common observation can acquire, seems to abound with events which appear solitary and incoherent... by representing the invisible chains which bind together all these disjointed objects, [philosophy] endeavours to introduce order into this chaos of jarring and discordent appearances (Smith, 1795, p. 45).

In short, 'equilibrium', if we may revert to the modern terminology for a moment, became the central organizing category around which economic theory was to be constructed. It is no accident that the formal introduction of the concept into economics is associated with those very writers whose names are closely connected with the foundation of 'economic science'. It could even be argued that its introduction marks the foundation of the discipline itself, since its appearance divides quite neatly the subsequent literature from the many analyses of individual problems which dominated prior to Smith and the Physiocracts.

Cementing this tradition, Ricardo spoke of fixing his 'whole attention on the permanent state of things' which follows from given changes, excluding for the purposes of general analysis 'accidental and temporary deviations' (1817, p. 88). Marshall, though substituting the terminology 'long-run normal conditions' for the older 'natural conditions', excluded from this category results upon which 'accidents of the moment exert a preponderating influence' (1890, p. vii). J.B. Clark followed suit and held that 'natural or normal' values are those to which 'in the long run, market values tend to conform' (1899, p. 16). Jevons (1871, p. 86), Walras (1874–7, p. 380), Böhm-Bawerk (1899, II, p. 380) and Wicksell (1901, I, p. 97) all followed the same procedure.

Not only was the status of 'equilibrium' as the centre of gravitation of the system (the benchmark case, so to speak) preserved, but it was defined in the manner of Smith. The primary theoretical object of all these writers was to explain that situation characterized by a uniform rate of profit on the supply price of capital invested in different lines of production. Walras, whose argument is quite typical, stated the nature of the connection forcefully:

> uniformity of…the price of net income [rate of profit] on the capital goods market…[is one] condition by which the universe of economic interests is governed (1874–7, p. 305).

From an historical point of view, the novelty of these arguments which were worked out in the 18th century by Smith and the Physiocrats, is not that they recognized that there might be situations which could be described as 'natural', but that they associated these conditions with the outcome of a specific process common to market economics (free competition) and utilized them in the construction of a general economic analysis of market society. Earlier applications of 'natural order' arguments were little more than normative pronouncements about some existing or possible state of society. They certainly made no 'scientific' use of the idea of systematic tendencies, even if these might have been involved. This is particularly apparent in the case of the 'natural law' philosophers, but is also true of the early liberals like Locke and Hobbes. Even Hume, who to all intents and purposes had in his possession all of the building blocks of Smith's position, drew back from the one crucial step that would have led him to Smith's 'method' – he was just not prepared to admit that thinking in terms of regularities, however useful it might prove to be in dispelling theological and other obfuscations (and thus in advancing 'human understanding'), was anything more than a convenient and satisfying way of thinking. The question as to whether the social and economic world was actually governed by such regularities, so central to Smith and the Physiocrats, just did not concern Hume.

Yet the earlier normative connotations of ideas like 'natural conditions', 'natural order', and the like, quite rapidly disappeared when the terminology was appropriated by economic theory. Nothing was 'good' simply by virtue of its being 'natural'. This, of course, is not to say that once the theoretical analysis of the natural tendencies operating in market economies had been completed, and the outcomes of the competitive process had been isolated in abstract, an individual theorist might not at that stage wish to draw some conclusions about the 'desirability' of its results (a normative statement, so to speak). But such statements are not implied by the concept of equilibrium – they are value judgements about the characteristics of its outcomes.

Indeed, contrary to the view sometimes expressed, even Smith's use of Deistic analogies and metaphors in the *Theory of Moral Sentiments*, where we read about God as the creator of the 'great machine of the universe', and where we encounter for the first time the famous 'invisible hand', is no more than the extraneous window-dressing which surrounds a well-defined *theoretical* argument based upon the operation of the so called 'sympathy' mechanism. Thus, as W.E. Johnson noted when writing for the original edition of Palgrave's *Dictionary*, 'the confusion between scientific law and ethical law no longer prevails', and he observes that 'the term normal has replaced the older word natural' – to be understood by this terminology as 'something which presents a certain empirical uniformity or regularity' (1899, p. 139).

While 'natural conditions' or 'long-run normal conditions' represent the original concept of 'equilibrium' utilized in economic theory, John Stuart Mill's *Political Economy* seems to have been the source from which the actual term equilibrium gained widespread currency (though, like so much else, it is also to be found in Cournot's *Recherches*). More significant, however, is the fact that in Mill's hands the meaning and status of the concept undergoes a modification. While maintaining the idea of equilibrium as a long-period position, Mill introduces the idea that the equilibrium theory is essentially 'static'. The relevant remarks appear at the beginning of the fourth book:

> We have to consider the economical condition of mankind as liable to change... thereby adding a theory of motion to our theory of equilibrium – the Dynamics of political economy to the Statics (Mill, 1848, IV.i, p. 421).

Since he retained the basic category of 'natural and normal conditions', Mill's claim had the effect of adding a property to the list of those associated with the concept of equilibrium. However, over the question of whether this additional property was necessary to the concept of equilibrium there was to be less uniformity of opinion. Indeed, this matter gave rise to a debate in which at one time or another (until at least the 1930s) almost all theorists of any repute became contributors. The problem was a simple one – are natural or long-period normal conditions the same thing as the 'famous fiction' of the stationary or steady state. Much hinged upon the answer; a 'yes' would have limited the application of equilibrium to an imaginary stationary society in which no one conducts the daily business of life.

On this question, as might be expected, Marshall vacillated. The thrust of his argument (as well as those of his major contemporaries, with the important exception of Pareto) seems to imply that such a property was not essential to his purpose, but as was his habit on so many occasions, in a footnote he qualified that position (1890, p. 379, n.1). In the final analysis, the answer seems to have depended rather more on the explanation given for the determination of equilibrium values, than upon the concept of equilibrium proper. It was not until the 1930s that the issue seems to have been resolved to the general satisfaction of the profession. But then its 'resolution' required the introduction of a new definition of equilibrium (the concept of intertemporal equilibrium) due in the main to Hicks.

However, some further embellishments and modifications were worked upon the concept of equilibrium before the 1930s. Here, two developments stand out. The first concerns the distinction between partial equilibrium analysis and general equilibrium analysis. The second concerns a trend that seems to have developed consequent upon Marshall's treatment of the element of time, which led him to his threefold typology of periods ('market', 'short', and 'long' – we shall leave to one side the further category of 'secular movement'). The upshot of this trend which is decisive, is that it became common to speak of the possibility of 'equilibrium' in each of these Marshallian periods.

The analytical basis for partial equilibrium analysis was laid down in 1838 by Cournot in his *Recherches*. Mathematical convenience, more than methodological principle, seems to have been responsible for his adopting it (see, for example, 1838, p. 127). Though this small volume failed to exercise any widespread influence on the discipline much before the present century, it was known and read by Marshall (who spoke of Cournot as his 'gymnastics master'), from whose *Principles* the popularity of partial equilibrium analysis is largely derived (though it would be remiss to overlook Auspitz, Lieben and von Mangoldt). Unlike the case of Cournot, however, it would be difficult to argue that Marshall came across the method in anything other than a roundabout way (though some have argued that its principal attraction for him lay in its facility in allowing him to express his theory in a manner which required little recourse to mathematics).

When Marshall first introduced the idea of assuming 'other things equal' in the *Principles*, the *ceteris paribus* condition which is taken as the hallmark of the partial equilibrium approach, he seems to have done so not in order to justify the procedure of analysing 'one bit at a time', but in order to make a quite different point – that a long-run normal equilibrium would only *actually* emerge if none but the most general causes were allowed to operate without interference (see, for example, 1890, p. 36, p. 366, and pp. 369–70). In other words, the 'other things' that were being held 'equal' were the given data of the theory and the external environment – if the data remained the same and the external environment was freely competitive, then a long-run normal equilibrium would result. Indeed, Walrasian general equilibrium holds 'other things equal' in this sense. To put it another way, in Marshall's initial argument nothing was said about the possibility of assuming the interdependencies between long-run variables themselves to be of secondary importance, as is customary in partial equilibrium analysis.

This latter requirement of Marshallian analysis, the idea of the negligibility of indirect effects when one looks at individual markets (1919, p. 677ff.), seems to have sprung from his habit of presenting equilibrium *theory* in terms of *particular* market demand and supply curves (with their attendant notions of representative consumers and firms). It is here, in fact, that Marshall's presentation of demand and supply theory differs so markedly from its presentation by Walras. To the extent that this is so, it would seem to be better to recognize that the idea of 'partial' versus 'general' equilibrium has more to do with the presentation of a particular theory, and Marshall's propensity to consider markets one at a time, than it has to do with the abstract category of equilibrium with which this discussion is concerned. This view would accord, incidentally, with the fact that the great disputes over the relative merits of these two modes of analysis (for example, that between Walras on the one hand, and Auspitz and Lieben on the other) were fought over the specification of demand and cost functions.

Another modification to the concept of equilibrium that has become more significant in recent literature also makes an appearance in Marshall; though it is not carried as far as it has been in recent literature. The second, third and fifth chapters of the fifth book of Marshall's *Principles* set out the conditions for the determination of what he calls the 'temporary equilibrium', the 'short-run equilibrium' and the 'long-run equilibrium' of demand supply. The last of these categories, as Marshall makes perfectly clear in the text, corresponds to Adam Smith's 'natural conditions' (1890, p. 347). The first two are to a greater or lesser degree 'more influenced by passing events, and by causes whose action is fitful and short lived' (p. 349). What is striking about Marshall's terminology is the fact that situations which from an analytical point of view would traditionally have been regarded as 'deviations' from long-period normal equilibrium (that is, disequilibria) are explicitly referred to as different cases of 'equilibrium'. This trend has taken on an entirely new significance in recent literature, and has had dramatic consequences for the meaning and status of the concept of equilibrium in economic theory. But just as important in comprehending this development is the introduction of the notion of intertemporal equilibrium into theoretical discourse.

The notion of intertemporal equilibrium (introduced by Hayek, Lindahl and Hicks in the inter-war years and developed in the 1950s by Malinvaud, Arrow and Debreu) warrants special consideration since 'equilibrium conditions' under this notion are defined quite differently from 'natural' or 'long-run normal' conditions. Intertemporal equilibrium defines as its object the determination of nt market-clearing prices (for n commodities over t elementary time periods commencing from an arbitrary short-period starting point). The chief implication of this definition of equilibrium conditions, and that which sets it apart from long-run normal conditions, is that not only will the price of the same commodity be different at different times but also that the stock of capital need not yield a uniform return on its supply price.

This fundamental change in the concept of equilibrium did not mean that intertemporal equilibrium positions were immediately divested of the status that had been given to 'equilibrium' ever since Adam Smith. In certain circles they continued to be regarded as positions towards which the economic system could actually be said to be 'tending' (or as benchmark cases).

However, once the *sequential* character of this equilibrium concept come to be better understood, it became apparent that there could be no 'tendency' towards it – at least not in the former meaning of that idea. One was either in it, in which case the sequence was 'inessential', or one was not, in which case the sequence was 'essential' (see Hahn, 1973, p. 16). And the probabilities overwhelmingly suggested the latter. Attention was thus turned to the individual points in the sequence; the temporary equilibria, as Hicks had dubbed them (applying the terminology of Marshal in a new context). A whole new class of cases, disequilibrium cases from the point of view of full intertemporal equilibrium, began to be examined. The discipline has now accumulated so many varieties that it is impossible to document them all here. Instead, two broad features of this development may be noted here, the first concerning the role that expectations were thereby enabled to play, the second the common designation now uniformly applied to all such cases: 'equilibrium'.

When equilibrium is interpreted as a solution concept in the sense that *all* solutions to *all* models (for which solutions exist) enjoy equal analytical status and differ only in that they become 'significant', as von Neumann and Morgenstern put it, when they are 'similar to reality in those respects which are essential in the investigation at hand' (1944, p. 32), it is sometimes said that economics has availed itself of a very powerful notion of equilibrium. On this line of argument, Walrasian equilibrium and, say, conjectural equilibrium compete with one another not for the title 'general' (since, in the traditional sense at least, there is no such category), but for the title 'significant'. Furthermore, at any given time they are competing for this title with as many other models as are available to the profession.

It seems to be the case that the status of equilibrium in economic analysis has come full circle since its introduction in the late 18th century. From being derived from the idea that market socieities were governed by certain systematic forces, more or less regular in their operation in different places and at different times, it now seems to be based on an opinion that nothing essential is 'hidden' behind the many and varied situations in which market economies might actually find themselves. In fact, it seems that these many cases are to be thought of as being more or less singular from the point of view of modern theory. From being the central organizing category around which the whole of economic theory was constructed, and therefore the ultimate basis upon which its practical application was premissed, equilibrium has become a category with no meaning independent of the exact specification of the initial conditions for *any* model. Instead of being thought of as furnishing a theory applicable, as Mill would have said, to the whole class of cases under consideration, it is increasingly being regarded by theorists as the solution concept relevant to a particular model, applicable to a limited number of cases. The present fashion for replacing economic theory proper by game theory, an approach which could be regarded by no less a theorist than Professor Arrow as contributing only 'mathematical tools' to economic analysis not many years ago (1968, p. 113), seems to exemplify the trend of modern economics.

BIBLIOGRAPHY

Arrow, K.J. 1968. Economic equilibrium. In *International Encyclopedia of the Social Sciences*, as reprinted in *The Collected Papers of Kenneth J. Arrow*, Volume 2, Cambridge, Mass.: Harvard University Press.

Böhm-Bawerk, E. von. 1899. *Capital and Interest*. 3 vols; reprinted, Ill.: Libertarian Press, 1959.

Clark, J.B. 1899. *The Distribution of Wealth*. London: Macmillan.

Cournot, A.A. 1838. *Researches into the Mathematical Principles of the Theory of Wealth*. Translated by N.T. Bacon with an introduction by Irving Fisher, 1897; 2nd edn, London and New York: Macmillan, 1927.

Garegnani, P. 1976. On a change in the notion of equilibrium in recent work on value. In *Modern Capital Theory*, ed. M. Brown et al., Amsterdam: North-Holland.

Hahn, F.H. 1973. *On the Notion of Equilibrium in Economics*. Cambridge: Cambridge University Press.

Hicks, J.R. 1939. *Value and Capital*. 2nd edn, Oxford: Clarendon Press, 1946.

Jevons, W.S. 1871. *Theory of Political Economy*. Edited from the 2nd edition (1879) by R.D.C. Black, Harmondsworth: Penguin, 1970.

Marshall, A. 1890. *Principles of Economics*. 9th (variorum) edition, taken from the text of the 8th edition, 1920. London: Macmillan; New York: Macmillan, 1948.

Marshall, A. 1919. *Industry and Trade*. 2nd edn. London: Macmillan.

Mill, J.S. 1844. *Essays on Some Unsettled Questions of Political Economy*. 2nd edn, 1874; reprinted, New York: Augustus M. Kelley.

Mill, J.S. 1848. *Principles of Political Economy*. 6th edn, 1871 (reprinted 1909), London: Longmans, Green & Company; New York: A.M. Kelley, 1965.

Palgrave, R.H.I (ed.) 1899. *Dictionary of Political Economy*, Vol. III. London: Macmillan.

Pareto, V. 1909. *Manual of Political Economy*. Translated from the French edition of 1927 and edited by A.S. Schwier and A.N. Page, New York: Augustus M. Kelley, 1971.

Ricardo, D. 1817. *The Principles of Political Economy and Taxation*. Edited from the 3rd edition of 1821 by P. Sraffa with the collaboration of M. Dobb, Vol. I of *The Works and Correspondence of David Ricardo*, 11 vols, Cambridge: Cambridge University Press, 1951–73; New York: Cambridge University Press, 1973.

Smith, A. 1759. *The Theory of Moral Sentiments*. Edited by D.D. Raphael and A.L. Macfie from the 6th edn of 1790, Oxford: Oxford University Press, 1976.

Smith, A. 1776. *An Inquiry into the Nature and Causes of the Wealth of Nations*. 2 vols, ed. E. Cannan, London: Methuen, 1961; Chicago: University of Chicago Press, 1976.

Smith, A. 1795. *Essays on Philosophical Subjects*. Edited by W.P.D Wrightman and J.C. Bryce, Oxford: Oxford University Press, 1980.

Von Neumann, J. and Morgenstern, O. 1944. *Theory of Games and Economic Behavior*. 3rd edn, Princeton: Princeton University Press, 1953.

Walras, L. 1874–7. *Elements of Pure Economics*. Translated and edited by W. Jaffé from the definitive edition of 1926, London: Allen & Unwin, 1954, Homewood, Ill.: R.D. Irwin.

Wicksell, K. 1901. *Lectures on Political Economy*. 2 vols, ed. L. Robbins, London: Routledge and Kegan Paul, 1934; New York: A.M. Kelley, 1967.

Adam Ferguson

NICHOLAS PHILLIPSON

Ferguson (1723–1815) was born in Perthshire and died in Edinburgh. He was educated at St Andrew's University for the Church of Scotland and became a leading member of the 'moderate' clergy which controlled its affairs from 1752 to 1805. He was a charismatic teacher who held the Moral Philosophy chair at Edinburgh from 1764 to 1785, transforming its curriculum and laying the foundations of its international reputation. As a moralist, Ferguson was worried by the materialism inherent in modern philosophy and modern life, and was anxious to show that the classical republicanism of the Machiavellians was still of value in analysing and resolving its problems. He presented human beings as active rather than passive agents who were motivated by a natural love of perfection that seemed to be in danger of extinction in a commercial world. In the process he showed that the mechanics of social bonding in primitive societies in particular were more complex than contemporaries realized, a demonstration that continues to be admired by anthropologists.

Marx admired Ferguson's discussion of the division of labour and the apparent alienation that accompanied its progress and he thought that Smith's treatment of the subject owed much to him. In fact the resemblances are only superficial, Ferguson's treatment of the subject and of political economy generally was derivative and shaped by the classical republican's traditional concern with virtue, corruption and the place of the heroic virtues in an age of commerce. *The Wealth of Nations* was to leave no significant marks on his thought. He was a moralist who sought to tighten, not loosen the ties which bound political economy to moral philosophy.

Ferguson's contemporary reputation rested on three frequently republished and translated works, *An Essay on the History of Civil Society* (1769) and *The History of the Progress and Termination of the Roman Republic* (1783). His lectures were published as *The Principles of Moral and Political Science* (1792).

SELECTED WORKS

1767. *An Essay on the History of Civil Society.* Ed. D. Forbes, Edinburgh: University Press, 1966.

BIBLIOGRAPHY

Kettler, D. 1965. *The Social and Political Thought of Adam Ferguson.* Columbus: Ohio State University Press.

William Godwin

PETER MARSHALL

The first and greatest exponent of philosophical anarchism, Godwin was born in Wisbech, Cambridgeshire in 1756. He was brought up in the Dissenting tradition in Norfolk, attended Hoxton Academy, and became a candidate minister. He gradually lost his faith, and in his late twenties turned to political journalism for the Whig cause. Inspired by the French Revolution, he wrote *An Enquiry concerning Political Justice* (1793). It earned him immediate recognition: 'no work in our time', Hazlitt wrote, 'gave such a blow to the philosophic mind of the country'. His novel *Caleb Williams* (1794) was considered no less of a masterpiece. But as the reaction to the French Revolution grew, so Godwin's reputation waned. Despite a long series of novels, histories, plays, essays, and children's books, he was unable to recapture the public imagination. He died in 1836, and was buried beside the feminist Mary Wollstonecraft, who had died in childbirth. Their daughter Mary eloped with Godwin's greatest disciple, Percy Bysshe Shelley.

Godwin's economics, like his politics, are an extension of his ethics. His starting point is a belief in the perfectibility of man: since man is a rational and voluntary being, education will suffice to make him enlightened, generous and free. In his ethics, he is a thoroughgoing and consistent utilitarian, defining good as pleasure and arguing that 'I should contribute everything in my power to the general good'. Indeed, his bold application of the principle of utility, coupled with the principle of impartiality, led him to condemn private affections, positive rights, promises, gratitude and patriotism. In his politics, he concluded that government and law are unnecessary evils and in their place proposed a decentralized and simplified society of autonomous communities.

Godwin considers the subject of property (or economics) as the keystone that completes the fabric of political justice. His treatment has a critical and a constructive phase. He sees a close link between property and power: the rich are always 'directly or indirectly the legislators of the state'. Moreover, accumulated property has disastrous effects on rich and poor alike: it creates a 'servile and truckling spirit', makes wealth the universal passion, and reduces society to the narrowest selfishness.

But since we have a common nature, it follows from the principle of impartial justice that the good things of the world are a 'common stock', upon which one man is as entitled as another to draw what he wants. Property therefore should be considered a trust to be employed in the best possible way in order to promote liberty, knowledge and virtue. Just as every man has a duty to help his neighbour, so his neighbour has a claim to assistance.

Developing the labour theory of value, Godwin further argues that money is only a means of exchange and that there is no wealth except the labour of man. The producer should therefore retain what is necessary for his subsistence from the produce of his labour and then distribute the surplus to the most needy. Godwin also distinguishes between four classes of things: the means of subsistence, the means of intellectual and moral improvement, inexpensive pleasures, and luxuries. It is the last which is the chief obstacle to the just distribution of the previous three.

In place of the capitalist economic system, Godwin looks to small-scale production for the local market in a decentralized society. Production would be organized voluntarily with the producers controlling distribution. There would be a voluntary sharing of material goods, without barter or exchange. Anticipating the liberating effects of new technology, Godwin suggests that if all able-bodied people worked, production time could be reduced drastically, thereby giving people the leisure to develop their intellectual and moral potential.

When Malthus asserted that such a scheme would result in over-population, Godwin replied with his doctrine of moral restraint or prudence as a check. In his *Of Population* (1820), he went on to question the validity of Malthus's ratios, and argued that people would tend to reproduce less as their living standards improved.

Godwin's economic theory is clearly both profound and original. He was the first to write systematically about the competing claims of capital, need and production. Marx and Engels recognized his importance in developing the theory of exploitation. He not only strongly influenced the early socialist thinkers Robert Owen, William Thompson and Thomas Hogdskin, but the Owenites and Chartists took note of what he had to say. While Malthus has been most remembered, it is arguable that Godwin will be proved right in the long run. His scheme of voluntary communism remains moreover a thoughtful and persuasive ideal.

SELECTED WORKS

1793. *An Enquiry concerning Political Justice and its Influence on General Virtue and Happiness.* 2 vols, London: Robinson.
1794. *Things as They Are; or, The Adventures of Caleb Williams.* 3 vols, London: B. Crosby.
1797. *The Enquirer: Reflections on Education, Manners and Literature.* London: Robinson.
1801. *Thoughts occasioned by the Perusal of Dr. Parr's Spital Sermon.* London: Robinson.

1820. *Of Population. An Enquiry concerning the Power of Increase in the Numbers of Mankind.* London: Longman, Hurst, Rees, Orme & Brown.

1831. *Thoughts on Man, his Nature, Productions and Discoveries.* London: Wilson.

BIBLIOGRAPHY

Brailsford, H.N. 1913. *Shelley, Godwin and their Circle.* Oxford: Oxford University Press.

Clark, J.P. 1977. *The Philosophical Anarchism of William Godwin.* Princeton: Princeton University Press.

Hazlitt, W. 1820. William Godwin. In *The Spirit of the Age*, Oxford: Oxford University Press, 1954; Garden City, New York: Doubleday, 1960.

Locke, D. 1980. *A Fantasy of Reason: The Life and Thought of William Godwin.* London, Boston and Henley: Routledge & Kegan Paul.

Marshall, P.H. 1984. *William Godwin.* New Haven and London: Yale University Press.

Monro, D.H. 1953. *Godwin's Moral Philosophy.* Oxford: Oxford University Press.

Paul, C.K. 1876. *William Godwin: his Friends and Contemporaries.* 2 vols, London: H.S. King.

Priestley, F.E.L. 1946. Introduction to *Enquiry concerning Political Justice.* Vol. III. Toronto: University of Toronto Press.

Friedrich August von Hayek

ROGER W. GARRISON AND ISRAEL M. KIRZNER

Friedrich August von Hayek, a central figure in 20th-century economics and foremost representative of the Austrian tradition, 1974 Nobel laureate in economics, a prolific author not only in the field of economics but also in the fields of political philosophy, psychology and epistemology, was born in Vienna on 8 May 1899. Following military service as an artillery officer in World War I, Hayek entered the University of Vienna, where he attended the lectures of Friedrich von Wieser and Othmar Spann and obtained doctorates in law and political science. After spending a year in New York (1923–4), Hayek returned to Vienna where he joined the famous *Privatseminar* conducted by Ludwig von Mises. In 1927 Hayek became the first director of the Austrian Institute for Business Cycle Research. On an invitation from Lionel Robbins, he lectured at the London School of Economics in 1931 and subsequently accepted the Tooke Chair. Hayek soon came to be a vigorous participant in the debates that raged in England during the 1930s concerning monetary, capital, and business-cycle theories and was a major figure in the celebrated controversies with John Maynard Keynes, Piero Sraffa and Frank H. Knight.

During the late 1930s and early 1940s Hayek's research focused on the role of knowledge and discovery in market processes, and on the methodological underpinnings of the Austrian tradition, particularly subjectivism and methodological individualism. His contributions in these areas were an outgrowth of his participation in the debate over the possibility of economic calculation under socialism.

In 1950 Hayek moved to the United States, joining the Committee on Social Thought at the University of Chicago. His research there engaged the broader concerns of social, political and legal philosophy. He returned to Europe in 1962 with appointments at the University of Freiburg, West Germany, and then (1969) at the University of Salzburg, Austria. Since 1977 Hayek has resided in Freiburg.

Hayek's scholarly output spans more than six decades. Still growing in the mid-1980s, his bibliography (Gray, 1984) includes 18 books, 25 pamphlets,

16 books edited or introduced, and 235 articles. Although these publications have brought Hayek international renown and honours in several disciplines, his contributions to other social sciences emerged, to a significant degree, as extensions of his scholarship in the field of economics and its methodological foundations. The following survey refers rather narrowly to the career and contributions of Hayek the economist.

ECONOMICS AS A COORDINATION PROBLEM. Throughout all of Hayek's writings, both the questions asked and the answers given reflect his general conception of economics as a coordination problem (O'Driscoll, 1977). Thoughtful observation of market economies suggests that they are characterized by order more complex and intricate than can be explained in terms of deliberate efforts to achieve coordination among individual activities. According to Hayek (1952, p. 39), it is precisely the existence of this 'spontaneous order' that provides the subject matter for the science of economics.

While market economies are better coordinated than can be accounted for by references to deliberate planning, they are always less than fully coordinated, hence the coordination *problem*. In one important sense, coordination failures are an integral part of an ongoing market process that iterates towards a greater degree of coordination. An oversupply or undersupply of some particular good, for instance, is evidence that the plans of producers and consumers of that good are not well coordinated one with the other. But the discoordination itself provides both an indication of the inconsistency in plans and the incentive for producers and consumers to make the appropriate adjustments.

But market economies do occasionally experience profound economy-wide coordination failures. Much of Hayek's research has been aimed, either directly or indirectly, toward discovering the set of circumstances or, more appropriately, the sequence of events that could cause such failures, i.e. that could cause an economy to collapse into economic depression. The focus of his research is *intertemporal* discoordination. The coordination of activities over time is inherently more difficult, more problematic, than the coordination of activities in a given period. Producers must make decisions now in anticipation of decisions that other producers and, ultimately, consumers will make sometime in the future. The fact that production is time consuming, the more so the more well developed the economy, figures importantly in Hayek's theorizing. This essential time element increases the likelihood of erroneous investment decisions and gives scope for cumulative investment errors. A spate of intertemporally discoordinated investments, whether triggered by a real or a monetary disturbance, can increase employment opportunities producing an artificial boom. But the eventual realization of the discoordination will necessitate a partial liquidation, which constitutes a bust. In this context, the Austrian theory is differentiated from other macroeconomic theories by its attention to the problem of intertemporal coordination *within* the investment sector. The more conventional treatments of macroeconomic coordination problems focus on the general *level* of investment in comparison with the level of saving or the size of the labour force.

Hayek adopted a two-tier approach to the study of business cycles. Prerequisite to the question of how an economy-wide coordination failure could occur is the question of how any degree of intertemporal coordination can be achieved at all in market economies. In Hayek's words, 'before we explain why people commit mistakes, we must first explain why they should ever be right' (1937, p. 34). His account first of how a market economy works to coordinate activities over time and then of what can go wrong draws from several different fields of study within the science of economics. In particular, it draws in fundamental ways from price theory, capital theory and monetary theory.

Each of these fields required further development before becoming part of Hayek's account. Price theory had to be recast so as to emphasize the role of the price system as a communication network and as the most efficient means of making use of economic information. Capital theory had to be detailed so as to give play to the individual elements of the capital structure, which is made up of heterogeneous pieces of capital of various degrees of specificity and durability and related to one another by various degrees of intertemporal substitutability and complementarity. And monetary theory had to be extended in scope so as to allow the identification of systematic relative price effects associated with the process of monetary expansion or contraction.

While Hayek contributed importantly to each of these fields of study, his ultimate achievement consists in the integration of price theory, capital theory and monetary theory. Hayek integrated his own developments in these fields into a cohesive account of a market process that tends towards intertemporal coordination and of central-bank policies that can interfere with that process in such a way as to cause artificial economic booms which are inevitably followed by economic busts. Hayek's business cycle theory provided a basis for interpreting much of 19th- and 20th-century economic history, for evaluating alternative macroeconomic theories – especially those of John Maynard Keynes – and for promoting institutional reform of the kind that will prevent or minimize intertemporal discoordination.

SUBJECTIVISM AND METHODOLOGICAL INDIVIDUALISM. The methodological norms adopted by Hayek are a direct reflection of his perception of the subject matter: economic phenomena as *spontaneous order*. Fundamental institutions in society owe their existence to no identifiable creator. They are the 'results of human action but not of human design'. The most obvious examples of spontaneous order are the use of language and, among economic phenomena, the use of money. Money, the most commonly accepted medium of exchange, came to be accepted, commonly accepted, and then most commonly accepted as a result of a long sequence of actions on the part of a multitude of individual traders none of whom *intended* to create the institution of money. Other economic phenomena – from the simple division of labour to the more broadly conceived organization of industry – are to be understood as instances of spontaneous order.

If there were no order in society except for what was consciously designed, Hayek argued, there would be no scope and no need for the social sciences. The task of these sciences in a world characterized by spontaneous order is precisely to account for those aspects of social order that were not consciously designed.

A central methodological theme that has consistently pervaded Hayek's investigation of spontaneous order stems from his insistence that it is inappropriate to apply uncritically the methods of the physical sciences to the phenomena of the social sciences. Hayek used the term *scientism* to refer to the slavish imitation of the methods of the physical sciences without regard for the innate differences between physical and non-physical reality. Scientism, which unavoidably overlooks crucial aspects of social reality, such as perception, intent and anticipation, was the focus of two long and critical articles published by Hayek during World War II. In these articles, which constitute the central core of his 1952 book, *The Counter-Revolution of Science: Studies on the Abuse of Reason*, Hayek spelled out the case for subjectivism and methodological individualism in the social sciences. 'It is probably no exaggeration,' according to Hayek, 'to say that every important advance in economic theory during the last hundred years was a further step in the consistent application of subjectivism' (1952, p. 31).

Classical economists had focused their attention on the *objects* using valued and had looked for common denominators of value in terms of labour input or costs of production. The Austrian economists, particularly, Menger, Mises and Hayek, are to be credited with shifting attention from the objects being valued to the subjects engaged in valuation. The value attributed to the various objects of economic actions, Hayek emphasized, can be accounted for only with reference to human purposes and in terms of the views that people hold about those objects.

Hayek's thoroughly subjectivist outlook and his adherence to the strictures of methodological individualism were mutually reinforcing. Methodological individualism is not a prescription of how to engage in economic research but rather a recognition of what counts as an economic explanation. To explain the undesigned aspects of a spontaneous order is to trace those aspects to the consciously taken individual actions that gave rise to that order. In Hayek's own words, 'it is the concepts and the views held by individuals which are directly known to us and which form the elements from which we must build up, as it were, the more complex phenomena...' (Hayek, 1952, p. 38).

The contention that Hayek's crusade against scientism has consistently informed his substantive work is at least partly in conflict with a recent argument by T.W. Hutchison, who has sought to establish that Hayek's 1937 article 'Economics and Knowledge' marked a sharp change in his methodology towards a 'falsificationist' approach to economic science (Hutchison, 1981). This argument has been effectively disputed by John Gray (1984, pp. 16–21), who recognizes that the 1937 article was intended to persuade Mises that, contrary to Mises' own 'praxeology', there is an essential empirical element in our understanding of economic phenomena. Further, Hayek's (1952) commitment to subjectivism and methodological individualism, and his emphasis on the fallacies of scientism suggest in fact a deepening, rather than an erosion, of his recognition of the extent to which economic theory is independent of – in fact a prerequisite for – empirical economic observation.

THE PRICE SYSTEM AS A COMMUNICATION NETWORK. It is a short step from Hayek's appreciation of the phenomenon of spontaneous order to his understanding of the price system as a communication network. The key contribution of the price system to social well-being consists, Hayek demonstrated, in the system's capacity to transmit information from one part of the market to another. In the event of a natural disaster which has curtailed the availability of a specific raw material, for example, the fact of a reduced supply will be effectively communicated to potential users through the medium of a higher price – which also provides the incentive for the socially desirable economizing of the particular raw material (Hayek, 1945, p. 85–6). The need for such a communication network arises out of the fact that the information to be communicated is dispersed throughout the society. This insight into the nature of prices as *signals* has, during the past decade and a half, come to be fairly widely recognized and expounded in modern textbooks.

In his treatment of the use of knowledge in society, Hayek made a sharp distinction between two kinds of knowledge: (1) scientific, or theoretical, knowledge and (2) the knowledge of the particular circumstances of time and place. The first-mentioned category is the proper concern of the economist; the second-mentioned category is the proper concern of the market participant. Failure to recognize this 'division of knowledge' can lead to one of two serious errors. The assumption that *economists* can assimilate both kinds of knowledge leads to the conclusion that 'rational planning' can outperform – or at least duplicate – the market itself; the assumption that *market participants* can assimilate both kinds of knowledge leads to the conclusion that 'rational expectations' can nullify the systematic effects of monetary manipulation.

Hayek recognized and emphasized that if a fully adjusted system of prices – one corresponding to attained equilibrium – can be held to offer a system of coordinated and mutually reinforcing signals, such as system must depend on some prior groping process of market *discovery*. Hayek saw this process as consisting of market *competition* – which meant for him not the state of affairs consistent with the conditions for so-called perfect competition, but rather the rough-and-tumble process of market agitation kept in motion by complete freedom for competitive entrepreneurial entry. What such a competitive process can accomplish, Hayek argued, is the discovery of possibilities and preferences that no one had realized hitherto (Hayek, 1968).

These insights concerning knowledge and discovery articulated by Hayek in a number of profound papers from the late 1930s to the mid-1940s (Hayek, 1948) were partly responsible for, and partly emergent from, Hayek's participation in the celebrated interwar debate over the possibility of economic calculation under a socialist system. In deepening and widening the case originally presented by Mises in 1920, which challenged the feasibility of such calculation in the absence of market prices for factors of production, Hayek came to perceive the market process itself as crucial for the generation of that very knowledge which it would be necessary for a central planning authority to possess *before* it could hope to achieve a successful and efficient allocation of societal resources.

It was especially this Hayekian appreciation of the market as a discovery process that has significantly contributed to the contemporary revival of interest in the Austrian paradigm. In this context the Austrian contribution is to be distinguished from the more formal, or mathematicall tractable, theories by its emphasis on the role of the entrepreneurial discovery in those systematic market processes upon which we must depend, in a world of ignorance and disequilibrium, for any possible tendency toward mutual coordination among the market participants. What Hayek showed was that much modern economics misconstrues the nature of the economic problem facing society by assuming away the problems raised by the fact of dispersed information. To imagine (as earlier critics of Mises and Hayek had proposed) that it would be possible to run a socialist system by simulating the market and promulgating non-market 'prices' for the guidance of socialist managers is to ignore the extent to which market prices – both of consumer goods and of the capital goods that constitute the economy's capital structure – *already* express the outcome of an entrepreneurial discovery procedure that draws upon scattered existing knowledge.

THE INTERTEMPORAL STRUCTURE OF CAPITAL. Hayek's contribution to the development of capital theory is commonly regarded as his most fundamental and pathbreaking achievement (Machlup, 1976). His early attention (1928) to 'Intertemporal Price Equilibrium and Movements in the Value of Money' (English translation in Hayek, 1984) provided both the basis and inspiration for many subsequent contributions in this area, most notably for those of John Hicks. The widely recognized but rarely understood Hayekian triangles, introduced in his *Prices and Production* (1935), provided a convenient but highly stylized way of describing the changes in the intertemporal pattern of the capital structure. The formal and comprehensive analysis in *The Pure Theory of Capital* (1941) fleshed out the earlier formulations and established the centrality of the 'capital problem' in questions about the market's ability to coordinate economic activities over time.

The essential element of time in the economy's production process coupled with the inherent complexities of the capital structure gives special significance to the problem of intertemporal coordination. Individual producers must commit resources in the present on the basis of some production plan. Intertemporal coordination in the strictest sense requires that all such plans be mutually compatible and that they be jointly consistent with resource availabilities. The extent to which such compatibility and consistency actually exists is determined only through the market process in which each producer attempts to carry out his own plan. The individual production plans take shape as non-specific capital (e.g. raw material) is committed to a specific use (e.g. a particular tool or machine); the passage of time and the efforts of each producer to secure the additional capital needed to complete his own production plans reveal the extent to which the capital structure is intertemporally coordinated or discoordinated. The actual availability of some raw material complementary to already-committed capital may be less, for instance, than the amount needed for each producer to carry out his plan. As such discoordination is revealed (by an increase in the price of the raw material), production plans are revised. In Hayek's formulation, the capital goods that make up the production process are neither so specific that such plan revision is impossible nor so non-specific that it is costless.

In his *Pure Theory of Capital* (1941), Hayek provides a detailed treatment of capital goods in terms of reproducibility, durability, specificity, substitutability and complementarity. These multifaceted characteristics of various capital goods and of relationships among them cause the structure of production, taken as a whole, to be characterized by a longer or shorter 'period of production', a greater or lesser degree of 'roundaboutness'. The degree of roundaboutness, the extent to which the production process ties up resources over time, is determined by the market rate of interest – with the 'market rate' broadly conceived as the terms of trade between goods available in the present and goods available in the future. The market process works to translate intertemporal preferences into production plans. For instance, a fall in the rate of interest reflecting an increased willingness to forgo present goods for future goods creates incentives for engaging in production processes of greater degrees of roundaboutness. The characteristics, mentioned above, of the individual capital goods and of the relationships among them determine the extent to which the existing capital structure is actually adaptable to changes in intertemporal preferences.

MONEY AND ITS EFFECTS ON PRICES. Hayek's contribution to monetary theory and to trade cycle theory are intertwined, a circumstance that reflects the nature of his contribution in both areas. In summary terms, Hayek's monetary theory consists of integrating the idea of money as a medium of exchange with the idea of the price system as a communication network. His trade-cycle theory consists of integrating monetary theory and capital theory – in which a particular aspect of the price system, namely the system of intertemporal prices, is emphasized.

Both in his *Monetary Theory and the Trade Cycle* (1933) and his *Prices and Production* (1935), Hayek argued against the then-dominant (and still-prevalent) idea that the appropriate focus of monetary theory is on the relationship between the quantity of money and the general level of prices. The kernel of truth in the quantity theory of money was not to be denied, but progress in monetary economics was to be made by moving beyond the simple proportionalities implied by a relatively stable velocity of circulation. According to Hayek (1935, p. 127), the proper task of monetary theory requires a thorough reconsideration of the pure theory of price determination, which is based on the assumption of barter, and a determination of what changes in the conclusions are made necessary by the introduction of indirect exchange.

Hayek introduced the concept of 'neutral money' in part as a means to contrast his own view of money with the more aggregative views. By definition, neutral money characterizes a monetary system in which money, while facilitating the coordination of economic activities, is itself never a source of discoordination. According to the aggregative views, money is neutral so long as the value of money (as measured by the general level of prices) remains unchanged. Thus, increases in economic activity require proportionate increases in the quantity of money in circulation. According to Hayek, monetary neutrality requires the absence of 'injection effects'. When the quantity of money is increased, the new money is injected in some particular way, which temporarily distorts relative prices causing the price system to communicate false information about consumer preferences and resource availabilities.

The contrasting views on the requirements for monetary neutrality had important implications for US monetary policy during the prosperous decade of the 1920s. The rate of monetary growth during that period was roughly equivalent to the rate of real economic growth, a circumstance which resulted in a near-constant price level. The absence of price inflation was taken by most monetary economists to be a sign of monetary stability. Hayek's contrary assessment (1925) that the injection of money through credit markets must result in a misallocation of resources despite the price-level stability was the basis for his prediction that the money-induced boom would eventually lead to a bust.

It should be noted that in other writings, both early and late in his career (e.g. 1933 and 1984), Hayek was ambivalent about the choice between a monetary policy that avoids injection effects (a constant money supply despite a positive real growth rate) and a monetary policy that avoids price deflation (a money growth rate that 'accommodates' real growth).

THE TRADE CYCLE AS INTERTEMPORAL DISCOORDINATION. Hayek's contribution to the theory of the trade cycle consists in his developing the idea that monetary injections can have a systematic effect on the intertemporal pattern of prices. The Austrian theory of the trade cycle was first formulated by Mises (1912), who showed that money-induced movements in the interest rate (as identified by Knut Wicksell) have identifiable effects on the capital structure (as conceived by Eugen von Böhm-Bawerk). Hayek's major contribution to the theory (1935), as well as many subsequent developments of it, was based on an extremely stylized portrayal of the economy's time-consuming production process. The relevant characteristics of the 'structure of production' were identified with the dimensions of a right triangle. One leg of the triangle represents the time dimension of the structure of production, the degree of roundaboutness; the other leg represents the money value of the consumer goods yielded up by the production process. Slices of the triangle perpendicular to the time leg represent stages of production; the heights of individual slices represent the money value of the yet-to-be-completed production process.

Resources are allocated among the different stages of production as a result of entrepreneurial actions guided by price signals. But because of the distinct temporal dimension of the structure of production, the supplies and demands for resources associated with the different stages are differentially sensitive to changes in the rate of interest: the demand for the output of extraction industries, for example, is more interest-elastic than the demand for the output of service industries. Changes in the rate of interest will have a systematic effect on the pattern of prices that allocates resources among the different stages of production.

A fall in the rate of interest, for instance, will strengthen the relatively interest-elastic demands drawing resources into the early stages of production. This modification is represented by a relative lengthening of the temporal dimension of the Hayekian triangle.

A crucial distinction is made between interest-rate changes attributable to changes in the intertemporal preferences of consumers and interest-rate changes attributable to central-bank policy. In the first instance (Hayek, 1935, pp. 49–54), entrepreneurial actions and resulting changes in the pattern of prices allow the structure of production to be modified in accordance with the changed consumer preferences; in the second instance (Hayek, 1935, pp. 54–62), similar changes in the pattern of prices induced by the injecting of new money through credit markets constitute 'false signals', which result in a misallocation of resources among the stages of production. The artificially low rate of interest can trigger an unsustainable boom in which too many resources are committed to the early stages of production. The market process triggered by the injection of money through credit markets, Hayek showed, is a self-reversing process. More production projects are initiated than can possibly be completed. Subsequent resource scarcities turn the artificial boom into a bust. Economic recovery must consist of liquidating the 'malinvestments' and reallocating resources in accordance with actual intertemporal preferences and resource availabilities.

Hayek (1939) recognized that expectations about future movements in the rate of interest and entrepreneurial interpretations of intertemporal price movements can have an important effect on the course of the trade cycle. That is, prices are signals, not marching orders. But Hayek did not assume, as some modern economists do, that falsified price signals plus 'rational' expectations are equivalent to unfalsified price signals. Such an equivalence would require that market participants make use of knowledge of the kind that they cannot plausible possess; it would require that they have knowledge of the 'real' factors independent of the price system that supposedly communicates that knowledge.

CRITIQUE OF KEYNESIANISM. Hayek's critique of Keynesian theory and policy followed directly from his own theories of capital and of money. Hayek argued that by ignoring the intertemporal structure of production that particularly the intertemporal complementarity of the stages of production, Keynes failed to identify the market process that could achieve intertemporal coordination: 'Mr Keynes's aggregates conceal the most fundamental mechanisms of change' (Hayek, 1931, p. 227). And by shifting the focus of analysis from money as a medium of exchange to money as a liquid asset, Keynes failed to see the harm caused by policies of injecting newly created money through credit markets or of spending it directly on public projects.

Hayek had emphasized that in functioning as a medium of exchange, money 'constitutes a kind of loose joint in a self-equilibrating apparatus to the price mechanism which is bound to impede its working – the more so the greater the play in the loose joint'. Keynesian theory and policy were the specific targets of Hayek's criticism when he warned that the existence of such a loose joint is no justification for concentrating attention on that loose joint and disregarding the rest of the mechanism, and still less for making the greatest possible use of the short-lived freedom from economic necessity which the existence of this loose joint permits (Hayek, 1941, p. 408).

In the decades that followed the debate between Hayek and Keynes, economic theory was dominated by Keynesianism, and the corresponding macroeconomic policies consisted precisely of those measures that Hayek had warned against: monetary manipulation for political advantage. Monetary injections during the Great Depression, conceived as 'pump priming', soon gave way to a more broadly conceived policy of 'demand management'. The short-run trade-off between inflation and unemployment were treated in the political arena – and in some academic circles – as a societal menu from which elected officials, and hence voters, could choose; deviations of the economy from some conception of full employment or from some long-run growth path were taken as mandates for macroeconomic 'fine tuning' to be implemented by the central bank in cooperation with the fiscal authority.

As Hayek clearly recognized in his critique of Keynes's theories and his analysis of the actual effects of Keynesian policies, the political exploitation of the monetary loose joint contains an inherent inflationary bias. Newly created money can be used to hire the unemployed and to finance politically popular spending programmes. Monetary injections through the commercial banking system can stimulate the economy by triggering an artificial economic boom. The undesirable effects of inflating the money supply, the eventual collapse of the artificial boom and the general increase in the level of prices, are removed in time from the initial, politically desirable effects and are less conspicuously identified with the elected officials who engineered the monetary expansion (Hayek, 1960, pp. 324–39). As the political process continues, elected officials face the choice of monetary passivity which would permit the market to undergo the painful adjustments to earlier monetary injections or further monetary injections which would reproduce the desirable effects in the short run while staving-off the eventual adjustment. The cumulative effects of the play-off between political advantage and economic necessity is the theme of Hayek's critique of Keynesianism. Excerpts of 'a forty years' running commentary on Keynesianism by Hayek, compiled by Sudha Shenoy, is appropriately entitled *A Tiger by the Tail* (1972).

DENATIONALIZATION OF MONEY. Hayek as a monetary reformer is interested in minimizing the potential for discoordination that is inherent in monetary mechanisms and precluding the manipulation of money for political advantage. He has long doubted that the government has either the will or the ability to manipulate the money supply in the public interest.

In his early writings, Hayek took for granted the existence of a central bank and focused his analysis on the consequences of different policy goals, for example, the goal of stimulating economic growth or the goal of stabilizing the general price level. In his later writings, he began to see the monopolization of the money supply as the ultimate cause of monetary disturbances. As early as 1960, though still

> convinced that modern credit banking as it has developed requires some public institutions such as central banks, [he was] doubtful whether it is necessary or desirable that they (or the government) should have the monopoly of the issue of all kinds of money (1960, p. 520, n.2).

In the mid-1970s Hayek's interest in the denationalization of money (1976) was renewed. Having lost all hope of achieving monetary stability through the instruments of highly politicized monetary institutions, Hayek suggested – by his own account, almost as a 'bitter joke' – that the business of issuing money be turned over to private enterprise. Soon taking this suggestion seriously, he began to explore the feasibility and the consequences of competing currencies.

Hayek's proposal for competition in the issue of money is not subject to the standard objection based on the so-called common-pool problem. The proposal is not that private issuers should compete by issuing some generic currency. Clearly, competition on this basis would produce an explosive inflation. The proposal, rather, is that each competitor issue his own trade-marked currency. Under this arrangement, each issuer would have an incentive to maintain a stable value of his own currency and to minimize the difficulties of using this currency in an environment where other currencies are used as well.

In spelling out just how such a system of competing currencies would or could work, Hayek has had to walk the fine line between constructivism on the one hand and blind faith in the market process on the other. His discussions of possible outcomes of the market process should not be taken as prescriptions for the provision of competing currencies, but rather as a basis for believing that competition between private issuers if feasible. Individuals may choose one currency over another on the basis of the issuer's demonstrated ability to achieve purchasing-power stability for that currency. Their choice may be influenced, Hayek has suggested, by what particular price level serves as the issuer's guide for managing the currency. Or it may be that public confidence can be maintained only by a currency that is convertible at a fixed rate into some stipulated commodity or basket of commodities. Hayek does doubt that a gold standard would re-emerge as a result of the competitive process, largely because the confidence and stability of gold was based upon beliefs and attitudes on the part of the public that no longer exist and cannot easily be recreated. But if gold did prevail in a competitive environment, there would be no basis for objection.

More importantly, Hayek's proposal for monetary reform should be seen not as an aberration from but as thoroughly consistent with his view of economics as a spontaneous order. Markets serve to coordinate the activities of individual market participants. The use of money, while greatly facilitating economic coordination, contains an inherent potential for discoordination. Competition in the market for money holds that potential in check and allows market participants to take the fullest advantage of the remaining elements of the spontaneous order.

SELECTED WORKS

1925. (In German.) The monetary policy of the United States after the recovery from the 1920 crisis. In F.A. Hayek, *Money, Capital, and Fluctuations*: *Early Essays*, ed. R. McCloughry, Chicago: University of Chicago Press, 1984.

1928. (In German.) Intertemporal price equilibrium and movements in the value of money. In F.A. Hayek, *Money, Capital and Fluctuations*: *Early Essays*, ed. R. McCloughry, Chicago: University of Chicago Press, 1984.

1931-2. Reflections on the pure theory of money of Mr J.M. Keynes I–II. *Economica*, Pt I, 11, August 1931, 270–95; Pt II, 12, February, 1932, 22–44.

1933. (In German.) On 'neutral money'. In F.A. Hayek, *Money, Capital, and Fluctuations*: *Early Essays*, ed. R. McCloughry, Chicago: University of Chicago Press, 1984.

1933. *Monetary Theory and the Trade Cycle*. New York: Augustus M. Kelley, 1975.

1935. *Prices and Production*. 2nd edn, New York: Augustus M. Kelley, 1967.

1937. Economics and knowledge. *Economica* NS 4, February, 33–54.

1939. Price expectations, monetary disturbances, and malinvestments. In F.A. Hayek, *Profits, Interest, and Investment*, Clifton, NJ: Augustus M. Kelley, 1975.

1941. *The Pure Theory of Capital*. Chicago: University of Chicago Press.

1945. The use of knowledge in society. *American Economic Review* 35, September, 519–30. Reprinted in F.A. von Hayek, *Individualism and Economic Order*, London: Routledge & Kegan Paul, 1949.

1949. *Individualism and Economic Order*. London: Routledge & Kegan Paul.

1952. *The Counter-Revolution of Science*: *Studies on the Abuse of Reason*. Glencoe, Ill.: Free Press.

1960. *The Constitution of Liberty*. Chicago: Henry Regnery & Co., 1972.

1968. Competition as a discovery procedure. In *New Studies in Philosophy, Politics, Economics and the History of Ideas*, Chicago: University of Chicago Press.

1972. *A Tiger by the Tail*. Ed. S. Shenoy, London: Institute for Economic Affairs.

1975. *Full Employment at Any Price*. Occasional Paper No. 45, London: Institute of Economic Affairs.

1976. *Denationalization of Money*. London: Institute of Economic Affiars.

1984. The future monetary unit of value. In *Money in Crisis*: *The Federal Reserve, the Economy, and Monetary Reform*, ed. B. Siegel, Cambridge, Mass.: Ballinger.

BIBLIOGRAPHY

Gray, H. 1984. *Hayek on Liberty*. Oxford: Basil Blackwell.

Hutchison, T.W. 1981. *The Politics and Philosophy of Economics*: *Marxians, Keynesians, and Austrians*. New York: New York University Press, ch. 7.

Keynes, J.M. 1936. *The General Theory of Employment, Interest, and Money*, London: Macmillan; New York: Harcourt, Brace.

Machlup, F. 1976. Hayek's contribution to economics. In *Essays on Hayek*, ed. F. Machlup, Hillsdale, Mich.: Hillsdale College Press.

Mises, L. von. 1912. *The Theory of Money and Credit*. New Haven: Yale University Press, 1953.

O'Driscoll, G. 1977. *Economics as a Coordination Problem*: *The Contribution of Friedrich A. Hayek*. Kansas City: Sheed Andrews & McMeel.

Thomas Hobbes

C.B. MACPHERSON

The greatest English political theorist and philosopher, Hobbes was born at Malmesbury and died at Hardwick, the seat of the Earl of Devonshire, who had been Hobbes's patron for many years. After attending Magdalen Hall, Oxford (BA, 1608), Hobbes entered the Devonshire household as tutor to the son, and made several trips to the Continent, on one of which (in 1636) he conversed with Galileo, whose resolutive-compositive method Hobbes took over, and whose laws of motion he later carried over and applied to the motions, internal and external, of men. In 1640, fearing that his earliest work would offend the Long Parliament, he went into voluntary exile in Paris, where for a time (1646–8) he tutored the future Charles II in mathematics. He returned to England in 1651 and from then on lived as inconspicuously as he could.

Economic insights are to be found in his three main works of political theory, *The Elements of Law, Natural and Politic* (1640); *De Cive* (1642), translated (by Hobbes) as *Philosophical Rudiments Concerning Government and Society* (1651); *Leviathan* (1651); and in his history of the Long Parliament and the Civil War, *Behemoth* (1682). Hobbes's great work was his political science, of which his economic ideas seem to be only an incidental part. Yet we may notice that his political edifice rested on economic assumptions, in that his model of society was the atomistic bourgeois market society whose seismic rise in England in his own time he had certainly noticed. However, he did not attempt anything along the lines of the classical political economy of the 18th century, or even of the political arithmetic of his own century: he offered neither a general theory of exchange value nor a theory of distribution, that is, of the determinants of rent, interest, profits and wages, nor even a theory of the balance of trade or of foreign exchange. But he did set down a few general economic principles. One is a supply and demand theory of exchange value, as in: 'The value of all things contracted for, is measured by the Appetite of the Contractors (*Leviathan*, ch. 15, p. 208) and in his more striking statement:

The *Value* or WORTH of a man, is as of all other things, his Price; that is to say, so much as would be given for the use of his Power: and therefore is not absolute; but a thing dependent on the need and judgement of another.... And as in other things, so in men, not the seller, but the buyer determines the price...(ibid., ch. 10, pp. 151–2).

The two statements are consistent only on the assumption of an endemic surplus of wage-labourers, an assumption which Hobbes did explicitly make. The able-bodied poor, who were expected to increase indefinitely,

are to be forced to work: and to avoyed the excuse of not finding employment, there ought to be such Lawes, as may encourage all manner of Arts; as Navigation, Agriculture, Fishing, and all manner of Manifacture that requires labour. The multitude of poor, and yet strong people still encreasing, they are to be transplanted into Countries not sufficiently inhabited: where neverthelesse, they are not to exterminate those they find there; but constrain them to inhabit closer together, and not range a great deal of ground, to snatch what they find; but to court each little Plot with art and labour, to give them their sustenance in due season (*Leviathan*, ch. 30, p. 387; cf. *Behemoth*, p. 126).

Another general proposition is that 'a mans Labour also, is a commodity exchangeable for benefit, as well as any other thing' (*Leviathan*, ch. 24, p. 295).

More important than such general principles are his many policy recommendations to the Sovereign, all of which are designed to increase the wealth of the nation by promoting the accumulation of capital by private enterprisers seeking their own enrichment. Typical are his recommendations about taxation. Taxes are justified only because they provide the income which enables the sovereign power to maintain the conditions for private enterprise: 'the Impositions that are layd on the People by the Soveraign Power, are nothing else but the Wages, due to them that hold the publique Sword, to defend private men in the exercise of severall Trades, and Callings' (ibid., ch. 30, p. 386). Taxes on wealth are bad, for they discourage accumulation. The best taxes are those on consumption, which discourage 'the luxurious waste of private men' (0. 387). Hobbes's recommendations to the Sovereign all follow from his most general rule, as set out in the opening paragraph of chapter 30:

The office of the Soveraign, (be it a Monarch, or an Assembly,) consisteth in the end, for which he was trusted with the Soveraign Power, namely the procuration of *the safety of the people*...But by Safety here, is not meant a bare Preservation but also all other Contentments of life, which every man by lawfull Industry, without danger, or hurt to the Common-wealth, shall acquire to himselfe (p. 376).

Most important of all was his insistence that the sovereign was above the law and could not be limited by any of the traditional rights of leasehold or copyhold tenants, or by any traditional limits on market transactions, or traditional protections of the poor: 'it belongeth to the Common-wealth, (that is to say, to the Soveraign), to appoint in what manner, all kinds of contract between Subjects, (as buying, selling, exchanging, borrowing, lending, letting, and taking to hire), are to bee made; and by what words and signes they shall be understood for valid' (ibid., ch. 24, p. 299).

In short, the job of the state was to clear the way for capitalism. It is evident that Hobbes's doctrine was particularly appropriate to the period of primary capital accumulation. It is scarcely too much to say that it was his perception of the needs of such a period which determined the main lines of his political theory. What was needed was a sovereign powerful enough to override all the protections of the common law, and, to justify such a power, a new, untraditional basis for political obligation. That is what Hobbes's doctrine provided. In effect, it is the legitimation of the early capitalist state.

SELECTED WORKS

1650. *Elements of Law, Natural and Politic*. Ed. F. Tonnies, Cambridge: Cambridge University Press, 1928.

1651. *Philosophical Rudiments Concerning Government and Society*. Published as *De Cive or The Citizen*. Ed. S.P. Lamprecht, New York: Appleton-Century-Crofts, 1949.

1651. *Leviathan*. Ed. C.B. Macpherson, Harmondsworth: Penguin, 1968.

1682. *Behemoth: or the Long Parliament*. Ed. F. Tonnies, London: Simpkin, Marshall & Co., 1889.

BIBLIOGRAPHY

Macpherson, C.B. 1983. Hobbes's political economy. *Philosophical Forum* 14 (3–4).

David Hume

EUGENE ROTWEIN

The economic essays of David Hume (1711–1776), which originally appeared in 1752 in a volume entitled *Political Discourses*, comprise a small portion of his writings. The scope of Hume's thought was vast. He wrote extensively in philosophy (the area in which his reputation primarily lies), explored several of the social sciences and the humanities, and was deeply interested in history. His multi-volume *History of England* (1754–61) was a pathbreaking work in the field. Nonetheless, in the literature Hume's economic writings have typically been treated as an entirely self-contained aspect of his work. This is not surprising, since in his economic essays he does not allude to his other writings, and subsequent disciplinary specialization has not encouraged consideration of any interrelationships between the two. For their part, philosophers have often treated Hume's philosophical writings in isolation from his other work.

For Hume, however, there was no such sharp disjunction. In the Advertisement prefixed to his first and major philosophical work – *A Treatise of Human Nature* (1739) – he states that he expects his philosophy to serve as the 'capital or centre' of all the 'moral' (i.e. psychological and social) sciences and that the hopes to expand the *Treatise* to accommodate a study of these areas. Owing perhaps to the poor reception accorded his *Treatise*, Hume did not carry out his original intention. His treatment of the moral sciences was left mainly to his essays. But there are many links between Hume's philosophical thought and his essays, and this is true with respect to his economic essays. Indeed, in light of the importance of these links, Hume may be regarded as the outstanding philosopher-economist of the 18th century.

Viewed in most general form, what is the nature of the relationship between Hume's economic and philosophical thought? Hume regarded the foundation of his entire philosophical system – its 'capital or centre' – as a body of 'principles of human nature', or elements and relations concerning human understanding and human passions that he believed to be irreducible and universal. These principles, which constitute the analytical phase of Hume's system of thought,

are treated in Books I and II of the *Treatise*. In the second and syn
Hume then relates various aspects of 'human nature' to environmen
seeking to frame laws of human behaviour, or generalizations indic
man may be expected to behave under different specific conditio
generalizations comprise the substance of the 'moral sciences' with
indicated, Hume dealt principally in the essays. An explicit and deep in
psychology is thus a salient characteristic of Hume's treatment of the
sciences' in general, and this is conspicuously evident in his economic a

What were Hume's views concerning the prospects of developing r
generalizations in the 'moral sciences'? That Hume should have distinct
on this issue is scarcely surprising in light of the depth of his interest,
philosopher, in the epistemological basis of science. As he had argued, the cont
of any generalization concerning relations between matters of fact is alw
conceivable and hence always possible. Consequently, the only way of develop
an understanding of these relations, he contended, is through empirical observatic
and this can only yield probabilities, never certainty. With respect to his ow
principles of human nature, Hume believed that his propositions carried th
highest order of probability because of the abundance of evidence on which they
rested.

On the other hand, recognizing the complexity of the interrelationships between
man's 'nature' and his environment, he stressed the difficulty in framing valid
laws of human behaviour. He calls attention to the effect on human behaviour
of imperceptible influences, emphasizes the extent to which it could be altered
by changing conditions and notes the impracticality of conducting controlled
experiments in the realm of psychological phenomena. He thus warns that in the
social sciences 'all general maxims... ought to be established with the greatest
caution' and states that 'I am apt... to entertain a suspicion that the world is
still too young to fix many general truths in [the area of the social sciences]
which will remain true to the latest posterity' (Hume, *Philosophical Works*, ed.
Green and Grose, vol. III, pp. 156–7). Of all the social fields, however, he believed
that a field such as economics lent itself especially well to scientific study, and
here he was cautiously optimistic concerning the possibility of developing reliable
generalizations through direct observation of man in the course of his day-to-day
affairs. As he argued, behaviour here was governed by mass passions, which were
'gross' or 'stubborn', or were not as affected by imperceptible influences as
passions governing the behaviour of small numbers of individuals. Uniformities
in behaviour therefore could here be more readily discerned (*Philosophical Works*,
p. 176). It should be noted that, in accord with this view, Hume introduces his
economic essays by contrasting the potential for scientific analysis in economics
with the very limited prospects for such analysis in a field such as foreign
diplomacy, where events are controlled by the behaviour of a small number of
individuals (*Writings on Economics*, ed. Rotwein, pp. 3–4).

To return to the substance of Hume's economic thought, in addition to
emphasizing psychological considerations Hume's analysis displays a deep
interest in historical sequence. Hume's interest in history developed at a very

early age, even before he undertook his *Treatise*. As it appears in his essays, however, his treatment of history differs from conventional historiography (with its concern with unique particulars) which predominates in his *History of England*. For, writing as a 'moral scientist', Hume sought to reduce historical sequences to generalizations which explain how transformations in human behaviour result from the impact of changing historical circumstance on 'human nature'. This type of study (which bore a relationship on the 'conjectural history' and the French '*histoire raisonée*' of the period) Hume termed 'natural history' – the term 'natural' here denoting the recurrent or probable, or the substance of laws of human behaviour. There are clusters of what Hume regards as historical laws of human behaviour in several of the essays. One essay bears the title 'The Natural History of Religion'. And in the economic essays the approach of 'natural history' is of fundamental importance.

This can be seen when Hume's economic essays are viewed on three different levels of analysis. The first is economic psychology, where Hume deals with economic motivation, or what he terms the 'causes of labour'. This is the most basic level of his economic analysis in the sense that here one finds the links between his economic thought and his treatment of 'human nature' in the *Treatise*. On this level the analysis takes the form of a natural history of 'the rise and progress of commerce'. In a word, Hume introduces the question of economic motivation in seeking to explain how changing environmental influences stimulated the economic growth of his general period through their impact on various human passions. Here Hume observes that there are four 'causes of labour' – the desire for consumption, the desire for action, the desire for liveliness and the desire for gain.

The first of these, which is commonly stressed by economists, simply denotes all the wants that may be gratified by consumption. The desire for action refers to a desire for challenging activity as such. However, its full effectuation, as Hume stressed, requires activity whose end or objective has independent value. Like hunting and gaming, economic pursuits (and especially the activities of the merchant and, more generally, the 'industrious professions') are seen as meeting these conditions. By the desire for liveliness Hume meant the desire for the experience of active passion as such (which he contrasts with a state of no passion, or in effect a state of waking sleep). This is not a completely independent cause of labour but is an important ingredient common to both consumption and interesting activity. The last cause of labour is the desire for monetary gain, which is a desire to accumulate the tokens of success is in the economic 'game'.

Hume argues that all these motives play a role in a nation's economic growth – the initial stimulus to which he finds in the expansion of international trade. As compared with the treatments of economic motivation by economists (which commonly record exclusive or overshadowing emphasis to the desire for consumption), a striking characteristic of Hume's treatment lies in its multi-dimensionality. This multi-dimensionality is also found in Hume's criticism of the doctrine of psychological hedonism. Here he argues that, in addition to seeking pleasure, man is driven by a variety of 'instincts' which lead him to do

things for their own sake, and therefore will not automatically lead him to act in his own best interests. Hume's position thus precludes any simple identification of wealth with welfare.

The second level of Hume's economic analysis is his political economy, or his treatment of market relations. It is this which makes up the bulk of his economic essays. Here Hume considers several of the major economic issues of his own period, including monetary theory, interest theory, the question of free versus regulated trade, the shifting and incidence of taxes, and fiscal policy. In this context the natural history of 'the rise and progress of commerce' plays a dominant role. For repeatedly in his critical treatment of the economic doctrines of his period Hume seeks to show that their major deficiency lies in a failure to give proper attention to the importance of economic growth and to the underlying psychological and other factors associated with this growth process.

Let us consider first Hume's quantity theory specie flow doctrine, which he presents (in the essay 'Of the Balance of Trade') in criticism of the mercantilist view that without restraints on international trade a nation would suffer losses in its money supply. Hume's position, which has been recognized as an early anticipation of the classical view, is that, owing to the effects of specie flows on price levels in trading nations, the amount of specie in each automatically tends towards an equilibrium at which its exports and imports are in balance. Any attempt through restraints on trade to increase the amount of specie beyond this equilibrium level, as Hume argues, is destined to fail (assuming the money circulates domestically) because the specie movement from abroad will raise the nation's prices relative to those abroad, reduce exports and increase imports, and generate a return outflow of specie.

The relationship of this analysis of Hume's historical perspective is evident in the purpose with which he introduces this doctrine. For in employing the quantity theory of money he is here arguing that the extent to which a specie inflow into a nation affects its prices depends on its total output. Consequently, as he is seeking to show, it is the level of a nation's economic development, or its productive capacity as determined by its population and the spirit of industry of its people, that controls the amount of specie a nation can attract and retain. As he states, 'I should as soon dread that all our springs and rivers should be exhausted as that money should abandon a kingdom where there are people and industry' (Hume, *Writings on Economics*, p. 61).

To consider another of Hume's anticipations of the classical position – his interest theory presented in his essay 'Of Interest' – here he attacks the mercantilist view that the rate of interest is determined by the money supply. On quantity theory grounds he argues that an increased money supply will simply raise all prices and, necessitating an offsetting increased demand for loans to finance expenditures, will leave interest rates unaffected. It is therefore the supply of real capital that determines interest rates. The bulk of Hume's discussion, however, is concerned with the factors affecting the supply of real capital itself; and here he turns to a historical analysis in which he considers the effect of economic growth on the class structure of society and, through this, on economic incentives.

In this context every 'cause of labour' considered in the natural history of 'the rise and progress of commerce' is brought into his treatment. In a feudal society, he points out, the supply of capital is low because there are only two classes – the peasants and the landed aristocracy. The peasants cannot save since they are poor. On the other hand, the landed aristocracy tend to be heavy borrowers. For, as they are idle and lack the sense of liveliness that interesting activity affords, they seek liveliness wholly through extravagant consumption expenditures. Capital is therefore scarce and interest rates are high. Economic development, however, spawns the growth of the merchant class and the industrious professions. These groups derive a sense of liveliness from economic activity. Consumption expenditure drops for this reason and also because the pursuit of profit nourishes a desire to accumulate gain as a token of success in the economic game. As the new industrious classes earn a substantial share of the growing national income, their disposition to save thus results in a significant increase in the capital supply and a decline in interest rates.

As noted, Hume employs the quantity theory of money in criticizing the mercantilist position. But Hume's monetary theory also exhibits a similarity to the mercantilist view. However, his treatment here too springs from an attempt to call attention to the importance of economic growth. Thus (in his essay 'Of Money') Hume – assuming a condition of less than full employment – grants that an increase in the quantity of money (as against a greater absolute quantity of money as such) need not simply raise prices but can stimulate economic activity. Here, in tracing the impact of the increased money supply as it courses through the economy, he presents a lucid description of the multiplier process. He denies, however, that the stimulating effect on industry – when resulting from a short-run increase in the money supply – can prove anything more than ephemeral. No justification for this view is given. But it serves to underscore the conclusion of his analysis. For he goes on to argue that if the increase in the money supply is gradual and continues over a long period of time, its sitimulating effects on output will prove enduring because it will nourish the 'spirit of industry' and therefore economic growth itself. Similarly, although Hume argued that an increase in the money supply does not affect interest rates, near the conclusion of his essay 'Of Interest' he points out that a long-run increase in the supply of money, by stimulating economic growth and inducing a change in spending and saving patterns, can increase the supply of capital and lower the interest rate.

Another noteworthy area of Hume's analysis is his treatment of the issue of free versus regulated markets. Since the relevant comments are not found in his economic essays but rather lie scattered through his *History of England*, the full extent to which Hume anticipated Adam Smith's 'invisible hand' argument has not been generally recognized. These comments make clear that Hume understood the role of a free price mechanism in governing the allocation of resources (*Writings on Economics*, pp. lxxviii–lxxx).

In applying the argument for free markets to the case of international trade, Hume emphasizes that free trade makes it possible for nations to enjoy the gains from an exchange of the products of their different resource endowments.

However, in his most thorough treatment of the issue of international free trade (in his essay 'Of the Jealousy of Trade') it is not this static approach to the question that predominates. Rather, once again, it is economic growth considerations that receive primary emphasis. For here, where Hume seems to meet the mercantilist argument that foreign economic development adversely effects home industry and employment, he takes the position that expansion abroad, on the contrary, commonly promotes economic development at home. By increasing foreign income, he argues, economic growth abroad not only leads to an expansion of foreign demand for domestic output but, through an emulation of foreign technological innovations, promotes the advance of technology at home. Hume goes on to argue that even when foreign expansion competes with domestic output, there is no need for concern provided the nation's 'spirit of industry' – which is itself nourished by foreign trade – is preserved. For as long as a nation remains industrious it need not fear that other nations will encroach on the market for its staple and, even in the unlikely event that this does occur, an industrious nation can readily divert its resources to other uses. Moreover, in stimulating the spirit of industry, foreign trade also promotes the diversification of a nation's resource use, and so reduces the impact of any shrinkage of demand that may occur from time to time in particular markets.

These are indications that Hume was more fully aware of the possible costs of free trade than one would gather from the main argument in the essay 'Of the Jealousy of Trade'. Elsewhere he treats the interests of poor and rich countries as incompatible, and in one place he also justifies the use of a tariff in specific cases (*Writings on Economics*, pp. 34–5, 76, 199–205). In the essay 'Of the Jealousy of Trade' itself he recognizes, in a modification of his main argument, that there are circumstances in which a nation facing a loss of markets to foreign countries may find resource diversion difficult (p. 81). The character of this essay as a whole (which appeared six years after the other economic essays) suggests, however, that after much reflection and groping Hume had concluded that free trade would have a markedly favourable effect on long-term economic growth for all nations, and that, with this end in view, any associated costs – which would be of a shorter-term nature – would be well worth sustaining.

A further illustration of the role of natural history in Hume's political economy is found in his treatment of the shifting and incidence of taxes (in his essay 'Of Taxes'), where he considers the view that an expansion of taxes creates an expanded ability to pay the levies by increasing 'proportionably the industry of the people'. This view was commonly held by the mercantilists and, in what came to be known as 'the utility of poverty' doctrine, was employed to justify the imposition of excises on goods consumed by the poor. Hume's position here is twofold. He points out that history shows that natural burdens, such as relatively infertile soil, often stimulate industry, and he argues that artificial burdens such as taxes may have the same effect. This position springs from Hume's view concerning the importance of a desire for interesting action as a 'cause of labour' since he here emphasizes that in order to prove interesting the activity must be difficult and challenging. On the other hand, he emphasizes that since economic activity is also motivated by a desire for consumption, increasing difficulty beyond a certain level in achieving consumption ends will lead to despair. From the viewpoint of its stimulating effect on industry there is thus an optimum tax level, and Hume takes the view that taxes on the poor throughout Europe had already so substantially exceeded that optimum that they were threatening to 'crush all art and industry'. Considered as a whole, Hume's position represents an amalgam of both the mercantilist and the later classical view. He rejects the mercantilist 'utility of poverty' doctrine with its unqualified endorsement of higher taxes on goods consumed by the poor, but also would reject the view (which is based on the subsistence or accustomed standard of living theory of wages found in the writings of Smith and Ricardo) that any tax on labour would inevitably result in a reduction in its supply.

Hume's treatment of fiscal policy – the last major aspect of his political economy – does not reveal significant relationships to his natural history of the rise and progress of commerce. Owing to space limitations, his analysis – contained in the long essay 'Of Public Credit' – cannot here be considered in detail. It should be observed, however, that this essay, which deals specifically with the question of large and continually mounting public debt, constitutes in all essential respects a 'natural history of the rise and collapse of public credit'. Particular noteworthy in this analysis are the extensive relationships Hume draws between economic and other social developments, especially of a political and sociological character. Of all aspects of his political economy, this essay most fully exhibits Hume's awareness, as a moral scientist, of significant interrelations between different realms of social experience.

The third and last level of Hume's economic thought is his economic philosophy, which is his appraisal, on ultimate moral grounds, of the desirability of a commercial and industrial society. In the light of his general concern, as a philosopher, with moral questions, it is hardly surprising to find that the question of the moral aspects of commercial and industrial growth was of basic importance for Hume. Appearing in the second of the economic essays – 'Of Refinement in the Arts' – he considers this question before turning to an analysis of market problems. Although the essay is brief, its scope is broad; for Hume discusses the impact of the development of an advanced economy both on the individual and on society as a whole.

The standard for moral judgement Hume employs is drawn from the utilitarian ethic – a position which he himself had expounded and defended in his philosophical analysis. And here the role played by his natural history of the rise and progress of commerce is fundamental. As observed, in this natural history Hume dealth with various 'causes of labour'. In his economic philosophy three of these motives – the desires for consumption, for interesting activity and for liveliness – are now treated as ends which are regarded as major ingredients of the happiness of the individual. Here he argues that – by providing new consumption experiences, enlarging the scope for the enjoyment of economic activity as a form of interesting action and (through both the latter) enhancing a sense of liveliness – economic growth advances the fulfilment of all these ends.

Economic growth, he contends, contributes to the fulfilment of a fourth end of importance to human welfare – a sense of peace and tranquility or a state of no passion – which he argues is enjoyable only in 'recruiting the spirits' after intensive indulgence in lively experiences. It is noteworthy that Hume's treatment of these ingredients of human happiness bears a direct relationship to the principal conceptions of the good life as Hume construes these in an earlier series of essays entitled 'The Epicurean', 'The Stoic' and 'The Platonist'. Further, the pluralism reflected in his multi-dimensional prescription for human happiness springs from the position taken in a fourth essay on the good life entitled 'The Sceptic' (Hume, *Writings on Economics*, pp. xcv–xcix).

Turning to a treatment of the effect of economic development on major aspects of social relations, Hume now expands the 'natural history' to ecompass non-economic considerations. He argues that economic growth contributes to the growth of knowledge in the liberal as well as the mechanical arts, nurtures a sense of humanity and fellow-feeling, enhances a nation's spiritual as well as its economic ability to defend itself and, through its impact on the growth of knowledge and fellow-feeling, advances an understanding of the art of government and political harmony. A final political consideration, to which Hume gives special attention, is the charge (drawn from the experience of Rome) that luxury is corrupting and debasing and therefore is inimical to liberty. Hume argues that history shows that precisely the opposite is true. For the growth of commerce brings the expansion of the merchant class – the 'middling rank of men' who above all are interested in uniform laws protecting their property; and it is this development, he emphasizes, which has led to the growth of parliamentary government and the associated respect for individual liberty. Hume thus perceived the link between the growth of economic individualism and political liberty that has drawn so much attention since his time. Although Hume recognized that the development of commerce and industry could produce evils of its own, he argued that these were outweighed by its benefits. Owing apparently to an overzealous desire to counter the common religious objections to luxury, Hume over-extends himself and leaves some of his arguments in support of economic growth open to criticism (Hume, *Writings on Economics*, pp. cii–civ). His treatment nonetheless stands as an unusually broad and penetrating appraisal of a wealth-orientated individualistic society. In light of this it deserves recognition as an early classic.

Throughout our discussion, attention has been given to Hume's interest in the psychological and historical aspects of economic activity. A similar interest – pursued in varying degree – is found among other writings of Hume's own period. However, owing to his own searching analysis as a philosopher and historian, Hume's treatment was of a particularly high order; equally extraordinary was the extent to which he employed the method of 'natural history' in the treatment of a wide range of issues of economic theory and policy.

Comparing Hume with Adam Smith (his close friend), one is struck by the brevity of Hume's economic writings. Hume wrote a series of relatively short 'discourses' on selected topics. Smith's *Wealth of Nations* (1776) is a general economic treatise. In contrast to Smith, Hume moreover gives little systematic attention to price and distribution theory, which was to become the major concern of classical and neoclassical economics. In point of the general analysis of psychological and historical influences on economic activity, however, Hume's work is more comprehensive, more highly organized and more penetrating than Smith's. When dealing with the subjective aspects of human behaviour, Smith not infrequently regards them as universals (e.g. his assertion that there is an innate disposition among men to 'truck and barter'), where Hume treats them as historical variables and himself seeks to explain the nature of the specific historical influences at work (Hume, *Writings on Economics*, pp. cvii–cx). In this Hume did not foreshadow the mainstream of subsequent economic thought; it was Adam Smith's tendency in his economic theory to abstract from history that was to become the dominant characteristic of later economic analysis. In point of general perspective (though often not its conceptual framework) Hume's economic thought bears a relation to other subsequent lines of development – to the historical and institutional schools of economics, to the more current revived analytical interest in economic growth along with its associated cultural aspects, to the concern with psychological factors in dealing both with macroeconomics and the economics of non-competitive markets, and to the normative appraisals of economic systems in their fuller social settings.

In the standard histories of economic thought Hume has been accorded relatively little attention. He is often ignored altogether or treated cursorily as a predecessor of Adam Smith. Various studies of the technical aspects of economic analysis have called attention to several of Hume's contributions. These aspects of Hume's analysis are noteworthy in their own right. Their significance deepens and broadens when they are related to Hume's work as a philosopher and historian and are seen to take form within the context of 'natural history'.

SELECTED WORKS

1752. *Political Discourses*. Edinburgh: A. Kincaid & A. Donaldson.
1875. *The Philosophical Works of David Hume*. Ed. with notes by T.H. Green and T.H. Grose, 4 vols, London: Longmans, Green & Co.
1955. *Writings on Economics*. Ed. Eugene Rowtein, London: Nelson.

Francis Hutcheson

ANDREW S. SKINNER

Hutcheson was born on 8 August 1694. His father, John, was a Presbyterian minister in Armagh, Ireland, and Francis spent his early years at nearby Ballyrea. In 1702 Francis and his elder brother Hans went to live with their grandfather, Alexander Hutcheson, at Drumalig in order to attend school near Saintfield. At the age of 14 he moved to a small denominational college or academy at Killyleagh, County Down.

In 1711 Hutcheson matriculated at Glasgow University where he was particularly influenced by Robert Simson (Mathematics), Gerschom Carmichael (Moral Philosophy), Alexander 'old' Dunlop (Greek) and John Simpson the 'heretical' divine. Hutcheson graduated in 1713 and embarked on a course of study in theology under Simpson's guidance. Hutcheson was back in Ireland by 1719, when he was licensed as a probationary minister, but moved to Dublin, where he set up an academy of which he remained head until 1730. It was during his period in Dublin that he was closely associated with Lord Molesworth, Edward Synge and James Arbuckle, all of whom had been influenced by the work of Shaftesbury.

His reputation established, Hutcheson was elected to the Chair of Moral Philosophy in Glasgow in 1730, when he delivered an inaugural lecture defending his principle of benevolence. It was as a lecturer that he made his mark on the University: brilliant and stylish, using English rather than Latin, Hutcheson's career amply confirms the accuracy of Adam Smith's reference to 'the abilities and virtues of the never to be forgotten' Francis Hutcheson (*Correspondence*, 1977, letter 274, p. 309).

Hutcheson lectured five days a week on Natural Religion, Morals, Jurisprudence and Government (Leechman, 1755, p. xxxvi). On three days, he lectured on classical theories of morality thus contributing (with Dunlop) to a revival of classical learning in Glasgow and forming an important channel for Stoic philosophy (Scott, 1937, pp. 31–2); a branch of philosophy which was to have

143

a profound influence on his pupil, Adam Smith. Hutcheson died on 8 August (his birthday) 1746 and was buried in St Mary's Churchyard, Dublin.

ETHICS AND JURISPRUDENCE. Hutcheson shared with his correspondent David Hume a concern with empirical study and an interest in elucidating the principles of human nature (1755, Book I, chapter 1). He noted that men are capable of acts of will which may be 'calm' or 'turbulent' where both may be selfish or benevolent, thus introducing the need for some means of control.

He argued that man is equipped with the faculty of reason and has powers of perception which 'introduce into the mind all its materials of knowledge' and which are associated with 'acts of the understanding' (1755, i. 7). This argument in turn led to the discussion of the senses of beauty, harmony and design. He added: 'Another important determination or sense of the soul we may call the *sympathetick*', which differs from *external* senses such as sight, sound, or taste and 'by which, when we apprehend the state of others, our hearts naturally have a fellow-feeling with them' (i. 19).

But in practice Hutcheson placed most emphasis on the *moral sense* representing a capacity for moral judgement, whose deployment (reinforced by the senses of honour or of shame) encourages the individual to virtuous actions. Hutcheson went on to distinguish the moral sense from the senses of decency and dignity. He added, in an important passage, that 'A penetrating genius, capacity for business, patience of application and labour...are naturally admirable, and relished by all observers; but with quite a different feeling from moral approbation' (i. 28).

The position is admirably summarized in the introduction to Smith's *Theory of Moral Sentiments*, where the editors note that Hutcheson 'held (against egoism) that moral action and moral judgement are disinterested and (against rationalism) that they both depend on natural feeling. Moral action is motivated by the disinterested feeling of benevolence', and since benevolence aims at producing happiness, 'the morally best action is that which procures the greatest happiness for the greatest number' (1976, p. 12).

It was Hutcheson's contention that men were inclined to, and fitted for, society: 'their curiosity, communicativeness, desire of action; their sense of honour, their compassion, benevolence, gaiety and the moral faculty, could have little or no exercise in solitude' (1755, i. 34).

This discussion was to lead to Hutcheson's treatment of natural rights and of the state of nature in a manner which is reminiscent of Locke. He also advanced the Lockean claim that the state of nature is a state not of war but of inconvenience which can only be resolved by the establishment of government in terms of a complex double contract:

Civil power is most naturally founded by these three different acts of a whole people. 1. An agreement or contract of each one with all the rest, that they will unite into one society or body, to be governed in all their common interests by one council. 2. A decree or designation, made by the whole people, of the form or plan of power, and of the persons to be intrusted with it. 3. A mutual agreement or contract between the governors thus constituted and the people, the former obliging themselves to the faithful administration of the powers vested in them for the common interest, and the latter obliging themselves to obedience' (ii. 227).

This has been described as the 'Real Whig position' (Winch, 1978, p. 46; Robbins, 1968) and may explain the considerable influence of Hutcheson's political ideas in the American Colonies (Norton, 1976). Hutcheson's 'warm love of liberty' was attested by Principal Leechman in his introduction to the *System* (1755, pp. xxxv–xxxvi); a sentiment which was echoed by Hugh Blair (Winch, 1978, pp. 47–8) in a contemporary review of the book.

The argument was developed in a number of directions which include the analysis of the 'Several Forms of Polity, with their Principal Advantages and Disadvantages' (Book III, ch. 6).

POLITICAL ECONOMY. The economic analysis, which is an important feature of the *System*, is woven into the broader fabric of the argument. It is concentrated primarily in Book 2, chapters 4, 6, 7, 12 and 13. Economic policy of a broadly 'mercantilist' tenor is discussed in Book 3, chapter 9, section 4 and taxation (including a discussion of the canons of taxation) is considered briefly in section 16 of the same chapter.

The argument is interesting in that it illustrates Hutcheson's concern with the advantages which accrue from the organised social state and further illustrates his grasp of the role of self-interest. The order of the argument is equally noteworthy.

Hutcheson effectively began his treatment of economic topics with a discussion of the division of labour (i. 287–9):

Nay, tis well known that the product of the labour of any given number, twenty for instance ... shall be much greater by assigning to one, a certain sort of work of one kind, in which he will soon acquire skill and dexterity, and to another assigning work of a different kind, than if each one of the twenty were obliged to employ himself, by turns, in all the different sorts of labour requisite for his subsistence, without sufficient dexterity in any. In the former method each procures a great quantity of goods of one kind, and can exchange a part of it for such goods obtained by the labours of others as he shall stand in need of (i. 288–9).

The discussion of the division of labour led in turn to Hutcheson's treatment of property and further illustration of the claim that men have a right to property which is important of itself and which, where respected, also provides a significant stimulus to economic activity (i. 320–24).

The longest continuous discussion is found in chapter 12 of the second Book (ii. 53–64) where Hutcheson, following the lead of Gershom Carmichael, introduced the discussion of value. Starting from the proposition that the 'natural ground of all value or price is some sort of use which goods afford in life' (ii. 53), 'usefulness' is then defined to include 'any tendency to give any satisfaction, by prevailing custom or fancy' (ii. 54). He concluded that:

> When some aptitude to human use is pre-supposed, we shall find that the prices of the goods depend on these two jointly, the *demand* on account of some use or other which many desire, and the *difficulty* of acquiring or cultivating for human use (ibid).

On the supply side, Hutcheson argued that 'value' is affected by the labour involved, the materials used, the ingenuity of the artist, the remuneration of the employer, rent and interest. He added that 'value is also raised, by the dignity of the station in which, according to the custom of a country, the men must live who provide us with certain goods or works of art' (ii. 55).

Hutcheson proceeded from this point to the discussion of the means of exchange (money) and to comment on the advantages of the metals and the need for coinage (ii. 56–8). The remainder of the chapter is largely concerned with the issue of debasement, and makes the point that money is not of itself an adequate measure of value.

The analytical section of the work is concluded in the following chapter where Hutcheson demonstrates the need for *interest*, since were it prohibited 'none would lend' (ii. 72). He argued that the rate would be determined by 'the state of trade and the quantity of coin' recognizing that 'as men can be supported by smaller gains in proportion upon their large stocks, the profit made upon any given sum employed is smaller, and the interest the trader can afford must be less' (ibid.) Hutcheson was well aware of the relationship between the rate of interest and other forms of return such as rent, and also introduced an allowance for risk. In sum, an interesting and often sophisticiated analysis which is likely to have made an important general impression on Adam Smith, while influencing his treatment of particular topics, such as the division of labour.

ADAM SMITH. There can be little doubt that Smith owed much to his teacher. There are marked parallels in the treatment of beauty (Scott, 1900, pp. 188, 284). In the ethics, there is the same emphasis on the role of immediate sense and feeling, on the point that moral judgement is disinterested, and further elaboration of the concept of the 'spectator'. It has also been noted that there is a marked parallel in the treatment of jurisprudence (see for example, Meek, 1976; Pesciarelli, 1986). The similarity in respect of the treatment of economic topics in Smith's lectures and in Hutcheson's work has been elaborated most notably by W.R. Scott (1900, 1937) and by W.L. Taylor (1965). Edwin Cannan went so far as to claim with respect to Hutcheson's treatment of price, that 'Probably it is in this chapter that the germ of the *Wealth of Nations* is to be found' (1896, p. xxvi).

At the same time there are differences of emphasis which are analytically interesting. While Smith admired benevolence, he rejected Hutcheson's claim that self-love cannot be 'in any case a motive for virtuous actions' (1759, VII, ii. 3.13), together with the view that moral judgement depended upon a special sense (1759, VII, iii. 3). If the economic analysis found in Smith's lectures follows the order of his master's treatment, the discourse is not only more elaborate, but also presented as a complete and self-contained account. But the most remarkable contrast is to be found in Hutcheson's acceptance, and Smith's rejection, of the contract theory of government. Hutcheson's radicalism has been contrasted with Smith's more conservative position (Winch, 1978, pp. 52–4). The same writer has also drawn attention to the associated point that Smith's treatment of jurisprudence was more explicitly historical (ibid., p. 65).

Yet a *System of Moral Philosophy* would have been as good a title for Smith's more ambitious programme, as it was for Hutcheson's summary of his lecture course; a course which embraced ethics, jurisprudence, government and political economy and which treated these different disciplines as the parts of a single, organic, whole (Scott, 1900, p. 227).

SELECTED WORKS All references to Hutcheson (and Leechman) in the text are to the *System of Moral Philosophy* (1755).

1725. *Inquiry into the Original of our Ideas of Beauty and Virtue*. London. 2nd edn, 1726.

1725–6. *Reflections upon Laughter and Remarks on the Fable of the Bees*. Dublin Journal No. 11 (5 June 1725); No. 12 (12 June); No. 13 (19 June) and No. 45 (5 February 1726); No. 46 (12 February); No. 47 (19 February). Also in *Hibernicus's Letters* (1729; 2nd edn, 1734).

1728a. *Essay on the Nature and Conduct of the Passions, with Illustrations upon the Moral Sense*. London and Dublin.

1728b. *Letters between the late Mr G. Burnet and Mr Hutcheson, London Journal*.

1730. *Hutchesoni Oratio Inauguralis*.

1735. *Considerations on Patronage addressed to the Gentlemen of Scotland*.

1742a. *The Meditations of M. Aurelius Antoninus. Newly Translated from the Greek, with Notes and an Account of His Life*. Glasgow.

1742b. *Metaphysicae Synopsis Ontologiam et Pneumatologiam complectens*. Glasgow. 2nd edn, 1744.

1742c. *Philosophiae Moralis Institutio Compendiaria, Ethices et Jurisprudentiae Naturalis Elementa continens, Libri Tres*. Glasgow. 2nd edn, 1745. Published as *A Short Introduction to Moral Philosophy in Three Books, containing the Elements of Ethics and the Law of Nature*. Glasgow. 1747.

1755. *A System of Moral Philosophy in Three Books, written by the late Francis Hutcheson, LL.D., Professor of Moral Philosophy in the University of Glasgow. Published from the original MS. by his son Francis Hutcheson, M.D. to which is prefixed Some Account of the Life, Writings, and Character of the Author. By The Reverend William Leechman, D.D., Professor of Divinity in the same University*. Glasgow.

1756. *Logicae Compendium, &c*. Glasgow. *Illustrations on the Moral Sense* was edited by Bernard Peach in 1971. Hutcheson's *Collected Works* are available in the Georg Olms Verlagsbuch-handlung edition (Hildesheim, 1969).

BIBLIOGRAPHY

Blackstone, W.T. 1975. *Francis Hutcheson and Contemporary Ethical Theory*. Athens, Georgia: University of Georgia Press.

Campbell, T.D. 1982. Francis Hutcheson. In *The Origins and Nature of the Scottish Enlightenment*, ed. R.H. Campbell and A.S. Skinner, Edinburgh: Edinburgh University Press.

Cannan, E. (ed.) 1896. *Adam Smith's Lectures on Justice, Police, Revenue and Arms*. Oxford: Clarendon Press.

McCosh, J. 1875. *The Scottish Philosophy From Hutcheson to Hamilton*. Princeton: Princeton University Press.

Meek, R.L. 1976. New light on Adam Smith's Lectures on Jurisprudence. *History of Political Economy* 8(4), Winter, 439–77.

Norton, D.F. 1976. Francis Hutcheson in America. in *Studies on Voltaire and the Eighteenth Century*, ed. T. Besterman, Vol. CLIV, Oxford: Voltaire Foundation.

Pesciarelli, E. 1986. On Adam Smith's Glasgow Lectures on Jurisprudence. *Scottish Journal of Political Economy* 33(1), February, 74–85.

Raphael, D.D. 1947. *The Moral Sense*. London: Oxford University Press.

Raphael, D.D. 1969. *British Moralists 1650–1800*. Oxford: Clarendon Press.

Robbins, C. 1954. When is it that colonies may turn independent: an analysis of the environment and politics of Francis Hutcheson. *William and Mary Quarterly* 11(2), 214–51.

Robbins, C. 1968. *The Eighteenth-Century Commonwealth Man*. New York: Antheneum.

Scott, W.R. 1900. *Francis Hutcheson, His Life, Teaching and Position in the History of Philosophy*. Cambridge: Cambridge University Press.

Scott, W.R. 1932. Hutcheson, Francis. In *Encyclopedia of the Social Sciences*, Vol. 7, ed. E.R.A. Seligman, New York: Macmillan.

Scott, W.R. 1937. *Adam Smith as Student and Professor*. Glasgow: Jackson, Son & Co.

Smith, A. 1759. *The Theory of Moral Sentiments*. Ed. D.D. Raphael and A.L. Macfie, Oxford: Clarendon Press, 1976.

Smith, A. 1977. *The Correspondence of Adam Smith*. Ed E. Mossner and I.S. Ross, London and New York: Oxford University Press.

Taylor, W.L. 1965. *Francis Hutcheson and David Hume as Predecessors of Adam Smith*. Durham, North Carolina: University of North Carolina Press.

Teichgraeber, R.E. 1986. *Free Trade and Moral Philosophy*. Durham, North Carolina: University of North Carolina Press.

Winch, D. 1978. *Adam Smith's Politics: An Essay in Historiographic Revision*. Cambridge: Cambridge University Press; New York: Cambridge University Press.

Individualism

C.B. MACPHERSON

Individualism is a social theory or ideology which assigns a higher moral value to the individual than to the community or society, and which consequently advocates leaving individuals free to act as they think most conducive to their self-interest. The term was also, as noted below, sometimes used in the 19th century as a name for an actual economic system. When so used, the term denoted the competitive market system which lets the direction of the economy be the unintended outcome of the decisions made by myriad individuals about the uses to which they will put their own labour and resources.

The first edition (1896) of Palgrave's *Dictionary of Political Economy* defined individualism in the latter, narrower sense. The article entitled Individualism began by reporting that John Stuart Mill had applied the term to 'that system of industrial organization in which all initiative is due to private individuals, and all organisation to their voluntary agreement'. The article then remarked: 'The natural antithesis to individualism is COLLECTIVISM or we may say SOCIALISM, a system under which industry is directly organized by the state, which owns all means of production and manages all processes by appointed officers.' The author defined the fundamentals of the system of individualism quite precisely:

> The essential features of individualism are, (1) private property in capital, to which are added almost of necessity the rights of bequest and inheritance, thus permitting unlimited transfer and accumulation. (2) competition, a rivalry between individuals in the acquisition of wealth, a struggle for existence in which the fittest survive.

There could hardly be a better definition of capitalism, at least of the neo-classical economists' model of capitalism. John Stuart Mill's *Socialism* is cited as authority for such a use of 'individualism', properly enough: his *Chapters on Socialism* (1879) does describe 'the principle of individualism' as 'competition, each one for himself and against all the rest. It is grounded on the opposition of interests, not the harmony of interests, and under it everyone is required to find his place by struggle, by punishing others back or being pushed back by them'; and later in the same work individualism is equated with 'quarelling about material interests'. One might also cite Mill's earlier (1851) 'Newman's Political Economy', where 'the existing individualism', described as 'arming one human being against another, making the good of each depend upon evil to others', is said to be so morally inferior to socialism that socialism is 'easily triumphant' over it.

It may be thought that the Palgrave definition of individualism is unduly narrow: a modern scholar (Lukes, 1973) has distinguished no less than eleven meanings the term may have, ranging from respect for human dignity, autonomy, privacy, and self-development, to epistemological and methodological individualism. Most of these meanings are indeed not considered in Palgrave's *Dictionary*, but since it is a dictionary *of political economy*, only meanings with an economic connotation can be expected to be treated. However, although that charge of undue narrowness may be dismissed, it may still appear that, considered historically, his usage is too narrow to be accurate for the whole modern Western tradition down to his own time.

The idea that the individual is morally more important than society goes back of course, in modern times, to the Renaissance. The same view, in religious terms, emerged at the Reformation, which made each individual, rather than the Church, the guardian of his own salvation; and this view got wider currency in 17th-century Puritanism. Neither the Renaissance nor the Reformation and the subsequent Puritanism reduced individuals to atoms of matter in motion, each seeking power and wealth at the expense of every other one. That step was taken by Hobbes in the mid-17th century: in his view, society was simply a congeries of colliding atoms in unceasing motion. That puts Hobbes's individualism close to, but leaves it broader than, Palgrave's concept.

In the 18th century Adam Smith gave full market individualism a more pleasant face, arguing that the most beneficent possible social result would be attained by leaving individuals free to make self-interested bargains in a competitive market: that was the doctrine of *laissez-faire*. And the market economy was solidly enough established in England by Smith's time that it could be accepted as a part of the natural order by that venerator of the traditional hierarchy of ranks, Smith's contemporary. Edmund Burke, though in Burke's hands the market economy became a much less pleasant affair. His *Thoughts and Details on Scarcity* (1795) was an unqualified endorsement of *laissez-faire*: it issued a shrill warning against 'breaking the laws of commerce, which are the laws of nature, and consequently the laws of God'. Governments must not interfere with 'the great wheel of circulation' even though it dooms 'so many wretches' to 'innumerable servile, degrading, unseemly, unmanly, and often most unwholesome and pestiferous occupations'.

In the 19th century, Bentham relentlessly restated and elaborated Hobbes's atomic individualism, and Benthamism became the dominant ideology. Its doctrine of human nature was summed up in its crudest form in James Mill's article *Government* (1820): 'The desire...of that power which is necessary to render the persons and properties of human beings subservient to our pleasures is a grand governing law of human nature.'

So we may say that historically, at least down to 1820 or so, the Palgrave definition is not at all too narrow. But it is too narrow for the latter part of the century, for it leaves out a quite different idea of individualism, one which John Stuart Mill promoted implicitly in his *Principles of Political Economy* (1848) and explicitly in his *On Liberty* (1859), with its opening laudatory quotation from Wilhelm von Humboldt: 'The grand, leading principle, towards which every argument unfolded in these pages directly converges, is the absolute and essential importance of human development in its richest diversity.'

Let us call this *developmental individualism*. It is the antithesis of *possessive individualism*, which assumes that the human being is essentially a striver for, and a receptacle for the acquisition of, material goods. The whole doctrine of *On Liberty* puts Mill squarely in the camp of developmental individualism. And the famous chapter 'Of the Stationary State' (*Principles*, Bk. IV, ch. 6) is eloquent testimony to the depth of his revulsion from the existing acquisitive individualism of the competitive market economy. So, although the developmental ideal of individualism is not found as positively in Mill's *Political Economy* as it is in his *On Liberty*, we may treat the former text also as being on the developmental side. If we do so, however, we must add that Mill was himself so confused a political economist that he did not see that the acquisitive behaviour he denounced was entailed in the capitalist structure he accepted: he did not see that it was that structure which effectively denied a developmental life to the bulk of the wage earners.

A greater political economist than Mill, namely Marx, saw through this confusion and took the logical way out. Marx may be classified as the ultra-collectivist but it is important to see that for him the collective control of the economy was simply a necessary means to an end which was ultra-individualistic, that is, to a flowering of individuality which would be possible when capitalism with its alienation of labour has been surpassed. Marx condemned capitalism morally because it defined any such flowering.

> In bourgeois society... the past dominates the present: in Communist society, the present dominates the past. In bourgeois society capital is independent and has individuality, while the living person is dependent and has no individuality. And the abolition of this state of things is called by the bourgeois, abolition of individuality and freedom! And rightly so. The abolition of bourgeois individuality, bourgeois independence, and bourgeois freedom is undoubtedly aimed at (*Communist Manifesto*, 1848, sect.2).

And the final outcome of the communist revolution was to be 'an association, in which the free development of each is the condition for the free development of all' (ibid.).

Similarly:

> In a higher phase of communist society... after labour has become not only a means of life but life's prime want; after the productive forces have also

increased with the all-round development of the individual, and all the springs of co-operative wealth flow more abundantly – only then can the narrow horizon of bourgeois right be crossed in its entirety and society inscribe on its banner: From each according to his ability, to each according to his needs! (*Critique of the Gotha Programme*, 1875, I, 3).

The *Manifesto's* vision of a fully developed individual as the highest human attainment, echoed in the *Critique of the Gotha Programme*, puts Marx as firmly as Mill in the developmental camp. And just as Mill is there not only by virtue of his *On Liberty* but also by virtue of his *Political Economy*, so Marx is there not only by virtue of the *Manifesto* but also of the *Critique*. And we may add that Marx is there just as firmly in Volume I of *Capital* (1867), where he refers scornfully to the capitalist mode of production as that 'in which the labourer exists to satisfy the needs of self-expansion of existing values instead of, on the contracy, material wealth existing to satisfy the needs of *development on the part of the labourer*' (emphasis added).

There is no warrant in any of this for trying, as some commentators used to do, to drive a wedge between the young 'humanist' Marx and the 'mature' political economist. And, of course, Marx had a strongly developmental vision in his earliest work, the *Economic-Philosophic Manuscripts of 1844*. Thus from his earliest to his latest economic writings there is this development vision. Developmental individualism is at the very heart of his political economy.

We find, then, that by the time of Mill and Marx developmental individualism is well established: in the liberal tradition it takes place alongside the continuing possessive individualism; in Marx's theory it was inherent from the beginning.

What of the late 20th century? The liberal tradition still contains the two strands of individualism. On the one hand, two of the most esteemed liberal individualists of our time – Isaiah Berlin and John Rawls – are clearly developmental individualists. And on the other hand, the two most noted economic individualists – Friedrich Hayek and Milton Friedman – are equally clearly possessive individualists. Friedman, who would dismantle the welfare state and leave the distribution of economic benefits to an unrestrained competitive market, may be cited as the very model of a possessive individualist. Hayek, whose economic philosophy was set out succinctly in his 1945 lecture *Individualism. True and False*, tries to give market individualism a more aggreeable image. He does this by claiming as 'true' individualists the great names in one line of the British tradition, a line from Locke through Mandeville, Hume, Tucker, Ferguson, Smith and Burke, down to Lord Acton, and by categorizing as false individualists the 19th-century Benthamists and Philosophical Radicals, and, on the continent, those infected by Cartesian rationalism, notably the Frency Encyclopaedists, Rousseau and the Physiocrats. True individualism, he says,

affirms the value of the family and all the common efforts of the small community and group, ... believes in local autonomy and voluntary associations ..., and ... its case rests largely on the contention that much for which the coercive action of the state is usually invoked can be done better by voluntary collaboration.

In sharp contrast, false individualism 'wants to dissolve all these smaller groups into atoms which have no cohesion other than the coercive rules imposed by the state...'. But Hayek's attempt to humanize market individualism cannot hide the fact that his 'true' individualism, being tied to the free market economy, compels everyone to compete atomistically. Both his kinds of individualism must be graded possessive. Market freedom, the individual freedom to choose between different uses of one's abilities and resources, is, he recognizes, 'incompatible with a full satisfaction of our individual views of distributive justice'. And the individual's freedom is limited by 'the hard discipline of the market'. Hayek's 'true' individualism, for all its smoothness, in the end comes down to the atomistic 'rugged individualism' of Calvin Coolidge and Herbert Hoover: it is rugged individualism with a smooth false front.

It is clear, then, that the liberal tradition in the late 20th century, including within itself both the developmental individualism of Berlin and Rawls and the possessive individualism of Hayek and Friedman, does contain two antithetical positions and cannot be reduced to either one.

We have said that the old Palgrave definition of individualism was an accurate enough description of the prevailing ideology in the earlier part of the 19th century but was too narrow for the latter part of the century, when the view we have called developmental individualism emerged alongside of the earlier purely possessive individualism. We may go on to ask, what brought about this change? What brought developmental individualism into the picture?

Clues are to be found in John Stuart Mill's own writings. In the first place is his perception that the unrestrained market economy had produced a kind of society which would no longer be tolerated by the working class it had produced. In his 1845 article 'The Claims of Labour' he took the rise of the Chartist movement, with its threat of physical force, to be evidence that the British working classes would no longer put up with things as they were, and he believed that 'the more fortunate classes' must see the writing on the wall: 'While some, by the physical and moral circumstances which they say around them, were made to feel that the condition of the labouring classes *ought* to be attended to, others were made to see that it *would* be attended to, whether they wished to be blind to it or not.'

In the second place, perhaps partly because of this apprehension of class violence, Mill became a more sensitive and humane liberal than his father or Bentham, denouncing as utterly unjust the existing relation of effort and reward, by which the produce of labour was apportioned 'almost in an inverse ratio to the labour' (*Principles of Political Economy*, Bk. II. ch. 1, sect.3), and deploring the fiercely competitive character of the market-dominated society of his day, 'the trampling, crushing, elbowing, and treading on each other's heels, which form the existing type of social life' (*Principles*, Bk. IV. ch. 6, sect.2). In reacting as early as 1848 against this kind of society, Mill was a harbinger of the more humane social conscience which became noticeable in early 20th-century liberal thinking and which in mid-20th century brought the welfare state.

We conclude that the old Palgrave definition of individualism, already too narrow when it was promulgated, became increasingly inadequate in the subsequent decades. It was made inadequate by the rise and growth of developmental individualism, which in turn was the result of two distinct but related phenomena – the apprehension by middle-class thinkers of a danger of working-class violence, and the somewhat delayed reaction of those same minds to the shocking brutality of the industrial *laissez-faire* society. The two factors together ensured that developmental individualism would coexist with possessive individualism in the heyday of free capitalist enterprise.

How much longer they will coexist is not readily predictable. The danger of class violence now within advanced capitalist welfare states is less than Mill thought it to be in the society of his time, but what may well be called class violence as between undeveloped (or misdeveloped) and developed states is not far to seek in our time. And the working and living conditions of wage-earners in developed countries are less savage now than they were in Mill's day, but the increasing speed and tension of much of the work presses heavily on them. All we can say is that the probability of our advanced societies continuing to afford any substantial measure of developmental individualism varies inversely with the degree of industrial speed-up and the amount of class violence, national and international.

BIBLIOGRAPHY

Burke, E. 1795. *Thoughts and Details on Scarcity, originally presented to the Right Hon. William Pitt, in the month of November, 1795*. London, 1800.

Hayek, F.A. 1946. *Individualism: True and False. The twelfth Finlay Lecture, 1945*. Dublin: Hodges, Figgis & Co.; Oxford: B.H. Blackwell.

Lukes, S. 1973. *Individualism*. Oxford: Blackwell; New York: Harper.

Macpherson, C.B. 1962. *The Political Theory of Possessive Individualism*. Oxford: Oxford University Press.

Marx, K. and Engels, F. 1848. *The Communist Manifesto*. London; New York: Russell & Russell, 1963.

Marx, K. 1867. *Capital*. London: Lawrence & Wishart, 1970.

Marx, K. 1891. *Critique of the Gotha Programme*. London: Lawrence & Wishart, 1938.

Marx, K. 1959. *Economic and Philosophic Manuscripts of 1844*. Moscow: Foreign Languages Publishing House.

Mill, J. 1820. *Government*. (Originally written for the supplement to the fifth edn of the *Encyclopaedia Britannica* which was completed in 1824.)

Mill, J.S. 1845. The claims of labour. *Edinburgh Review*. In *Collected Works of John Stuart Mill*, Vol. IV, ed. J.M. Robson, Toronto: University of Toronto Press, 1967, 363–89.

Mill, J.S. 1949. *Principles of Political Economy*. 2 vols, London: J.W. Parker.

Mill, J.S. 1851. Newman's political economy. *Westminster Review*. In *Collected Works of John Stuart Mill*, Vol. V, ed. J.M. Robson, Toronto: University of Toronto Press, 1967, 439–57.

Mill, J.S. 1859. *On Liberty*. London: J.W. Parker; Chicago, H. Regnery, 1955.

Mill, J.S. 1879. Chapters on socialism. *Fortnightly Review*. In *Collected Works of John Stuart Mill*, Vol. V, ed. J.M. Robson, Toronto: University of Toronto Press, 1967, 703–53.

Palgrave, R.H.I. (ed.) 1894–9. *Dictionary of Political Economy*. London: Macmillan & Co.

Interests

ALBERT O. HIRSCHMAN

'Interest' or 'interests' is one of the most central and controversial concepts in economics and, more generally, in social science and history. Since coming into widespread use in various European countries around the latter part of the 16th century as essentially the same Latin-derived word (*intérêt, interesse*, etc.), the concept has stood for the fundamental forces, based on the drive for self-preservation and self-aggrandizement, that motivate or should motivate the actions of the prince or the state, of the individual, and later of groups of people occupying a similar social or economic position (classes, interest groups). When related to the individual, the concept has at times had a very inclusive meaning, encompassing interest in honour, glory, self-respect, and even after-life, while at other times it became wholly confined to the drive for economic advantage. The esteem in which interest-motivated behaviour is held has also varied drastically. The term was originally pressed into service as a euphemism serving, already in the late Middle Ages, to make respectable an activity, the taking of interest on loans, that had long been considered contrary to divine law and known as the sin of usury. In its wider meanings, the term at times achieved enormous prestige as a key to a workable and peaceful social order. But it has also been attacked as degrading to the human spirit and corrosive of the foundations of society. An inquiry into these multiple meanings and appreciations is in effect an exploration of much of economic history and in particular of the history of economic and political doctrine in the West over the past four centuries.

The concept, moreover, still plays a central role in contemporary economics and political economy: the construct of the self-interested, isolated individual who chooses freely and rationally between alternative courses of action after computing their prospective costs and benefits to him or herself, that is, while ignoring costs and benefits to other people and to society at large, underlies much of welfare economics; and the same perspective has yielded important, if disturbing, contributions to a broader science of social interactions, such as the

Prisoner's Dilemma theorem and the obstacles to collective action because of free riding.

Two essential elements appear to characterize interest-propelled action: *self-centredness*, that is, predominant attention of the actor to the consequences of any contemplated action for himself; and *rational calculation*, that is, a systematic attempt at evaluating prospective costs, benefits, satisfactions, and the like. Calculation could be considered the dominant element: once action is supposed to be informed only by careful estimation of costs and benefits, with most weight necessarily being given to those that are better known and more quantifiable, it tends to become self-referential by virtue of the simple fact that each person is best informed about his *own* satisfactions and disappointments.

INTEREST AND STATECRAFT. Rational calculation also played the chief role in the emergence of the concept of interest-motivated action on the part of the prince in the 16th and 17th centuries. It accounts for the high marks interest-governed behaviour received during the late 16th- and early 17th-century phases of its career in politics. The term did duty on two fronts. First, it permitted the emergent science of statecraft to assimilate the important insights of Machiavelli. The author of *The Prince* had almost strained to advertise those aspects of politics that clashed with conventional morality. He dwelt on instances where the prince was well advised or even duty bound to practise cruelty, mendacity, treason, and so on. Just as, in connection with money lending, the term interest came into use as a euphemism for the earlier term usury, so did it impose itself on the political vocabulary as a means of anaesthetizing, assimilating and developing Machiavelli's shocking insights.

But in the early modern age, 'interest' was not only a label under which a ruler was given *new latitude* or was absolved from feeling guilty about following a practice that he had previously been taught to consider as immoral: the term also served to impose *new restraints* as it enjoined the Prince to pursue his interests with a rational, calculating spirit that would often imply prudence and moderation. At the beginning of the 17th century, the interests of the sovereign were contrasted with the wild and destructive passions, that is, with the immoderate and foolish seeking of glory and other excesses involved in pursuing the by then discredited heroic ideal of the Middle Ages and the Renaissance. This disciplinary aspect of the doctrine of interest was particularly driven in home in the influential essay *On the Interest of Princes and States of Christendom* by the Huguenot statesman the Duke of Rohan (1579–1638).

The interest doctrine thus served to release the ruler from certain traditional restraints (or guilt feelings) only to subject him to new ones that were felt to be far more efficacious than the well-worn appeals to religion, morals, or abstract reason. Genuine hope arose that, with princely or national interest as guide, statecraft would be able to produce a more stable political order and a more peaceful world.

INTEREST AND INDIVIDUAL BEHAVIOUR. The early career of the interest concept with regard to statecraft finds a remarkable parallel in the role it played in shaping behaviour codes for individual men and women in society. Here also a new licence went hand in hand with a new restraint.

The new licence consisted in the legitimation and even praise that was bestowed upon the single-minded pursuit of material wealth and upon activities conducive to its accumulation. Just as Machiavelli had opened up new horizons for the Prince, so did Mandeville two centuries later list a number of 'don'ts' for the commoner, in this case primarily in relation to money making. Once again, a new insight into human behaviour or into the social order was first proclaimed as a startling, shocking paradox. Like Machiavelli, Mandeville presented his thesis on the beneficial effects on the general welfare of the luxury trades (which had long been strictly regulated) in the most scandalous possible fashion, by referring to the activities, drives and emotions associated with these trades as 'private vices'. Here again, his essential message was eventually absorbed into the general stock of accepted practice by changing the language with which he had proclaimed his discovery. For the third time, euphemistic resort was had to 'interest', this time in substitution for such terms as 'avarice', 'love of lucre', and so on. The transition from one set of terms to the other is reflected by the first lines of David Hume's essay 'On the Independency of Parliament':

> Political writers have established it as a maxim, that, in contriving any system of government and fixing the several checks and balances of the constitution, every man ought to be supposed a *knave*, and to have no other end, in all his actions, than private interest. By this interest we must govern him, and, by means of it, make him, notwithstanding his insatiable avarice and ambition, cooperate to public good (Hume, 1742, vol. I, pp. 117–18, emphasis in the original).

Here interest is explicitly equated with knavishness and 'insatiable avarice'. But soon thereafter the memory of these unsavoury synonyms of interest was suppressed, as in Adam Smith's famous statement about the butcher, the brewer and the baker who are driven to supply us with our daily necessities through their interest rather than their benevolence. Smith thus did for Mandeville what the Duke of Rohan had done for Machiavelli. His doctrine of the Invisible Hand legitimated total absorption of the citizen in the pursuit of private gain and thereby served to assuage any guilt feelings that might have been harboured by the many Englishmen who were drawn into commerce and industry during the commercial expansion of the 18th century but had been brought up under the civic humanist code enjoining them to serve the public interest *directly* (Pocock, 1982). They were now reassured that by pursuing gains they were doing so *indirectly*.

In fact, Adam Smith was not content to praise the pursuit of private gain. He also berated citizens' involvement in public affairs. Right after his Invisible Hand statement he wrote 'I have never known much good done by those who affected to trade for the public good' (1776, p. 423). Ten years before, Sir James Steuart had supplied an interesting explanation for a similar aversion toward citizens' involvement in public affairs.

> ... were everyone to act for the public, and neglect himself, the statesman would be bewildered ... were a people to become quite disinterested, there would be no possibility of governing them. Everyone might consider the interest of his country in a different light, and many might join in the ruin of it, by endeavouring to promote its advantages (1767, vol. I, pp. 243–4).

In counterpart to the new area of authorized and recommended behaviour, these statements point to the important *restraints* that accompanied the doctrine of interest. For the individual citizen or subject as for the ruler, interest-propelled action meant originally action informed by rational calculation in any area of human activity – political, cultural, economic, personal and so on. In the 17th century and through part of the 18th, this sort of methodical, prudential, interest-guided action was seen as vastly preferable to actions dictated by the violent, unruly and disorderly passions. At the same time, the interests of the vast majority of people, that is of those outside of the highest reaches of power, came to be more narrowly defined as economic, material or 'moneyed' interests, probably because the non-elite was deemed to busy itself primarily with scrounging a living with no time left to worry about honour, glory, and the like. The infatuation with interest helped bestow legitimacy and prestige on commercial and related private activities, that had hitherto ranked rather low in public esteem; correspondingly, the Renaissance ideal of glory, with its implicit celebration of the public sphere, was downgraded and debunked as a mere exercise in the destructive passion of self-love (Hirschman, 1977, pp. 31–42).

THE POLITICAL BENEFITS OF AN INTEREST-BASED SOCIAL ORDER. The idea that the interests, understood as the methodical pursuit and accumulation of private wealth, would bring a number of benefits in the political realm took various distinct forms. There was, first of all, the expectation that they would achieve at the macrolevel what they were supposed to accomplish for the individual: hold back the violent passions of the 'rulers of mankind'. Here the best-known proposition, voiced early in the 18th century, says that the expansion of commerce is incompatible with the use of force in international relations and would gradually make for a peaceful world. Still more utopian hopes were held out for the effects of commerce on domestic politics: the web of interests delicately woven by thousands of transactions would make it impossible for the sovereign to interpose his power brutally and wantonly through what was called '*grands coups d'autorité*' by Montesquieu or 'the folly of despotism' by Sir James Steuart. This thought was carried further in the early 19th century when the intricacies of expanding industrial production compounded those of commerce: in the technocratic vision of Saint-Simon the time was at hand when economic exigencies would put an end, not just to *abuses* of the power of the state, but to any power whatsoever of man over man: politics would be replaced by administration of 'things'. As is well known this conjecture was taken up by Marxism with its prediction of the withering away of the state under communism. An argument that a century earlier had been advanced on behalf of emergent capitalism was thus refurbished for a new, *anti*-capitalist utopia.

Another line of thought about the political effects of an interest-driven society looks less at the constraints such as society will impose upon those who govern than at the difficulties of the task of governing. As already noted, a world where people methodically pursue their private interests was believed to be far more predictable, and hence *more governable*, than one where the citizens are vying with each other for honour and glory.

The stability and lack of turbulence that were expected to characterize a country where men pursue singlemindedly their material interests were very much on the minds of some of the 'inventors' of America, such as James Madison and Alexander Hamilton. The enormous prestige and influence of the interest concept at the time of the founding of America is well expressed in Hamilton's statement:

> The safest reliance of every government is on man's interests. This is a principle of human nature, on which all political speculation, to be just, must be founded (Hamilton [1784], cited in Terence Ball, 1983, p. 45).

Finally, a number of writers essentially extrapolated from the putative personality traits of the individual trader, as the prototype of interest-driven man, to the general characteristics of a society where traders would predominate. In the 18th century, perhaps as a result of some continuing disdain for economic pursuits, commerce and money-making were often described as essentially innocuous or 'innocent' pastimes in contrast no doubt with the more violent or mor strenuous ways of the upper or lower classes. Commerce was to bring 'gentle' and 'polished' manners. In French, the term innocent appended to commerce was often coupled with *doux* (sweet, gentle) and what has been called the thesis of the *doux commerce* held that commerce was a powerful civilizing agent diffusing prudence, probity and similar virtues within and among trading societies (Hirschman, 1977, 1982a). Only under the impact of the French Revolution did some doubt arise on the direction of the casual link between commerce and civilized society: taken aback by the outbreak of social violence on a large scale, Edmund Burke suggested that the expansion of commerce depended itself on the *prior* existence of 'manners' and 'civilization' and on what he called 'natural protecting principles' grounded in the 'spirit of a gentleman' and 'the spirit of religion' (Burke, 1790, p. 115; Pocock, 1982).

THE INVISIBLE HAND. The capstone of the doctrine of self-interest was of course Adam Smith's Invisible Hand. Even through this doctrine, being limited to the economic domain, was more modest than the earlier speculations on the beneficient *political* effects of trade and exchange, it soon came to dominate the discussion. An intriguing paradox was involved in stating that the *general* interest and welfare would be promoted by the self-interested activities of innumerable decentralized operators. To be sure, this was not the first nor the last time that such a claim of identity or coincidence or harmony of interests of a part with those of a whole has been put forward. Hobbes had advocated an absolute monarchy on the ground that this form of government brings about an identity of interest between ruler and ruled; as just noted, the writers of the Scottish Enlightenment saw an identity of interest between the general interests of British society and the interests of the middle ranks; such an identity between the interests of one class and those of society became later a cornerstone of Marxism, with the middling ranks having of course been supplanted by the proletariat; and finally, the American pluralist school in political science returned essentially to the Smithian scheme of harmony between many self-interests and the general interest, with Smith's individual economic operators having been replaced by contending 'interest groups' on the political stage.

All these *Harmonielehren* have two factors in common: the 'realistic' affirmation that we have to deal with men and women, or with groups thereof, 'as they really are', and an attempt to prove that it is possible to achieve a workable and progressive social order with these highly imperfect subjects, and, as it were, behind their backs. The mixture of paradoxical insight and alchemy involved in these constructs makes them powerfully attractive, but also accounts for their ultimate vulnerability.

THE INTERESTS ATTACKED. The 17th century was perhaps the real heyday of the interest doctrine. Governance of the social world by interest was then viewed as an alternative to the rule of destructive passions; that was surely a lesser evil, and possibly an outright blessing. In the 18th century, the doctrine received a substantial boost in the economic domain through the doctrine of the Invisible Hand, but it was indirectly weakened by the emergence of a more optimistic view of the passions: such passionate sentiments and emotions as curiosity, generosity and sympathy were then given detailed attention, the latter in fact by Adam Smith himself in his *Theory of Moral Sentiments*. In comparison to such fine, newly discovered or rehabilitated springs of human action, interest no longer looked nearly so attractive. Here was one reason for the reaction against the interest paradigm that unfolded toward the end of the 18th century and was to fuel several powerful 19th-century intellectual movements.

Actually the passions did not have to be wholly transformed into benign sentiments to be thought respectable and even admirable by a new generation. Once the interests appeared to be truly in command with the vigorous commercial and industrial expansion of the age, a general lament went up for 'the world we have lost'. The French Revolution brought another sense of loss and Edmund Burke joined the two when he exclaimed, in his *Reflections on the Revolution in France*, 'the age of chivalry is gone; that of sophisters, economists and calculators has succeeded; and the glory of Europe is extinguished for ever' (1790, p. 111). This famous statement came a bare 14 years after the *Wealth of Nations* had denounced the rule of the 'great lords' as a 'scene of violence, rapine and disorder' and had celebrated the benefits flowing from everyone catering to his interests through orderly economic pursuits. Now Burke was an intense admirer of Adam Smith and took much pride in the identity of views on economic matters between himself and Smith (Winch, 1985; Himmelfarb, 1984). His 'age of chivalry' statement, so contrary to the intellectual legacy of Smith, therefore signals one of those sudden changes in the general mood and understanding from one age to the next of which the exponents themselves are hardly aware. Burke's lament set the tone for much of the subsequent Romantic protest against an order based on the interests which, once it appeared to be dominant, was seen by many as lacking nobility, mystery, and beauty.

This nostalgic reaction merged with the observation that the interests, that is, the drive for material wealth, were not nearly as 'innocuos', 'innocent' or 'mild', as had been thought or advertised. To the contrary, it was not the drive for material dvantage that suddenly loomed as a subversive force of enormous power. Thomas Carlyle thought that all traditional values were threatened by 'that brutish god-forgetting Profit-and-Loss Philosophy' and protested that 'cash payment is not the only nexus of man with man' (1843, p. 187). This phrase – cash-nexus – was taken over by Marx and Engels who used it to good effect in the first section of the *Communist Manifesto* where they painted a lurid picture of the moral and cultural havoc wrought by the conquering bourgeoisie.

Many other critics of capitalist society dwelt on the destructiveness of the new energies that were released by a social order in which the interests were given free rein. In fact, the thought arose that these forces were so wild and out of control that they might undermine the very foundations on which the social order was resting, that they were thus bent on self-destruction. In a startling reversal, feudal society, which had earlier been treated as 'rude and barbarous' and was thought to be in permanent danger of dissolution because of the unchecked passions of violent rulers and grandees, was perceived in retrospect to have nurtured such values as honour, respect, friendship, trust and loyalty, that were essential for the functioning of an interest-dominated order, but were relentlessly, if inadvertently, undermined by it. This argument was already contained in part in Burke's assertion that it is civilized society that lays the groundwork for commerce rather than vice versa; it was elaborated by a large and diverse group of authors, from Richard Wagner via Schumpeter to Karl Polanyi and Fred Hirsch (Hirschman, 1982a, pp. 1466–70).

THE INTERESTS DILUTED. While the interest doctrine thus met with considerable opposition and criticism in the 19th century, its prestige remained nevertheless high, particularly because of the vigorous development of economics as a new body of scientific thought. Indeed, the success of this new science made for attempts to utilize its insights, such as the interest concept, for elucidating some non-economic aspects of the social world. In his *Essay on Government* (1820), James Mill formulated the first 'economic' theory of politics and based it – just as was later done by Schumpeter, Anthony Downs, Mancur Olson etc. – on the assumption of rational self-interest. But this widening of the use of the concept turned out to be something of a disservice. In politics, so Mill had to recognize, the gap between the 'real' interest of the citizen and 'a false supposition [i.e. perception] of interest' can be extremely wide and problematic (1820, p. 88).

This difficulty provided an opening for Macaulay's withering attack in the *Edinburgh Review* (1829). Macaulay pointed out that Mill's theory was empty: interest 'means only that men, if they can, will do as they choose...it is...idle to attribute any importance to a proposition which, when interpreted, means only that a man had rather do what he had rather do' (p. 125).

The charge that the interest doctrine was essentially tautological acquired greater force as more parties climbed on the bandwagon of interest, attempting to bend the concept to their own ends. As so many key concepts used in everyday discourse, 'interest' had never been strictly defined. While individual self-interest in material gain predominated, wider meanings were never completely lost sight of. An extremely wide and inclusive interpretation of the concept was put forward at a very early stage in its history: Pascal's Wager was nothing but an attempt to demonstrate that belief in God (hence, conduct in accordance with His precepts) was strictly in our (long-term) self-interest. Thus the concept of *enlightened* self-interest has a long history. But it received a boost and special, concrete meaning in the course of the 19th century. With the contemporary revolutionary outbreaks and movements as an ominous backdrop, advocates of social reform were able to argue that a dominant social group is well advised to surrender some of its privileges or to impove the plight of the lower classes so as to insure social peace. 'Enlightened' self-interest of the upper classes and conservative opinion was appealed to, for example, by the French and English advocates of universal suffrage or electoral reform at mid-century; it was similarly invoked by the promoters of the early social welfare legislation in Germany and elsewhere toward the end of the century, and again by Keynes and the Keynesians who favoured limited intervention of the state in the economy through countercyclical policy and 'automatic stabilizers' resulting from welfare state provisions. These appeals were often made by reformers who, while fully convinced of the intrinsic value and social justice of the meaures they advocated, attempted to enlist the support of important groups by appealing to their 'longer-term' rather than short-term and therefore presumably *shortsighted* interests. But the advocacy was not only tactical. It was sincerely put forward and testified to the continued prestige of the notion that interest-motivated social behaviour was the best guarantee of a stable and harmonious social order.

Whereas enlightened self-interest was something the upper classes of society were in this manner pressed to ferret out, the lower classes were similarly exhorted, at about the same epoch but from different quarters, to raise their sights above day-to-day pursuits. Marx and the Marxists invited the working class to become aware of its *real interests* and to shed the 'false consciousness' from which it was said to be suffering as long as it did not throw itself wholeheartedly into the class struggle. Once again, the language of interests was borrowed for the purpose of characterizing and dignifying a type of behaviour a group was being pressed to adopt.

Here, then, was one way in which the concept of interest-motivated behaviour came to be diluted. Another was the progressive loss of the sharp distinction an earlier age had made between the passions and the interests. Already Adam Smith had used the two concepts jointly and interchangeably. Even though it became abundantly clear in the 19th century that the desire to accumulate wealth was anything but the 'calm passion' as which it had been commended by some 18th-century philosophers, there was no return to the earlier distinction between the interests and the passions or between the wild and the mild passions. Money-making had once and for all been identified with the concept of interest so that all forms of this activity, however passionate or irrational, were automatically thought of as interest-motivated. As striking new forms of accumulation and industrial or financial empire-building made their appearance, new concepts were introduced, such as entrepreneurial leadership and intuition (Schumpeter, 1911) or the 'animal spirits' of the capitalists (Keynes, 1936, pp. 161–63). But they were not contrasted with the interests, and were rather assumed to be one of their manifestations.

In this manner the interests came to cover virtually the entire range of human actions, from the narrowly self-centred to the sacrificially altruistic, and from the prudently calculated to the passionately compulsive. In the end, interest stood behind anything people do or wish to do and to explain human action by interest thus did turn into the vacuous tautology denounced by Macaulay. At about the same time, other key and time-honoured concepts of economic analysis, such as utility and value, became similarly drained of their earlier psychological or normative content. The positivistically oriented science of economics that flourished during much of this century felt that it could do without any of these terms and replaced them by the less value- or psychology-laden 'revealed preference' and 'maximizing under constraints'. And thus it came to pass that interest, which had rendered such long and faithful service as a euphemism, was not superseded in turn by various even more neutral and colourless neologisms.

The development of the self-interest concept and of economic analysis in general in the direction of positivism and formalism may have been related to the discovery, toward the end of the 19th century, of the instinctual-intuitive, the habitual, the unconscious, the ideologically and neurotically driven – in short, to the extraordinary vogue for the nonrational that characterized virtually all of the influential philosophical, psychological and sociological thinking of the time. It was out of the question for economics, all based on rationally pursued self-interest, to incorporate the new findings into its own apparatus. So that discipline reacted to the contemporary intellectual temper by withdrawing from psychology to the greatest possible extent, by emptying its basic concepts of their psychological origin – a survival strategy that turned out to be highly successful. It is of course difficult to prove that the rise of the non-rational in psychology and sociology and the triumph of positivism and formalism in economics were truly connected in this way. Some evidence is supplied by the remarkable case of Pareto: he made fundamental contributions both to a sociology that stressed the complex 'non-logical' (as he put it) aspects of social action and to an economics that is emancipated from dependence on psychological hedonism.

CURRENT TRENDS. Lately there have been signs of discontent with the progressive evisceration of the concept of interest. On the conservative side, there was a return to the orthodox meaning of interest and the doctrine of enlightened self-interest was impugned. Apart from the discovery, first made by Tocqueville, that reform is just as likely to unleash as to prevent revolution, it was pointed out that most well-meant reform moves and regulations have 'perverse' side effects which compound rather than alleviate the social ills one had set out to cure. It was best, so it appeared, not to stray from the narrow path of narrow self-interest, and it was confusing and pointless to dilute this concept.

Others agreed with the latter judgement, but for different reasons and with different conclusions. They also disliked the manoeuvre of having every kind of human action masquerade under the interest label. But they regarded as relevant for economics certain human actions and activities which cannot be accounted for by the traditional notion of self-interest: actions motivated by altruism, by commitment to ethical values, by concern for the group and the public interest, and, perhaps most important, the varieties of non-instrumental behaviour. A beginning has been made by various economists and other social scientists to take these kinds of activities seriously, that is, to abandon the attempt to categorize them as mere variants of interest-motivated activity (Boulding, 1973; Collard, 1978; Hirschman, 1985; Margolis, 1982; McPherson, 1984; Phelps, 1975; Schelling, 1984; Sen, 1977).

One important aspect of these various forms of behaviour which do not correspond to the classical concept of interest-motivated action is that they are subject to considerable variation. Take actions in the public interest as an example. There is a wide range of such actions, from total involvement in some protest movement down to voting on Election Day and further down to mere grumbling about, or commenting on, some public policy within a small circle of friends or family – what Guillermo O'Donnell has called 'horizontal voice' in contrast to the 'vertical' voice directly addressed to the authorities (1986). The actual degree of participation under more or less normal political conditions is subject to constant fluctuations along this continuum, in line with changes in economic conditions, government performance, personal development, and many other factors. As a result, with total time for private *and* public activity being limited, the intensity of citizens' dedication to their private interests is also subject to constant change. Near-total privatization occurs only under certain authoritarian governments, for the most repressive regimes do not only do away with the free vote and any open manifestation of dissent, but also manage to suppress, through their display of terrorist power, all *private* expressions of nonconformity with public policy, that is, all those manifestations of 'horizontal voice' that are actually important forms of public involvement.

An arresting conclusion follows. That vaunted ideal of predictability, that alleged idyll of a privatized citizenry paying busy and exclusive attention to its economic interests and thereby serving the public interest indirectly, but never directly, becomes a reality only under wholly nightmarish political conditions!

More civilized political circumstances necessarily imply a less transparent and less predictable society.

Actually, this outcome of the current inquiries into activities not strictly motivated by traditional self-interest is all to the good: for the only certain and predictable feature of human affairs is their unpredictability and the futility of trying to reduce human action to a single motive – such as interest.

BIBLIOGRAPHY

Ball, T. 1983. The ontological presuppositions and political consequences of a social science. In *Changing Social Science*, ed. D.R. Sabia, Jr. and J.T. Wallulis, Albany: State University of New York Press.

Boulding, K.E. 1973. *The Economy of Love and Fear: A Preface to Grants Economics.* Belmont, California: Wadsworth.

Burke, E. 1790. *Reflections on the Revolution in France.* Chicago: Regnery, 1955.

Carlyle, T. 1843. *Past and Present.* New York: New York University Press, 1977.

Collard, D. 1978. *Altruism and Economy: A Study in Non-selfish Economics.* Oxford: Robertson.

Collini, S., Winch, D. and Burrow, J. 1983. *That Noble Science of Politics: A Study in Nineteenth-century Intellectual History.* Cambridge: Cambridge University Press.

Hamilton, A. 1784. Letters from Phocion, Numer I. In *The Works of Alexander Hamilton*, ed. John C. Hamilton, New York: C.S. Francis, 1851, Vol. II, 322.

Himmelfarb, G. 1984. *The Idea of Poverty: England in the Early Industrial Age.* New York: Knopf.

Hirschman, A.O. 1977. *The Passions and the Interests: Political Arguments for Capitalism Before its Triumph.* Princeton: Princeton University Press.

Hirschman, A.O. 1982a. Rival interpretations of market society: civilizing, destructive, or feeble? *Journal of Economic Literature*, 20(4), December, 1463–84.

Hirschman, A.O. 1982b. *Shifting Involvements: Private Interest and Public Action.* Princeton: Princeton University Press.

Hirschman, A.O. 1985. Against parsimony: three easy ways of complicating some categories of economic discourse. *Economics and Philosophy*, 1, 7–21.

Hume, D. 1742. *Essays Moral, Political and Literary.* Ed. T.H. Green and T.H. Grose, London: Longmans, 1898.

Keynes, J.M. 1936. *The General Theory of Employment, Interest and Money.* London: Macmillan; New York: Harcourt, Brace.

Macaulay, T.B. 1829. Mill's Essay on Government. In *Utilitarian Logic and Politics*, ed. J. Lively and J. Rees. Oxford: Clarendon, 1978.

McPherson, M.S. 1984. Limits on self-seeking: the role of morality in economic life. In *Neoclassical Political Economy*, ed. D.C. Colander, Cambridge, Mass.: Ballinger, 71–85.

Margolis, H. 1982. *Selfishness, Altruism and Rationality.* Cambridge: Cambridge University Press.

Meinecke, F. 1924. *Die Idee der Staatsträson in der neueren Geschichte.* Munich: Oldenburg.

Mill, J. 1820. *Essay on Government.* In *Utilitarian Logic and Politics*, ed. J. Lively and J. Rees, Oxford: Clarendon, 1978.

O'Donnell, G. 1986. On the convergences of Hirschman's *Exit, Voice and Loyalty* and *Shifting Involvements.* In *Development, Democracy and the Art of Trespassing: Essays in Honor of A.O. Hirschman*, ed. A. Foxley, et al., Notre Dame, Ind.: University of Notre Dame Press.

Phelps, E.S. (ed.) 1975. *Altruism, Morality and Economic Theory*. New York: Russell Sage Foundation.

Pocock, J.G.A. 1982. The political economy of Burke's analysis of the French Revolution. *Historical Journal* 25, June, 331–49.

Rohan, H., Duc, de. 1638. *De l'interêt des princes et états de la chrétienité*. Paris: Pierre Margat.

Schelling, T.C. 1984. *Choice and Consequence*. Cambridge, Mass.: Harvard University Press.

Schumpeter, J.A. 1911. *The Theory of Economic Development*. Cambridge, Mass.: Harvard University Press, 1951.

Sen, A. 1977. Rational fools: a critique of the behavioral foundations of economic theory. *Philosophy and Public Affairs* 6(4), Summer, 317–44.

Smith, A. 1776. *An Inquiry into the Nature and Causes of the Wealth of Nations*. Ed. E. Cannan, New York: Modern Library, 1937.

Steuart, J. 1767. *Inquiry into the Principles of Political Oeconomy*. Ed. A.S. Skinner, Chicago: University of Chicago Press, 1966.

Winch, D. 1985. The Burke–Smith problem and late eighteenth century political and economic thought. *Historical Journal* 28(1), 231–47.

Invisible Hand

KAREN I. VAUGHN

'The invisible hand' was a metaphor used by Adam Smith to describe the principle by which a beneficient social order emerged as the unintended consequences of individual human actions. Although Smith used the specific term 'invisible hand' in this sense only twice in his writings, once in the *Theory of Moral Sentiments* and once in *The Wealth of Nations*, the idea the metaphor connotes permeates all of his social and moral theories. Indeed, it was the notion of the invisible hand that enabled Smith to develop the first comprehensive theory of the economy as an interrelated social system. It is not much of an exaggeration to say that the invisible hand made theoretical social science itself possible.

In the *Theory of Moral Sentiments*, Smith, expounding on how the desire for wealth and luxury spurs men to great industry and production, points out that those who become rich from all this effort are not much better off in the things of this world that really count than the poor who work for them. The rich landlord, for example, desires many trivial luxuries, but can only consume a modest portion of the food his efforts produce; the rest must be paid to those who serve him. Rich landlords:

> ...in spite of their natural selfishness and rapacity, though they mean only their own conveniency, though the sole end which they propose from the labours of all the thousands whom they employ be the gratification of their own vain and insatiable desires, they divide with the poor the produce of all their improvements. They are led by an invisible hand to make nearly the same distribution of the necessaries of life which would have been made had the earth been divided into equal portions among all its inhabitants; and thus, without intending it, without making it, advance the interest of the society, and afford means to the multiplication of the species (*Moral Sentiments*, IV, 1, pp. 304–5).

In the *Wealth of Nations*, Smith uses the term 'invisible hand' in the context of explaining why restrictions of imports or on the use of one's capital are

168

unnecessary:

> As every individual, therefore, endeavours as much as he can both to employ his capital in the support of domestick industry, and so to direct that industry that its produce may be of the greatest value; evey individual necessarily labours to render the annual revenue of the society as great as he can. He generally, indeed, neither intends to promote the publick interest, nor knows how much he is promoting it. By preferring the support of domestick to that of foreign industry, he intends only his own security; and by directing that industry in such a manner as its produce may be of the greatest value, he intends only his own gain, and he is in this, as in many other cases, led by an invisible hand to promote an end which was no part of his intention (*Wealth and Nations*, IV, ii, p. 456).

The underlying notion of unintended orders that the invisible hand captures was not new in Smith. There were glimmerings of the idea in the 17th century in the writings of Petty and Locke. One of the earliest 18th-century forerunners to Smith's invisible hand was Bernard Mandeville. While there is some controversy as to whether Mandeville had any concept of a self-ordering system comparable to Smith's, it is clear that his infamous statement that private vices of greed, luxury and avarice lead to public benefits of abundant wealth (*Fable of the Bees*, 1714) stirred a great deal of debate. The philosophers of the Scottish Enlightenment, of whom Smith was one, rejected Mandeville's sensational equating of self-interest with greed, but they developed as a major theme of their writing the underlying idea that private actions can have beneficial public effects that were not intended by the actors. Adam Ferguson, for instance, described private property and political institutions in general as 'the results of human action, but not the execution of any human design' (*An Essay on the History of Civil Society*, 1767). David Hume appealed to the same notion when he explained how a system of justice emerges as the by-product of a series of individual self-interested decisions about the disposition of particular disputes, and when he argued that human institutions like money and language arose from the actions of individuals directed toward another end (*Treatise of Human Nature*, 1740).

Adam Smith, like Mandeville, Ferguson and Hume, based his system on the observation that man is motivated by self-love. To Smith, however, self-love was potentially an admirable human characteristic that reflected a man's concern for his honour as well as his material welfare. Even more importantly, for Smith, self-love was the 'principle of motion' in social theory much as attraction is the principle of motion in Newton's physics. Those who believed that government was free to make any laws it chose to regulate society, Smith believed did not understand a most basic feature of human nature. The 'man of system', as Smith called him,

> seems to imagine that he can arrange the different members of a great society with as much ease as the hand arranges that different pieces upon a chess-board; he does not consider that the different pieces upon a chess-board have no other

principle of motion besides that which the hand impresses upon them; but that, in the great-chess board of human society, every single piece has a principle of motion of its own, altogether different from that which the legislator might choose to impress upon it (*Theory of Moral Sentiments*, pp. 380–81).

The 18th century was, of course, the century immediately following Newton's great discovery. The scientific and moral consequences of Newton's universe were still being debated, and Newtonian ideas and patterns of thought were finding their way into all areas of intellectual activity. Not only was Adam Smith familiar with Newton's ideas but he had even written, early in his career, a history of astronomy, the last ten pages of which praised Sir Isaac Newton's system. Hence, it is plausible to see Adam Smith's economic system in a 'Newtonian' context as an attempt to explain a complex social order on the basis of a few simple principles of human action. The economic system that Smith in fact described is a product both of man's self-love and his peculiarly human propensity to 'truck, barter and exchange one thing for another' (*Wealth of Nations*, I, 2, p. 25). Exchange leads to the division of labour and the division of labour enables workers to take advantage of economies of scale with the unintended result that greater aggregate wealth is produced than if there were no exchange. Hence, the wealth of nations depends not on conscious governmental planning, but on the freedom of individuals to exchange, specialize and extend their markets. Furthermore, the overall beneficial nature of Smith's 'simple system of natural liberty' depends not on the benevolence of individuals, but upon the operation of self-love in a system of free exchange. Smith points out that in an exchange, we obtain our ends neither from coercing our partner nor from appealing to his sense of charity, but by engaging his own self-love in the exchange process. Two people trade because there are mutual gains from trade. Or as Smith puts it:

> ...man has almost constant occasion for the help of his brethren, and it is vain for him to expect it from their benevolence only. He will be more likely to prevail if he can interest their self-love in his favour, and show them that it is for their own advantage to do for him what he requires of them.... It is not from the benevolence of the butcher, the brewer, or the baker, that we expect our dinner, but from their regard to their own interests (*Wealth of Nations*, I, 2, p. 26).

In general, the concept that the invisible hand so graphically captures – a concept Carl Menger restated as an 'organic understanding of social phenomena' ([1883] 1963, p. 127ff) and Hayek more recently referred to as a 'spontaneous order' (1973, vol. 1) – is composed of three logical steps. The first is the observation that human action often leads to consequences that were unintended and unforseen by the actors. The second step is the argument that the sum of these unintended consequences over a large number of individuals or over a long period of time may, given the right circumstances, result in an order that is understandable to the human mind and appears as if it were the product of some intelligent planner. The third and final step is the judgement that the overall order is beneficial to the participants in the order in ways that they did not intend but nevertheless find desirable.

The first of these steps must have been obvious to human beings since they became capable of articulating their observations. The capriciousness of nature and the fallibility of human plans has been the theme of religious doctrine, philosophy and dramatic literature since the beginning of recorded time. It is only with the introduction of the notion that the independent actions of individual human beings can inadvertently give rise to an understandable and orderly social process that the unintended consequences of human plans becomes scientifically interesting. Clearly, without some notion of an invisible hand in human actions, social science would be impossible. The only alternative to describing social processes as the unintended by-products of purposeful human actions would be to view all social institutions and practices either as the predicted unfolding of conscious human plans or as the results of natural or supernatural phenomena beyond human experience. It is for this reason that Hayek has referred to spontaneous orders as a third category of phenomena between consciously planned organization and the physical world (1973, vol. I, p. 20).

The third step in the 'invisible hand' formulation is not as uncontroversial as the other two nor is it even necessary to the description of a social order. To judge a spontaneous order to be benevolent, as Smith obviously did, is to judge it from a particular moral perspective and within a particular political and historical context. Smith's moral perspective was that of the participants in the system, and his judgement was that they would be better off under a predominantly free market system than under the system of mercantilist regulation that was still in force in 18th-century England. However, one could easily imagine a spontaneous order in which people were led as if by an invisible hand to promote a perverse and unpleasant end. The desirability of the order that emerges as the unintended consequence of human action depends ultimately on the kind of rules and institutions within which human beings act, and the real alternatives they face.

Spontaneous orders can be thought of in two, related ways. They can describe a set of regularities in a social system that is self-organizing in some way within the context of a set of social rules. In this interpretation, the constraints in the system could well be set by human design and can work for good or ill. Alternatively, spontaneous orders can be thought of as evolved orders where the rules themselves are the unintended products of human actions. For example, we think of a market economy as functioning according to a set of 'rules of the game' that permit allocative errors to be self-correcting within the system. The rules (laws, customs, the dictates of political organizations, and property rights) would be thought of as products of conscious human plans as in specific legislation and constitutional design, or alternatively, they could be thought of as themselves the unintended products of human action aimed at specific and narrow ends. In Adam Smith's writings, both interpretations of spontaneous orders can be found. In his moral philosophy, in the same manner as David Hume, Smith argues that our moral rules gradually evolve from the accumulation of individual experiences and jugements of individuals in concrete situations, while the rules themselves as evolved have the unintended results of promoting social stability. In his economic theory described in the *Wealth of Nations*, money prices and profit and loss provide the signals that lead to corrections in resource misallocations and to economic growth, while the economic institutions of markets, money and division of labour all emerged in an evolutionary process. How one views the institutions of society makes a different not only to one's political views, but also to how one evaluates an economic system.

The notion of spontaneous order in the sense of a self-ordering system continued to provide the foundation of economic science and especially general equilibrium theory throughout the 19th century and up to the present. In the general equilibrium formulation self-love is translated into preference orders defined over all goods (but not benevolence or honour), and the political and social institutions of society are alterable by government corrective action. In this view, the invisible hand still makes the system run, but the optimality of the result is not necessarily guaranteed. Indeed, if one follows the logic of the argument to its conclusion, the invisible hand is palsied at best since it really only operates benevolently under conditions that are impossible to meet in the real world (Hahn, 1982).

An alternative formulation of the invisible hand that found its way from Adam Smith to Carl Menger views the economic institutions of a society as the unintended by-products of self-interested economic behaviour and sees these institutions as crucial to the self-ordering process. Hence, instead of asking what institutions would be necessary to make the invisible hand work perfectly, this view poses the question, what are the economic reasons why existing market institutions emerged and what unperceived purposes do they serve? Here, the attempt is to show how existing market institutions arise as the unintended consequences of human action. This, together with the argument that such institutions serve more ends than are known by planners, makes one more chary of 'fixing up' market arrangements.

BIBLIOGRAPHY

Ferguson, A. 1767. *An Essay on the History of Civil Society.* Edinburgh: Edinburgh University Press, 1966.

Hahn, F. 1982. Reflections on the invisible hand. *Lloyds Bank Review* 144, April, 1–21.

Hayek, F. von. 1973. *Law, Legislation and Liberty.* Vol. 1, Chicago: University of Chicago Press.

Hume, D. 1740. *Treatise of Human Nature.* Oxford: Oxford University Press, 1978.

Mandeville, B. 1714. *The Fable of the Bees: or, Private Vices, Public Benefits.* Oxford: Oxford University Press, 1924.

Menger, C. 1883. *Problems of Economics and Sociology.* Urbana: University of Illinois Press, 1963.

Smith, A. 1759. *The Theory of Moral Sentiments.* New York: Liberty Classics, 1969.

Smith, A. 1776. *An Inquiry into the Nature and Causes of the Wealth of Nations.* Ed. R.H. Campbell and A.S. Skinner, New York: Liberty Press, 1981.

Law and Economics

DAVID FRIEDMAN

The economic analysis of law involves three distinct but related enterprises. The first is the use of economics to predict the effects of legal rules. The second is the use of economics to determine what legal rules are economically efficient, in order to recommend what the legal rules ought to be. The third is the use of economics to predict what the legal rules will be. Of these, the first is primarily an application of price theory, the second of welfare economics and the third of public choice.

PREDICTING THE EFFECT OF LAWS. Of the three enterprises, the least controversial is the first – the use of economic analysis to predict the effect of alternative legal rules. In many cases, the result of doing so is to show that the effect of a rule is radically different from what a non-economist might expect.

Consider the following simple example. A city government passes an ordinance requiring landlords to give tenants three months notice before evicting them, even if the lease agreement provides for a shorter period. At first glance, the main effect is to make tenants better off, since they have greater security of tenure, and to make landlords worse off, since they now find it more difficult to evict undesirable tenants.

The conclusion is obvious; it is also false. The new ordinance raises the demand curve; the price at which tenants choose to rent any given quantity of housing is higher, since they are getting a more attractive good. It also raises the supply curve, since the cost of producing rental housing is now higher. If both the supply and the demand curve rise, so does the price. In the short run, the regulation benefits the tenant at the expense of his landlord. Once rents have had time to adjust, the tenant is better off by the improved security of his apartment but worse off by the higher rent he pays for it; the landlord is worse off by the increased difficulty of eviction and better off by the increased rent he receives.

One can easily construct specific examples in which such a regulation makes both landlords and tenants worse off, by adding to the lease terms which increase the landlord's costs by more than they are worth to the tenant and increase the

173

market rent by more than enough to eliminate the tenants' gain but too little to compensate the landlords' loss. One can also construct examples in which both parties are better off, because the regulation saves them the cost of negotiating terms which are in fact in their mutual interest. Thus economic analysis radically alters the grounds on which the regulation can be defended or attacked, eliminating the obvious justification (helping tenants at the expense of landlords) and replacing it with a different and much more complicated set of issues.

In this example, and in many similar ones, the two parties are linked by a contract and a price. In such cases, the first and most important contribution of economics to legal analysis is the recognition that a legally imposed change in the terms of the contract will result in a change in the market price. Typically, the result is to eliminate the transfer that would otherwise be implied by the change.

This is not true for cases, such as accidents and crimes, where there is no contract and no price. In analysing such situations, the essential contribution of economics is to include explicitly the element of rational choice involved in producing outcomes that are commonly regarded as either irrational or not chosen.

Consider automobile accidents. While a driver does not choose to have an accident, he does make may choices which affect the probability that an accident will occur. In deciding how fast to drive, how frequently to have his brakes checked, or how much attention to devote to the road and how much to his conversation with the passenger next to him, he is implicitly trading off the cost of an increased risk of accident against the benefit of getting home sooner, saving money, or enjoying a pleasant conversation. The amount of 'safety' the driver chooses to 'buy' will then be determined by the associated cost and benefit functions. Thus, for example, Peltzman (1975) demonstrated that safer autos tend to result in more dangerous driving, with the reduction in death rates per accident being at least partly balanced by more accidents, as drivers choose to drive faster and less carefully in the knowledge that the cost of doing so has been lowered.

This way of looking at accidents is important in analysing both laws designed to prevent accidents, such as speed limits, and liability laws designed to determine who must pay for accidents when they occur. From the economic perspective, the two sorts of laws are alternative tools for the same purpose – controlling the level of accidents.

A driver who knows he will be liable for the costs of any accidents he causes will take that fact into account in deciding how safely he should drive. Elizabeth Landes, in a study of the shift to no-fault auto insurance, concluded that one effect of the reduction in liability was to increase highway death rates by about 10–15 per cent.

The advantage of liability over direct regulation is that the knowledge that if he causes an accident he must pay for it gives the driver an incentive to modify his behaviour in any way that will reduce the chance of an accident, whether or not others can observe it. Regulations such as speed limits control only those elements of driver behaviour which can be easily observed from the outside –

speed but not attention, for example. The disadvantage of liabilitity is that if forces drivers, who may well be risk averse, to participate in a lottery – one chance in two thounsand, say, of causing an accident and having to pay all of its costs.

An accident is one example of an involuntary interaction; a crime is another. Economic analysis of crime starts with the assumption that becoming a criminal is a rational decision, like the decision to enter any other profession. Changes in the law which alter either the probability that the perpetrator of a crime will be punished for it or the magnitude of the punishment can be expected to affect the attractiveness of the profession, hence the frequency with which crimes occur – as demonstrated empirically in Ehrlich (1972). Similarly, changes in crime rates will, via the rational decisions of potential victims, affect expenditures on defending against crime.

Another area of law, in which the application of economic analysis is less novel, is anti-trust. One important contribution of economic analysis has been to suggest that some elements of anti-trust law may be based on an incorrect perception of how firms get and maintain monopoly power.

McGee (1958) used arguments originally proposed by Aaron Director to show that if, as commonly alleged, Standard Oil had attempted to maintain its market position by predatory pricing – cutting the price of oil below cost in order to drive out smaller but equally efficient rivals – the effort would probably have failed. Standard's larger assets would be balanced by a larger volume of sales, and hence larger losses when those sales were at a price below cost. Even if the smaller firm had gone bankrupt first, its physical plant would have remained, to be purchased by some new competitor. Based on a study of the record of the Standard Oil anti-trust case, McGee concluded that predatory pricing was a myth: Rockefeller had in fact maintained his position by buying out rivals, usually at high prices.

The argument, if correct, implies that some conventional anti-trust activity is misplaced. Pricing policies which are attacked as predatory may in fact be ways in which new firms break into existing markets, using low prices to induce potential customers to try their products. If so, prohibiting such policies reduces competition and encourages the monopoly that the law is intended to prevent.

EFFICIENCY: PRESCRIBING LAWS. The use of economic analysis to determine what the law ought to be starts with one simple and controversial premise – that the sole purpose of law should be to promote economic efficiency. There are two problems with this premise. The first is that it depends on the utilitarian assumption – that the only good is human happiness, defined not as what people should want but as what they do want. The second is that economic efficiency provides at best a very approximate measure of what most of us understand by 'total human happiness', since it assumes away the problem of interpersonal utility comparisons by, in effect, treating people as if they all had the same marginal utility of income.

One reply to this criticism is that while few people believe that economic efficiency is all that matters, most people who understand the concept would agree that it is either an important objective or an important means to other objectives. Hence while maximizing economic efficiency may not be the only purpose of laws, it is an important one – and one that economic theory can, in principle, tell us how to achieve. Further, economic theory suggests that an improvements in efficiency may be something that courts can achieve, whereas redistribution, for reasons suggested in the discussion of landlord–tenant relations, may not be.

Once one accepts economic efficiency as the objective, the standard tools of welfare economics can be used to analyse a wide variety of legal issues. Consider, for example, the eviction regulation discussed earlier. If the additional security of tenure is worth more to the tenant than it costs the landlord to produce, then landlords will find in their interest to include that condition in the lease contract whether or not the law requires them to; the additional rent they will be able to charge will more than make up for the cost of delays in evicting undesirable tenants. If, on the other hand, security of tenure costs the landlords more than it is worth to the tenants, then they will not choose to offer it – and, viewed from the standpoint of economic efficiency, a regulation compelling them to do so is undesirable.

So one conclusion suggested by such analysis is a strong case for freedom of contract – allowing the parties to a lease, or any other contract, to include any terms mutually agreeable. To the extent that one accepts that argument, the function of legal rules is simply to specify a default contract – a set of terms that apply unless the parties specify otherwise. If the default contract closely approximates what the parties would agree to if they did specify all the details of their agreement, it serves the useful purpose of reducing the cost of negotiating contracts.

An important example of such analysis occurs in the case of product liability law. Just as with lease contracts, the first step is to observe that changes in who bears the liability for product defects will produce corresponding changes in market price, so that shifting liability from, say, buyer to seller will not in general result in the buyer being better off and the seller worse off. Changes in liability law will, however, change the incentives facing both buyer and seller with regard to decisions they make that affect the damage produced by defects. To the extent that a buyer cannot judge the quality of a product before he buys it, a rule of *caveat emptor* gives the seller an inefficiently weak incentive to prevent defects, since he pays the cost of quality control and receives no corresponding benefit. On the other hand, a rule of *caveat venditor* provides the seller with the appropriate incentive, since he ends up paying, via damage suits, for the cost of defects, but it gives the buyer an inefficiently low incentive to try to use the product in a way that will minimize the damage from defects – by, for example, driving an automobile in a way that does not rely too heavily on the brakes always working perfectly.

This suggests that different legal rules may be appropriate for different sorts of goods. It also suggests that some intermediate rule, such as contributory negligence, in which the producer of a defective good may defend himself against a damage suit by showing the accident was in part the result of imprudent use by the purchaser, may be superior to both *caveat emptor* and *caveat venditor*.

Just as in the case of tenant and landlord, the analysis suggests that while the law may set a default rule, it ought to permit freedom of contract. Sellers can then convert *caveat emptor* into *caveat venditor* by offering a guarantee, and buyers can convert *caveat venditor* into *caveat emptor* by signing a waiver.

Another area of interest is corporate law. Here the central problem is that of structuring the contract which defines the corporation so as to control the principal–agent problem resulting from the separation of ownership and management. One solution, missed in Smith's classic statement of the problem (Smith, 1776), is the takeover bid, used to discipline managers who do not maximize the value of the assets they manage. The question of whether the law should assist or oppose managers in their attempt to prevent takeovers has been a lively issue in the recent literature.

Freedom of contract is of no use where there is no voluntary agreement among the parties. The law must somehow specify who is responsible under what conditions for the cost of accidents, and what the punishment is to be for crimes. One traditional approach to this problem is the 'Hand formula', according to which someone is judged negligent, hence legally responsible for an accident, only if he could have prevented it by precautions that would have cost less than the expected cost (probability times damage) of the accident. This seems to fit very neatly into the economic analysis of law, since it punishes someone only if he has acted inefficiently by failing to take a cost-justified precaution.

It has, however, two serious difficulties. One is that 'accidents' are usually the result of the joint action of two or more parties. My bad brakes would not have injured you if you had not chosen to ride a bicycle at night wearing dark clothing – but your bicycle riding would not have put you in the hospital if my car had had good brakes. In such a situation, the efficient solution is to have precautions taken by whichever party can take them most cheaply – even if the other party could prevent the accident at a cost lower than the resulting damage. This suggests that the Hand formula should be interpreted as making the party liable who could have avoided the accident at the lower cost. Situations in which the probability and cost of accidents are continuous functions of both my level of precaution and yours require additional elaborations of the formula.

A second problem is that the Hand formula requires the court to make judgements, both about the probability of accidents given various levels of precaution and about the cost of both precautions and accidents to the parties involved, which it may not be competent to make. This suggests the desirability of legal rules which are sufficiently general so that they do not depend on a court making case-by-case evaluations of cost and benefit, but which give the parties incentives to use their private knowledge of costs and benefits to produce efficient outcomes. The attempt to construct such rules, for a wide variety of legal problems, makes up a considerable part of the law and economics literature.

Crimes, like accidents, involve involuntary interactions. The economic analysis of crime focuses on two related issues – the incentives facing the criminal and the incentives facing the system of courts and police. The first leads to the question of what combination of punishment and probability of apprehension would be applied, for any crime, in an efficient system; the answer involves trading off costs and benefits to criminals, victims and the enforcement system. The second leads to questions about the procedures used by the court system to determine guilt or innocence (also an issue in other parts of the law), and of the relative advantages of private enforcement of law, as in our civil system, in comparison to public enforcement, as in our criminal system.

ECONOMISTS LEARNING FROM LAW: THE COASE THEOREM. So far, all of the examples of economic analysis of law have involved using existing economic theory to analyse the law. There is at least one area, however, where the interaction of law and economics has resulted in a substantial body of new economic theory. This is the set of ideas originating in the work of Ronald Coase and commonly referred to as the Coase Theorem.

According to the traditional analysis of externalities associated with Pigou, an externality exists where one party's actions impose costs on another, for which the first need not compensate him. This leads to an inefficient outcome, since the first party ignores the costs to the second in making his decision. Thus, for example, a railroad company may permit its locomotives to throw sparks, even though they cause occasional fires in the neighbouring corn fields. The cost of modifying the engine to prevent sparks would be borne by the company; the cost of the fires is an externality imposed on the adjacent farmers. The traditional solution is a Pigouvian tax. The railroad company is charged for the damage done, and can either pay or stop doing the damage, whichever costs less.

Coase pointed out that in this and many other cases, the cost is not simply imposed by one party on the other, rather, it arises from incompatible activities by two parties. The fires are the result both of the railroad company using a spark-throwing locomotive and of the farmers choosing to grow inflammable crops near the rail line. The efficient solution might be to modify the locomotive, but it also might be to grow different crops. In the latter case, a Pigouvian tax on the railroad leads to an inefficient outcome.

Hence the first step in Coase's analysis suggests that there is no general solution to the problem of externalities. The legislature, in setting up general laws, cannot know which party, in any specific case, will be able to avoid the problem at the lowest cost. If it attempts to solve that problem by a law making whichever party can avoid the problem at the lower cost liable, the court is left with the problem of estimating the costs. Each party has an incentive to misrepresent the cost of its potential precautions, in order to make the other party liable for preventing the damage.

The second step is to observe that both this argument and the traditional analysis of externalities ignore the possibility of agreements between the parties. If the law makes the railroad liable for the damage when the farmers can prevent it at a lower cost, it will be in the interest of both farmers and railroad to negotiate an agreement in which the railroad pays the farmers to grow clover rather than corn along the rail line. Hence this line of analysis leads to the conclusion that whatever the initial definition of rights – whether the railroad has the right to throw sparks or the farmers to enjoin the railroad or collect damages – market transactions among the participants will lead to an efficient outcome.

The final step in the argument is to observe that inefficient outcomes do in fact occur, and that the reason is transaction costs. If, for example, any farmer can enjoin the railroad from throwing sparks, then the railroad, in dealing with the farmers, is faced by a hold-out problem. A single farmer may try to collect a large fraction of what the railroad saves by not modifying its locomotive, using the threat that if his demands are not met he can enjoin the railroad, whatever the other farmers do. If, on the other hand, the railroad is free to throw sparks and it is up to the farmers to offer to pay for the modifications, then in raising the money to do so they face a public good problem; a farmer who does not contribute still benefits. Transaction cost problems of this sort may prevent the process by which bargaining among participants would otherwise lead to an efficient outcome.

The conclusion of all of this is the Coase Theorem, which states that in a world of zero transaction costs any initial definition of rights will lead to an efficient outcome. It is important not because we live in such a world, but because it shows us a different way of looking at a large range of problems – as resulting from the transaction costs that prevent the parties affected from bargaining their way to an efficient outcome.

This approach represents both an important change in the traditional economic analysis of externalities and a powerful tool for analysing legal institutions. Many such issues can be seen as questions of how property rights are to be bundled. When I acquire a piece of land, does what I by include the right to make loud noises on it? To prevent passing locomotives from throwing sparks on it? To leave objects lying about that might be hazardous to neighbours who accidentally trespass? From the perspective of the Coase Theorem, all such questions can be approached by asking first what bundling of rights would lead, under various circumstances, to an efficient outcome, and second, if a particular initial bundling of rights leads to inefficient outcomes, how easy will it be for the parties to negotiate a change, with the party who has a greater value for one of the rights in a bundle purchasing it from its initial owner.

One example is the law of attractive nuisance. Does the ownership of a piece of land include the right to put on it open cement tanks full of deadly chemicals, protected only by large signs – which are no barrier at all to a trespasser too young to read? The immediate answer is that the right to decide whether the tanks are fenced is worth more to the neighbourhood parents than to the owner of the property. The further answer is that if the law gives the right to the owner, including it in the bundle labelled 'ownership of land', it will be difficult for the parents to buy it, since the parents face a public good problem in purchasing an agreement from the owner to put high fences around his tanks. Hence we have an argument for the existing law of attractive nuisance, under which the parent can enjoin the property owner from leaving the tanks unfenced, or sue for damages if his child is injured. This is one example of the way in which the Coase Theorem approach helps illuminate a wide range of legal issues.

PREDICTION: WHAT THE LAW WILL BE. Economic analysis, of law or anything else, can be viewed either as an attempt to learn what should be or as an attempt to explain what is and predict what will be. In the case of the economic analysis of the law, attempts to explain and predict have taken two rather different forms.

On the one hand, there is the argument of Richard Posner, according to which the common law tends, for a variety of reasons, to be economically efficient. The analysis of what legal rules are efficient thus provides an explanation of what legal rules exist – and the observation of what legal rules exist provides a test of theories about what rules are efficient.

On the other hand, there is the approach associated with public choice theory, which views legislated, administrative and perhaps even common law as outcomes of a political market on which interest groups seek private objectives by governmental means. Since the amount a group is willing to spend in order to get the laws it favours depends not only on the value of the law to that group but also on the group's ability to solve the public good problem of inducing its members to contribute, expenditures in the political market will not accurately represent the value of the law to those affected, hence inefficient laws – laws which injure the losers by more than they benefit the gainers – may well pass, and efficient laws may well fail. The most obvious implication of this line of analysis is that laws will tend to favour concentrated interests at the expense of dispersed interests, since the former will be better able to raise money from their members to lobby for the laws they prefer.

CONCLUSIONS. In looking at economic analysis of law, one striking observation is the way in which economists tend to convert issues from disputes about equity, justice, fairness or the like into disputes about efficiency. In part, this is because economists do, and traditional legal scholars often do not, take account of the effect of legal rules on market prices. The result of taking these effects into account is frequently to eliminate the distributional effects of changes in such rules. In part, it is because economists do, and legal scholars sometimes do not, assume that rules modify behaviour. If so, then in evaluating the rules we must ask not only whether they produce a just outcome in a particular case, but whether their effects on the behaviour of those who know of the rules and modify their actions to take account of them is in some sense desirable.

A second observation is that economic analysis frequently demonstrates the existence of efficiency arguments for rules usually thought of as based entirely on considerations of justice. One simple example is the law against theft. At first glance, theft appears to involve no question of economic efficiency at all; the thief is better off by the same amount by which the victim is worse off, hence the transaction, however unjust, is not inefficient.

That conclusion is wrong. The opportunity to gain by stealing diverts resources to that activity. In equilibrium, the marginal thief receives the same income from stealing (net of risk of imprisonment, cost of tools, etc.) as he would in some alternative productive activity; there is no gain to the marginal thief to balance the cost to the victim. Hence theft can be condemned as inefficient with no reference to issues of justice.

A third observation is the degree to which the examination of real legal issues and real cases forces the economist to take account of some of the complexities of real-world interactions which he might otherwise never notice, and thus provides him with the opportunity to increase the depth and power of his analysis.

A final, and important, observation is that economics provides a unity among disparate fields of law which is lacking in much traditional legal analysis. In the words of one of the field's leading practitioners:

> Almost any tort problem can be solved as a contract problem, by asking what the people involved in an accident would have agreed on in advance with regard to safety measures if transaction costs had not been prohibitive.... Equally, almost any contract problem can be solved as a tort problem by asking what sanction is necessary to prevent the performing or paying party from engaging in wasteful conduct, such as taking advantage of the vulnerability of a party who performs his side of the bargain first. And both tort and contract problems can be framed as problems in the definition of property rights; for example, the law of negligence could be thought to define the right we have in the safety of our persons against accidental injury. The definition of property rights can itself be viewed as a process of figuring out what measures parties would agree to, if transaction costs weren't prohibitive, in order to create incentives to avoid wasting valuable resources (Posner, 1986).

Any note as short as this can provide only a very incomplete description of the field, and one heavily biased towards the author's own interests. The references cited below, and the references in Posner (1986) and Goetz (1984), provide a much more extensive survey.

BIBLIOGRAPHY

Becker, G. 1968. Crime and punishment: an economic approach. *Journal of Political Economy* 76, March, 169–217.

Becker, G. 1976. *The Economic Approach to Human Behavior*. Chicago: University of Chicago Press.

Calabresi, G. 1961. Some thoughts on risk distribution and the law of torts. *Yale Law Journal* 70, March, 499–553.

Calabresi, G. and Melamed, A.D. 1972. Property rules, liability rules, and inalienability: one view of the cathederal. *Harvard Law Review* 85(6), 1089–182.

Coase, R.H. 1960. The problem of social cost. *Journal of Law and Economics* 3, October, 1–44.

Demsetz, H. 1967. Toward a theory of property rights. *American Economic Review, Papers and Proceedings* 57(2), May, 347–59, especially 351–3.

Ehrlich, I. 1972. The deterrent effect of criminal law enforcement. *Journal of Legal Studies* 1(2), 259–76.

Goetz, C.J. 1984. *Cases and Materials on Law and Economics*. St Paul, Minn.: West.

Landes, E.M. 1982. Insurance, liability, and accidents: a theoretical and empirical investigation of the effect of no-fault on accidents. *Journal of Law and Economics* 25(1), April, 49–65.

Landes, W. and Posner, R. 1978. Salvors, finders, good samaritans, and other rescuers: an economic study of law and altruism. *Journal of Legal Studies* 7(1), 83–128.

McGee, J.S. 1958. Predatory price cutting: the Standard Oil (N.J.) case. *Journal of Law and Economics* 1, October, 137–69.

Peltzman, S. 1975. The effects of automobile safety regulations. *Journal of Political Economy* 83(4), 677–725.

Posner, R. 1986. *Economic Analysis of Law*. Boston: Little, Brown.

Smith, A. 1776. *An Inquiry into the Nature and Causes of the Wealth of Nations*. London: W. Strahan & T. Cadell.

Tullock, G. 1971. *The Logic of the Law*. New York: Basic Books.

Liberalism

RALF DAHRENDORF

Liberalism is the theory and practice of reforms which has inspired two centuries of modern history. It grew out of the English Revolutions of the 17th century, spread to many countries in the wake of the American and French Revolutions of the 18th century, and dominated the better part of the 19th century. At that time, it also underwent changes. Some say it died, or gave way to socialism, or allowed itself to be perverted by socialist ideas; others regard the social reforms of the late 19th and 20th centuries as achievements of a new liberalism. More recently, interest in the original ideas of liberals has been revived. Thus, classical liberals, social liberals and neoliberals may be distinguished.

Classical liberalism is a simple, dramatic philosophy. Its central idea is liberty under the law. People must be allowed to follow their own interests and desires, constrained only by rules which prevent their encroachment on the liberty of others. Early liberals before and after John Locke liked to use the metaphor of a social contract to express this view. Society can be thought of as emerging from an agreement among its members to protect themselves against the selfish desires of others. Man's 'unsociable sociability' (Kant) makes rules necessary which bind all, but requires also the maximum feasible space for competition and conflict.

In fact, of course, early liberals were not concerned with building societies from scratch. They were concerned with forcing absolute rulers to yield to demands for liberty. The rule of law envisaged by liberals was a revolutionary force which heralded the enlightened phase of modernity.

The notion, rule of law, is not without ambiguity. It is, in the first instance, largely formal. One thinks of rules of the game applying to all and regulating the social, economic and political process. In theory, such rules are intended not to prejudge the outcome of the game itself. Still, even their formal conditions, equality before the law and due process, involved fundamental changes which justify speaking of a movement of reform. Throughout the history of liberalism, however, the question of certain substantive rights of man has been an issue. The inviolability of the person and the rights of free expression have been liberal causes along with constitutional rules. Liberals have rarely found it easy to reason for such substantive rights to their own satisfaction. A certain tension between liberal thought and the notion of natural rights in unmistakable.

The modern debate of these issues began in Scotland and England. John Locke, David Hume and Adam Smith are but three of many names to consider. From Britain, the ideas spread to the United States and to continental Europe. Montesqieu and Kant borrowed some of their ideas from British liberals. The American Declaration of Independence and the Constitution, and the Declaration of the Rights of Man three years after the French Revolution are only two practical illustrations of the effect of the new ideas. If one wants to, one can distinguish, with Friedrich von Hayek, between a British 'evolutionary' and a continental 'constructivist' concept of liberalism. Either or both, however, became the dominant reform movements of the early 19th century and determined the dynamics of Europe and North America between the 1780s and the 1840s or 1850s.

Liberalism had consequences for economic, social and political thought. Its economic application was the most obvious and remains the most familiar. If rules of the game are all that can be justified whereas otherwise interests should be allowed a free reign, the scene is set for the operation of the market. It is the forum where equal rights of access and participation but divergent and competing interests lead, through the operation of an 'invisible hand' (Adam Smith), to the greatest welfare for all. Liberalism and market capitalism are inseparable, much as later European theorists (notably in Germany and Italy) have tried to dissociate the two.

The social application of liberalism analogously leads to the emergence of the public, if by 'public' we understand the meeting place of divergent views from which a 'public opinion' emerges. On the continent, a more emphatic language is often preferred; here, one likes to speak of the emergence of society from under the state. Either way, the basic idea involves the same departure from an all-embracing system of domination by traditional authorities to one in which public authority is confined to certain tasks of regulation, and thus bound to grant and defend the freedom of individuals to express their views.

This is the point at which classical liberalism was not only instrumental for the promotion of market capitalism and social participation, but also for the development of what is today called democracy. Again, the term is anything but clear. It can be understood to mean a system of government which is based on the competition of divergent views – individual views or group views – for power, constrained by rules which limit the instruments used in the process, and stipulate the possibility for change. In this sense, a variety of constitutional forms of democracy respond to liberal views, including versions of representative government as well as forms of plebiscite. Liberalism is not anarchism, but anarchism is in some ways an extreme form of liberalism. The law has a key role in liberal thinking, but for a long time the prevalent interest of liberals was that of liberating people from the fetters of control imposed by the tangible force of the state (and the church) or the abstract force of tradition. Not surprisingly, some authors took this intention of liberation to its extreme. If they believed in the essential goodness of man, they advocated the abolition of all social restraint; at times, Jean-Jacques Rousseau seems to argue this way. If, on the other hand, they believed in the ambivalence of human nature, they were not afraid to demand unlimited room for manoeuvre for 'the singular one and his property' (Max Stirner).

Perhaps this anarchist strain in early liberal thinking can be said to have been one of the reasons for the counter-reaction of the 19th century. Marx was the first to point out the historical advance brought about by 'bourgeois' equality before the law, including the contractual basis of economic action, but also the price paid by many for the 'anarchic' quality of the resulting market. The market – it was increasingly argued – was in fact not neutral, but favoured certain players to the systematic disadvantage of others. Mass poverty, conditions of labour, the state of industrial cities were cited as examples. Nor was this merely a view of anti-liberals. The great ambiguities in the thinking of John Stuart Mill tell the same story.

There are two ways of describing the resulting history of thought and of social movements. One is to say that as the 19th century progressed, and certainly in the early decades of the 20th century, liberalism was replaced by socialism as a dominant force. People began to shrink back from the unconstrained market and sought new kinds of intervention. Today, authors would add that the 'structural change of the public' (J. Habermas) and the bureaucratization of democracy followed suit. Liberalism died a 'strange death'; it ceased to be a source of reform and became a defence of class interest.

Another view ascribes the new reforms to liberals also, albeit to a different kind of liberalism. In his Alfred Marshall Lectures of 1949, T.H. Marshall argued that the progress of citizenship rights had to involve, from a certain point onwards, their extension from the legal and the political to the social realm. Social citizenship rights turned out to be a necessary prerequisite for the exercise of equality before the law and universal suffrage. Thus, the social, or welfare state was no more than a logical extension of the process which began with the revolutions of the 18th century.

There is much to be said for this line of argument, if one considers that the two men who above all determined the climate of political thought and action from the 1930s to the 1970s, John Maynard Keynes and William Beveridge, were both self-declared Liberals. In effect if not in intention, they advanced ideas which led to restrictions on the operation of markets. One will be remembered as the author of economic policy as a deliberate effort by governments, the other has contributed much to the creation of transfer systems which are operated by governments in the light of an assumed common interest. In other words, these were liberals who pursued policies which led to strengthening rather than limiting the power of public authorities. Theirs was a substantive, a social liberalism.

Liberal parties have found it difficult to follow the twists of theoretical liberalism. Before World War I, when socialist parties were still in their infancy and unable to determine policy in any major country, they were often the spokesmen of the deprived and underprivileged. At least one strand of the liberal tradition continued to be reformist. However, after World War I, socialists or social democrats came to form governments in many countries. Their gain was the Liberals' loss. Liberal parties declined to the point of insignificance, unless they merely kept the name and changed their policies out of recognition, either in the direction of social democracy (Canada) or in that of conservatism (Australia). Indeed, as a practical political movement, liberalism came to present such a confused picture that Hayek could argue that liberalism has become a mere intellectual, and not a political, force.

The experience of totalitarianism interrupted this process without stopping it altogether. To the dismay, but also to the surprise of many, basic human rights and the rules of the game of civil government became an issue again in the 1930s and 1940s. This gave rise to an important literature in which the underlying values of liberal thought were spelt out anew. Hayek's *Road to Serfdom* is one example, but the most important one is probably Karl Popper's *Open Society and its Enemies*. Popper developed above all what might be called the epistemology of liberalism. We are living in a world of uncertainty. Since no one can know all answers, let alone what the right answers are, it is of cardinal importance to make sure that different answers can be given at any one time, and especially over time. The path of politics, like that of knowledge, must be one of trial and error. The principle can be applied to economy and society as well.

The liberal revolt against totalitarianism waned with the memory of totalitarianism itself. While the term 'social market economy' was coined for Germany in the 1950s, the quarter-century of the economic miracle was in fact a social-democratic quarter-century. In it, economic growth was combined almost everywhere with a growing role of government and with the extension of the social state. Entitlements came to matter as much as achievements. Consensus counted for more than competition or conflict. Despite variations, this was a very successful period in the countries of the First World. But by the 1970s, the side-effects of success had become major problems in their own right. These were not only obvious problems like environmental and social 'limits to growth', but systematic ones arising from the role of the state. Both Keynes and Beveridge gave rise to new questions. Neither stagflation in the 1970s, nor boom unemployment in the 1980s seemed amenable to government intervention. The social state had got out of hand; it became harder and harder to finance, and its bureaucracies robbed it of much of its plausibility. There were demands for a reversal of trends.

Where such a reversal happened, it remained bitty, halting and inconsistent. However, the new climate gave rise also to elements of a new theory of liberalism. In one sense, this was, and is a return to the original project of asserting society against the state, the market against planning and regulation, the right of the individual against overpowering authorities and collectivities. American authors in particular re-stated the theory. Milton Friedman tried to show in a series of arguments that the role of government is usually contrary to the interests of people. Robert Nozick made a strong case for the 'minimal state' and against the arrogance of modern state power. James Buchanan and the 'constitutional economists' reconstructed the social contract and argued for severely limited rules and regulations, using the fiscal system as one of their main examples. This trend, more than the notion of supply-side economics (which in some ways is merely Keynes stood on his head) signifies the revival of liberalism.

There are other facets of the many-facted term. For many, the extension of civil rights to hitherto disadvantaged groups is a liberal programme. Others still concentrate on the separation of church and state and the reduction of church influence. Again others regard liberalism as an advocacy of cultural values, including pluralism and creativity. It is not difficult to see the connection of such preferences with the mainstream of liberal thought.

This mainstream has three elements. Liberalism is a theory and a movement of *reform* to advance *individual liberties* in the horizon of *uncertainty*. This means by the same token that the prevailing theme of liberalism cannot be the same at all times. In the face of absolutism, it is liberty under the law; in the face of market capitalism, it is the full realization of citizenship rights; in the face of the 'cage of bondage' (Max Weber) of modern bureaucratic government, it is the optimal, if not the minimal state. The struggle for the social contract has become virulent in the advanced free societies. The crisis of the social state, the new unemployment, issues of law and order all raise basic questions of what is Caesar's and what are therefore the proper limits of individual desires. It is no accident that constitutional questions have come to the fore in several countries. At such a time, liberalism is gaining new momentum. It will not solve all issues, but it will remain a source of dynamism and progress towards more life chances for more people.

BIBLIOGRAPHY

Buchanan, J. 1975. *The Limits of Liberty*. Chicago: University of Chicago Press.
Habermas, J. 1962. *Strukturwandel der Öffentlichkeit*. Neuwied: Luchterhand.
Hayek, F. von. 1944. *The Road to Serfdom*. Chicago: University of Chicago Press.
Hume, D. 1740. *A Treatise of Human Nature*. Ed. L.A. Selby-Bigge, Oxford: Clarendon Press, 1888.
Kant, I. 1784. Idee zu einer allgemeinen Geschichte in weltbürgerlicher Absicht. In *Kants Populäre Schriften*, ed. P. Menzer, Berlin: Georg Reimer, 1911.
Locke, J. 1690. *Second Treatise of Government*. Ed. T.P. Peardon, New York: Liberal Arts Press, 1952.
Marshall, T.H. 1950. *Citizenship and Social Class*. Cambridge: Cambridge University Press.
Popper, K.R. 1952. *The Open Society and its Enemies*. 2nd edn, London: Routledge & Kegan Paul.
Smith, A. 1776. *An Inquiry into the Nature and Causes of the Wealth of Nations*. Oxford: Oxford University Press, 1976.
Stirner, M. 1845. *Der Einzige und sein Eigentum*. Leipzig: D. Wigand.
Weber, M. 1922. *Wirtschaft und Gesellschaft*. 4th edn, Tübingen: Mohr/Siebeck, 1956.

Liberty

ALAN RYAN

In *The Philosophy of History* Hegel declared that the history of the world was the history of freedom. Human history had been a process of education and self-discovery at the end of which men could see that freedom and reason were their very essence. But Hegel was conscious of the fact that 'freedom' was not the same thing at all stages of its history – a truth which is reflected in the inconclusiveness of philosophical attempts to answer the question 'what is freedom?'.

The first discussions of freedom in Western political thinking occur among the Greeks. Aristotle, for instance, defines politics as a way of life in which free men rule one another in turn; freedom is a matter of citizenship. The 'unfree' are all those who are subject to an authority to which they have not given their consent. The Persians are ruled despotically and are unfree; women have no role in politics and are dependent on their husbands; slaves are in all things dependent on their owners; and if manual workers are not exactly unfree, they cannot share in the freedom of citizenship because they lack the leisure and intelligence so to do. Freedom is a uniquely Greek possession, for only among the Greeks is politics possible.

Aristotle's discussion did not reflect a Greek consensus; Pericles' 'Funeral Speech' praised Athens's freedom, but used the term in a way any 20th-century reader understands – the Athenians were tolerant of diversity, and did not think that political unity depended on depriving themselves of a vigorous private life. But like Aristotle, Pericles took it for granted that women and slaves were condemned to obscurity and that their freedom raised no questions. Plato was positively hostile to freedom, which he identified with an unbridled opportunity to do whatever we liked; democracy was addicted to liberty – so much so, he said in *The Republic*, that in the streets of Athens even the donkeys will not move out of your way. It was not freedom but discipline based on philosophical illumination which would make individuals good and society stable.

Roman political thinking made three crucial contributions to the discussion.

One was a sophistication of the argument about the best way to avoid the tyranny of one man or of a social class; republican freedom was best preserved by a 'mixed constitution' with elements of monarchy, aristocracy and democracy. A second was the Roman Law concern with the status and the nature of slaves; they were archetypically unfree, being as the lawyers said 'legally dead', or 'always children'. They had no legal personality and were always (even when they were rich and powerful administrators) vulnerable to the loss of everything they possessed, since they had no legal protection. The third was the development of an unpolitical conception of freedom, epitomized by the declaration of the Stoic emperor Marcus Aurelius that the slave could be as free as the emperor. A slave who was sufficiently immune to the ills of this life could exercise 'self-control' – and what was freedom if not the condition of autonomy, or controlling oneself?

The rediscovery of both the Greek and the Roman interests in freedom had to wait until the end of the medieval period; but arguments about political liberty did not. Under the often notional overlordship of the Holy Roman Empire, 'free cities' sprang up, and in Northern Italy independent republics never quite severed their links with the ancient tradition. In Florence or Venice, liberty was well understood to be a condition of self-government immune from the interference of foreign powers or from the tyranny of local aristocrats and despots. It is to be noticed that in no discussion of liberty in this sense is there any suggestion that economic freedom or an approach to laissez-faire is part of freedom so understood. Indeed, since the crucial issues were how to secure a reliable militia on the one hand and a non-tyrannical ruling class on the other, the search for public-spirited citizens and rulers generally resulted in the condemnation of self-interest and the lure of wealth.

But an alternative conception of liberty was slowly growing as the feudal and military basis of land ownership was eroded, and something closer to modern commercial relations grew up. Dating the stages of this transformation is difficult, but it is not implausible to talk of the emancipation of English landed property from its feudal past from the 13th century onwards. Allied to this process was an extension of the scope of centralized justice and a sophistication of procedures for protecting legal rights, such that their joint effect was to bring into existence the idea that liberty was above all a matter of being able to enjoy one's rights as a private person, and to know that these rights set limits to what the holders of power could do and to how they could do it.

There were thus two competing ways of thinking about political freedom waiting to be taken up in the 16th and 17th centuries, while political practice was also affected by Protestant antinomian doctrines, which held that true freedom was not of this world but of the next, a view which might lead to political quietism or to radical outbreaks such as the Anabaptists' revolution in Munster. All could legitimately claim to be theories of liberty; but they naturally led in very different directions. Those who looked back to the ancient republics for their image of liberty thought the triumph of laissez-faire and security for the individual a triumph for 'corruption'. Their opponents thought them nostalgic and unrealistic. The unworldly were attacked as disturbers of the peace when they insisted on following their own consciences rather than their rulers' edicts, condemned as apathetic if they were quietist.

Serious political writers of the 18th century were pulled in different directions. Adam Smith's attitude towards laissez-faire is now generally recognized to be ambivalent; the simple system of natural liberty has its drawbacks, and these drawbacks are explained in 'republican' terms. They include the inability of the common man to display the military valour of his Roman forebears and the danger that wealth will corrupt the institutions which protect us from tyranny. Rousseau anathematized the 18th century's concern with private welfare rather than public spirit and hankered after Spartan simplicity – but agreed that Sparta could not easily be rebuilt in modern Europe. To him we owe a strikingly lucid categorization of liberty: natural liberty is what we enjoy when we are subject to no restraint, moral liberty what we enjoy when we only follow rules which an impartial benevolence would urge upon us, and civil liberty what we enjoy when we are citizens participating in the creation of the laws we obey. It cannot be said that he is wholly successful in explaining which of these we can expect to achieve in the modern European state; he may have hoped that the rule of law would realize moral liberty – his Jacobin readers hoped to recreate Roman civil liberty in a virtuous republic.

The disasters of the Revolution provoked Benjamin Constant to write his *Essai sur la liberté des anciens comparée à celle des modernes*, in which he contrasted the freedom enjoyed by the citizens of the ancient city states with that enjoyed by modern man. Theirs was essentially political, a matter of the right to take part in politics and be a member of the sovereign authority; ours is essentially private, a matter of security under the law and the right to pursue our own goals without interference. Since we cannot recreate the social conditions of the Greek city state, we cannot have ancient liberty. Nor do we really want it, since we want neither the slavery on which liberty for the male citizen population depended nor the continual wars in which the ancient republics engaged. Political rights of the kind enshrined in the American Constitution are essential to preserve modern freedom, but they are needed for self-defence, not to turn us into Roman citizens.

Much subsequent argument has concentrated on the question of how much freedom modern man enjoys in fact. The argument has moved away from political liberty to a wider and less precisely delimited concern with social, economic and psychological constraints. Mill's *Liberty* was dedicated to the proposition that although the English enjoyed political freedom, they did not enjoy social freedom. Public opinion constrained all but the very boldest spirits; the threat of social disapproval made most people afraid to think differently from the majority on any issue whatever. In some ways this tyranny was worse than many forms of political tyranny because it aroused less opposition and worked silently and insidiously. Mill opposed this conformism with two principles – negatively, we must coerce others only in self-defence and not merely for the sake of having them think like us; positively, we must see that individuality is the distinguishing mark of humanity and that we are only free when our ideas and lives are our own. Similar views have been put forward by sociologists and psychologists ever since; many have thought the tyranny of the majority less impressive than our capacity to take away our own liberty by one means or another, but all have held that political liberty, vital as it is, can only be the beginning of complete liberty.

The claim that under laissez-faire there is less freedom than its defenders suppose goes back to the 18th century. But it has been the central issue between defenders of capitalism and their socialist critics for the past century and a half. Those who identify liberty and 'free enterprise' argue that the man who has no property or no marketable skills is worse off than the man with property or abilities to his name, but no less free. Liberty is counterfactual: *if* he were able to make his way in the world, nobody would prevent him. The poor man cannot dine at the Ritz, but that is not because he is not free to do so. To this is often added a claim which has been popular since Sir Isaiah Berlin's *Two Concepts of Liberty* (1958): freedom is negative, a matter of the absence of coercion. We must not confuse the negative matter of what we are at liberty to do with the positive matter of what we are able to do.

Opponents have seized on different issues. Marx, for instance, claimed that the distinction between rich and poor under capitalism originated in the forcible expropriation of the small freeholder, so that coercion underpinned 'free exchange'. Mill argued that the range of choice open to the poorest manual worker was as limited as that of the slave. Many writers have denied that the distinction between the presence of opportunities and abilities on the one hand and the absence of coercion on the other is as important as has been made out. Others have widened the argument, pointing out that we talk of 'having no choice' where circumstances as well as people dictate what we must do. Following Marx, their strictures on the unfreedom of capitalism sometimes imply a tyranny of capital over all its victims, sometimes a tyranny of capitalists over workers, and sometimes that capital itself forces capitalists to force workers into exploited labour. The attempts of philosophers to show that this is not an argument about liberty – as opposed to justice or happiness or self-respect – have been unsuccessful, but this is far from saying that anyone has a clear idea of just what *would* constitute economic freedom.

BIBLIOGRAPHY

Berlin, I. 1969. *Four Essays on Liberty.* Oxford: Oxford University Press.
Hegel, G.W.F. 1822–30. *Lectures on The Philosophy of World History: Introduction.* Trans. H.B. Nisbet, Cambridge and New York: Cambridge University Press, 1975.
Lukes, S.M. 1985. *Marxism and Morality.* Oxford: Oxford University Press.
Macpherson, C.B. 1973. *Democratic Theory.* Oxford: Clarendon Press.
Mill. J.S. 1859. *On Liberty.* Harmondsworth: Penguin Books, 1974.
Nozick, R. 1974. *Anarchy, State and Utopia.* New York: Basic Books; Oxford: Basil Blackwell.

John Locke

KAREN I. VAUGHN

John Locke (1632–1704), the philosopher and author of *Essay Concerning Human Understanding*, *Two Treatises of Government* and *A Letter Concerning Toleration*, was educated at Westminster School and Christ Church, Oxford, where he received a BA in 1656 and an MA in 1659. He lectured in Greek and Moral Philosophy, studied experimental medicine on his own initiative and attended Robert Boyle's unorthodox experimental group in his spare time. In 1666 he joined the household of Anthony Ashley Cooper, the first Earl of Shaftesbury, where he developed an interest in political and economic matters. Locke's cautious political involvements caused him to spend a brief period of exile in Holland during the 1680s until James II abdicated and William and Mary ascended the British throne. Locke was known as both a philosopher and a public servant. Among his contributions to public life was his organizing of the Board of Trade in 1695 and his subsequent service as a commissioner of the Board until 1700.

Locke's contributions to economic thought consisted of two major essays and a minor pamphlet. Locke's first economic essay, *Some Considerations of the Consequences of the Lowering of Interest, and Raising the Value of Money*, was also his most important. Although he worked on drafts of this essay for more than twenty years, he only published it in 1691 in an attempt to influence Parliament to defeat a bill to lower the legal rate of interest from 6 per cent to 4 per cent. Although the essay, being too complicated and analytic for successful polemic, failed to persuade Parliament, its very failures as political persuasion make it an interesting essay in the history of economic thought.

In an age of mercantilist confidence in the importance of economic regulation, Locke, the natural law philosopher, began his essay with the question, 'Whether the price of the hire of money (the rate of interest) can be regulated by law?' (*Some Considerations*, p.1). His answer was that 't'is manifest it cannot' because interest is a price and all prices are determined by laws of nature that are beyond the control of mere political law. Politicians can pass interest rate legislation, but they are powerless to effect the results they intend. People unwilling to give up the 'chance of gain' will evade the interest rate ceilings in ways that will drive the effective interest rate higher than the market rate would have been in the absence of legislation and cause shortages of loanable funds, hamper trade and redistribute wealth in undeserved ways.

Locke based his conclusions on a carefully developed theory of price determination which he applied to all exchangeable goods. His price theory, while primitive by modern standards, was nevertheless remarkably accurate in predicting the correct direction of change of price in response to changes in underlying variables. He clearly showed that quantity demanded is inversely related to price, while quantity supplied is directly related. He had the concept of an equilibrium price and in fact used the term equilibrium in several contexts. The fact that the price with which he was most concerned was the interest rate also led him to develop a very advanced monetary theory, probably his most important contribution to the development of economic thought.

Locke's theory of value starts from the premise that only relative values are important to economic exchange. There are no intrinsic values that make some quantity of one good always exchange for some quantity of another good. Exchange value depends exclusively upon the proportion between the quantity of a good offered for sale and its vent, the quantity of the good demanded. The same principles applied to the value of money. Money was a special good in that it had two values: a value in use and a value in exchange. Its value in use was as money capital and its price was the rate of interest. The rate of interest, then, depended not upon legislation but upon the profitability of investment and the alternative uses of money to individuals. The value of money in exchange, however, was a special case of the value of goods because while its quantity was variable, its vent was 'always sufficient' (*Some Considerations*, p. 71), by which Locke meant that the public would be willing to hold any amount of money in circulation. Hence, he argued, the value of money, or its purchasing power was solely an inverse function of the quantity of money in circulation. The quantity of money, however, also depended upon its 'quickness of circulation' (ibid., p. 33), which he analysed as a function of the relatively stable payments habits of the community. It is easy to see an early statement of the quantity theory in Locke's analysis.

Locke applied his quantity theory of money to the problem of international price levels and specie flows. His analysis here is interesting because he argued that 'any quantity of money...would serve to drive any proportion of trade' (ibid., pp. 75-6) and hence the absolute amount of specie in any one country is irrelevant to its welfare. However, he also believed that countries which were involved in world trade needed to maintain a certain proportion between the quantity of money and the volume of trade so that it would not be disadvantaged relative to its trading partners. While this position is inconsistent with a simple quantity theory of money (as Hume was to point out in the next century), Locke assumed that unfavourable terms of trade would lead to depression and the emigration of skilled labour. In other words, he assumed output effects consequent on changes in the money supply that made him reject an untrammelled reliance on the price-specie-flow mechanism to maintain a balance of trade.

Locke's second major essay, *Further Considerations Concerning Raising the Value of Money* (1695), while it reiterated many of his earlier arguments, was most concerned with the issue of recoinage. Locke took issue with a proposal to devalue the official coinage by 20 per cent and argued strongly for recoining at the old standard the currently circulating coins debased by clipping and normal wear and tear. Money, Locke argued, was equivalent to gold and silver. People contracted for gold and silver and a government stamp was simply an assurance of the specie content of official coins. Hence, a devaluation would only confuse trade and cause an increase in prices denominated in terms of pounds and shillings.

It had been pointed out that a 20 per cent official devaluation would simply have ratified a de facto devaluation that had taken place through clipping and wear and tear, and so Locke's arguments were not pertinent to the problem. While that may well have been correct, Locke's real agenda was to argue that money was the private property of citizens and not a creation of government. He was making a moral argument that was consistent with the political philosophy he espoused in his *Second Treatise of Government*.

From the point of view of the economist, Locke's *Second Treatise* is interesting primarily because of the theory of property developed therein. Locke argues that individuals earn the right to private property by virtue of the fact that in order to survive, they must mix their own labour with unowned resources. Locke goes on to argue that one has a right to create as much property (in land as well as in goods) as one can for one's use as long as nothing is wasted and as long as there are sufficient resources left for others also to make a living. From this basis, Locke developed a theory of the origin of money where money arises out of man's efforts to provide a store of value to prevent waste and a theory of the origin of the state based on scarcity of land.

In the course of making his point, Locke argued that private property is not only moral, it is also practical since labour is productive and the accounts for 99/100 of the value of things 'useful to the life of man' (*Second Treatise*, p. 314). While this statement was only illustrative and was not meant to suggest any casual relationship between labour input and market price, it did provide a starting point for later labour theories of value.

SELECTED WORKS

1690. *Two Treatises of Government*. Ed. Peter Laslett, 2ne edn, Cambridge: Cambridge University Press, 1953.
1696. *Several Papers Relating to Money, Interest and Trade, etcetera*. New York: Augustus M. Kelley, 1968.

BIBLIOGRAPHY

Laslett, P. 1957. John Locke, the great recoinage, and the origins of the board of trade, 1695–1698. *William and Mary Quarterly* 14, July, 370–92.

Leigh, A.H. 1974. John Locke and the quantity theory of money. *History of Political Economy* 6, Summer, 200–19.

Letwin, W. 1964. *The Origins of Scientific Economics*. Garden City, NY: Anchor Books.

Vaughn, K.I. 1980. *John Locke: Economist and Social Scientist*. Chicago: University of Chicago Press.

Bernard Mandeville

N. ROSENBERG

Mandeville was born in or near Rotterdam in 1670 and died in Hackney, London, in 1733. He was awarded the degree of Doctor of Medicine from the University of Leyden in 1691. He took up the practice of medicine, specializing in the 'Hypochondriack and Hysterick Diseases', a subject on which he later published a treatise. Mandeville travelled to England, married there in 1699, and lived in England for the rest of his life. He was very widely read in the 18th century. His writings have often led to his being referred to as a satirist, but that is an inadequate and misleading classification.

Although Mandeville was not an economist, his writings were influential in shaping the direction of economic thinking in the 18th century. In 1705 he published a pamphlet, in doggerel verse, under the title *The Grumbling Hive: Or Knaves turn'd Honest*. In 1714 it was republished under its better-known title, *The Fable of the Bees: or, Private Vices, Publick Benefits*. This and subsequent editions included extensive expansions, clarifications and 'vindications' of his earlier themes. The grumbling hive was originally a thriving and powerful community. When, however, its inhabitants were suddenly and miraculously converted from a vicious to a virtuous moral condition, the community was swiftly reduced to an impoverished and depopulated state.

Mandeville's central theme is that public benefits are the product of private vices and not of private virtues. His paradox, which was widely regarded as scandalous, was achieved by employing a highly ascetic and self-denying definition of virtue. Since behaviour that could be shown to be actuated by even the slightest degree of self-regarding motive – pride, vanity, avarice or lust – was classified as vice, Mandeville had little difficulty in concluding that a successful social order must inevitably be one where public benefits are built upon a foundation of private vices.

> ...I flatter myself to have demonstrated that, neither the Friendly Qualities and kind Affections that are natural to Man, nor the real Virtues he is capable

of acquiring by Reason and Self-Denial, are the Foundation of Society; but that what we call Evil in this World, Moral as well as Natural, is the grand Principle that makes us sociable Creatures, the solid Basis, the Life and Support of all Trades and Employments without Exception: That there we must look for the true Origin of all Arts and Sciences, and that the Moment Evil ceases, the Society must be spoiled, if not totally dissolved (Mandeville, 1732, vol. I, p. 369).

What was of more enduring significance in Mandeville's views was his forceful and unapologetic popularization of the belief that socially desirable consequences would flow from the individual pursuit of self-interest. It is an essential part of Mandeville's argument that a viable social order can emerge out of the spontaneous actions of purely egoistic impulses, requiring neither the regulation of government officials, on the one hand, nor altruistic individual behaviour, on the other.

As it is Folly to set up Trades that are not wanted, so what is next to it is to increase in any one Trade the Numbers beyond what are required. As things are managed with us, it would be preposterous to have as many Brewers as there are Bakers, or as many Woolen-drapers as there are Shoe-makers. This Proportion as to Numbers in every Trade finds it self, and is never better kept than when nobody meddles or interferes with it (Mandeville, 1732, vol. I, pp. 299–300).

Thus, Mandeville enunciates a vision of an economy that organizes itself and that allocates resources through the market place. Although there is no serious analysis of the workings of the market mechanism, there is the clear assertion that the unregulated market provides a system of signals and inducements such that the interactions of purely egoistic motives will somehow produce results that will advance the public good.

In developing his views, Mandeville offered many acute observations on the causes as well as the consequences of the division of labour in society. He regarded the division of labour as the great engine of economic improvement over the ages. It is the most reliable way for 'savage People' to go about 'meliorating their Condition'. For

...if one will wholly apply himself to the making of Bows and Arrows, whilst another provides Food, a third builds Huts, a fourth makes Garments, and a fifth Utensils, they not only become useful to one another, but the Callings and Employments themselves will in the same Number of Years receive much greater Improvements, than if all had been promiscuously follow'd by every one of the Five (Mandeville, 1729, vol. II, p. 284).

Although one can identify a number of possible precursors to Adam Smith's celebrated views on the division of labour, it is well established that Smith had in fact read and digested Mandeville carefully. Smith's marvellous description of the extensive division of labour involved in the production of a day-labourer's coat, with which he closes the first chapter of the *Wealth of Nations*, may be traced to Mandeville's earlier treatment of the same subject – a treatment which, indeed, Smith extensively paraphrases. Moreover, the passage in the *Wealth of Nations* containing the often quoted statement that 'It is not from the benevolence of the butcher, the brewer, or the baker, that we expect our dinner, but from their regard to their own interest' (Smith, p. 14) is in a direct lineage from Mandeville's earlier observation:

> ...The whole Superstructure [of Civil Society] is made up of the reciprocal Services, which Men do to each other. How to get these Services perform'd by others, when we have Occasion for them, is the grand and almost constant Sollicitude in Life of every individual Person. To expect, that others should serve us for nothing, is unreasonable; therefore all Commerce, that Men can have together, must be a continual bartering of one thing for another (Mandeville, 1729, vol. II, p. 349).

Thus Mandeville was, in some important respects, an early advocate of laissez-faire (although this advocacy did not extend to foreign trade, where Mandeville's views were still distinctly Mercantilist). He articulated a vision of the role of the division of labour in society, and of the forces making for social change and evolution, as well as for social cohesion, that were in many respects distinctly precocious, and that exercised a powerful influence in shaping the intellectual agenda of economists and other social scientists later in the 18th century.

SELECTED WORKS

1714. *The Fable of the Bees.* 2 vols, ed. F.B. Kaye, London: Oxford University Press. (This is the definitive edition.)

BIBLIOGRAPHY

Hayek, F.A. 1978. Dr. Bernard Mandeville. In F.A. Hayek, *New Studies in Philosophy. Politics, Economics and the History of Ideas*, Chicago: University of Chicago Press.

Primer, I. (ed.) 1975. *Mandeville Studies*. The Hague: Martinus Nijhoff.

Rosenberg, N. 1963. Mandeville and laissez-faire. *Journal of the History of Ideas* 24(2), April, 183–96.

Smith, A. 1776. *An Inquiry into the Nature and Causes of the Wealth of Nations*. New York: Modern Library, 1937.

Stephen, L. 1876. *History of English Thought in the Eighteenth Century*. 2 vols, London: Smith, Elder.

Viner, J. 1953. *Introduction to Bernard Mandeville, A Letter to Dion*. Los Angeles: Augustan Reprint Society, Publication No. 41.

a record of the development of his intellectual and political outlook. He was born in London in May 1806. His father James Mill was in the process of writing the *History of British India* which made him famous and a power in the East India Company, but had thus far led a precarious existence as a journalist. John was the oldest of six children. His mother, who is never mentioned in his *Autobiography*, was born Harriet Burrows; her mother kept an asylum and must have been modestly well off. The non-appearance of Mrs Mill in her son's record of his life is easily, if unhappily explicable. In an early draft of the *Autobiography*, her son dwelt at length on the deficiencies which made her unfit to be his father's wife. She was uneducated and weakly good-natured; she had no opinions of her own. James Mill was evidently bored and irritated by her, and she could do nothing about it but retreat into being a *Hausfrau*. She therefore exerted no influence on her oldest son, who was left entirely to the educational programme of his father.

We may speculate that two added reasons explain Mill's harsh account of her in his draft – kinder second thoughts removed the account when he revised it just before his death. He wrote his draft in 1854, not long after he married Harriet Taylor; at the time of their marriage, he fancied that his mother had insulted his new wife and broke off relations with her. It seems plausible that one reason for the harshness was this resentment, and that the other was the feeling that it was her inadequacies that had abandoned him to the exceedingly fierce education he had had from his father. For the moral of Mill's *Autobiography* is that an education of the intellect alone must result in emotional deprivation, and that a proper education must be an education of the feelings as well as of the brain. When he sat down to record an education whose most memorable product, it seemed to him, was a breakdown in his twenties, his resentment must have been extreme. Objectively, his mother was a casualty of the domestic tyranny which *The Subjection of Women* was written to condemn; subjectively, the knowledge that her inadequacies were hardly her fault made no difference to his reactions.

His early life, then, was an educational experiment. He learned Greek at three – from 'flash cards' of the kind still used by psychologists; he went on to read omnivorously in history and literature; he learned mathematics readily and even a little science at second hand; in his early teens he learned logic, assisted his father in preparing his *Elements of Political Economy*, and finally read Bentham's defence of utilitarianism. By his sixteenth year, he was everything his father had hoped – an enlightened young man whose intellect was that of a forty-year-old.

At sixteen he joined his father at the East India Company – which by this time was important as the government of India, not as a trading company; he served the Company for thirty-six years, until 1858, when the British Government finally took over a government it had supervised for so long. For most of that time, he organized the Political Department's dealings with the independent princely states; at the end he held his father's old position, 'Examiner of India Correspondence', or to all intents and purposes the senior permanent post in the government of the subcontinent. Unlike his father, whose legacy still exists in the Indian legal and educational systems, Mill did not much affect policy. His experience, however, reinforced his views about self-government and bureaucracy, and *Liberty* and *Representative Government* would have been thinner without that experience behind them.

The East India Company did not take up all his time. In his early twenties he worked for two years as secretary and amanuensis to Bentham in the preparation of his *Rationale of Judicial Evidence*. It was this which seems to have provoked his nervous breakdown. The collapse seems to have been noticed by nobody else, but it is the central event in the *Autobiography*. It has a symbolic importance which goes beyond the acute misery Mill no doubt felt at the time. Mill says that the event which provoked the collapse was asking himself whether the success of all the schemes he and his utilitarian friends had would make him happy. Consciousness irresistibly answered 'No' and his world crumbled. How long the depression endured it is impossible to say; what cured it was reading the memoirs of Marmontel and bursting into tears. The proof that he was a being with genuine feelings restored his happiness. It also spawned a theory.

The theory is central to all Mill's work. He thought that the 18th century had been a destructive century – but a valuably destructive one; the institutions of the *ancien régime* in France and the legal abuses on which Bentham had trained his weapons epitomized arrangements which could not stand up to rational criticism. But the analytical intelligence which sees through old abuses is not well equipped to construct something with which to replace them. Some years later, his essays on 'Bentham' and 'Coleridge' summed up the position to which he worked his way. Bentham always asked – does it work? and thought that simple efficiency was everything; what he was no good at was asking what the ends of life were for the sake of which it was worth asking such a question. Coleridge asked – what does it mean? and tried to see the rationality buried in customary ways of doing things. But this conserved too much, and allowed too little room for a scientific approach to social progress. If social progress was to be moral and spiritual progress rather than the mere accumulation of wealth, men needed a synthesis of the analytical and imaginative mind. Even if his own talents were inadequate to the task, Mill now knew what was wanted – politics and economics had to be discussed in a historically sensitive way, utilitarianism had to be enlarged to make sense of the varieties of human happiness, authority and liberty had each to receive their due. This was not mere eclecticism; it was following Goethe's motto of 'many-sidedness'.

If this discovery was one source of happiness, Mill's friendship and eventual marriage with Harriet Taylor was the other. They met in 1830; she was a married lady, bored by domestic life and full of an intellectual passion quite unlike anything Mill knew. Although their friendship was entirely chaste, it was not exactly respectable, and the fact reinforced Mill's sense of the deadening weight of Victorian respectability – a major of theme of *Liberty*. They married in 1851 after the death of her husband; but Harriet was already ill, and died herself in 1858. Thereafter Mill was looked after by his stepdaughter, the formidable Helen Taylor, and lived half the year in Avignon to be near Harriet's grave. This was no obstacle to his leading an active public life in his last fifteen years. In 1865 he was elected MP for Westminster and proved to be no mean debater and no gentle critic of his Tory opponents. He lost to W.H. Smith in 1868 and retired to write about religion, trade unionism, the reform of Irish land tenure and much else. He died in Avignon in May 1873.

Although Mill's banner was 'many-sidedness', it is the way his major writings fit together which is impressive. In the *Autobiography* Mill denounces what he terms 'the intuitive school' of philosophy, and that hostility holds Mill's work together. The 'intuitive school' held that the basic truths of logic, mathematics, science and morality were self-evident, and were guaranteed true by the 'inconceivability' of their opposites. Mill's aim was to drive the doctrine out of ethics; to do so, he had to begin with logic and mathematics because this was the enemy's strongest point. It is to this task that *A System of Logic* is devoted. Mill returned to the attack in his *Examination of Sir William Hamilton's Philosophy* (1865), but the *Logic* went into eight editions as Mill revised it during his lifetime.

Mill held that 'inconceivability' has nothing to do with truth, but everything to do with intellectual habit. The King of Siam thought ice was 'inconceivable' because he could not imagine an elephant walking on solid water. All truths about the world were vulnerable to experience; none could be proved by appealing to 'intuition'. In defending this position, Mill rashly argued that even the truths of arithmetic were generalizations of experience, in this case of the results of counting different groups of objects and finding, say, that pairs of pairs always made fours. He agreed, as he had to, that this meant that it was possible that in some distance reach of the universe the laws of arithmetic and geometry might break down. The fact that we cannot now say what it would be like if they did so does not show that they cannot. Although this doctrine has generally been disliked by empiricists as much as by Mill's opponents, it has enjoyed something of a revival in the work of Quine.

But Mill's main concern in his *Logic* is to give an account of causal explanation and of how we establish causal laws. Mill offers several different accounts, but generally argues as follows. To explain anything is to show its cause; to say that a man died because he ate cyanide is to say that eating cyanide is the cause of his death, and this in turn is to appeal to a generalization of the form 'if anyone eats cyanide, then he dies'. He denies that causes necessitate their effects, and denies that we can or need to go further than establishing that as a matter of fact causes do invariably precede their effects. It is generally agreed that his treatment of the difference between genuinely causal generalizations ('cyanide eating is followed by death') and non-causal generalizations ('night follows day') is not very satisfactory; there is no agreement on what is needed instead.

The object of science is to establish true generalizations. Mill calls the methods by which we do this 'inductive', as if their nature was to allow us to extrapolate successfully from partial evidence to true generalizations; if this was his aim, he would have been in difficulties of a familiar kind, for no finite set of statements of the form 'this *A* is *B*', 'that *A* is *B*' and so on can *prove* that all *A*s are *B*. In fact, Mill's canons of induction are canons of eliminative deduction. That is, what Mill supposes is that we employ his canons to eliminate false claims of causal connection; what survives the tests is not proved true. Thus, the so-called 'method of difference' imagines that we have a set of antecedent B, C and a set of consequents b, c and we add the antecedent A; if the consequents are now a, b, c we can infer that neither B nor C caused a, since they existed when a did not. Can we infer that A caused a? We cannot do so conclusively. It may be that in introducing A we introduced something we knew nothing of which caused a; so the method is not conclusive unless we know that the conditions are fully described. As Mill's great opponent William Whewell observed, by that time we know that the game is over. Again, even with proviso we cannot decide on this one experiment that A caused a, since it may be that it is only $A + B$ which does the trick, or $A + C$, or $A + B + C$. In short, Mill's canons formalize *part* of the procedures of experimental science; they are not canons of experimental proof in a strict sense.

The *Logic* culminates in Book VI, 'The Logic of the Moral Sciences'; by 'Moral Sciences' Mill meant all disciplines which depend on the laws of mind as well as the laws governint physical nature. Mill did not distinguish 'social' and 'natural' sciences, since the polemical point of the book was to insist that all science is natural science. He distinguished 'physical' and 'moral' science, the former being whatever did not involve the laws of mind. The moral sciences include psychology, economics, political science – and a discipline Mill hoped to see established, but one we wait for still, the science of 'ethology', that is, the science of the development of individual and national character. It was, of course, the science which was needed if the social sciences were to be historically self-conscious in the way Mill hoped. Mill's other concern was with the scope and limits of economics; economics, he thought, was rather like geometry in being an 'abstract' science. It was therefore not a model for political science, which had to be concrete, and in Mill's terms 'physical' rather than 'geometrical'. This was a coded criticism of his father's *Essay on Government*, which had attempted to derive an argument for universal suffrage from the simple premise of universal self-interest. But Mill also savaged his father's main critic, T.B. Macaulay, who had complained of James Mill's *a prior* approach; political science was more than case by case description – what Mill condemned as the 'chemical method'.

A final chapter of the *Logic* briefly tackles the distinction between science and morality. Mill says, as Hume had done before him, that there is a logical gap between statements about what *is* the case and statements about what *ought* to be the case. The latter are, implicitly, imperative rather than declarative; they are rules rather than generalizations. Mill's view is that all rules belong to what he calls 'art'; thus, to take an easy example, architecture is an art – that is a system of instructions for building commodious buildings – founded on the science of materials. Progress in any art must depend on progress in the corresponding science; the art of morality is susceptible of progress, which is the crux of the attack on intuitionist theories, and that progress depends on a deeper understanding of the sciences corresponding to it, namely psychology and ethology.

Although *Utilitarianism* was written after most of Mill's other major works, its logical place in his intellectual system is before them – since it supplies the moral theory which lies behind the defence of freedom and his doubts about democratic government. Mill's essay is notorious for its attempt to 'prove' the 'greatest happiness principle'; but concentration on that issue distorts our understanding of Mill's aims. Moreover, Mill himself says at the beginning of the essay that questions of ultimate ends are not susceptible of proof, so much of the 20th-century criticism of the essay has been misdirected. Mill has three main aims in *Utilitarianism*. The first is to defend ethical rationalism against intuitive theories of ethics; the second is to defend utilitarianism against the charge that it cannot allow an independent value to virtuous action, and cannot explain why anyone ought to do his or her duty; the last is to show that utilitarianism can explain justice, that is, that utilitarianism can justify our conviction that the rules of justice take priority over all other rules, and can given an account of moral rights.

Mill's case is that rational argument is a matter of justifying beliefs – moral or practical – by appealing to principles which support them. Since principles themselves often conflict, we need some way of reconciling them. Intuitive theories cannot provide this and are thus defective. Utilitarianism provides a rational scheme of argument; the ultimate principle, that actions, institutions, principles and anything else are good in proportion as they increase the happiness of all sentient creatures and bad in proportion as they diminish it, is itself not provable, but justifies the judgements made in accordance with it. Mill thinks that people will resist this for two reasons, the first their conviction that courage, sympathy, honesty and the rest are good independently of their results, the second that happiness cannot really be the spur to action, since people so often act in ways which cause them no happiness. Mill partly accepts the first point. That is, unless people took honesty, courage and the rest as their targets regardless of their results, the practice of these virtues would not have such good results. But what makes them virtues is the good results of people practising them; otherwise, they are pointless asceticism. Mill defeats the second point by claiming that to call a man courageous is to say that he would be unhappier acting in a cowardly fashion; 'happiness' is not a simple state of feeling, but a way of summing up a person's goals. So Socrates did not risk his life for the truth as he saw it *as a means* to happiness, rather it was that the pursuit of truth in the face of death was *part of* happiness for him. This allows Mill to make his memorable distinction between quantitative and qualitative estimates of happiness – better a man dissatisfied than a pig satisfied, better Socrates dissatisfied than a fool satisfied. If we ask, who is to judge, Mill's answer is; those who know both sides of the question.

This in turn allows Mill to argue that what makes people act morally, that is, with proper concern for the interests of others, is in essence socialization into associating their happiness with the happiness of others. It is not a matter of perceiving the object 'rightness' of some course of action as the intuitionists would have it, but of having been brought up in such a way that we not only respect the interests of others for instrumental reasons but because we now find it painful to do anything else. This naturalistic account of moral sanctions id doubly important to Mill; it defeats intuitionism, and it also explains why individual freedom is so important. Socialization is such a powerful force that it must be handled with care; we must mould people's reactions only where it is essential to do so.

It is at this point that Mill turns to offer his famous 'proof'; most of the persuasive task has been accomplished when Mill has shown that utilitarianism can defend itself against criticism – we now know that we need a first principle in ethics and that utility does not have absurd results. The 'proof' adds a positive argument. If we ask how we know that something is visible, the reply that we've seen it is enough; if we ask how we know something is desirable, says Mill, the proof is that people desire it. The obvious complaint that 'visible' means '*can* be seen' while 'desirable' means '*should* be desired' rather than 'can be desired' has never been satisfactorily answered. But Mill seems not to have attached much weight to the claim in any case. He laid more stress on two thoughts, the first that anything desirable is either a means to happiness or a part of it, the second that if my happiness is a good, everybody's happiness is a good. It goes without saying that these also are highly debatable claims.

In keeping with his, rather than our, sense of where the argument lay, Mill ends *Utilitarianism* with a chapter on justice. The man in the street distinguishes between expediency and justice, between the obligatory and the supererogatory; he thinks it is good to give to charity, but obligatory to pay one's debts, that fairness is part of justice, but kindness not. Mill departs from Bentham in agreeing that there are moral rights as well as legal ones; justice is about the realm of people's rights. The question is what picks out that realm. Mill's reply is that it is the fact that we distinguish those parts of our duties which particularly promote security and distinguish them by their greater stringency, and treat the interests which they serve as rights. It is not a wholly convincing answer, though it covers much of the proper ground. That is, the rights to life, liberty, a fair trial and to receive debts due seem to relate to security, though not always to justice; the right to be treated fairly in minor matters seems to relate to justice but not especially to security.

One objection to utilitarianism that has recently been current is that utilitarianism is liberticide. Benevolent despotism would be approved by the utilitarian, deplored by the libertarian. Mill's *Liberty* is the most highly regarded of all his works, and deeply controversial just because its defence of liberty is couched in utilitarian terms. Mill had learned from de Tocqueville's *Democracy in America* a deep suspicion of the egalitarian and democratic pressures of the age. Like de Tocqueville, he feared the coming of a 'society of industrious sheep'; he did not fear the sort of democratically backed dictatorship which 20th-century liberals fear, so much as a society in which freedom was sacrificed to comfort and conformity. *Liberty* is a sermon on the need to control public opinion before public opinion takes away all freedom of thought.

Mill thought that the movement towards democracy had begun in justified self-defence; unless the whole people could exercise enough power to control their rulers, they would be at their mercy. But what we have discovered is that 'self-government' is not the government of each of us by himself or herself, but the government of each of us by all the rest. People increasingly take as their only rule of conduct the need to think like everybody else. There is no universally acknowledged principle about when it is right for social pressure to be exerted to secure uniformity of conduct, and as a result our freedom is at the mercy of the 'likings and mislikings' of society.

Three things are important about Mill's case. First, he is more anxious about public opiniong than about law; in England at least political liberty is well protected, but moral and intellectual liberty not. Public opinion is a greater danger than political oppression because it works its way into our minds whereas brute repression tends to arouse resistance. Second, Mill confines his discussion to society's right to *coerce* its members into any particular line of conduct. Most commentators accuse Mill of ignoring all the non-coercive ways of influencing each other; but Mill does not ignore them. He insists that we may encourage, advise, exhort and entreat each other in any matter whatever. But, we may not coerce anyone else except in self-defence. Third, he insists that the right to liberty in any matter which does not threaten the legitimate interests of other people is a right which rests on utility. It is not a 'natural' or, as he says, an 'abstract' right.

Liberty defends what Mill calls 'one very simple principle', which is to replace the mere likings and mislikings of society. That principle, which we may summarize as 'no coercion except in self-defence', prohibits interferences with free speech (though not with incitement), prohibits paternalistic legislation, prohibits what we, though not Mill himself, would call 'victimless crimes'. Mill's defence of his principle rests on two things; the first is the utilitarian account of rights which he gives in *Utilitarianism*, which implies that it is the security of others which we are obliged to respect, the second, which is much more characteristically 'Millian', is an account of the development of individual character as a vital element in utility. Personality is a part of happiness; only a person who feels that his thoughts and feelings are truly his own is truly happy.

It is noticeable that Mill dissociates his defence of individual liberty from *laissez-faire*. Mill never thought that property rights and freedom of contract had very much to do with liberty; *Liberty* is wholly consistent with his defence of worker cooperatives in the *Principles* and with his discussion of government activity in that work. Trade and ownership were essentially social matters and could be regulated by society; they ought, however, to be regulated in a way that promoted freedom and individuality – Mill thought a decentralized socialism could do precisely that.

This raises the question of what form of politics Mill advocated, and to this there is no very simple answer. As a young man, Mill was a straightforward democrat, thinking that annual parliaments, universal suffrage and the secret ballot would allow 'the people' to pursue the public interest and defeat aristocratic and other forces which were pursuing 'sinister interest' (as his father had called all interests opposed to the public interest). As he became more anxious about the tendency of public opinion to stifle dissenting views, and more sceptical of any government's ability to govern without a great deal of help from a professional administrative class, Mill moved towards a complicated theory of what he wished to call 'representative government' to mark the distance between himself and the enthusiasts for simple majority rule.

Considerations on Representative Government sums up Mill's mature thoughts. He begins by arguing that the crucial question in politics is the question of progress; the best form of government for any country is that which makes the most of the citizen's present abilities and encourages the development of more – here is the argument of the last book of the *Logic* in direct application. But, representative government is the absolutely best form of government because it both demands the most from the citizenry and encourages them to develop their intelligence and energy in a way no other government does. Would not benevolent despotism be even better? No, says Mill, for two reasons. In the first place, the whole idea of benevolent despotism is incoherent; suppose the despot and his subjects disagree over what is good for them, who then is to decide? If it is the despot, then it has ceased to be benevolent despotism; if it is the people, it is no longer despotism at all. In the second place, governments which concentrate on doing things *for* their subjects deprive them of the stimulus which doing things for themselves provides. Only self-government can prod people into self-improvement.

The only alternative to self-government is the government of a disinterested and public-spirited bureaucracy, such as the Venetian aristocracy once supplied. But bureaucracies need to be kept vigorous or they relapse into the stagnant state that the Chinese mandarins exhibited. In any case each individual has the right to defend himself and to give his opinion on how he is governed, so in principle and in terms of its consequences some sort of self-government is essential. It cannot be direct democracy, since modern states are too large and various to permit that; it must be a parliamentary democracy.

Mill then sets out the desiderata of a lively democracy, in which good order can be combined with the 'antagonism of opinions' on which progress depends. There is to be universal suffrage, women to be admitted on the same terms as men; no one who does not support himself can be given the vote – since no one has the right to vote on how to spend other people's incomes without putting his own at risk – but some simple, small tax ought to be universal in order to incorporate everyone. But if everyone should have a vote, it is far from obvious that each should have one vote only; Mill suggests an educational franchise, in which the better educated have more votes, in order to balance the votes of the uneducated labouring classes. This is not a way of securing the rule of the middle classes, since anyone can demand an extra vote whenever he or she has the qualifications, and Mill is emphatic that the weighting of the system is warranted only to protect society against class legislation, not in order to allow the middle class to dominate instead. Mill's concern for expertise and leadership appears when he argues that parliament ought not to try to govern; it must scrutinize those who do, but cannot do the job itself. It ought not to legislate, either; or, rather, it ought to hand over the job of drawing up legislation to a commission of expert draftsmen, and should then vote for or against what was proposed. It ought not to try to amend on the floor of the house. Carlyle's complaint that parliament is a talking shop is cheerfully accepted by Mill; parliament ought to be a talking shop.

Mill is famous for his defence of proportional representation; having observed that democracy is generally not self-government but government by everyone else, he follows Thomas Hare in advocating a system of proportional representation – a version of the single transferable vote system. This would achieve two things; each voter would have helped to elect someone, and individuals of national distinction who would not appeal to the voters of a particular area might none the less attract a personal vote spread through the country. He ought to be better known for his attack on the secret ballot; Mill denied that the way a voter voted was in any sense a private matter. Voting for an MP was voting for something which affected the interests of others, and they had every right to ask how we had done it. They must not intimidate or bully the voter, but they might certainly entreat, exhort and encourage him or her. He ought also to be better known for his emphasis on the direct participation of the citizens in local government; he thought that local administration might be turned into a civic duty like jury service, on the grounds that there was nothing to match doing the job to teach people how it was done. In general, Mill advocated as much decentralization as was consistent with reasonable efficiency; the slogan was centralize information, decentralize power, so that central governments could advise and assist but not preempt local initiative. An application of Mill's approach is easily found in his own views on education. Parents had a duty to educate their children and might be legally compelled to do so; it was obviously intolerable to make them pay for this education if they were already poor; it was dangerous for the state to take over education as a centralized activity. The remedy was to enforce the duty on parents, give grants to individuals to pay the charges of schools, leave most education in private hands, but set up some state schools as models of good practice.

All of this struck his contemporaries as either good sense but somewhat visionary, or as excessively rationalistic. Of his views on religion and on relations between the sexes they were more disapproving. Mill was unusual in that he was brought up an agnostic and so never experienced the loss of faith which was such an important experience for many of this contemporaries. But he was well enough acquainted with Comte and the Saint-Simonians to have clear views about religion and its social role. In his essay 'Nature' – one of his *Three Essays on Religion* – he argued fiercely that nature was amoral and far from a model for humans to emulate; no torture dreamed up by a sadist was absent from nature's repetoire of disease. In 'Theism' he discussed the probability of the existence of God, and while dismissing the prospects of an all-loving and omnipotent deity who somehow still allowed evil to exist, surprised his friends by thinking it probable that a less than omnipotent and on the whole benevolent God did – finding some plausibility in the argument from design, and remaining surprisingly unaffected by the damage Darwin had recently wrought upon it. 'The Utility of Religion' reiterated the view he had expressed in discussing Comte; orthodox religion did as much harm as good, and its usefulness was in any case secondary to its truth – but mankind would find use for something like religion, that is the habit of venerating great men such as Socrates and Washington, and reflection on the way our goals transcend our own lives. A man whose projects have humanity at large for their object will die happier than a selfish man, for he knows that most of what he values will live on.

Mill's unorthodox views on sex, marriage and the legal status of women were well known. As a youth of 16 he had spent a night in prison after being caught trying to distribute birth control pamphlets to the City of London poor. (Half a century later, the discovery of this fact was enough to persuade Mr Gladstone to resign from the committee which was raising money to commemorate Mill with a statue in Temple Gardens.) In *The Subjection of Women* he put forward no unorthodox views on sex or marriage at all. He stuck to a simple task, that of showing that there was no evidence that the legal inferiority of women and their legal and political dependence on men stemmed directly from their natural inferiority. Although his personal opinion was that divorce ought to be allowed on the mere say-so of childless couples, he put forward no such view in this essay; he affected to do no more than put forward a negative case, that is to show that everything his opponents said about the natural inferiority of women could be explained by the way women had been treated. But Mill ends with two arguments which sum up his enthusiasm for freedom in a way that even the essay on liberty did not. Addressing the man who observes that women seem happy enough in their dependent state, and, anyway that he cannot see why he should disturb them, Mill replies first that men are bored with women as they are, but would not be bored by genuinely independent beings, and second, that freedom does not need to be argued for – everyone remembers how pleased he was to leave school, nobody would voluntarily live under parental tutelage once having escaped it, no country would trade its freedom for any amount of prosperity; even if women are happy as they are, they would, once free, never regret the change. In that claim, Mill sums up not only the emotional mood behind his *Autobiography* and *Liberty*, but all that has made most commentators say that he is a better defender of liberty than of the implausible proposition that liberty is itself one of the elements in utility.

SELECTED WORKS

1843. *A System of Logic.* 2 vols, London: John W. Parker.

1848. *Principles of Political Economy, with some of their applications to Social Philosophy.* 2 vols, London: John W. Parker.

1859. *On Liberty.* London: J.W. Parker; Chicago, H. Regnery, 1955.

1861. *Considerations on Representative Government.* London: Parker, son, and Bourn.

1863. *Utilitarianism.* London: Parker, son, and Bourn. First published in *Fraser's Magazine*, October–December 1861, vol. 64, 383–4.

1865. *Auguste Comte and Positivism.* London: N. Trübner. First published in the *Westminster Review.*

1869. *The Subjection of Women*. London: Longmans, Green, Reader and Dyer.
1873. *Autobiography*. London: Longmans, Green, Reader and Dyer; New York: Columbia University Press, 1948.
1874. *Three Essays on Religion*. New York: H. Holt.
1963–84. *Collected Works of John Stuart Mill*. 21 vols, Toronto: University of Toronto Press; London: Routledge and Kegan Paul.

BIBLIOGRAPHY
Berger, F.R. 1984. *Happiness, Justice and Freedom*. Berkeley: University of California Press.
Packe, M. St J. 1954. *The Life of John Stuart Mill*. London: Secker & Warburg.
Robson, J.M. 1968. *The Improvement of Mankind*. Toronto: University of Toronto Press; London: Routledge and Kegan Paul.
Ryan, A. 1974. *J.S. Mill*. London: Routledge and Kegan Paul, Boston, Mass.: Routledge and Kegan Paul.

John Millar

NICHOLAS PHILLIPSON

Born in Lanarkshire, the son of a Presbyterian minister, Millar (1735–1801) was educated at Glasgow University for the Scottish Bar. He became a protégé of Adam Smith and Lord Kames, both of whom were instrumental in securing his appointment as Professor of Civil Law at Glasgow, a post he held until his death. He was a charismatic teacher who transformed the civil law curriculum by placing it on the jurisprudential foundations Smith had created for his moral philosophy lectures. He was a radical Foxite Whig and a member of the Society of the Friends of the People.

Millar is now much admired by historians of social thought for his *Origin of the Distinction of Ranks* (1771) in which he appeared to develop the sociological implications of Smith's account of the progress of civilization in a history of different systems of social authority. Unfortunately this view will not stand. The publication of the text of Smith's *Lectures on Jurisprudence* in 1978 showed that Millar's apparently original analysis, for all its closeness of texture and acuity, was intellectually entirely dependent on Smith's earlier work.

He never gave a separate course of lectures on political economy and dealt with that subject in unpublished lectures on government whose character can be inferred from a series of essays first published in the posthumous edition of his *Historical View of the English Government* (1803). His Smithian interest in the natural history of property led him to formulate a distinctive theory of profit as the wage of the manufacturer plus the saving he derived from investing in the division of labour, a subject which also interested his pupil, the Earl of Lauderdale. The attraction of this theory lay in its radical political implications. It allowed Millar to show that the attributes of property ownership and personal independence which lay at the heart of contemporary ideas of political rights extended to all of those who participated in the productive relationships of a commercial society. It led him to campaign for the radical reform of parliament in order to adjust the old whig constitution to the social and economic changes of the past century.

SELECTED WORKS
1771. *The Origin of the Distinction of Ranks*. 4th edn, Edinburgh: William Blackwood;
    London: Longman, Hurst, Rees & Orme, 1806.
1803. *An Historical View of the English Government*. 4 vols. London: J. Mawman.

BIBLIOGRAPHY
Ignatieff, M. 1983. John Millar and individualism. In *Wealth and Virtue: the Shaping of
    Political Economy in the Scottish Enlightenment*, ed. I. Hont and M. Ignatieff, Cambridge:
    Cambridge University Press.
Lehmann, W.C. 1960. *John Millar of Glasgow. 1735–1801: His Life and Thought and His
    Contributions to Sociological Analysis*. Cambridge: Cambridge University Press.

Moral Philosophy

R.S. DOWNIE

Some idea of the nature of moral philosophy is provided by considering the analogies which philosophers have used over the centuries to explain their aims. This entry will give a brief account of these and then a longer one of the preoccupations of moral philosophers this century.

For Plato (4th century BC), the moral philosopher is the *authoritative guide* to the good life. Asserting the premise that virtue is knowledge, Plato goes on to develop a view on the nature of such knowledge and how it can be acquired. The conclusion is that only certain people are fitted by natural endowment to attain it, and then only after a prolonged period of intellectual, physical and moral education. But, granted they have gone through the process, Plato regards them as fitted to determine the laws and to govern; they are the 'philosopher kings'. Plato is clearly ascribing to moral philosophy the strongest possible normative function, but apart from any philosophical problems attached to his ideas, we have difficulty in a democratic age with his general approach.

Aristotle (4th century BC) seems more plausible. His method is to examine the current views on any topic – what he calls the views of the many and the wise – and then to sift them with the aim of uncovering the general principles embodied in them. Aristotle is therefore inviting us to see the aim of the moral philosopher on the analogy of the *interpreter*. The assumption is that the first principles of conduct are not easily picked out because they are immersed in the details, but the moral philosopher can do so provided he accepts the general opinions of mankind on right and wrong and then uses a process of philosophical analysis to purge these opinions of inconsistency.

A third and totally different analogy is that of the '*razor*'. The principle – *entia non sunt multiplicanda* – commonly associated with the medieval philosopher William of Ockham, has been used as a philosophical razor to cut out what are thought to be redundant concepts, often in practice concepts in ordinary moral and political thinking which cannot be analysed in terms of sense-experience. Concepts such as 'moral obligation' or 'natural law' have sometimes been cut out by those who are using this philosophical razor. There are general difficulties in the basic doctrine, and the artificial limbs which must be manufactured when concepts such as 'moral obligation' are cut off are not more serviceable. Undoubtedly, however, the analogy has been an important one in the behaviourism or positivism which has sometimes appealed to social scientists. The razor can be seen in a characteristic destructive use in David Hume (1748, section XII, Part III). In a famous purple passage he invites us to ask of any volume: 'Does it contain any abstract reasoning concerning quantity or number? *No.* Does it contain any experimental reasoning concerning matter of fact and existence? *No. Commit it then to the flames: for it can contain nothing but sophistry and illusion.*'

A fourth and again a typically modern way of depicting the relationships between moral philosophy and the facts of the moral life can also be illustrated by David Hume, this time in his analogy with a *microscope* (1748, section VII, Part I). The philosopher takes the concepts used by the moral agent (or the social scientist) and looks at them through his philosophical microscope, thereby achieving a better understanding of their meaning. This is in some ways like the 'razor' approach because, although less destructive in intent, if often has had the same result of casting doubt on the validity of what cannot be empirically supported. Nevertheless, it is a view of the relationship between theory and practice which has been and still is philosophically influential.

A fifth analogy is that of *cartography*. The philosopher, it has been said, should be concerned with the logical mapping of concepts in a particular area, and so the moral philosopher will be concerned with the mapping of concepts in the moral and political life. This approach, as a supplement to Aristotle's, has a lot to be said for it. It suggests that the moral philosopher must himself learn from the moral agent or the practitioners of special subjects the procedures and types of argument actually used, and it discourages philosophers from abstracting a concept from its context and examining it in terms of some artificially imported criterion of meaningfulness. Moral philosophers inspired by Wittgenstein were encouraged to see moral concepts as interdependent, like those of a game, and as part of a total way of life (Wittgenstein, 1953).

It will be noted that of the five analogies the first two assign to moral philosophy some sort of normative function while the other three assign it an analytical function. In the period from 1945 to the present that distinction appeared in the literature as one between 'normative ethics' and 'meta-ethics'. Some philosophers even took the line that only the analytical approach was properly philosophy, and that moral philosophy should be entirely neutral on first-order moral questions. This doctrine went in conjunction with a second – that moral philosophy should be sharply distinguished from anything empirical – psychology, economics, sociology, etc. These two doctrines – of the moral neutrality and non-empirical nature of moral philosophy – were at the root of a style of philosophy, known as linguistic analysis, which was the dominant one in Anglo-Saxon philosophy during the period 1945–65.

From the mid-1960s cracks began to appear in this solid front. Some philosophers questioned whether meta-ethics or analytical moral philosophy could be value-neutral even if its practitioners tried. It was argued that apparently neutral, logical analysis of the language of morals presupposed a particular moral stance, liberalism, say. This debate was parallelled by the debate as to whether there could be a value-neutral social science. The conclusion that began to emerge – that meta-ethics cannot be morally neutral – had a liberating effect on practitioners of normative ethics, and the 1970s saw a resurgence of interest in normative questions. Moreover, the second pillar of the analytical approach weakened also, and there was a consequent development within professional philosophy of areas which had been out in the cold for several decades, such as political philosophy and the philosophy of education. It is true that some practitioners of philosophy of education (say) argued that they were just applying to other subject-matters the techniques of analytical philosophy, but the distinction between philosophy and empirical subject-matters was by now blurred, and new areas of interest to moral philosophers were opened up, such as social work ethics and medical ethics. At the time of writing, in the mid-1980s, the normative aspect to moral philosophy is if anything the dominant one, and philosophers produce books with titles like *What Sort of People Should There Be?* (Glover, 1984), without any suggestion that they have stayed away from the central concerns of moral philosophy.

Let us now examine in more detail the typical problems and theories of 20th-century moral philosophy. It is convenient for expository purposes to accept the distinction between 'normative' and 'meta-ethical' theories. Normative theories are concerned with attempts to answer the questions, 'What makes right actions right?' or 'What makes actions duties?' The answers fall into two broad categories: the teleological, and the deontological. In other words, for some philosophers actions are right if they produce some sort of good state of affairs, while for others rightness is in some way intrinsic to the right action and independent of what the action might produce. In expounding teleological theories we must note a distinction, often overlooked, between consequentialist and non-consequentialist versions of teleology. A consequentialist sees the good to be brought about as being externally related to the right action; actions are right if they are instrumental in bringing about good states of affairs.

The most common and influential of these consequentialist theories is hedonistic utilitarianism, familiar in the slogan associated with J.S. Mill (1863): 'Seek the greatest happiness of the greatest number.' The theory has two components – a doctrine of right action (that actions are right if they produce the best possible consequences for the majority) and a doctrine of the good, or of the nature of these consequences (pleasure or happiness). The latter doctrine has been criticized on the grounds that not all pleasures are equally good, or that happiness is not the only thing good in itself. J.S. Mill was himself fully aware of the force of this sort of point and tried to defend the theory by introducing a qualitative distinction between pleasures (Mill, 1863). Whereas Bentham had maintained the consistent view that, if the amount of pleasure were the same, push-pin was as good as poetry, Mill tried to argue that some pleasures were *qualitatively* better than others. It is generally thought that Mill's argument is in itself circular, and also inconsistent with the rest of his theory. More recent hedonistic utilitarians have dropped the reference to pleasure or happiness and speak simply of people's 'interests' or 'preferences'. But it can still be argued that some things are better worth having than others regardless of whether or how much people might prefer them, or how much they might claim that these things were in their interests. This anti-hedonist argument, even if thought successful, need not lead to the abandonment of utilitarianism, but can (and historically did) lead to the development of non-hedonistic or 'ideal' forms of utilitarianism.

The utilitarian doctrine of right action, which is the crux of the theory, has been criticized on various grounds. First, it might be held to be radically unclear. The criterion refers to the best possible consequences 'for the majority'. But how is this to be interpreted? As referring to a small group (a family), or a community, or a race, or the whole of mankind? Does it include future persons? Does it include animals? The answers to these questions have important social and economic consequences, but there are no clear lines of guidance from the theory.

Second, supposing the theory could be stated so as to meet these criticisms of internal detail, we must still consider whether it can meet criticisms from the other main group of normative theories – the deontological ones. Theories of this type claim that certain types of action are just right or just obligatory, regardless of the consequences. Some deontological theories claim that no actions are right or are duties because of their consequences. In so far as Kant's moral philosophy is deontological he holds this position (Kant, 1785). Other deontologists allow that some actions are right for utilitarian reasons and simply deny that all actions are right for utilitarian reasons (Ross, 1939). But all deontologists would agree that duties of justice cannot be accommodated on any utilitarian scheme. For example, a deontologist would argue that the utilitarian idea of maximizing good seems to sanction the possibility of unequal distribution of good, and so could conflict with widespread and basic intuitions of equality or fairness, or *distributive justice.* Again, deontologists would argue that a utilitarian is committed to the punishment of the innocent if that would (as sometimes it might) maximize good. But this conflicts with our basic intuition of *retributive justice.* Yet again, the deontologist would stress that whereas the utilitarian is necessarily committed to the view that *duties of truth-telling* or *promise-keeping* are dependent on the maximization of good, the ordinary person's view is that such requirements seem to be moral duties regardless of the consequences.

Theories which stress the importance of *rights* can also be included under the umbrella of deontology. Indeed, theories stressing rights and deontological theories stressing duties both arose historically from doctrines of natural law going back to the Greeks. Theories of rights became popular in the 17th and 18th centuries as doctrines of 'natural rights' or the 'rights of man', and have again become popular in this half of the 20th century in the vocabulary of human rights. Many moral causes are supported by invoking human rights. Theories of rights have this in common with all deontological theories that they insist that rights can be held by individuals regardless of the interests of the majority.

One of the interests in normative moral philosophy during the period 1960–75 was the rise and fall of utilitarian attempts to come to terms with deontological criticisms of their theory. Those attempts were expressed in a theory known as 'rule-utilitarianism' (as distinct from 'act-utilitarianism'). Rule-utilitarians distinguished rules of two sorts. The first were sometimes called 'regulative', such as 'People ought not to lose their tempers'. These were said to be rough guides, rules of thumb, to the likely best consequences of individual actions, and had no other force. The second were sometimes called 'constitutive' or rules which define a 'practice', such as 'One ought to keep one's promise', or 'One ought to tell the truth'. Property rules and rules of justice would also come into this category. The point to notice about the second category, according to the rule-utilitarian, is that we must distinguish two questions which were not distinguished by either the act-utilitarian or the deontologist: why ought we to perform certain individual actions? and, why ought we to agree to having certain sorts of rule? The deontologist correctly answers the first question by saying that we ought to keep our promise (say) simply because a promise is a promise, but he cannot on his theory explain how we can justify accepting the whole practices of promising, or of owning property, etc. The act-utilitarian, on the other hand, who does see the importance of good consequences for morality, does not see that a 'practice' will be undermined and rendered useless if people decide for themselves on each occasion whether or not the best consequences will come about by their actions. The solution according to the rule-utilitarian, is to insist with the deontologist that we keep to the rule because it is a rule, but then to go on to say that the existence of the rule can be justified, if it can, to the extent that its operation as a whole produces the best possible consequences for the majority. This theory is associated with the name of John Rawls (Rawls, 1955), but it can be found as powerfully expressed in David Hume (Hume, 1739).

Rule-utilitarianism was much criticized during the 1970s. The usual line was to note that it tends to inconsistency. The rule-utilitarian tells us that we should keep to a rule, say that we should keep a promise or observe a right, even when we know for sure that doing so will not maximize the best consequences in the given case, for otherwise we shall undermine the rule or the 'practice'. But if the promise has been made in secret, as promises often are, then it is not clear how we would be undermining the practice if we broke the promise. Many other examples can be used to make the point that the attempt to combine the views of the act-utilitarian with those of the deontologist results in inconsistency.

There is a third sort of criticism which can be made of any kind of utilitarianism. We can put it in terms of rights, although it can be put in other ways and does not depend on accepting deontology. If A injures B in some way – assaults him or slanders him – then this may have bad consequences for the majority. For example, it might encourage similar sorts of bad behaviour. But that is not what is mainly wrong with A's action. What A has done is wrong, if it is wrong, not because of the effect of his action on the *majority* but simply because he has injured B. If we put this in terms of rights we can say that B's rights have been violated.

There is a fourth sort of criticism of utilitarianism, which refers to the moral position of the agent of the action, as distinct from the recipient. The concept often invoked is 'integrity'. For example, let us suppose that A is on a bus party and is captured by bandits. The bandit chief (a man of honour) promises to release A plus all the other members of the bus party provided A agrees to shoot any one member of it. If A does not agree then the bandit chief will himself shoot everybody. Now on utilitarian terms there is no doubt that A should agree to shoot one person if the others can go free; but it is at the very least not morally unintelligible if A should think he ought to refuse, on the grounds that *he* ought not to kill someone himself even at the cost of some one else's killing far more people (Smart and Williams, 1973).

In general terms, what is lacking in utilitarianism is some sort of appreciation of the essential connection between morality and the nature of a person. The theory is at its most plausible if it is considered as an administrator's or legislator's theory, but it lacks any grasp of the inward, or personal, or face to face, aspects of morality.

A possible way forward is to return to the distinction between consequentialist and non-consequentialist teleology and to consider the latter. The Greeks provided one sort of non-consequentialist teleology, and the Idealists of the 19th century provided a slightly different sort. Common to both was the idea of morality as being an expression of essential aspects of human nature and social life. For the utilitarians, morality was simply a device, instrumental in producing a harmonious society; and human beings were conceived as being simply consumers of happiness. To put it in another way, the consequentialist teleology of utilitarianism is external to the self. But it is possible to see morality in terms of an internal teleology. An analogy might help here. When a house is built the lorries which bring the materials, the cement-mixers, the scaffolding, are all necessary means to the final product, which is the house. They have a value in their use, but are externally related to the product and have no part in it when it is finished. By contrast, the bricks and cement and tiles, while they too are necessary means for the creation of the final product, are also internally related to it; indeed, they are part of it, and it displays its character through them. In an analogous way, I suggest, morality should be seen not just as a means necessary for the good life for man, but as itself an expression of it. Human beings have a moral nature as well as a capacity for happiness, and it is this that the utilitarians ignored. The deontologists were correct in seeing that morality cannot be justified simply in terms of the good things it might produce, but they too (although we must except Kant) lacked a grasp of the connection between morality and the self. Insights into this connection are, curiously, shown by J.S. Mill. He stresses the importance of the 'flourishing' of the self, a Greek idea which he sees in non-hedonistic terms. As he puts it, 'It really is of importance not only what men do, but also what manner of men they are that do it' (Mill, 1859, chapter 3).

In other words, morality must be seen not simply as a technical device, but as a humane practice.

Let us move from normative questions to meta-ethical ones, bearing in mind that they too presuppose views about the nature of man and are far from being morally neutral. Within the broad area of meta-ethics three types of question are often discussed and not always distinguished. First, there are questions of what is sometimes called the 'logic of moral language'. These are often thought to be questions of the meanings of moral words. Secondly, there are questions of moral epistemology, of how we can be said to know the difference between right and wrong, or whether the vocabulary of knowing is appropriate. Thirdly, there are questions of the metaphysics of morality. Is it just an expression of human emotion or is it somehow part of the fabric of things? The questions are all interconnected, in that answers to one of the sets of questions have implications for the others. Let us begin with the logical questions, but note that they will slide into the others.

Three possibilities have been discussed this century: that moral judgements are statements of fact, that they are expressions of emotion, and that they are commands or prescriptions.

The view that they are statements of natural fact has been called 'naturalism', for it is along the lines that moral judgements are in some way 'reducible to' or 'analysable in terms of' some sort of fact, such as 'what gives pleasure'. G.E. Moore (1903) went as far as to say that philosophers who held this view had committed a logical fallacy, which he named 'the naturalistic fallacy'.

This was the alleged fallacy of defining 'good' in terms of something other than itself, and Moore thought that the fallacious nature of this definition could be brought out by what came to be known as the 'open question' test. For any attempted definition of 'good' in terms of properties x, y, z, it is possible to say, 'This is x, y, z, but is it good?', and the fact that this question remained open (or at least meaningful) was thought to indicate that the definition could not be correct. Moore concluded that 'good' did not name a natural property, but was indefinable and irreducible (although other moral words like 'right' could be defined as 'what realizes good'). He inferred from his conclusion, that 'good' does not name any natural property, that it must name a *non-natural* property. This was said to be in some ways like a natural property such as 'yellow', but in other ways quite different. In Moore, then, we find a logical view – that 'good' is the name of an indefinable property – which commits us to a metaphysical view – for since the property is non-natural it cannot be understood by any of the sciences, but it is still part of the fabric of things. This metaphysical view in turn commits us to an epistemological view, for since the property is non-natural it cannot be known by any of the senses, so must be known by an 'intuition'.

All three of these aspects of Moore's position were heavily criticized. For example, some philosophers argued that Moore had an inadequate view of language, since he thought that adjectives must always name properties. It was argued that 'good' does not name any sort of property, but rather commends, or expresses favourable emotion, or a pro-attitude, to something. This argument was based both on a philosophy of language, and also on a revived awareness of the action-guiding nature of moral judgements. The action-guiding nature of moral judgements is not explained if they are taken to state facts or name properties, but seems to be better explained if they are taken to express attitudes.

Out of this came the theory known as 'emotivism', which was immensely influential in the 1940s and 1950s. For the emotivist, moral sentences do not primarily state facts; they express attitudes. The expression of attitudes in moral utterances has a 'magnetic' effect – the hearer is moved to act by them. To support a moral utterance with a reason is to mention a (natural) fact which will causally influence an attitude (Stevenson, 1937). This view also was criticized in many ways. For instance, we often make moral judgements with no intention of influencing other people's attitudes, as when someone says to a vegetarian that eating meat is wrong. Again, it is not clear how emotivism can cope with moral doubt, as when I *wonder* whether I ought to do X or not. But, above all, emotivism does seem to do justice to the apparent rationality of morality. We argue with people and give reasons for our positions, and we think other people are mistaken. But how can a person be mistaken is his moral view is just a matter of causally induced emotion?

In an effort to regain the rationality of morality, while preserving the practicality stressed by emotivism, R.M. Hare developed a theory which became known as 'prescriptivism' (Hare, 1952, 1963). The prescriptivist line on practically was that the moral agent chooses his ultimate moral principles, and to choose a principle is to commit oneself to what the principle enjoins. 'I ought to do x' is seen as being like a command expressed to oneself, or like a firm statement of intention. The *practical force* of moral judgements then is expressed *via* the logical thesis that to assent to a moral judgement is to be committed to acting in terms of it; if one does not so act then one does not hold the principle. Such a position gave rise to many problems over weakness of will. Can I not still be said to hold a principle even if sometimes I weakly and blindly, or even perversely and deliberately, act against it?

Hare was emphatic that the rationality of moral judgements could not be explained by showing them as deducible from any set of factual premises – a moral 'ought' logically cannot be deduced from any set of 'is' propositions. This argument, which originated in Hume, was used as an apparent trump card against naturalists. It was Hare's version of Moore's 'naturalistic fallacy'. The rationality of moral judgements was said by Hare rather to be expressed *via* the idea of the 'universalizability' of moral judgements. If I say that I ought or ought not to do X then I am logically committed to saying that anyone in a similar position ought or ought not to do likewise. But this provides only a thin account of rationality. The account is correct in insisting that singular 'oughts' must be capable of being made universal by being connected with general rules, but those who see morality as rational are claiming to see more than consistency in it. For example, if I say that I ought not to walk on the cracks of the pavement then I am certainly committed to the rule that no one ought to, but the rule itself does not sound justifiable. Hare thinks that in practice people will not prescribe rules which are not in their self-interest, and dubs those who do 'fanatics'. But he cannot show that the fanatic is mistaken; all he can do is to weaken the appeal of fanaticism by invoking the utilitarian's generalized self-interest.

Dissatisfied with prescriptivism and its many difficulties, and with the aim of restoring rationality to morality in a sense stronger than consistency, some philosophers such as Philippa Foot (1958) or G.J. Warnock (1971) revived naturalism. What these forms of naturalism had in common was the attempt to show how morality was logically connected with concepts of harm and benefit. This certainly brought back objectivity and rationality to morality. To use Warnock's example, to triumph over one's enemies may be a splendid thing, but it must, objectively, be morally wrong, granted the premise that morality is logically connected with the concepts of harm and benefit plus some incontestable empirical premises about human reactions.

But neo-naturalism still has difficulties with the practical force of moral judgements. How do natural facts provide reasons for action unless we assume dubious premises such as that we all desire each other's benefit, or that my own benefit is furthered by that of others? The main problem with this neo-naturalism, however, is that either it makes morality too narrow in scope – confining it to matters of human harm and benefit – or it makes the conceptions of harm and benefit so wide that they are emptied of all meaning. For example, two consenting single adults who have a sexual encounter and who take contraceptive precautions cannot be said to be harming anyone (if 'harm' is to mean anything). Yet some people might condemn what they do on moral grounds. Now, whether or not we agree with this condemnation, we cannot rule it out on logical grounds as not being a moral condemnation. But this is precisely what we are committed to if morality is narrowly defined in terms of human harm and benefit. And what about harm and benefit to animals?

It should be noted that the moral philosophers after Moore – the emotivists, the prescriptivists and the neo-naturalists – all have in common that they assume a *metaphysical* naturalism. In other words, they all assume that the whole phenomenon of morality can be explained in terms of some combination of psychology, economics and sociology (plus, nowadays, socio-biology). At the moment, however, there are faint signs of a revival of interest in non-naturalistic view of morality. This has been brought about partly by the rediscovery of Hegel, and partly by a revival of Natural Law studies. At any rate, it provides a welcome shake to the kaleidoscope of moral philosophy.

No account of the subject would be complete without some reference to Existentialism. Continental philosophy has never been part of the main stream of Anglo-Saxon philosophy, but many of the concepts of Existentialism have been accepted by moral philosophers. For example, the idea of 'bad faith', of pretending to oneself that one is determined, that one has no choices so must just accept a way of life, was one discussed by J.-P. Sartre (1943) in a series of illuminating examples. Indeed, one beneficial influence which Existentialism exerted on Anglo-Saxon philosophy was *via* its more dramatic examples. This encouraged moral philosophers to abandon the thin examples offered by duties of returning library books or the rules of cricket in favour of more extended and full-blooded ones.

This use of more realistic examples, plus the desire to be applied to other subject-matters (such as medicine), plus the availability of more sophisticated logical techniques, all make moral philosophy a more worthwhile subject than it was 40 years ago.

BIBLIOGRAPHY

Aristotle. *Nicomachean Ethics*. Translated by Sir David Ross, London: Oxford University Press, 1954.

Foot, P. 1958. Moral beliefs. *Aristotelian Society Proceedings*. Collected in P. Foot, *Virtues and Vices*, Oxford: Blackwell, 1978; Berkeley: University of California Press.

Glover, J. 1984. *What Sort of People Should There Be*? Harmondsworth: Pelican Books.

Hare, R.M. 1952. *The Language of Morals*. Oxford: Clarendon Press; New York: Oxford University Press, 1964.

Hare, R.M. 1963. *Freedom and Reason*. Oxford: Clarendon Press; New York: Oxford University Press, 1965.

Hume, D. 1739. *A Treatise of Human Nature*. Ed. L.A. Selby-Bigge, Oxford: Clarendon Press, 1896. 2nd edn, 1978.

Hume, D. 1748. *An Enquiry Concerning Human Understanding*. Ed. L.A. Selby-Bigge, 2nd edn, Oxford: Clarendon Press, 1902. Revised by P.H. Nidditch, 1975.

Kant, I. 1785. *Groundwork of the Metaphysic of Morals*. Translated by H.J. Paton as *The Moral Law*, London: Hutchinson's University Library, 1948.

Mill, J.S. 1859. *Essay on Liberty*. Ed. M. Warnock, London: Collins, 1962.

Mill, J.S. 1863. *Utilitarianism*. Ed. M. Warnock, London: Collins, 1962.

Moore, G.E. 1903. *Principia Ethica*. Cambridge: Cambridge University Press.

Plato. *Republic*. Translated by Benjamin Jowett, 3rd edn, revised, Oxford: Clarendon Press, 1888. Reprinted New York: Sphere Books, 1970.

Rawls, J. 1955. Two concepts of rules. *Philosophical Review* 64, January, 3–32.

Ross, W.D. 1939. *Foundations of Ethics*. Oxford: Clarendon Press.

Sartre, J.-P. 1943. *Being and Nothingness*. Translated by Hazel Barnes, London: Methuen, 1957.

Smart, J.J.C. and Williams, B. 1973. *Utilitarianism: For and Against*. Cambridge: Cambridge University Press; New York: Cambridge University Press.

Stevenson, C.L. 1937. The emotive meaning of ethical terms. *Mind* 46(181), 14–31.

Warnock, G.J. 1971. *The Object of Morality*. London: Methuen; New York: Barnes and Noble.

Wittgenstein, L. 1953. *Philosophical Investigations*. Translated by G.E.M. Anscombe, Oxford: Blackwell.

Natural Law

N.E. SIMMONDS

It is not uncommon to find the term 'natural law' being applied to any philosophical theory that espouses a belief in the 'objectivity' of moral standards, or the possibility of moral knowledge. If we avoid this inflated usage, however, and seek to identify a natural law tradition that is to some extent distinct from other cognitivist moral theories, it is probably best to identify such a tradition in terms of three basic features. First, natural law theories regard morality as, in some sense, a body of precepts. Even if the theory has a broadly teleological character, it will not have a nakedly maximizing structure: rather, the teleology will serve to justify a body of rules or standards. Secondly, natural law theories take juridical equality as a fundamental assumption: men are assumed to be of equal standing before the law of nature. Even when the theory serves to justify unequal rights in the real circumstances of society, those unequal rights are justified by reference to principles that treat everyone equally. The tension between natural rights and positively established rights which is therefore implicit in the idea of juridical equality finds expression in the third basic feature of natural law theories: the way in which they approach the relationship between natural law and the positive law enacted by men. Natural law represents the ultimate objective foundation by reference to which positive laws must be evaluated. But positive law is nevertheless necessary, and is far more than just an imperfect reflection of natural law. Positive laws are required in part to induce compliance with standards that would not otherwise receive the obedience of weak or evil men; but they are required also to give concrete detail to the general requirements of natural law. Natural law may require, for example, that conduct in certain areas of social life should be coordinated, but it will not necessarily specify the precise form that coordination should take: natural law therefore requires the existence of positive law as a body of publicly ascertainable rules making coordination possible.

Perhaps the most significant metamorphosis of the natural law tradition is to be found in the shift from the position of Aquinas, which achieved pre-eminence in the later Middle Ages, to the theories of Grotius and Pufendorf in the 17th century. Most commentators have been struck by the change in character that natural law theory undergoes over this period, but there has been less agreement about what features actually mark the essential difference. One one view, the 17th-century writers put forward a theory of natural rights rather than a theory of natural law. But, although the 17th-century theories certainly display a more individualistic character, this is not invariably associated with the development of a rights-based theory: Pufendorf, for example, takes 'duty' as his basic concept rather than 'right'. On another view, the 17th-century writers offer a secular theory which can be contrasted with the theo-centric approach of Aquinas. For reasons that will be explained, this view must be rejected. A better way of comprehending the change of tone and approach that separates Aquinas from Grotius is by reference to the role that notions of 'good' play in their theories. For Aquinas, an account of what is good for man forms the central pillar around which an understanding of natural law must be constructed. The role of positive law is to provide for the good, thus considered. For Grotius and Pufendorf, on the other hand, the role of law is to provide a framework within which men who are self-seeking and who live in conditions of scarcity may live together in a social order that enables each to pursue his own good as he conceives it. Although it would clearly be absurd to portray writers such as Grotius and Pufendorf in the guise of fully fledged liberals making a dramatic break with the past, it is nevertheless some such change of emphasis and orientation that marks the distinctive character of the theories that emerged in this period.

Given the way in which natural law theories depend upon some deep notion of human equality, and yet frequently adopt a conservative standpoint towards the material inequalities of social life, various stratagems have been adopted in order to bridge the gap between ideal and reality. Thus, in 17th-century thought, a basic right to appropriate and enjoy the resources of the natural world is possessed by men equally, yet it serves to justify the unequal division of wealth and resources in established society. In Aquinas the tension appears and is resolved in a different form, within his central notion of the good. The Aristotelian view, that the best life for man is a life of philosophic contemplation accessible only to a leisured elite, is replaced in Aquinas by the idea that man's ultimate good lies in a beatific vision of God that is potentially accessible to everyone, but only in a life after death: the postulate of equality is preserved by moving its centre of gravity to another world. It is in this recurring tension between the ideal realm of equality and the material world of inequality that we find the basis for Marxist critiques of natural law theory and, indeed, of bourgeois legal thought more generally.

The orthodox position for the natural lawyers of the 17th century was that the content of natural law could be determined by reason, but that it derived its binding force from the divine will. The role of the notion of divine will within such theories was, in effect, to preserve a deontological character for natural law within a basically teleological form of argument. According to both Grotius and Pufendorf, reason shows us that human nature and circumstances being what they are, man can live in society only if certain basic rules are observed, e.g. rules defining and protecting rights of property. But this establishes only that such rules are requirements of utility: it does not show that they are requirements of natural law. Thus Pufendorf is careful to point out that, considered apart from the divine will, the precepts of natural law are merely 'like the prescriptions of physicians for the regimen of health' but are not laws (*De Officio Hominis et Civis*, 1682, 1.3.10). Actions are right and wrong (as opposed to wise and foolish) only in relation to a law: and a law, Pufendorf holds, presupposes the will of a superior. Natural law binds by virtue of the divine will. Given that we know certain rules to be necessary for social life, we know that such rules must be willed by God. Since God created our nature and fitted us with the capacities that make social life possible, it must be his will that we should live in society and observe those rules that are necessary for the existence of social life.

Grotius is often regarded as denying the role of the divine will in natural law, and he was so interpreted by Pufendorf, who attacked him on precisely this point. It is in fact unlikely that Grotius intended any such radical move away from the theo-centric approach. He says that natural law arguments would have a degree of validity even if God did not exist: but this may simply mean that the rules of natural law are not arbitrary but are founded on the nature of man and of his circumstances. In fact the idea of the divine will could not be so easily discarded, since it was employed in these theories to solve a number of fundamental problems. First was the question of how an action being obligatory differs from an action being one that we merely have good reason to perform. Second was the question of how moral reasons are related to prudential reasons: a problem that became particularly acute once morality was conceived of as a body of rules rather than as based on certain virtues as aspects of character. Lastly, and most significantly for our purposes, the notion of the divine will preserved a deontological character for natural law even while the reasoned arguments being offered were arguments of a basically utilitarian character. As we shall see, it was this feature of natural law thought that was later to bring about a dramatic transformation that some have seen as the death of natural law.

It might at first be thought that Hobbes represents an exception to the argument that 17th-century natural law theories ascribed a vital role to the divine will. There are of course large questions about whether Hobbes forms part of the natural law tradition at all. But it should be noted that, on the *concept* of natural law, Hobbes puts forward the orthodox view that precepts of reason can only be thought of as laws if they are considered to be products of the divine will (see ch. 15 of *Leviathan*, 1651).

As we have seen, the theo-centric framework of natural law theory preserved a deontological form for the precepts of natural law while allowing the substantive arguments (the need for certain rules given the known features of human nature, etc.) to take on a basically utilitarian character. What is often described as the 'critique' of natural law produced by David Hume in the 18th century is really best understood as a removal of the deontological framework, leaving only the utilitarian arguments in place. Hume removed God from the picture and offered a justification for rules of justice and property that appealed straightforwardly to arguments of 'convenience' or utility. Once this move was made, however, a dramatic sea-change was in process, for if the rules of justice and property are not prescribed by God, they are simply justified by utility. Of course, when Hume spoke of utility he did not have in mind a simple maximizing structure with a clearly defined maximand. But in the hands of Bentham, the notion of utility was developed in precisely that way.

Hume's removal of God from the picture of natural law was undoubtedly a decisive move. Yet the underlying utilitarian cast of much natural law writing meant that there was a good deal of continuity between Hume's predecessors and his immediate heirs. There had always been a tendency for the separate precepts of natural law to collapse into a general injunction to maximize utility, so that natural law ideas could continue to live a ghostly afterlife in the writings of utilitarians. Moreover, the reliance on speculative histories of, for example, the rise of private property, which had characterized the writings of Grotius and Pufendorf, was to take on a more descriptive and naturalistic character in the work of Adam Smith and the writers of the Scottish Enlightenment.

BIBLIOGRAPHY

Cairns, H. 1949. *Legal Philosophy from Plato to Hegel.* Baltimore: Johns Hopkins Press.

Crowe, M.B. 1977. *The Changing Profile of the Natural Law.* The Hague: Nijhoff.

d'Entreves, A.P. 1970. *Natural Law.* 2nd edn, London: Hutchinson.

Finnis, J. 1980. *Natural Law and Natural Rights.* Oxford: Clarendon Press; New York: Oxford University Press.

Forbes, D. 1975. *Hume's Philosophical Politics.* Cambridge: Cambridge University Press; New York: Cambridge University Press.

von Gierke, O. *Natural Law and the Theory of Society.* Trans. E. Barker, Cambridge: Cambridge University Press, 1958.

Haakonssen, K. 1981. *The Science of a Legislator: The Natural Jurisprudence of David Hume and Adam Smith.* Cambridge: Cambridge University Press.

Jones, J.W. 1940. *Historical Introduction to the Theory of Law.* Oxford: Clarendon Press.

O'Connor, D.J. 1967. *Aquinas and Natural Law.* London: Macmillan.

Simmonds, N.E. 1984. *The Decline of Juridical Reason.* Manchester: Manchester University Press.

Strauss, L. 1953. *Natural Right and History.* Chicago: Chicago University Press.

Tuck, R. 1979. *Natural Rights Theories.* Cambridge: Cambridge University Press; New York: Cambridge University Press.

Property

ALAN RYAN

Property rights are as fundamental to economics as scarcity and rationality. Unless some human agency has the right to control the use of whatever resource is in question nobody can set prices, and there will be no incentive for anyone to calculate costs of production. In much of their work, economists can, and do, take it for granted that everything of value (both tangible goods and intangible objects such as skills) has an owner, and that the owner's powers of control will correspond to the motivational assumptions of orthodox economic theory. That the free market and 'the liberal concept of ownership' (Honoré, 1961) imply one another is obvious enough, and rightly allows most economists to feel free to leave the nature of ownership to others, while they tackle the intricacies of market interactions. Although Mill and Marx accused their contemporaries of discussing economics as if all the world had the legal institutions of the North Atlantic seaboard, the accusation is not wholly just – and both of them willingly exempted Smith in any case. For many purposes, the economy an investigator is concerned with can be assumed to have the legal background of the countries of the North Atlantic littoral. Nor have economists been reluctant to broaden their interest in property. Speculation about the possibilities of socialism, the analysis of the economics of slavery, inquiries into the agriculture of developing countries and very much more besides have all provoked investigations into the effects of particular systems of property rights. Defences of the free market based on individual private property (A. Buchanan, 1985), explorations of the outlook for workers' cooperatives (Vanek, 1970), assessment of the efficiency of American slavery (Fogel and Engerman, 1974) and the literature provoked by Coase's demonstration of the irrelevance to overall welfare of the distribution of property rights are only a fraction of what economists have done.

No definition of ownership is wholly satisfactory for all purposes; 'the right of property is the right of dealing with things in the most absolute fashion the law allows', declares the French civil code, and it is echoed in many other codes. That seizes on two crucial things. First, it is not an infringement of my *ownership* of this knife that I may not stick it in your chest. The law allows nobody to stick a knife in anybody's chest, but whatever anyone may lawfully do with any knife, I (and nobody else) may do with this one. Second, the owner must have *all* the rights anyone can have over the things in question. The suggestion sometimes encountered in textbooks that ownership can be reduced to a 'right to an income' is inadequate, because it mistakes one element in ownership for the whole. Ownership certainly grounds the right to an income, but many rights to an income are grounded on something other than ownership, and ownership embraces other rights than the right to an income. The *code civile* is right to emphasize this, but does not deal with our intuition that if the law circumscribed too closely what an owner might do with his 'property', we might hesitate to call it his property at all. If, for instance, nobody could leave land to their children, or sell a freehold in it, or raise a mortgage on it, we should be doubtful whether individuals could be said to 'own' it at all. The crucial element in the '*ius utendi et abutendi*' is the ultimate power of disposal. It is, therefore, not only a question of having all the rights the law allows, but of the law conferring on some person or institution the right of disposal. The same observation casts doubt on theories of so-called 'new property rights'. As did theorists of the 'new class', writers who have claimed to identify 'new property rights' have observed, rightly, that in a socialist society where there is supposedly no private ownership of the means of production, individuals in favoured positions may exert the same power as did capitalist owners of businesses in the past or have the same security of occupation and income as did those owners; similarly, those protected by trade unions in mixed economies may have the same security as those who purchased military commissions or government offices in the 18th century. Where they have gone wrong is in thinking of these as property rights. For they have simply ignored the question of who has the right of disposal. The may well be right to think that these new powers are as important as ownership and even that they confer on people powers similar to those which ownership confers. They are wrong to think that they amount to ownership.

Until the 18th century, and perhaps later, property was a central concern of political theorists. Plato began a long tradition in demanding that the rulers of the ideal republic should have no property. They should possess in common the common property of the republic, to separate their private interests from the public interest. He was not concerned, as St Paul was, to condemn avarice and urge men to set their hearts on the goods of the next world; rather he was concerned to avoid class warfare and to secure uncorrupt leadership. The lower classes were welcome to engage in their usual occupations and hang on to whatever few possessions those occupations yielded. Aristotle began an equally long tradition by observing that common property would not be regarded as 'belonging to us all' but as 'belonging to no one'. Unless owned as private property, land and other resources would be neglected. But although private property was essential if people were to live in moderate comfort, Aristotle did not approave of the market; he complained that profit making was a distraction from the proper use of goods – which existed to be consumed not traded – and that lending money at interest was doubly wicked, because it was setting barren metal to breed. Ownership, and especially land ownership, existed in order to give the better sort of people the leisure to cultivate their talents and govern wisely.

Neither the Greeks nor the Romans had much use for the conception of individual rights which provides the framework of modern discussions of property. None the less, it was the Roman Law conception of ownership that bred modern theories of natural right and of a natural right of property, just as it was Roman thinking about practical politics that bred a rival habit of thought. This is the tradition of 'statecraft' and is exemplified in the work of Machiavelli and Harrington, and to a lesser extent in Hume and Smith. A crucial question to be asked of any system of property rights is whether it favours political stability and political liberty. The question is one of political sociology – what kind of property encourages public spirit in the citizen, and what kind encourages 'corruption' in the ruling class? The exemplary figure of the Roman farmer, who kept his weapons over his fireplace and would fight for republican institutions against enemies from without and would-be tyrants from within, haunts this tradition. Adam Smith, who is rightly thought of as the apostle of the modern economy, was equally taken with the ancient conviction that military valour, public spirit and free institutions were inconsistent with a wholly commercial economy. Small, independent farmers were the source of republican virtue. Their independence was not the same thing as modern individualism; they must be independent of the wealthy but they would not think of their land as theirs so much as their family's. In Machiavelli, the argument is entirely nostalgic; by the time of Harrington, there is more understanding of the impossibility of simply recreating the Roman republic; Hume and Smith saw that the modern, fluid, commercial world in which money is the great solvent of other forms of property cannot be escaped and cannot be wholly regretted. It is then an open question what balance of social forces can preserve freedom. It goes without saying that this 'political' conception of liberty with its roots in stable, landed property is not congenial to critics to the welfare state and socialism, who identify freedom with what Smith termed 'the simple system of natural liberty' or freedom of contract.

The 'statecraft' tradition does not enquire into the origins of property rights, nor into the justice of present distributions of property, but only into their political results. The natural law tradition (and its successors) is concerned with justice, and with what Locke called the 'original' of property. By 'original' he did not mean its historical origins but its moral logic. The crucial questions which this tradition faces are not sociological but moral – what grounds a valid claim to ownership; is there a conflict between the goals of property as an institution and the distribution of property rights in practice? From Locke, through Hume, Rousseau, Kant, Hegel, Mill and their successors, a variety of answers was offered, some of which had a clear tendency to justify the status quo, some of which, as in Rousseau on the one hand and Mill on the other, led to its rejection. Natural rights theories like Locke's held that each individual had a right to appropriate and use the unowned bounty of nature; the exercise of his natural liberty was enough to give him the ownership of it. Did it follow that the propertyless labourer in contemporary society had been cheated? Locke thought not; so long as he can earn a livelihood by his labour, he can 'appropriate' what he needs. But it does follow that owners who fail to provide employment commit an injustice. Rousseau held the same view, but complained that in practice the owners reduced the propertyless to near slavery and that even where they did not they corrupted them in other ways.

Hume and Mill offered a utilitarian justification for property. Unless these are rules of 'meum et tuum', there will be no efficient employment of the world's resources; as to what rules should govern ownership, that is a matter of expediency. But where Hume thought that expediency favoured custom and prescription even at the price of considerable inefficiency, Mill argued for positive governmental pressure by way of the law on property to promote efficiency on the one hand and the creation of an economy of producer cooperatives on the other.

In a very different idiom, Kant and Hegel also explained property as the expression of human freedom. Human beings, who alone possessed free-will, conferred value on the merely material objects they took into ownership. Without ownership, the world of mere material objects is inert, useless and of no value. But if property in some form or other is essential, the particular form is a matter for different governments to decide for themselves. Kant and Hegel were fierce enemies of the feudal hangovers which disfigured the German states of their day. Neither advocated complete laissez-faire, but since property expresses human sovereignty over nature, it must be open to any individual to acquire property his own work. This rather romantic justification of property rights was turned on its head by Marx, when he declared that the irrationality of capitalism and its evident moral failings showed that so long as there was property at all, things would be sovereign over men and men would continue to suffer alienation. On the whole this argument has appealed to Marxist philosophers rather than Marxist economists; the economist feels he can analyse the consequences of different systems of public ownership, but has little to say about what a world without the very concept of property would be like.

In the mixed economies of the West, some kind of utilitarian justification of property is the 'common sense' of politics, even if most writers now acknowledge that the defence of private property needs to take into account questions of justice as well as questions of overall efficiency. John Rawls's insistence on appraising economic institutions from the standpoint of the representative least-favoured person (Rawls, 1972) has captured the imagination of writers of a broadly, but uneasily utilitarian persuasion. The least abashed intellectual heirs of 18th- and 19th-century utilitarianism are the defenders of the so-called 'economic theory of property rights'. In this account the property rights characteristic of developed capitalist economies came into existence by an evolutionary process which allowed production to proceed in ever more efficient ways. The capitalist firm, say, exists because a system of property rights developed which allowed entrepreneurs to act swiftly and decisively. One implication is that a government which forced some other ownership pattern on the economy would find that evolutionary pressures would gradually reintroduce de facto capitalism and that only political repression could preserve socialism. The value of property rights lies in the pattern of resource management (in the widest sense) that they promote; what Marx condemned as 'bourgeois' forms of ownership create the most efficient management. Critics complain that this suffers from the same defects as other doctrines of the 'survival of the fittest' – it takes its standard of fitness from the behaviour of the institutions it explains. But this is certainly one place where the discussion of property rights most vividly engages the concerns of lawyers, economists and philosophers alike.

BIBLIOGRAPHY

Alchian, A. and Demsetz, H. 1972. Production, information costs, and economic organization. *American Economic Review* 62(5), December, 777–95.

Buchanan, A. 1985. *Ethics, Efficiency and the Market.* Totowa, NJ: Rowman & Allanheld; Oxford: Clarendon Press.

Buchanan, J.M. 1986. *Liberty, Market and State.* Brighton: Wheatsheaf Books.

Coase, R. 1960. The problem of social cost. *Journal of Law and Economics* 3, 1–44.

Demsetz, H. 1967. Towards a theory of property rights. *American Economic Review*, Papers and Proceedings, 57, May, 347–59.

Fogel, R.W. and Engerman, S.L. 1974. *Time on the Cross.* New York: Little Brown.

Honoré, A.M. 1961. Ownership. In *Oxford Essays in Jurisprudence*, ed. A.G. Guest, London: Oxford University Press.

Rawls, J. 1972. *A Theory of Justice.* Oxford: Clarendon Press; Cambridge, Mass.: Harvard University Press, 1971.

Vanek, J. 1970. *The General Theory of Labour-managed Market Economies.* Ithaca and London: Cornell University Press.

Property Rights

ARMEN A. ALCHIAN

PRIVATE PROPERTY RIGHTS. A property right is a socially enforced right to select uses of an economic good. A private property right is one assigned to a specific person and is alienable in exchange for similar rights over other goods. Its strength is measured by its probability and costs of enforcement which depend on the government, informal social actions and prevailing ethical and moral norms. In simpler terms, no one may legally use or affect the physical circumstances of goods to which you have private property rights without your approval or compensation. Under hypothetically perfect private property rights none of my actions with my resources may affect the physical attributes of any other person's private property. For example, your private property rights to your computer restrict my and everyone else's permissible behaviour with respect to your computer, and my private property rights restrict you and everyone else with respect to whatever I own. It is important to note that it is the physical use and condition of a good that are protected from the action of others, not its exchange value.

Private property rights are assignments of rights to choose among inescapably incompatible uses. They are not contrived or imposed restrictions on the feasible uses, but assignments of exclusive rights to choose among such uses. To restrict me from growing corn on my land would be an imposed, or contrived restriction denying some rights without transferring them to others. To deny me the right to grow corn on my land would restrict my feasible uses without enlarging anyone else's feasible physical uses. Contrived or unnecessary restrictions are not the basis of private property rights. Also, because those restrictions typically are imposed against only some people, those who are not so restrained obtain a 'legal monopoly' in the activity from which others are unnecessarily restricted.

Under private property rights any mutually agreed contractual terms are permissible, though not all are necessarily supported by governmental enforcement. To the extent that some contractual agreements are prohibited, private property rights are denied. For example, it may be considered illegal to agree to work for

232

over 10 hours a day, regardless of how high a salary may be offered. Or it may be illegal to sell at a price above some politically selected limit. These restrictions reduce the strength of private property, market exchange and contracts as means of coordinating production and consumption and resolving conflicts of interest.

ECONOMIC THEORY AND PRIVATE PROPERTY RIGHTS. A successful analytic formulation of private property rights has resulted in an explanation of the method of directing and coordinating uses of economic resources in a private property system (i.e. a capitalistic or a 'free enterprise' system). That analysis relies on convex preferences and two constraints: a production possibility and a private property exchange constraint, expressible biblically as 'Thou Shall Not Steal', or mathematically, as the conservation of the exchange value of one's goods.

For the decentralized coordination of productive specialization to work well, according to the well known principles of comparative advantage, in a society with diffused knowledge, people must have secure, alienable private property rights in productive resources and products tradeable at mutually agreeable prices at low costs of negotiating reliable contractual transactions. That system's ability to coordinate diffused information results in increased availability of more highly valued goods as well as of those becoming less costly to produce. The amount of rights to goods one is willing to trade, and in which private property rights are held, is the measure of value; and that is not equivalent to an equal quantity of goods not held as private property (for example, government property). It probably would not be disputed that stronger private property rights are more valuable then weaker rights, that is, a seller of a good would insist on larger amounts of a good with weaker private property rights than if private property rights to the goods were stronger.

FIRMS, FIRM-SPECIFIC RESOURCES AND THE STRUCTURE OF PROPERTY RIGHTS. Though private property rights are extremely important in enabling greater realization of the gains from specialization in production, the partitionability, separability and alienability of private property rights enables the organization of cooperative joint productive activity in the modern corporate firm. This less formally recognized, but nevertheless important, process of cooperative production relies heavily on partitioning and specialization in the components of private property rights. Yet, this method is often misinterpreted as unduly restrictive and debilitating to the effectivness and social acceptability of private property rights. To see the error, an understanding of the nature of the firm is necessary, especially in its corporate form, which accounts for an enormous portion of economic production. The 'firm', usually treated as an output-generating 'blackbox', is a contractually related collection of resources of various cooperating owners. Its distinctive source of enhanced productivity is 'team' productivity, wherein the product is not a sum of separable outputs each of which is attributable to specific cooperating inputs, but instead is a nondecomposable, non-attributable value produced by the group. Thus, for something produced jointly by several separately owned resources, it is not possible to identify or define how much of the final output value each resource could be said to produce separately. Instead, a marginal product value for each input is definable and measurable.

Whereas specialized production under comparative advantage and trade is directed in a decentralized process by market price and spot exchanges, productivity in the team, called the firm, relies on long-term, constraing contracts among owners who have invested in resources specialized to the group of inputs in that firm. In particular, some of the inputs are specialized to the team in that once they enter the firm their alternative (salvage) values become much lower than in the firm. They are called 'firm-specific'. In the firm, firm-specific inputs tend to be owned in common, or else contracts among separate owners of the various inter-specific resources restrict their future options to those beneficial to that group of owners as a whole rather than to any individual. These contractual restrictions are designed to restrain opportunism and 'moral hazard' by individual owners, each seeking a portion of each other's firm-specific, expropriable composite quasi-rent. Taking only extremes for expository brevity, the other 'general' resources would lose no value if shifted elsewhere. A firm, then, is a group of firm-specific and some general inputs bound by constraining contracts, producing a non-decomposable end-product value. As a result, the activities and operation of the team will be most intensively controlled and monitored by the firm-specific input owners, who gain or lose the most from the success or failure of the 'firm'. In fact, they are typically considered the 'owners' or 'employers' or 'bosses' of the firm, though in reality the firm is a cooperating collection of resources owned by different people.

Firm-specific resources can be non-human. Professional firms – in law, architecture, medicine – are comprised of teams of people who would be less valuable elsewhere in other groups. They hire non-human general capital, for example building and equipment. The contract, which defines 'hiring', depends on the specificity and generality, not on human or non-human attributes nor on who is richer. Incidentally, 'industrial democracy' arrangements are rare, because the owners of more general resources have less interest in the firm than those of specific resources.

THE CORPORATION AND SPECIALIZATION IN PRIVATE PROPERTY RIGHTS. In a corporation the resources owned by the stockholders are those the values of which are specific to the firm. The complexities in specialization in exercise of the components of property rights and the associated contractual restraints have led some people to believe that the corporation tends to insulate (e.g. 'separate') decisions of use from the bearing of the consequences, (i.e. control from ownership) and thereby has undermined the capacity of a private property system to allocate resources to higher market value uses. For example, it has been argued that diffused stock ownership has so separated management and control of resources from 'ownership' that managers are able to act without sufficient regard to market values and the interests of the diffused stockholders. Adam Smith was among the first to propound that belief. Whatever the empirical validity, the logical analysis underlying those charges rests on misperceptions of the structure of private property rights in the corporation and the nature of the competitive markets for control and ownership, which tend to restrain such managers. What individual managers seek, and what those who survive are able successfully to do in the presence of competition for control, are very different things.

An advantage of the corporation is its pooling of sufficient wealth in firm-specific resources for large-scale operations. Pooling is enabled if shares of ownership are alienable private property, thereby permitting individuals to eliminate dependence of their time path of consumption on the temporal pattern of return from firm-specific investments. Alienability is enabled if the shares have limited liability, which frees each stockholder from dependence on the amount of wealth of every other stockholder. The resultant ability to tolerate anonymity, that is, disinterest in exactly who are the other shareholders, enables better market alienability.

When voluntary separability of decision authority over firm-specific resources from their market value consequences is added to alienability, the ability to specialize in managerial decisions and talent (control) without also having to bear the risk of all the value consequences, enables achievement of beneficial specialization in production and coordination of cooperative productivity. Specialization is not necessarily something that is confined to the production of different end products; it applies equally to different productive inputs or talents. Voluntary partitionability and alienability of the component rights enable advantageous specialization (sometimes called 'separation') in (a) exercise of rights to make decisions about uses of resources and of (b) bearing the consequent market or exchange values. The former is sometimes called 'control' and the latter, 'ownership'. Separability enables the achievement of the gains from specialization in selecting and monitoring uses, evaluating the results, and bearing the risk of consequent future usefulness and value. Because different uses have different prospective probability distributions of outcomes, and because outcomes are differentially sensitive to monitoring the prior decisions, separability and alienability of the component rights permit gains from specialization in holding and exercising the partitionable rights.

Thus, the modern corporation relies on limited liability to enhance alienability and on partitionability of components of private property rights in order to achieve gains from large-scale specialization in directing productive team activity and talents. Rather than destroying or undermining the effectiveness of private property rights, the alleged 'separation' enables effective, productive 'specialization' in exercising private property rights as methods of control and coordination.

GOVERNMENT PROPERTY RIGHTS. It might be presumed that government property rights in a democracy are similar to corporate property with diffused stockholdings and should yield similar results. The analogy would be apt if each voting citizen had a share of votes equivalent to one's share of the wealth in the community, and if a person could shift wealth among governments, as one can among different corporations. If, for example, one could buy and sell land (as assets capturing essentially most of the value of whatever the government does in that particular state) in several different governments and could vote in each in proportion to the value of that 'land', then government property would be closer to private property in its effects. But it is difficult to take that possibility seriously. The nature of government, public, or communal property rights surely depend on the kind of government. Because these are so vaguely and indefinitely defined, attempts to deduce formally the consequences of resource allocation and behaviour under each have been hampered.

NON-EXISTENT PROPERTY RIGHTS. Not all resources are satisfactorily controlled by private property rights. Air, water, electromagnetic radiation, noises and views are some examples. Water under my land flows to yours. Sounds and light from my land impinge on yours. Other forms of control are then designed, for example, political or social group decisions and actions, though these other forms are sometimes employed for ideological or political purposes, even where private property rights already exist.

If these other forms permit open, free entry with every user sharing equally and obtaining the average return, use will be excessive. Extra uses will be made with an increased realized total value that is less than the cost added, that is, the social product value is not maximized. This occurs because the marginal yield is less than the average to each user, to which each user responds. So, use occurs to the point where the average yield is brought down to marginal cost, with the consequence that the marginal yield is less than the marginal cost – often exampled as excessive congestion on a public road or public park, or over-fishing of communal, free access fishing areas. The classic 'communal property' implication that apples on the public apple tree are never allowed to ripen is an extreme example of the proposition that property rights, other than private, reduce conformity of resource uses to market revealed values. Alternatively, if communal property rights mean that incumbent users can block more users, the resource will be under-utilized as incumbents maximize their individual yield, which is the average, not the marginal. This results in fewer users. Though more users or uses would lower the average value to the incumbents and hence dissuade a higher rate of use, the addition to the total group value (of the extra use) exceeds the extra costs. Examples are public, low tuition colleges that restrict entry to maximize the 'quality' of those who are educated – that is, to maximize the average yield of those admitted. Some labour unions (i.e. teamsters) are examples of similar situations.

A mistaken inference commonly suggested by the example of fishermen who overfish unowned lakes is that independent sellers with open access to customers will 'over-congest' in product variety and advertising to catch customers, with unheeded costs borne by other sellers. If, for example, Pall Mall cigarettes attract some customers from Camel, the loss to Camel is the reduced value of Camel-specific resources, not its lost sales revenue. General resources will be released from making Camels for use elsewhere with no social loss. But Camel-specific resources fall in value by the extent to which Pall Mall's product is better or cheaper. Camel's loss is more than offset by the sum of Pall Mall's increased net income plus the transfer gain to customers from lower prices or better quality. The loss to Camel is not from new entry itself, but from its incorrect forecasts of its earlier investment value. It is presumed here that mistaken forecasts should not be protected by prohibiting the unexpected future improvements. This differs from the over-fishing case in that consumers, in contrast to fish, have property rights in what they pay and what they buy. If every fish had a separate owner or owned itself, none would allow it to be caught unless paid enough, and over-fishing would not occur. One owner of all the fish is unnecessary; it suffices that each fish (or potential customer) be owned by someone who can refuse to buy. (Of course, unless the lake were owned, the lake surface might be overcongested with too many fishermen, each fishing to a lesser area, even if the fish were owned.)

Ownership of tradeable rights by customers is the feature that is missing in the over-fishing, over-congestion case. Because rights to (or 'of') the fish or whales need not be bought, over-fishing does not imply over-customering where customers own rights to what the competing sellers are seeking. Otherwise, customers could be caught like fish, wherein sellers would be competing both to (1) establish property rights over the customers and to (2) possess those rights. Costly redundant competition for initial establishment of rights could be avoided simply by establishing customers' rights to themselves, as in fact done. If the preceding seems fanciful, replace 'fish' with people and the lake surface with streets on which taxi-drivers cruise for customers. Excessive costs will be incurred in competition for use of unowned, valuable resources, in this case, the streets.

MUTUAL PROPERTY RIGHTS. 'Mutual' forms of organization are used apparently in order to sustain the maximum average per member, or to reserve for the incumbent members any greater group value from more members. Mutual private property, a form that has barely been analysed, does not permit anonymous alienability of interests in what are otherwise private property rights. A 'mutual' member can transfer its interest to other people only upon permission of the other mutually owing members or their agents. Fraternal, social and country clubs are examples. These activities have not typically been viably organized and their services sold, as for example, in restaurants and health and exercise gymnasia. The intragroup-specific resources are themselves the members (erstwhile customers) who interact and create their social utility. More members affect each incumbent's realized utility in two ways: by social compatibility and by congestion. An outside, separate owner interested in the maximum value of the organization, but not the maximum average per member, could threaten to sell more memberships which, although enabling a larger total social value with more members, would reduce the average value to the existing members. This is an example of the earlier analysed difference between maximizing the average yield per input rather than the total yield by admitting more members, who while they would be made better off than if not admitted nevertheless reduce the average value to the incumbent members. In addition, the ability of newcomers to compensate incumbents for any loss in the individual (average) value to incumbent members is restrained if

237

the membership fee were to go instead to an outside owner of the club. To the extent that a pecuniary compensation, via an initiation fee, were paid to an outside owner and exceeded the reduction in their average individual and total group utility, newcomers would be admitted, and the outside owner would gain, but incumbent members would lose their composite quasi-rent of their interpersonal sociability. (It is not yet well understood why, aside from tax reasons, the mutual form occurs in savings and loans and insurance firms.)

TORTS, CONDITIONAL AND UNASSIGNED PROPERTY RIGHTS. Private property rights may exist in principle, but, quite sensibly, not be blindly and uncompromisingly enforced against all possible 'usurpers'. For example, situations arise in which someone's presumed private property rights do not exclude an 'invader's' use. Accidental or emergency use of some other person's private property without prior permission constitutes an example, sometimes called a 'tort'. Another possibility is that the property rights are so ill-defined that whether a right has been usurped or already belonged to the alleged 'usurper' is unclear. For example, my newly planted tree may block the view from your land. But did you have a right to look across my land? If the rights to views (or light rays) were clearly defined and assigned, we could negotiate a price for preserving the view or my putting up a tree, depending upon which was more valuable to the both of us and with payment going to whoever proved to have the rights. Or, while sailing on a lake, to escape a sudden storm and save my boat and life, I use your dock without your prior permission. Did I violate any of your rights, or did your rights not include the right to exclude users in my predicament? If such emergency action is deemed appropriate, then rights to use of the dock are not all yours, as you may have thought. Whereas in the tree and view case, where a prior negotiation might have avoided a 'tort' (except that initially we did not agree about who had what rights), in the emergency use of the dock, prior negotiation was unfeasible. If prior negotiation is uneconomic, rights to that emergency use 'should' and will exist if that use is the most valuable use of the resource under the postulated circumstances. And compensation may or may not be required to the erstwhile 'owner'. The principle underlying such a legal principle seems straightforward and consistent with principles of efficient economic behaviour. It suffices for present purposes merely to call attention to this aspect of economic efficiency underlying the law.

Scottish Enlightenment

JOHN ROBERTSON

Between 1740 and 1790 Scotland provided one of the most distinguished branches of the European Enlightenment. David Hume and Adam Smith were the pre-eminent figures in this burst of intellectual activity; and around them clustered a galaxy of major thinkers, including Francis Hutcheson, Lord Kames, Adam Ferguson, William Robertson, Thomas Reid, Sir James Steuart and John Millar. The interests of individual thinkers ranged from metaphysics to the natural sciences; but the distinctive achievements of the Scottish Enlightenment as a whole lay in those fields associated with the enquiry into 'the progress of society' – history, moral and political philosophy and, not least, political economy.

In the European context, Scotland's was a characteristically 'provincial' Enlightenment. Conscious of their membership of a wider movement, the Scottish thinkers cultivated connections with Paris, the Enlightenment's acknowledged metropolitan centre. But the Scottish Enlightenment is perhaps best understood when it is compared with the Enlightenment in France's provinces, or in the provincial states of Italy and Germany. The concern with economic improvement and its moral and political conditions and consequences was as urgent, for instance, in the distant Kingdom of Naples as in Scotland; and political economy was equally absorbing to the Neapolitan philosopher-reformers Genovesi and Galiani.

At the same time, the experience of Scotland in the 18th century was distinctive in a number of respects, which offered a particular stimulus to Scottish thinkers. First of all, there was the actual achievement of economic growth. Slow in coming, but increasingly perceptible, it gave Scottish thinkers an unusually direct acquaintance with the phenomena of development. Political change was also significant. The Union of 1707 with England was in no simple sense the cause of Scotland's economic growth (or the precondition of its Enlightenment). But the sacrifice of the nation's independent parliament for the opportunity of free trade with England and its empire highlighted the problem of the institutional conditions of economic development. Most dramatic of all were the changes in religion and culture. The fierce, convenanting presbyterianism of the 17th century was dissipated, as the 'Moderate' group of clergy rose to power in the Kirk. The four universities of Edinburgh, Glasgow, Aberdeen and St Andrews were reformed, allowing professorial specialization; and around the universities flourished a vigorous informal culture of voluntary clubs, most famous of which was the Select Society of Edinburgh. Together these changes secured for Scottish thinkers unprecedented intellectual freedom and social support; and they provided an object lesson in the importance of the moral and cultural as well as the material dimensions of progress.

Nothing in Scotland's comparatively successful provincial experience, moreover, inclined its Enlightenment in a very radical direction. It was not that the Scottish thinkers were complacent: on particular issues they were anxious to influence the leaders of Scottish society. But where in backward provinces like Naples, Enlightenment thinking was programmatic, even utopian, the thought of the Scottish Enlightenment was characterized by a relatively detached, analytic interest in the underlying mechanisms of society's development.

Against the background of Scotland's particular provincial experience, it was natural for the Scottish thinkers to study economic phenomena in the framework of a wider enquiry. There were three principal dimensions to that enquiry: the historical, the moral and the institutional.

The historical theory of the Scottish Enlightenment developed a line of argument from later 17th-century natural jurisprudence, a tradition made familiar to the Scots by its incorporation in the moral philosophy curriculum of the reformed universities. Discarding the older jurisprudential thesis of the contractual foundations of society and government, the Scots focused on the new insights of Pufendorf and Locke into the origin and development of property. According to Pufendorf, there had never been an original state of common ownership of land and goods; from the first, property was the result of individual appropriation. As increasing numbers made goods scarce, individual property became the norm, and systems of justice and government were established to secure it. What the Scots added to this argument was a scheme of specific stages of social development: the hunting, the pastoral, the agricultural and the commercial. At each of these four stages the extent of property ownership was related to the society's means of subsistence, and both shaped the nature and sophistication of the society's government. Different versions of the theory were offered by Adam Ferguson in his *Essay on the History of Civil Society* (1767) and by John Millar in his *Origin of the Distinction of Ranks* (1770), and underlay Lord Kames's investigations into legal history and William Robertson's historical narratives. The *locus classicus* of the theory, however, was Adam Smith's *Lectures on Jurisprudence*, delivered to his students in Glasgow in the early 1760s.

As Smith's exposition makes particularly clear, the stages theory of social development provided the historical premises for political economy. An explicitly conjectural theory – a model of society's 'natural' progress – it provided a framework for a comparably theoretical treatment of economic development as 'the natural progress of opulence'. By positing the systematic interrelation of economic activity, property and government, with consequences which could be neither foreseen nor controlled by individuals, the theory also established the essential irreversibility of the development process. Short of a natural catastrophe, it demonstrated, the advent of commercial society was unavoidable.

The moral thought of the Scottish Enlightenment was closely related to the historical, sharing a common origin in 17th-century natural jurisprudence. Here the inspiration was the jurisprudential thinkers' increasingly sophisticated treatment of needs. These, it was recognized, could no longer be thought of primarily in relation to subsistence; with the progress of society, needs must be understood to cover a much wider range of scarce goods, luxuries as well as necessities. The potential of this insight was seen by every Scottish moral philosopher, but again it was Smith who exploited it to the full, in the *Theory of Moral Sentiments* (1759). Beyond the most basic necessities, Smith acknowledged, men's needs were always relative, a matter of status and emulation, of bettering one's individual condition. But it was precisely the vain desires of the rich and the envy of others which served, by 'an invisible hand', to stimulate men's industry and hence to increase the stock of goods available for all ranks.

Such an argument, however, had to overcome two of the most deeply entrenched convictions of European moral thought: the Aristotelian view that the distribution of goods was a matter for justice, and the classical or civic humanist view that luxury led to corruption and the loss of moral virtue. The Scots answered the first more confidently (but perhaps less satisfactorily) than the second. Following Grotius, Hobbes and Pufendorf, they defined justice in exclusively corrective terms, setting aside questions of distribution. On the issue of corruption, they were divided. Hume, who ridiculed fears of luxury, was the most confident; Ferguson, who defiantly reasserted the ideal of virtue, the least. Smith was closer to Hume in preferring propriety to virtue, at least for the great majority; but he showed that he shared Ferguson's doubts when he added, at the end of his life, that the disposition to admire the rich and the great did tend to corrupt moral sentiments. At a fundamental level, however, there was general agreement. As a consequence of the progress of society, the multiplication of needs was not only irreversible; it was the essential characteristic of a 'cultivated' or 'civilized' as distinct from a 'barbarian' society. And civilization, however morally ambiguous, was preferable to barbarism. With consensus on this, the moral premises of political economy were secure.

The definition of justice in simple corrective terms provided the starting-point for the institutional dimension of the Scottish enquiry. The priority of any government, the Scots believed, must be the security of life and property, ensuring every individual liberty under the law. This, as Smith put it, was freedom 'in our present sense of the word'; and there was a general confidence that it was tolerably secure under the governments of modern Europe, including the absolute monarchies. In principle, individual liberty was a condition of a fully commercial society: its provision, therefore, was the institutional premise of political economy.

Few of the Scots took institutional analysis beyond this relatively simple, if vital, point; the theory of the modern commercial state was not a Scottish achievement. But Hume and Smith did get further than the rest, identifying and exploring a two-fold problem in the government of commercial society. Most urgently, they argued that it was necessary to limit the opportunities for governmental aggrandizement at the expense of 'productive' society, by confining government to the minimum necessary provision of justice, defence and public works. In the longer run, as the lower ranks of society acquired material and moral independence, it would also be necessary to satisfy their demands for an extension of citizenship and enlargement of political liberty. It was the responsibility of legislators, Hume and Smith believed, gradually to adapt institutions to meet these needs. Both outlined models by which legislators might proceed, Hume reworking the institutional concepts of the classical, civic tradition in his 'Idea of a perfect Commonwealth', Smith elaborating the principles of parliamentary sovereignty in his exemplary vision of British–American imperial union.

A large part of the originality of the Scottish Enlightenment's conception of political economy lay in this exploration of the historical, moral and institutional framework of economic activity. But of course the Scots also engaged directly in economic analysis; and one such work of analysis, Adam Smith's *Wealth of Nations* (1776), so outshone all others that it seemed to establish political economy as a science in its own right.

The Scots' attention naturally focused on growth. In contemporary terms, the issue was the means by which a poor country (such as Scotland) could best hope to catch up on a rich country (such as England). The alternatives, canvassed afresh by Hume in his *Political Discourses* (1752), were those aired in the Scottish debate before the Union, fifty years earlier: free trade to take advantage of the poor country's lower wages, or protection and credit creation to assist its manufactures. An optimist, Hume favoured the free trade alternative. Sir James Steuart countered in his *Principles of Political Economy* (1767) that rich nations would not permit free trade to their disadvantage, and that protection and credit creation were therefore essential. Unfortunately for Steuart, his arguments were simply ignored in the *Wealth of Nations*. Smith was agnostic about the prospects for poor countries; but he was unequivocal about free trade. The uninhibited expansion of the market was necessary, he explained, to achieve the maximum extension of the division of labour and the optimum allocation of capital, the twin motors of growth.

Smith's confidence in the powers of the market was the cornerstone of more than his explanation of growth. It shaped his entire presentation of political economy. In writing the *Wealth of Nations*, Smith consciously set himself to achieve the standards of simplicity, coherence and comprehensiveness which he associated with succesful philosophical systems, and with the Newtonian philosophy in particular. What gravity was to Newton's astonomy, the market was to Smith's political economy. For the market was not simply the matrix of growth. It was also, he believed, the mechanism by which the fruits of growth were distributed, so that the unprecedented inequality of commercial society was offset by an equally unprecedented increase in the standard of living of even the lowest and poorest ranks. (As a means of improving the condition of the poor, in other words, the market was far more effective than any previous arrangement guided by the notion of distributive justice. It was the 'invisible hand' through which the vain desires of the rich were transformed into an increased stock of goods for all). In addition, the market could help to check the growth of unproductive government, since in Smith's view most institutions could be subjected to some degree to its disciplines. The market, in short, was cast in the *Wealth of Nations* as the hub of a complete, virtually self-sustaining economic system.

It was the systematic and comprehensive analysis which this faith in the market made possible, rather than simply the account of growth, which set the *Wealth of Nations* above any other work of Enlightenment political economy, Scottish or European. To be systematic and comprehensive had earlier been the ambition, at least, of Quesnay's *Tableau Economique* (1758–9), Genovesi's *Lezioni di Commercio* (1765) and Steuart's *Principles*; but the *Wealth of Nations* elipsed them all. Its success, moreover, was such as to suggest that political economy had an identity all of its own. Smith himself did not admit such an implication, continuing to insist that political economy was but 'a branch of the science of a statesman or legislator': his own work in jurisprudence and moral philosophy left him disinclined to drop the wider intellectual framework in which political economy had been conceived. But when the single concept of the market made possible an analysis at once so extensive and so self-contained, it was at least plausible to suppose that what was being presented in the *Wealth of Nations* was a distinct, autonomous science of political economy.

Smith's death in 1790 coincided with the end of the Scottish Enlightenment. In Scotland as throughout Europe, the French Revolution transformed the conditions and assumptions of intellectual life, while political economy had to come to terms with machinery. Within Scotland Dugald Stewart set himself to adapt the Enlightenment conception of political economy to these new circumstances; but his expansive, didactic approach had few imitators. Another Scot, Thomas Chalmers, took the lead in attaching political economy to newly urgent theological concerns, while in England Ricardo and his followers simply took a narrower view of the subject. Even so, it would be a mistake to see 19th-century classical political economy as a new departure. As the philosophical analysis of Hegel (who learnt much from Steuart) and the radical critiques of Marx and the early socialists pointed out, the historical, moral and institutional premises on which political economy rested were still those elucidated by the Scots. In any case, it was the Scottish Enlightenment, and specifically the *Wealth of Nations*, which had first shown how political economy might be presented as an independent science.

BIBLIOGRAPHY

Bryson, G. 1945. *Man and Society: the Scottish Enquiry of the Eighteenth Century*. Princeton: Princeton University Press.

Campbell, R.H. and Skinner, A.S. 1982. *The Origins and Nature of the Scottish Enlightenment*. Edinburgh: John Donald.

Hont, I. and Ignatieff, M. (eds) 1983. *Wealth and Virtue. The Shaping of Political Economy in the Scottish Enlightenment.* Cambridge: Cambridge University Press.

Medick, H. 1973. *Naturzustand und Naturgeschichte der bürgerlichen Gesellschaft.* Göttingen: Vandenhoeck and Ruprecht.

Phillipson, N.T. 1981. The Scottish Enlightenment. In *The Enlightenment in National Context*, ed. R. Porter and M. Teich. Cambridge: Cambridge University Press; New York: Cambridge University Press.

Sher, R.B. 1985. *Church and University in the Scottish Enlightenment.* Princeton and Edinburgh: Princeton: Princeton University Press; Edinburgh: Edinburgh University Press.

Self-Interest

D.H. MONRO

Two of the basic questions with which moral philosophers have been concerned are: (a) What are the fundamental principles of morality? (b) Why should we obey them? One tempting answer to the second question is: because obeying them is in your own interest. Tempting, because any other answer simply invites a further 'why?'. For example, 'why bother about helping others to get what they want?' clearly demands an answer. But 'why bother about getting what *you* want?', though of course it can be *asked*, hardly makes sense.

Self-interest as the answer to the second question, however, implies a similar answer to the first. Self-interest can only be a reason for obeying moral principles if those principles do always benefit us as individuals, so that the fundamental one becomes: Do whatever will enable you to satisfy your own desires. And this seems perverse, since most moralists tell us to consider others rather than ourselves. Self-sacrifice, we are told, is noble, and self-seeking base.

Thomas Hobes answers this objection by pointing out that, while human desires are diverse, so that there is no common end, there is a single means common to all ends. They all require the cooperation of other people, or at least their non-interference. Everyone has an interest in maintaining a peaceful and harmonious society. Moral principles are simply the rules which everyone must follow in order to obtain such a society. We should obey them because obeying them makes for peace and security, and without peace and security no one has much chance of satisfying *any* desires. If morality requires us to consider others and not ourselves, it is for our own sakes in the long run.

To suppose that men imposed moral restraints on themselves for this reason might suggest a far-sightedness greater than most of us are capable of. Bernard Mandeville suggested that men are motivated less by this consideration than by vanity. Morality, he conjectured, came abough through the artifice of a relatively few far-sighted men who, in order to make men useful to their fellows, spread the myth that man is somehow different from the other animals and shows his superiority by being able to conquer his desires. 'Moral Virtues', he says, 'are the Political Offspring which Flattery begot upon Pride' (Mandeville, 1724, vol. 1, p. 51). Part of Mandeville's purpose is to satirize the doctrine that no action is virtuous unless it involves self-denial. If that is true, he argues, then virtue does not exist, since all actions aim at some gratification, if only an increase in self-esteem. Civilization did not come about through self-denial, but through what moralists regard as moral weaknesses: avarice, vanity, luxuriousness, ambition and the rest. Hence his famous paradox: 'Private Vices, Publick Benefits.' In developing it he gives an example which has often been quoted: the many materials garnered from all over the world, and the toil and hardship endured by a multitude of workmen, in order to produce a scarlet coat. Even a tyrant, Mandeville says, would be ashamed 'to exact such terrible Services from his Innocent Slaves' merely for 'the satisfaction a Man receives from having a Garment made of Scarlet or Crimson Cloth'. Yet in pursuit of their own private ends men perform feats of endurance which neither their own benevolence nor the tyranny of others would drive them to (Mandeville, 1724, vol. 1, pp. 357–8). This passage has often been used to illustrate the efficiency and smooth working of a market economy; but, looked at in a slightly different way, it would really fit just as well into the first book of Marx's *Das Kapital*, which is full of atrocity stories about the sufferings of workers under capitalism.

Mandeville distinguishes between virtue and goodness. Virtue, in the sense of complete self-denial, is an illusion, since all actions spring from self-interest. It is not possible to subdue the passions, but only to set one passion against another. No action is completely virtuous, but (he seems to imply) it may be good, if it is useful to others. Mandeville, then, agrees with Hobbes that self-interest is the ultimate motive for all actions, but probably does not agree with his other thesis, that self-interest, as distinct from the general happiness, is ultimately the sole good.

The first of these two theses is ambiguous, because 'self-interest' as ambiguous, in more ways that one. If the thesis is that every action springs from some desire or other, including disinterested desires for the welfare of others, then it is probably a truism and in any case of very little interest. If it means that in every action the agent is aiming at his own greatest happiness in the long run ('enlightened self-interest' or 'cool self-love'), then it is significant but false. Actually Hobbes seems to mean something else again: that there are no altruistic or disinterested desires. Apparent altruism turns out on examination to be selfish or interested in the ordinary sense of those words, aiming perhaps at public acclaim or enhanced self-esteem.

It was argued against Hobbes that benevolence, the disinterested desire for the welfare of others, is as basic a part of human nature as self-interest. But, if there are two basic human instincts instead of one, which should we follow when they conflict? The stronger? But it would be rash to claim that benevolence is a stronger feature of human nature than selfishness. Shaftesbury and Hutcheson detected a third instinct, an innate moral sense which requires us to prefer benevolence to self-interest when they conflict. But why should we prefer *that* instinct? As an answer to the question 'why be moral?' this is hardly more satisfactory than to say (with other philosophers) that it is an eternal and immutable truth, known by intuition, that we should allow benevolence to prevail over self-interest.

David Hume and Adam Smith, while agreeing with Hutcheson in the main, try to make his position more plausible by going more deeply into the psychological sources of benevolence. An important one, they say, is sympathy, the tendency to enter into the joys and sorrows of others. Mandeville had regarded pity as a weakness, because it is a passion, though an amiable one: a self-indulgent desire to rid ourselves of a particular kind of uneasiness. Adam Smith insists that sympathy is disinterested, and suggests that 'that whole account of human nature... which deduces all sentiments and affections from self-love... seems to me to have arisen from some confused misapprehension of the system of sympathy' (Smith, 1759, p. 317).

Smith called attention to another tendency in human nature; the aesthetic delight in 'the fitness of any system or machine to produce the end for which it was intended', leading, very often, to the means being valued for its own sake, quite apart from the original end. (Smith would have understood the secretary of a home for unmarried mothers who said in an annual report: 'It would be a great pity if, after so much devoted work by so many people, this home had to close for lack of girls needing help'.) Although he regards this tendency as distinct from both self-interest and benevolence, consideration of it leads Smith to conclusions curiously like Mandeville's. One manifestation of it, he says, is the heaping up of riches far beyond the needs of the rich themselves:

> The rich only select from the heap what is most precious and agreeable. They consume little more than the poor, and in spite of their natural selfishness and rapacity, though they mean only their own conveniency, though the shole end which they propose from the labours of all the thousands which they employ be the gratification of their own vain and insatiable desires, they divide with the poor the product of all their improvements. They are led by an invisible hand to make nearly the same distribution of the necessaries of life which would have been made had the earth been divided into equal portions among all its inhabitants, and thus, without intending it, without knowing it, advance the interest of the society, and afford means to the multiplication of the species (Smith, 1759, pp. 184–5).

It is clear from this that Smith, like Mandeville, sees that the actual consequences of actions may be quite different from those intended. The bees in Mandeville's fable intended merely to lead virtuous and abstemious lives; they did not foresee that this would lead to the ruin of dressmakers, milliners, lawyers, turnkeys, footmen, courtiers, cooks and many others, and eventually to the economic collapse of the hive. Mandeville concludes that public benefits flow from public vices; but obviously the practitioners of those vices are not thinking of the public benefit, but solely of their own gratification.

Adam Smith, in his other reference to the invisible hand, says that most individuals, in their economic transactions, neither intend to promote the public interest nor realise that they are doing so. 'He intends only his own gain, and he is in this, as in many other cases, led by an invisible hand to promote an end which was no part of his intention'. He adds that this is on the whole a good thing. 'By pursuing his own interest he frequently promotes that of the society more effectually than when he really intends to promote it. I have never known much good done by those who affected to trade for the publick good. It is an affectation, indeed, not very common among merchants, and very few words need be employed in dissuading them from it' (Smith, 1776, p. 456).

Nor is that all. It is not only that the pursuit of wealth or power leads the ambitious to promote the public interest while seeking only their own; the aesthetic tendency to value a means for its own sake causes them to have false notions about where their own real interests lie. The pleasures of wealth and greatness, which do not really add much to happiness,

> strike the imagination as something grand, and beautiful, and noble, of which the attainment is well worth all the toil and anxiety which we are so apt to bestow on it. And it is well that nature imposes upon us in this manner. It is this deception which rouses and keeps in continual motion the industry of makind (Smith, 1759, p. 183).

But perhaps the most optimistic version of the theory of the invisible hand is put forward by T.H. Green. The actions of bad men, he says (at least when they are also powerful) are 'overruled for good'. There is, he tells us, nothing supernatural about this; it simply one of the beneficent effects of living in society, and particularly in a nation-state. He gives Napoleon as an example:

> With all his egotism, his individuality was so far governed by the national spirit in and upon him, that he could only glorify himself in the greatness of France; and though the national spirit expressed itself in an effort after greatness which was in many ways of a mischievous and delusive kind, yet it again had so much of what may be called the spirit of humanity in it, that it required satisfaction in the belief that it was serving humanity. Hence the aggrandisement of France, in which Napoleon's passion for glory satisfied itself, had to take at least the semblance of a deliverance of oppressed peoples, and in taking the semblance it to a great extent performed the reality...(Green, 1882, p. 134).

One may doubt whether the world's experience of dictators would yield much evidence of such overruling.

For Hobbes, moral principles ('laws of nature') are sociological laws about how men may cooperate peacefully. For Hume and Smith they are rather psychological truths about what men have come to approve, given their peculiar amalgam of dispositions (of which self-interest is merely one) and also the social need (which Hobbes had stressed) for some fixed standards of behaviour.

The psychological approach was also taken by the early Utilitarians. They were, however, less unwilling to found morality on self-interest, because the alternatives, 'intuition', 'the moral sense', 'natural law' and the rest, seemed to them to be merely an excuse for deifying one's own prejudices. 'Nature', Bentham said, 'has placed mankind under the governance of two sovereign masters, pain and pleasure. It is for them to point out what we ought to do, as well as to determine what we shall do' (Bentham, 1789, p. 11). These masters might have been expected to order each individual to pursue his own greatest happiness. But, according to Bentham, they set a different goal, the happiness of *everybody*. Bentham does not explain this transition.

Mill attempts to explain it, in a brief and much-criticized argument. Like Adam Smith, he appeals to the tendency for a means to become an end in itself. Virtue, he says, the desire to promote the general happiness, originally cultivated as a means to one's own happiness, comes to be aimed at for its own sake. From being a means to happiness, it has become a part of that happiness. G.E. Moore dismisses this contemptuously as a blatant failure to distinguish two very different things, a part and a means. Mill's argument may, however, be more subtle than that (Moore, 1903, pp. 71–2).

According to Hobbes, moral rules state the way men must behave if society is to be possible. Needing society, the individual accepts as his aim, not self-interest merely, but a compromise between his own interests and those of everybody else. He accepts the compromise because half a loaf is better than no bread. Consequently he feels obliged to subordinate his own interests to the compromise when they conflict. But he obeys moral rules only as a means, in order to induce others to obey them too. Having others obey them is his reward; obeying them himself is the price he pays. But it may be objected that we do not think of morality like that. We want to do the right thing for the sake of doing it. It would seem to follow from Hobbes's account that it would be more rational to be a successful hypocrite than a genuinely good person.

Consider, however, what happens once the compromise is accepted. Since society depends on that acceptance, society will take pains to inculcate in each new generation the importance of accepting it. To anyone so trained, the compromise will not be thought of *as* a compromise, but simply as the right thing to do. Moreover, he will feel uneasy at the prospect of attaining his personal ends in a way that could run counter to the compromise. In Mill's words, he comes to think of himself as a being who *of course* pays regard to others (Mill, 1863, p. 232). Conformity with morality, aiming at the general happiness, has become part of his private happines and not just a means to it.

Mill's answer to the question, what is the fundamental moral principle? is: do whatever makes for the greatest happiness all round. His answer to the other question (why obey it?) is: because you have been socially conditioned to associate your own happiness with that of other people. If you had not been so conditioned, there would be no stable society, and your life would be miserable. Moreover (and Mill learned this from David Hartley rather than Hobbes) greater satisfaction is to be derived from our socially conditioned desires than from our primary or biological ones.

Later Utilitarians have not usually followed Mill in this. Henry Sidgwick, indeed, in spite of Bentham, founded the greatest happiness principle on a rational, self-evident intuition. Moral philosophers of other persuasions have either accepted some form of intuitionism or have argued (unconvincingly) that 'why be moral?' is a nonsensical question.

BIBLIOGRAPHY

Bentham, J. 1789. *An Introduction to the Principles of Morals and Legislation*. Ed. J.H. Burns and H.L.A. Hart, London: Athlone Press, 1970.

Green, T.H. 1886. *Lectures on the Principles of Political Obligation*. London: Longmans, 1941.

Hobbes, T. 1651. *Leviathan, or The Matter, Forme & Power of a Commonwealth, Ecclesiasticall and Civill*. Oxford: Clarendon Press, 1909; New York: E.P. Dutton & Co., 1934.

Hume, D. 1739. *A Treatise of Human Nature*. Ed. L.A. Selby-Bigge, Oxford: Clarendon Press, 1896.

Hume, D. 1751. *Enquiries Concerning the Human Understanding and Concerning the Principles of Morals*. Ed. L.A. Selby-Bigge, Oxford: Clarendon Press, 1902.

Hutcheson, F. 1728. *An Essay on the Nature and Conduct of the Passions, with Illustrations upon the Moral Sense*. Facsimile edn prepared by B. Fabian, Hildesheim: G. Olms, 1971.

Mandeville, B. 1724. *The Fable of the Bees, or Private Vices, Publick Benefits*. Ed. F.B. Kaye, Oxford: Clarendon Press, 1924.

Mill, J.S. 1863. *Utilitarianism*. In *Essays on Ethics, Religion and Society*, ed. J.M. Robson, Toronto: University of Toronto Press; London: Routledge & Kegan Paul, 1969.

Moore, G.E. 1903. *Principia Ethica*. Cambridge: Cambridge University Press.

Shaftesbury [A.A. Cooper], 3rd Earl. 1699. *An Inquiry Concerning Virtue or Merit*. Ed. D. Walford, Manchester: Manchester University Press, 1977.

Sidgwick, H. 1907. *The Methods of Ethics*. 7th edn, ed. E.E.C. Jones, London: Macmillan, 1962.

Smith, A. 1759. *The Theory of Moral Sentiments*. Ed. A.L. Macfie and D.D. Raphael, Oxford: Clarendon Press, 1974.

Smith, A. 1776. *An Inquiry into the Nature and Causes of the Wealth of Nations*. Ed. R.H. Campbell, A.S. Skinner and W.B. Todd, Oxford: Clarendon Press, 1976.

Social Cost

J. DE V. GRAAFF

The idea underlying the notion of social cost is a very simple one. A man initiating an action does not necessarily bear all the costs (or reap all the benefits) himself. Those that he does bear are *private* costs; those he does not are *external* costs. The sum of two constitutes the *social* cost.

Behind this apparently straightforward statement lies a host of difficulties of definition, valuation and aggregation. They are considered in Section I. Section II discusses very briefly certain contexts in which, despite the ambiguities, the concept is often used.

I. PROBLEMS OF DEFINITION

Private cost is usually defined in opportunity-cost terms as the highest valued (or most preferred) option necessarily forgone. In practice this usually means no more than that the private cost of an object is the money paid for it. The definition works because the individual (or firm) is assumed to be optimizing. Every choice entails a sacrifice. There is always an option 'necessarily forgone'.

The external costs imposed on others by the initiator of an action are imposed on optimizing agents, so the definition works for them too. But it does not work for social cost because there is no reason to suppose that society is optimizing. Society may, without giving up leisure or anything else, be able to get more guns *and* more butter. Technically, this will be possible whenever it is operating 'within' (rather than 'on') its social production frontier – a situation as likely to be the norm as the exception. There would, in these circumstances, be no option forgone and therefore no cost.

If society does happen to be 'on' its production frontier, there is at least a cost. But its significance may depend on who bears it. Is butter forgone by A (who is rich) as important as that forgone by B (who is poor)? Can the two amounts simply be added together to get the cost to society?

The definition of social cost as the sum of private and external costs avoids the difficulty that society may not be optimizing but not the one that costs borne by different people have to be added together. Nor does it avoid certain other difficulties. We shall discuss these under separate headings, starting with the least troublesome.

(1) *Scope of society*. If I build a house that obstructs my neighbour's view, but affects no one else, it is fairly clear that the external cost I impose on him is the only one to be added to my own in determining the cost of my action to society. He will suffer an immediate loss of amenity, which may or may not be easy to value, and a decline in the resale value of his property which, if the market functions as it should, will be a reasonable estimate of the loss to his successors in title.

In other situations the position may not be so simple. Pollution of the atmosphere, or of a common waterway, may affect several nations. Are we interested in the cost to *our* society, or to the world community? What of activities that may affect unborn generations? How is the cost to them to be estimated? If one is dealing with questions such as the social cost of nuclear energy, these matters may be very relevant.

We must be clear about the scope, in time and space, of the society in which we are interested before talking about social cost. When we are, we can proceed to the other difficulties.

(2) *Costs and benefits*. The external costs imposed on others by the initiator of some action need not all be positive. Some may be negative costs, or benefits. (If I paint my house bright yellow it may horrify Jones, but delight Smith.) It is largely a matter of convention whether we reckon these negative costs separately, and call them benefits, or set them off against the positive ones immediately, to arrive at a figure for *net* cost.

In Cost Benefit Analysis the usual practice is to deal with the two categories separately, and then to weigh the one against the other. But in other branches of the subject it is common to reckon costs net of benefits. An example is the proposition, advanced in many standard texts, that *social cost excludes rent*. What is meant is that the increased rents earned by factors whose prices have risen in the face of increased demand for their services represent mere transfers of wealth, not costs to society.

If a project creates a demand for labour and other factors that results in higher wages and prices, these of course mean higher private costs for the entrepreneur who initiates it. But they are offset by negative external costs in the form of benefits to the factors (or their owners). The two balance out, so that when private and external costs are summed there is no net contribution to social cost. The increased rents enter into both private and external costs (with opposite signs), and – as the proposition says – not into the cost to society.

When costs borne by individuals are not costs to society it is often proper to call them *losses*, and their counterpart *gains*. If I own a shop next to yours and take away your trade by cutting prices, you will suffer a loss that is counterbalanced by the gain to consumers and my profit (if there is any) on the extra sales. Gains and losses due to price changes are not costs to society.

Implicit in the assertion that price changes do not give rise to social costs is the assumption that we are dealing with a closed economy. In an open economy, a movement in the international terms of trade may either impose real costs on nationals or enable them to earn rents at the expense of foreigners. Also implicit in the assertion is the assumption that the problems of measurement and aggregation have been solved.

(3) *Short- and long-run costs.* When measuring costs it is essential to state the time period under consideration. There is a tendency for most to be lower in the long run than in the short, and this applies with especial force to external ones. Injured parties are at first taken by surprise, but then will try to reduce costs imposed on them by adjusting their operations to the new circumstances. If the laws of society are such that they have a claim against the initiator of the activity that precipitated the external costs, the victims may succeed in getting him to modify his actions in a way that reduces the costs still further. Of course the *sum* of private and external costs (i.e. the social cost) may not reduce to the same extent – but that is another matter.

An old example (Pigou, 1932, p. 134) can be adapted to illustrate the point. If sparks from a railway engine increase the probability of fire damage to crops planted by a farmer whose land the line traverses, a sudden doubling of the number of trains will impose additional external costs on him. Over time he may be able to mitigate these by planting evergreens near the line, or leaving a strip of land fallow. If the law allows, he may be able to sue the railway company for any damage actually caused, or claim compensation for loss of profit on land put to inferior use. This may eventually persuade the company to fit spark suppressors to the locomotives or reduce the number of trains. These factors all combine to make it probable that external costs will decrease with time.

In an example such as this, where only two parties are involved, negotiation might be expected to be a real alternative to legal action. The division of the gains would of course depend on the bargaining strength of the negotiators, which would in part be determined by their rights, but the outcome would be much the same: a reduction in the sum of private and external costs until a further reduction would bring about a greater reduction in benefits. As negotiation is always time-consuming, one would again expect the result to be a social cost that was lower in the long run than the short.

(4) *Aggregation.* When we add external costs to private costs to get social cost we are adding costs borne by different people. In the last resort this amounts to saying that, all else being equal, a cost of $10 borne by A represents a greater cost to society than one of $9 borne by B, no matter who A and B might be. There are really only two possible justifications for this procedure.

The first is along *utilitarian* lines, with full interpersonal comparability and an assumption that the marginal utility of money is the same to everyone. Lower social cost then represents a lower loss of aggregate satisfaction.

The second is in terms of *compensation tests* (Graaff, 1957, chap. 5). Very briefly, these tests use as a criterion of social desirability the possibility of those who benefit from some change being able to compensate those who lose by it, without themselves becoming losers. Obviously, the lower the sum of private and external costs, the greater the possibility of being able to compensate those who bear them.

Neither justification is entirely satisfactory. Utilitarianism still has its adherents, but few among them would lightly assume that the marginal utility of money was the same to rich and poor. And the *possibility* of compensation means very little unless the compensation is actually carried out. (What does it help to say that, although several men will starve, the cost to society is low, because they *could* be given sufficient food to prevent their starving?) If, on the other hand, the compensation is paid, price changes can lead to *reversals* of the sort analysed by Scitovsky (1941). The social cost of activity A may then be lower than that of B before compensation, higher after it. Choosing the activity with the lower cost entails a prior choice between two distributions of wealth. Otherwise we go round in circles.

II. APPLICATIONS

The principal application of the notion of social cost is in the field of Cost Benefit Analysis. Valuation problems abound. How, for instance, does one value the cost of a human life, if the probability is that an extra one will be sacrificed when savings are made on safety or design specifications for a new highway? And how does one value other goods for which there are no markets? (In practice one uses prices in related markets; but these are what they are precisely because there are no prices for the goods one is trying to value!) Cost Benefit analysts handle these matters with great skill, and if they were the only problems they had to content with, would emerge with great credit.

But the theory also has to face the aggregation problems just mentioned. The utilitarian approach tends to use 'distributional weights' to indicate the analyst's rough assessment of differences in the marginal utility of money to different people. In this way $1 borne by a poor man can be made to contribute more to social cost than $2 borne by someone rich. It is almost fair to say that social cost then becomes what the analyst wants it to be.

Those who use the compensation-test approach tend to hope that price changes following hypothetical compensation would not be large enough to bring about embarrassing reversals. The matter cannot be disposed of that easily. Comparing social costs with social benefits to determine social choice is an exercise subject to all the impossibility theorems of Social Choice Theory. Reversals that give rise to intransitive choices can be expected unless our assumptions are rich enough to exclude them. Utilitarians recognize this when they boldly allocate distributional weights. Without a similar boldness those who base their analysis on the possibility of compensation leave the signifance of the costs they calculate in considerable doubt.

Social cost theory has also been used in the analysis of *market failure*. Without too much regard for the niceties of definition, the older theory (Pigou, 1932) went something like this. Maximization of the national dividend requires the equality of marginal social costs and benefits. Optimizing behaviour in markets secures the equality of marginal private costs and benefits. Unless the two sets of costs and benefits coincide, market behaviour will not maximize the national dividend. Divergences between private and social costs (and benefits) are the cause of failure. Various measures are available to correct these divergences.

A more modern statement would be that a market fails when it clears without all mutually advantageous bargains having been struck. This is most likely to happen when a transaction affects parties other than those directly involved in its negotiation. The existence of the external costs and benefits borne by them entails a divergence between private and social costs and benefits. (This follows directly from the definition.)

The more modern version brings out the central problem. *Why* are the 'other parties' not directly involved in the negotiations? Even if they have no legal standing (which, if property rights are clearly defined, they may well have), they can never be worse off negotiating. The answer, of course, lies in *transaction costs*. Bargaining is a costly and time-consuming procedure, especially when large numbers of people are involved. In addition, to get full benefit from deals struck, it may be necessary to take expensive steps to exclude freeloaders. (I may make it worth my neighbour's while not to park in front of my house, but unless I can stop others using the vacant space it will help me very little.) Any analysis of market failure that does not explicitly recognize the role played by the costs of bargaining is severly flawed.

If bargaining were costless and without legal impediment, optimising behaviour by market participants would automatically imply that all mutually advantageous bargains were struck. With zero transaction costs, market failure is impossible. This result, often attributed to Coase (1960), has been described as the Say's Law of Welfare Economics (Calabresi, 1968). But it might be fairer to reserve that accolade for the version of it that says that, if a bargain is *not* struck, it can only be because optimizing agents, in their wisdom, have decided that the transaction cost would exceed the benefit. It would be nice if the world were really like that.

A treatment of social cost that deals adequately with the costs of bargaining has not yet been developed. That, and the unsolved problems of aggregation, should make us wary of using the concept without the necessary circumspection.

BIBLIOGRAPHY

Calabresi, G. 1968. Transaction costs, resource allocation and liability rules: a comment. *Journal of Law and Economics* 11, April, 67–73.

Coase, R.H. 1960. The problem of social cost. *Journal of Law and Economics* 3(1), October, 1–44.

Graaff, J. de V. 1957. *Theoretical Welfare Economics*. Cambridge: Cambridge University Press.

Pigou, A.C. 1932. *The Economics of Welfare*. 4th edn, London: Macmillan; New York: St. Martin's Press, 1952.

Scitovsky, T. 1941. A note on welfare propositions in economics. *Review of Economic Studies* 9(1), 77–88.

Utilitarianism

C. WELCH

Intense, long, certain, speedy, fruitful, pure –

Such marks in *pleasures* and in *pains* endure.
Such pleasures seek if *private* by thy end;
If it be *public*, wide let them *extend*.
Such *pains* avoid, whichever be thy view;
If pains *must* come, let them *extend* to few.

Jeremy Bentham added these 'memoriter verses' to a revised edition of *An Introduction to the Principles of Morals and Legislation* to fix in the reader's mind those points 'on which the whole fabric of morals and legislation may be seen to rest' (Bentham, 1789, p. 38). And indeed, although his formulation equates utility with pleasure in a way that many contemporary utilitarians would reject, Bentham does implicitly identify the central propositions that continue to inform philosophical utilitarianism today: i.e. (1) individual well-being ought to be the end of moral action; (2) each individual is to 'count for one and no more than one'; and (3) the object of social action should be to maximize general utility (or, in Bentham's phrase, to promote the greatest happiness of the greatest number).

This moral position was not, of course, original to Bentham. It was held in some form by a wide array of 18th-century writers – the English theologians Brown, Tucker and Paley, as well as the French *philosophes* Helvetius and Holbach. The distinctive doctrine associated with Bentham and James Mill, however, was first labelled *utilitarianism*. Originally coined by Bentham, and subsequently rediscovered by John Stuart Mill in a novel by Galt, the term entered the general lexicon in the 1820s. It connoted a systematic ideology composed of sensationalist psychology, ethical hedonism, classical economics and democratic politics. Early utilitarianism – also known as Philosophical Radicalism – inspired an influential movement of reform in English law and politics during the early 19th-century. But more important, the philosophy of utility as articulated by Bentham and revised by his successors has retained a central place in the theoretical debates that have dominated economics, sociology and moral and political philosophy into the 20th century.

BENTHAM'S THEORY OF UTILITY. Bentham's theoretical innovations were not striking; like earlier utilitarians he stated both that men are in fact pleasure-seeking creatures and that the promotion of general pleasure or happiness should be the criterion of moral goodness. But Bentham's utilitarianism aspired to be both scientific and systematic. It derived these scientific pretensions from three tendencies that were particularly pronounced in his thought. First, he held a reductionist version of the empiricist theory of mind in which ideas – born of sensations – were formed by mental associations prompted by the urges of pleasure and pain. Bentham assumed that there was a correct association of ideas that would yield a correspondingly rationalized language. He believed that this rationalization of language was a necessary prerequisite to the proper calculation of self-interest, and always held to the Enlightenment hope that moral language could be made scientific by purging it of irrationalities and illusions. Second, Bentham stated unequivocally that pleasure is homogeneous and thus quantifiable. He used mathematical 'metaphors' – the felicific calculus, axioms of mental pathology, the table of the springs of action – images that suggested concreteness and precision. Finally, he gave detailed and systematic attention to 'sanctions', i.e. painful disincentives to action. Unlike the theological utilitarians, he neglected the godly sanction and concentrated on those earthly penalties of public opinion and legal punishment that could be placed under the influence or control of the legislator.

Bentham's importance lay not in these refinements of utilitarianism, except insofar as they apparently strengthened its claim to certainty, but rather in his lucid and single-minded application of the doctrine to criticize the 'fallacies' of English public discourse. In this crusade he attacked both the authority of custom and the 'anarchical' philosophy of natural rights. Bentham's rhetorical assault on the French Declarations of Rights was occasioned by his recoil from the Terror, but his arguments against the language of rights remained consistent throughout his life. He makes two powerful claims: (1) rights are not anterior to political society but are created by law; hence an inalienable or non-legal right is a self-contradictory notion; and (2) a philosophy of natural rights offers no way to adjudicate the competing claims of such rights to priority; a non-legal moral right is a 'criterionless notion' (Hart, 1982, p. 82). This distinction between law and morals is further developed by Austin and is fundamental to the legal positivist tradition, as well as to contemporary criticisms of rights-based moral theories.

If natural rights offered no clear theory to guide moral or social choice, utility, according to Bentham, did offer such guidance. The main body of his work lay in substituting utility for alleged logical fictions as a rationale for legislation. In his extensive writings on penal law, for example, he attempted to provide a 'calculus of harm' to facilitate the legislator's task of imposing the minimum sanction that would deter certain undesirable actions. Because Bentham's reformist ambitions encompassed civil and constitutional law, his work also touched directly on contentious public issues, such as abolition of the corn laws and reform of the suffrage. Bentham was a Smithian in economics and became a radical democrat in politics, but the logic of the original connections between utilitarianism and economic and political reform become clearer by considering the contributions of James Mill.

JAMES MILL AND PHILOSOPHICAL RADICALISM. According to J.S. Mill, 'it was my father's opinions which gave the distinguishing character to the Benthamic or utilitarian propagandism of the time' (Mill, 1873, p. 72). This propagandism was energetically carried out by a small group of self-styled Philosophical Radicals, including Francis Place, Joseph Hume, George Grote, Arthur Roebuck, Charles Buller, Sir William Molesworth and – most important – John Stuart Mill. In a series of articles in the *Westminster Review* (beginning in 1824), they launched a political movement to begin the radical revitalization of English public life.

Bentham's work on sanctions (and some of his theoretical statements) suggest that individual interests would have to be associated 'artificially' through the manipulation of legal penalties. At the same time his faith in the general harmony between individual interests and the public interest implies that interests are harmonized 'spontaneously' (see Halévy, 1903). Among Bentham's political disciples, and largely through the influence of James Mill, this tension was resolved decisively in favour of the latter conception. Underlying the Philosophical Radical's programme lay a dogmatic belief that the sum of enlightened self-interests would yield the general interest, in both economics and politics. It was the scientific reformer's job to attack the systematic distortions of self-interest that were charged to the account of 'King and Company', i.e. to the crown, the aristocracy, and the church.

In economics, the Philosophical Radicals endorsed the 'system of natural liberty' and the classical economic programme of competition, minimal state interference, free trade and the abolition of monopolies. Given the rule of law necessary to produce a sense of individual security, men would be spurred to productive labour and to a rational pursuit of their interests by the operation of the natural sanctions of hunger and desire for satisfaction. Self-interested exchanges would then lead to the establishment of ever-wider markets and eventually to the production of the greatest possible satisfaction of wants. The principle of 'utility' was thus linked to an economic programme; however, the central problem of theoretical economics, i.e. the notion of 'value', was not conceptualized directly in utilitarian terms.

One could argue that there is an inherently democratic and critical dimension to the politics of utilitarianism because of the assumption that every man is the best judge of his interest, and because of the perception that individual freedom is necessary to recognize and formulate 'rational' interests. But the democratic logic of the original utilitarian radicals, put forward most forcefully in James Mill's *Essay on Government* (1820) was tailored closely to the historical problem

259

of reforming the British aristocratic polity. James Mill argued that government is by definition rule by some group that is less than the whole 'people'. The circumstances of power, however, tempt these rulers to aggrandize themselves in a fashion neither in their own nor the people's long-term interests. They develop corporate, or in Bentham's terms, 'sinister' interests. This aristocratic corruption can be checked only through democratic representative institutions. Philosophical Radicals insisted on breaking the hold of Britain's aristocratic elite through education of the electorate, extension of the suffrage, frequent Parliaments and the secret ballot. This sort of radicalism was distinguished from that of other democrats by its appeal to a science of politics rather than to the rights – natural or prescriptive – of Englishmen, and from that of liberal Whigs by its ahistorical and doctrinaire view of that 'science'. In the wake of the highly charged but inconclusive debates of the French revolutionary period, the appeal of a rational arbiter in politics was very attractive, especially to Britain's small emerging 'intelligentsia'. The Radicals' endorsement of the neutral standard of utility had strong affinities with the view of certain continental radicals who attempted to exorcize the terrors of the French Revolution by repudiating its language while retaining the substance of moderate republicanism (Welch, 1984). In both cases, however, the reformers overestimated the attractions of their programme for the middle classes, and underestimated the possibility of the growth of a distinctively working-class consciousness. In England, the Philosophical Radicals never achieved their goal of creating a fundamental political realignment, although they clearly had an ideological impact much greater than their immediate political one.

J.S. MILL. The most famous proselytizer of Philosophical Radicalism, and its most notable apostate, was John Stuart Mill. Although Henry Sidgwick has often been called the last 'classical' utilitarian, the name can better be applied to Mill in the sense that he was the last thinker to attempt to integrate a utilitarian moral and social theory with a full-blown psychology and a theory of politics. In politics Mill came to question the iron-clad logic of his father's *Essay*, to distrust the tendency to uniformity that he perceived in democracy and to seek a theory of counterpoise and leadership. In economics he was both the last important thinker in the classical tradition and a sharp critic of existing capitalism. But his intent in all of his writings was, as he said, to modify the structure of his beliefs without totally abandoning the foundations.

An important discussion of the moral foundations of those beliefs can be found in *Utilitarianism* (1861). The argument here rests, inauspiciously enough, on the 'naturalistic fallacy' that underlay the work of Bentham and so many other 18th-century moralists; Mill's case for the moral worth of happiness rests on the 'fact' that people desire it:

> ...the sole evidence it is possible to produce that anything is desirable, is that people do actually desire it... No reason can be given why the general happiness

is desirable except that each person, so far as he believes it to be attainable, desires his own happiness (p. 44).

By 'desirable' Mill clearly seems to mean 'ought to be desired' rather than the less problematical 'can be desired'. Mill, then, was not unduly troubled by Bentham's psychological hedonism, which he largely shared, or by the derivation of ethical hedonism from this descriptive theory. Rather what bothered Mill was the suggestion that this psychological theory implied (1) a narrow materialistic view of pleasure, and (2) *egoistic* hedonism (i.e. the notion that every person ought to maximize his own pleasure). Egoistic hedonism, Mill correctly intuited, is not an ethical theory at all. To meet the first problem Mill proposed his notorious defence of qualitative differences in pleasure, a defence that only contributed to the common view that *Utilitarianism* is a casebook of logical blunders. For if there are higher and lower pleasures, it has often been pointed out, another standard than pleasure is clearly implied as the criterion of judgement between them. This tension between 'utility' and some notion of 'moral perfection' runs unresolved through most of Mill's mature works, and reappears in his defences of liberty and of democracy. To meet the second objection, Mill is careful to state, more clearly than his predecessors, that utilitarianism is a system of *ethical* hedonism, i.e. that the criterion applied to individual moral action is general happiness not individual interest. The difficult question, of course, is how to account for the motivation to moral action, given the psychological assumption that people act only to increase their own satisfactions. Mill moves away from Bentham's tendency to see the problem as one of 'conditioning' the agent to recognize the general interest as his self-interest, and offers a more sophisticated theory (reminiscent of Hume) of sympathy or disinterested altruism and its empirical connections with a sense of justice.

The power of Philosophical Radicalism as it entered the ideological arena (in a time when seismic political and industrial change had unsettled forms of social intercourse) was that it fused psychology, economics and moral and political theory into a compelling 'fit', just how compelling a study of J.S. Mill's intellectual development would confirm. But this synthesis soon began to unravel in the hands of both friends and critics.

UTILITARIANISM: RECONSTRUCTIONS AND INFLUENCE

If utilitarianism were only the doctrine of an unsuccessful 19th-century sect of reformers, it would hardly be of much contemporary interest. But as the exemplar of a 'type' of analysis, a type often held to be radically defective, it has served and continues to serve as a point of departure in discussions of economic, social and moral theory.

Utilitarianism and economics. Utilitarianism has overtly triumphed in only one area of what were once termed the moral sciences, namely, economics. Indeed, the idea of welfare economics, i.e. of determining a 'welfare function', is irreducibly utilitarian in the sense that it seeks to measure individual want-satisfaction and to construct indices of utility. The principle of decreasing marginal utility, which was to give a decisive turn to the evolution of modern economics when applied to the determination of value, was clearly stated by Bentham for the case of money (*Principles of the Civil Code*, 1802). Paradoxically, however, the roots of the marginalist revolution cannot be traced to the formulations of the original utilitarians in any straightforward way. The technical innovations of Gossen, Jevons, Menger and Walras seem to have come at least in part from a greater sensitivity to the market position of consumers. Since then, the increasingly sophisticated mathematical structure of utility theory has generated many of the innovations that have dominated debates within the field.

The early marginalists, however, continued to think of utility in terms of the pleasurable sensations associated with consuming a good. They generally defended the cardinal measurability of utility; some even dreamed of a 'hedomiter' to measure it. The important theoretical break with the classical tradition was to abandon this notion of pleasure as a quality inherent in a good that could be measured in favour of a theory of choice based on the possibility of ranked individual preferences. However, although the problem underlying welfare economics is today construed differently – not as measurement of pleasure but as ranking of preferences – the analysis is still fundamentally akin to Bentham's calculus. Indeed, insofar as economists have addressed the larger issue of intellectual debts and affinities, they have acknowledged the formative influence of the classic utilitarians (see Harsanyi, 1977). The issue that philosophically-inclined economists must address is that of the reach of this sort of analysis. Deep divisions remain about what sorts of issues a utilitarian theory of social choice can illuminate, and about whether the attempted solutions are morally compelling. The former issue has been posed most trenchantly by sociologists; the latter by moral philosophers.

Utilitarianism and sociology. If the hypothesis of the rational economic maximizer has been retained in economics because of its heuristic strength in addressing a range of econometric questions, it was abandoned by the earliest of 'sociologists' because of its perceived heuristic weakness. From the beginning of the 19th century, social theorists have criticized methodological 'individualism' as incapable of generating insights into social life because such a vew does not attribute constitutive power to social forces, but rather takes individual desires, purposes and aspirations as the starting point of social analysis.

Sociology was born of the perceived problematic status of order in societies that had, at least in theory, repudiated the ties of 'tradition'. From St Simon and Comte through Durkheim to Talcott Parsons, sociologists have singled out utilitarianism as singularly incapable of illuminating this problem. For these theorists, utilitarianism represents the notion of society conceived as a set of competing egoisms; this notion is thought to be peculiarly congenial to the English-speaking world and is often loosely and simplistically equated with liberalism. On this view, the utilitarian pedigree includes Hobbes, Locke and Smith, and its progeny the evolutionary utilitarianism of Spencer and McDougall.

Durkheim's attack on Herbert Spencer (in *The Division of Labour*, 1893) can be taken as paradigmatic of the sociological critique.

Spencer was greatly attracted by organic analogies, but he applied them to social analysis in a way that radically maintained the notion that consciousness exists only in the individual 'parts' of society. He developed a strict utilitarian theory of ethics, which described the moral ideal as the individual pursuit of long-term pleasures (a calculation that involved cooperation with others through self-interested exchanges). The relative predominance of this sort of calculus over one in which individuals sought immediate gratification distinguished advanced from primitive societies. Durkheim argues that Spencer, and by extension individualist social theory, is not only inadequate but incoherent conceptually in its reliance on the notion of exchange to comprehend the patterning of social life. Formalized exchange makes sense only against the background of a culture that has internalized a particular set of social norms. Talcott Parsons takes up the theme insistently in *The Structure of Social Action* (1937). He argues that any theory which postulates the 'randomness of ends' cannot account for the ultimate reconciliation of those ends in society except by unacknowledged assumptions, sleight of hand, or a providential *deus ex machina*. Thus, on Parsons' view, an analogous function is served by the Leviathan (for Hobbes); God and natural law (for Locke), the invisible hand (for Smith); and the necessities of evolution (for Spencer). Bentham's utilitarian policy oscillates uneasily between Leviathan and the prior assumption of a natural harmony.

According to many sociologists, then, utilitarianism as the quintessential 'individualist' social theory is fundamentally wrongheaded because individuals are defined, shaped and constrained within social structures. Nevertheless, a reconstructed and simplified 'utilitarianism' remains the indispensable foil from which they delineate and justify the constritions of their own discipline.

Utilitarianism and philosophy. The debate engaged between utilitarians and sociologists is between an intentionalist versus a structuralist theory of action, between a theory that heuristically treats individual preferences as random and one that emphasizes the determining constraints on those preferences. The moral philosopher engaged with utilitarianism – either as advocate or critic – has a rather different perspective and set of questions, although the philosophic criticism, especially those of 'communitarian' critics, sometimes overlaps with those of sociologists. In general, however, the debates within moral philosophy take place within the camp of liberal 'individualism', in the sense that they have focused on the problems of individual moral agency. Philosophers do not ask how we can understand social order, but rather how we can judge the rightness or wrongness of individual action. The utilitarian answer (i.e. by the goodness or badness of the action's consequences) can be taken as the starting point for constructing both an analysis of moral judgements and a system of normative ethics. The utilitarian tradition of the philosophers, however, differs from that of the sociologists; it harks back to Hume and Shaftesbury rather than to Hobbes, and forward to Sidgwick, Edgeworth and Moore, rather than to Spencer. In an attempt to give a general account of moral thinking, modern philosophers have drawn on this tradition to refine ever more subtle versions of utilitarianism.

Much of this literature focuses on the arena of personal ethics. However, the public dimension – so obvious among the Philosophical Radicals who employed utility principally as an argument for or against public rules, institutions and policies – has always been implicit. Contemporary discussion of the issue occurs largely within an overlapping group of practically minded philosophers and philosophically minded welfare economists. A utilitarian theory of social justice has been explicitly argued for in the works of such thinkers as R.M. Hare, J.J.C. Smart, P. Singer and J. Harsanyi. They endorse utility, as did the classical thinkers, as the only reasonable criterion of justice in a secular society.

Philosophical utilitarianism. There are three separate but related issues that have been crucial in the evolution of utilitarian moral theories. The first, that of justifying the imperatives of utility, has produced a measure of agreement among contemporary utilitarians and at least some of their critics. The second and third, how to decide what is a good consequence, and how to determine the right way to assess these consequences, have spawned a host of subtle distinctions that continue to preoccupy and provoke theoretical argument.

The problem of justification in utilitarianism is best approached through the work of Henry Sidgwick (*The Methods of Ethics*, 1874). Unlike Bentham or J.S. Mill, Sidgwick did not base his utilitarianism on the psychological theory that individuals always act to obtain their own good. He does argue that desirable or pleasant states of consciousness are the only intrinsic good, and that an act is objectively right only if it produces more good than any other alternative act open to the agent, but he presents these principles as moral imperatives, implicit in common sense morality, not descriptions of actual behaviour. They come to us through a sort of moral intuition that is self-evident and not susceptible of further analysis. Sidgwick narrowed the focus of utilitarianism to a theory of moral choice, theoretically separable from any particular metaphysical doctrine, psycholigical theory, or political and institutional programme. He distanced himself not only from the sensationalist psychology of the earlier radicals, but also from their democratic reformism. This narrowed field is still characteristic of much, though not all, contemporary utilitarian theory. However, the arguments advanced for why we should accept utilitarian moral precepts have changed. Although he clarified the problem of justification by recognizing the illegitimacy of the slide from 'is' to 'ought', Sidgwick's own theory of moral intuitions proved extremely vulnerable.

The 20th-century analytic movement in philosophy has tended to discredit the notion of a proof of normative ethics altogether, and to disregard 'intuition' as vague and arbitrary. Nevertheless, the analytic philosopher's preoccupation with the meaning of moral language and the types of moral reasoning that are valid has led to a widespread belief that, even in the absence of epistemological certainty, good moral arguments can be distinguished from bad ones, fallacious statements from true ones. It is on this basis (greater plausibility or reasonableness) that arguments for utility are generally defended. Given some ultimate attitude that is acknowledged to be shared (usually generalized benevolence), the utilitarian hopes to convince others that his system of ethics is more plausible, that is, less prone to conceptual confusions and more coherent, than either unreflective moral sentiments, or some alternative general account of these sentiments. Insofar as some moral critics share the desire to apply to moral argument the established canons of rationality, there is common ground for discussion of the utilitarian viewpoint. John Rawls's *Theory of Justice* (1971) is developed largely through an antagonistic dialogue with utilitarianism on just this common ground.

A second issue that has been important in debates within the utilitarian moral tradition is the problem of how consequences are to be defined. A 'consequentialist' moral theory is one in which the results of action, not the motives to action, are the objects of rational assessment. Bentham, for example, stated that 'there is no such thing as any sort of motive that is in itself a bad one' (1789, p. 100). The classic discussion of this issue took place within the rubric of hedonism; pleasure – in narrow or more expansive senses – was the desired end of moral action. G.E. Moore (*Principia Ethica*, 1903), building on the dissatisfactions already expressed by J.S. Mill, offered a theory of 'ideal' utilitarianism that was consequentialist, but not hedonistic. Moore argued that pleasure was but one of many desirable goods, among which he included truth and beauty. Another answer to this question arises from the attempt to accommodate the common sense moral judgement that it is better to relieve suffering than to promote pleasure. Hence the so-called 'negative' utilitarianism attributed to Karl Popper, which argues that moral experience is uniquely concerned with the prevention of harm to others.

Among many contemporary thinkers the problem of defining the good is thought to be obviated by considering the good in terms of maximizing 'preferences'. The power of legitimation falls, in this view, on the process of choice, not on what is chosen; it is 'topic neutral'. Despite the intuitive appeal and apparent methodological advantages of this reformulation, the constraints imposed by the process of 'sum-ranking' and by the theory of rationality, as well as by common empirical assumptions about what people *do* in fact choose, lead choice-based utilitarianism inexorably back to the notion of maximizing 'well-being' or 'interest'.

The most important distinction developed within modern utilitarianism is that between 'act' and 'rule' utilitarianism, or 'unrestricted' and 'restricted' utilitarianism. This distinction has to do with the proper procedure for determining consequences. The modern statement of the problem dates back to R.F. Harrod (1936), but the intuitive sense of the distinction is quite old and is certainly present in the classical thinkers, who are usually classed as act utilitarians.

An act utilitarian assesses the rightness of an action directly by its consequences, i.e. he judges that action A is to be chosen because the total happiness expected to be produced by A exceeds that of any alternative action open to the agent. This position has been criticized in a number of ways (for instance, it is said to hold the agent to an impossibly exigent standard of behaviour), but the most serious objections have centred on the possibility that the course of action that would be chosen on act utilitarian principles would clash violently with common sense moral judgements. Two examples, separated by two centuries, bring out the nature of this objection.

The utilitarian William Godwin (1793) argued that, if given a choice between saving one's mother from a burning building or saving a great man whose works were more likely to benefit mankind, one ought to save the great man and leave one's mother to the fire. A modern critic of utilitarianism, H.J. McCloskey (1963), offers one version of a familiar example involving not personal but public ethics. A small-town sheriff would be able to prevent serious public disturbances (in which hundreds would surely die) if he were to execute an innocent person as a scapegoat. (One could present the case, McCloskey argues, in such a way that the sheriff is certain both that his act will not be found out and and that the riots will occur.) A strict utilitarian would have to recognize that, on his principles, the correct moral choice would be to kill an innocent person. Or at least he would have to recognize that such a judgement was theoretically possible. Utilitarianism, then, seems to commit one to the possibility of acting in ways abhorrent to the common sense of domestic obligation and justice. To avoid these implications, many have proposed differing versions of rule utilitarianism.

A rule utilitarian assesses the rightness of an action by asking whether it would have good consequences if it became part of general practice. Thus general rules, like 'promises must be kept', are given moral status indirectly through their role in fostering long-term utility. All utilitarians have recognized the indirect utility of rules like promise-keeping, if only as short-cuts ('rules of thumb') to the process of calculating consequences. Bentham and Mill, for example, distinguished between first-order harm and the second-order evil that comes from the example of law-breaking. However, attempts to defend a distinctive rule-utilitarian position have proved problematical. Either rule-utilitarianism collapses into act-utilitarianism in disputed cases (e.g. when general rules conflict), or it departs from the particular utilitarian viewpoint by asserting that some rules are so necessary as to become good in themselves. Many have attempted to gain a foothold on the slippery slope between these two possibilities and the issue has generated a substantial literature.

CRITICISMS. One line of criticism of moral utilitarianism has always been 'technical', i.e. it has referred to the impossibility of inter-personal comparisons of utility. In 1879 a now-forgotten professor of jurisprudence argued:

> There is an illusive semblance of simplicity in the Utilitarian formula...it assumes an unreal concord about the constituents of happiness and an unreal homogeneity of human minds in point of sensibility to different pains and pleasures...Nor is it possible to weigh bodily and mental pleasures and pains one against the other; no single man can pronounce with certainty about their relative intensity even for himself, far less for all his fellows (T.E. Cliffe Leslie, 1879, 45–6).

The idea that utility is cardinally measurable was basic to Bentham's enterprise, and has always been criticized on the grounds that pleasures are incommensurable. Far from resolving these problems, the economic theory of social choice has merely transposed them into different terms. Many versions of the theory depend heavily on a system of cardinalization derived from the work of von Neumann and Morgenstern on decisions taken under uncertainty. Yet these arguments have always encountered great scepticism (Georgescu-Roegen, 1954). At issue is the notion of the substitutability of satisfactions. Many would argue that altruistic preferences, or preferences that are 'public', cannot be translated into preference schedules. And a persistent problem is the inability to deal in a satisfactory way with equity in distribution.

A related but more fundamental line of criticism asserts that utilitarians radically misconstrue the moral experience. If sociologists are concerned with the alleged poverty of social insight that a theory of utility-maximizing individuals offers, moral philosophers have been haunted by the unnecessary impoverishment of those individuals, and by the narrowing and distorting of individual moral judgement. When Themistocles proposed to burn the ships of Athens' allies in order to secure Athenian supremacy, Aristides is supposed to have answered, 'The project would be expedient but it is unjust.' The fundamental insight that expedience and justice are at some level qualitatively distinct forms the essence of this critical perspective. 19th-century critics focused on the inability of utilitarians to comprehend duties to God and country, and hence emphasized the virtues of 'excellence', 'reverence', 'nobility' and 'honour'. 20th-century critics focus on the lack of understanding of the moral person and of duties to oneself (hence their emphasis on 'integrity', 'commitment' and 'self-respect'). Implicit in both these views is the judgement that the psychological assumptions that utilitarianism must make are so narrow and implausible as to render the theory either inadequate, or positively pernicious.

Finally, there is the problem of the cultural and institutional correlates that might accompany the adoption of utilitarianism as the criterion of social justice. Utilitarianism as a practical movement was wedded to a particular theory of politics. Yet this connection between utilitarianism and liberal democracy was largely historical and fortuitous rather than logical. The institutional implications of preference utilitarianism have not been extensively discussed, but they have aroused numerous fears and doubts among its critics. One approach to the problem is to consider again the ambiguity present in Bentham's use of the concept of interests. On the one hand, he takes interests 'as they are'. On the other, he distinguishes between existing interests, and interests that are 'well-understood'. Both conceptions have led to misgivings about the institutional implications of utilitarianism.

The idea of giving people what they happen to desire, or what they 'prefer', has much to recommend it; it seems both benevolent and non-intrusive. Yet, as social theorists have long pointed out, what grounds do we have for accepting the 'givenness of wants'? Within debates over social choice this issue has reemerged in the form of the question 'why should individual want satisfaction be the criterion of justice and social choice when individual wants themselves may be shaped by a process that preempts the choice?' (Elster, 1982, p. 219). The use of existing preferences – especially given the severe restrictions on the types of preferences that can usefully be considered – may be a way of predetermining certain outcomes, of reinforcing what people regard as likely or possible in their present situation. Or so argue many critics who have seen in utilitarianism a complacent one-dimensional defense of the status quo.

Yet the concept of 'well-understood interests' (or the analogous 'true preferences') raises the question of the conditions under which these interests and preferences are revealed to be rational or true. One image that has reappeared – especially in the literature on private ethics – is the notion of the rational utilitarian floating in a sea of traditional moralists. Because the notion of a social utility function seems to imply the need for a central directing agency – an assumption itself often challenged from a pluralist perspective – the elitism implicit in the preceding image has often suggested the idea of a manipulating elite, or at best of a benevolent despotism.

CONCLUSION. Utilitarianism began and continues to be developed on the premise that intuitions of the divine, of tradition, or of natural law and rights have been discredited beyond rehabilitation as criterions of moral choice in a secular world shorn of metaphysics. Yet this view has always been challenged, and is today sharply contested by a resurgence of 'discredited' views. Insights into the underlying structure of social life are again sought in 'contract', 'rights' or 'community' by thinkers (one might mention such different theorists as Rawls, Nozick, McIntyre and Walzer) who argue that other traditions of thought correspond better to the articulation of the dilemmas of moral and public life. These same theorists, however, share a preoccupation with disposing of the claims of utilitarianism as a necessary prelude to developing their own positions. Indeed, utilitarianism apparently has a special status in the evolution of modern social inquiry, not just because well-being is the modern obsession, or because the model of the 'science' of economics is seductive in an age of science, but because utilitarians claim to offer a criterion of neutrality among competing conceptions of the good life in a pluralistic and antagonistic world. Thus, to many, some version of the theory of utility has a compelling claim on our intellectual attention. If it is ultimately rejected, the imagery is nevertheless that of a 'journey away from' or 'beyond' utilitarianism (see Sen and Williams, 1982). Utilitarianism has achieved a paradoxical status; it dominates the landscape of contemporary thought in the social sciences not because of its own commanding presence, but because it has been necessary to create and recreate it in order to map out the relevant terrain. Its critics claim to look forward to the day when 'we hear no more of it' (Smart and Williams, 1973, p. 150), yet it continues to figure as the alter-ego of much modern moral and social inquiry.

BIBLIOGRAPHY
Bentham, J. 1789. *An Introduction to the Principles of Morals and Legislation.* Ed. J.H. Burns and H.L.A. Hart, London: Athlone Press, 1970.

Bentham, J. 1802. *Principles of the Civil Code*, Vol. 1. In *The Complete Works of Jeremy Bentham*, 11 vols, ed. J. Bowring, New York: Russell & Russell, 1962.

Cliffe Leslie, T.E. 1879. *Essays in Political and Moral Philosophy*. London: Longmans, Green.

Durkheim, E. 1893. *The Division of Labour in Society*. New York: Free Press, 1964.

Elster, J. 1982. Sour grapes – utilitarianism and the genesis of wants. In Sen and Williams (1982).

Georgescu-Roegen, N. 1954. Choice, expectations, and measurability. *Quarterly Journal of Economics* 68, 503–34. Reprinted in N. Georgescu-Roegen, *Analytical Economics*: *Issues and Problems*, Cambridge, Mass.: Harvard University Press, 1966.

Halévy, E. 1903. *The Growth of Philosophical Radicalism*. Trans. M. Morris, Boston: Beacon, 1960.

Hamburger, J. 1965. *Intellectuals in Politics: John Stuart Mill and the Philosophical Radicals*. New Haven: Yale University Press.

Harrod, R.F. 1936. Utilitarianism revised. *Mind* 45, 137–56.

Harsanyi, J.C. 1977. Morality and the theory of rational behaviour. *Social Research*, Winter. Reprinted in Sen and Williams (1982).

Hart, H.I.A. 1982. *Essays on Bentham*: *Studies in Jurisprudence and Political Theory*. Oxford: Clarendon Press.

Lyons, D. 1965. *Forms and Limits of Utilitarianism*. Oxford: Clarendon Press.

McCloskey, H.J. 1963. A note on utilitarian punishment. *Mind* 72, 599.

Mill, J.S. 1861. *Utilitarianism*. New York: Bobbs-Merrill, 1957.

Mill, J.S. 1873. *Autobiography*. New York: Columbia University Press, 1944.

Moore, G.E. 1903. *Principia Ethica*. Cambridge: Cambridge University Press.

Parsons, T. 1937. *The Structure of Social Action*: *A Study in Social Theory with Special Reference to a Group of Recent European Writers*. Glencoe, Ill.: Free Press.

Plamenatz, J. 1970. *The English Utilitarians*. Oxford: Blackwell.

Rawls, J. 1971. *A Theory of Justice*. Cambridge, Mass.: Harvard University Press.

Ryan, A. 1974. *J.S. Mill*. London: Routledge; Boston: Routledge.

Sen, A.K. 1970. *Collective Choice and Social Welfare*. San Francisco: Holden-Day.

Sen, A.K. and Williams, B. 1982 (eds). *Utilitarianism and Beyond*. Cambridge: Cambridge University Press.

Sidgwick, H. 1874. *The Methods of Ethics*. 7th edn, London: Macmillan, 1907.

Smart, J.J.C. and Williams, B. 1973. *Utilitarianism*: *For and Against*. Cambridge: Cambridge University Press; New York: Cambridge University Press.

Stephen, L. 1900. *The English Utilitarians*. 3 vols, New York: Peter Smith, 1950.

Welch, C. 1984. *Liberty and Utility*: *the French Ideologues and the Transformation of Liberalism*. New York: Columbia University Press.

Utopias

GREGORY CLAEYS

The word 'utopia' is derived from a Greek term meaning 'no place'. A utopia is a fictional account of a perfect or ideal society which in its economic aspect is usually stationary and often includes community of goods. Many proposals for social reform have included elements inspired by utopias, and most utopias at least tacitly plead for social change. There is no single utopian tradition and thus no unilinear relationship between 'utopia' and the history of economic thought. Insofar as the provision of a subsistence for mankind has been the aim of all forms of normative economic thought, however, the mode of thinking about perfect or harmonious societies termed 'utopian' has usually presented itself as the most comprehensive answer to the riddles offered by economic writers. Particularly in the modern period this has involved the use of science and technology to solve economic problems. In turn, the most ambitious plans to settle all economic difficulties have themselves often verged upon the utopian (in the sense of being particularly fanciful or unachievable). A clarification of this relationship requires distinguishing utopian thought from at least four related modes of speculation. In millenarianism, all social problems are disposed of through divine intervention, often in the form of the Second Coming of Christ, at which time a perfect society is founded. In the medieval English poetic vision described in the 'Land of Cockaygne' and similar works, all forms of scarcity are dissolved in a fantasy of satiety, where desires remain fixed while their means of satisfaction increase without labour and are consumed without effort. In arcadias, a greater stress is given to the satisfaction of 'natural' desires alone and to the equal importance of a spiritual and aesthetic existence. In what has been termed the 'perfect moral community' the necessity for a prior change in human nature and especially in human wants is also assumed and more attention is given to spiritial regeneration as the basis of social harmony.

In all forms of ideal societies the problem of wants or needs is central. The utopian tradition has tended to accept the central tension between limited resources and insatiable appetites, neither ignoring the problem nor assuming

270

any essential change in human nature. Fuz (1952) has termed 'utopias of escape' those which begin with the assumption of plenty, 'utopias of realization' those which presume scarcity as a starting-point. Most utopias attempt instead to control the key forms of social malaise (crime, poverty, vice, war, etc.) which result from human frailty, giving greater stress to the best organization of social institutions rather than idealizing either nature (as in the 'Land of Cockaygne') or man (as does the perfect moral commonwealth), and relying upon designs fostered by human ingenuity rather than those derived from divine foresight. In economic as well as other aspects, utopias seek the perfection of a completely ordered and detailed social model rather than an interim solution to or partial reform of present disorders. In the imaginative grasp of possibility and presumptive omniscience of exactitude lies the charm and utility as well as the overperfectionist dangers of utopian schemes. Seeking at once to preserve the best of the past and to design an ideal future, utopias have themselves often served as models for judging the adequacy of the present as well as – particularly in the areas of science and technology – its logical linear development.

As a general rule the economic aspect of the utopian tradition can be understood as moving from a central concern with the maintenance of limited wants and (very often) a community of goods to solve problems of production and distribution, to a greater reliance upon the productive powers provided by science, technology and new forms of economic organization, with less strenuous demands being made for a denial of 'artificial' needs. In this sense the history of utopias mirrors both economic history and the history of economic thought insofar as the latter has legitimized that potential for satisfying greater needs for which scientific and technological developments have provided the chief basis. As mainstream liberal political economy came to relinquish the ideal of economic regulation in the 18th century, relying instead upon the development of the market to overcome scarcity, utopianism also shifted its emphasis away from the creation of virtue and towards that of organized superfluity and affluence, often in combination with centralized economic planning and organization. Technology has been presumed to have brought a diminution in the amount of socially necessary labour without the necessity for a concomitant reduction in wants. The inevitability of an extreme division of labour has also been supplanted by the vision of alternating forms of more interesting and creative employment in many modern utopias. Contemporary utopianism both builds upon the promises of technology, and remains critical of forms of social organization which fail to develop this potential or to curb its harmful excesses. No longer content to offer a transcendent image of possibility, modern utopianism is moreover committed to the problem of actualizing planned and ideal societies.

Though the utopian genre is usually dated from the publication of Thomas More's *Utopia* (1516), the proposal of a community of goods as a major element in the solution to economic disorder is much older. An important antecedent was Plato's *Republic* (c360 BC), in which the ruling Guardians alone shared their goods in common as a means of ensuring the least conflict between private and public interest. At the end of the 2nd century AD Plutarch wrote his life of the

271

mythical Spartan legislator Lycurgus, who ended avarice, luxury and inequality by an equal division of lands, the replacement of gold and silver by iron coinage and various sumptuary laws. Though Aristotle was an early and influential critic of Plato's communism, the idea that a community of goods was the ideal state of property survived in various forms in the early Christian era. The very ancient image of a mythical Golden Age of flowing milk and honey which appeared in Hesiod (c750 BC), Ovid and the Stoic-influenced account of the Isles of the Blessed here found a counterpart in the imagery of Paradise and the Garden of Eden, and it was universally assumed that the institution of private property could only have resulted from the Fall and the expulsion of Adam and Even from Paradise. Some community of goods existed among the Jewish sect of the Essenes, in the early Christian Church as well as later monastic movements, and there was later considerable debate as to whether the Apostles had intended this to hold amongst themselves or for all mankind. But early on the Church offered a robust defence of the naturalness of private property on the grounds that it produced greater peace, order and economic efficiency. Charity, however, and especially the support of the poor in times of necessity, was regarded as the duty accompanying the private ownership of goods on an earth intended by God to be sufficient for the sustenance of all.

This was the tradition which Thomas More, with one eye on Plato and another, perhaps, on the potential of the New World, was to overthrow. In More the possibility of secular, social improvement was revived and now recrafted in a new image of fantasy. Both at this time and later, rapid economic change in Britain was a key reason for the Anglo-centric character of much of the utopian tradition. No doubt angered by the effects of land enclosures on the poor, More gave to the Utopians not only equality but also plenty, six hours' daily work (and more dignity to their activity than had done the ancient utopias) and a rotation of homes every ten years and of town and country inhabitants more frequently. Public markets made all goods freely available, while public hospitals cared for the sick. National plenty and scarcity were to be balanced by compensatory distribution, while the surplus was in part given away to the poor of other countries and in part sold at moderate rates. Iron was to be esteemed higher than silver or gold, while jewels and pearls were treated as mere baubles fit only for children. Needs were clearly fixed and limited to the level of comforts. With the conquest of the fear of want, greed was largely eliminated, while pomp and excess derived from pride alone were prohibited by law.

The mid-16th century saw a variety of radical Protestant attempts and plans to emulate the purported communism of the early Church (e.g. in the Hutterite Anabaptism of Peter Rideman), and a considerable augmentation to anti-luxury sentiments within a few of the Protestant sects. A preference for agriculture and hostility to luxury typifies most Renaissance utopias, for instance Johan Günzberg's *Wolfaria* (1621), Andreae's *Christianopolis* (1619) (in which a guild model was of some importance), Campanella's *City of the Sun* (1623) (in which slave labour was first abolished in a utopia) and Robert Burton's *Anatomy of Melancholy* (1621) which included a powerful attack upon avariance as well as a national plan for land utilization, the management of economic resources by a bureaucracy, communal granaries and the public employment of doctors and lawyers. Francis Bacon's *New Atlantis* (1627) was less concerned with the details of economic organization than with the justification of the rule of scientists, and established a paradigmatic attitude towards technology often repeated in later utopias. Bacon also paid some heed to the dangers posed by novelties generally to social order, while Samuel Gott's *Nova Solyma* (1648) was more severe in its condemnation of luxury and intolerance of waste. Of the utopias of the English civil war period, two are particularly worthy of note. Gerrard Winstanley's *The Law of Freedom in a Platform* (1652) developed the Diggers' efforts to reclaim common land for the poor into a scheme for the communal ownership of all land which included universal agricultural labour to age 40. Public storehouses were to make all necessary goods freely available as needed, while domestic buying and selling and working for hire were prohibited. Gold and silver were to be used for external trade alone. Better known was James Harrington's *Oceana* (1656), which popularized the proposal for agrarian laws in order to prevent the predominance of the aristocracy and urged a limit upon dowries and inheritance for similar reasons.

The late 17th century occasioned a profusion of welfare or full-employment utopias in Britain (only in the following century would France see as rich a development of the genre). At this time schemes for practical, immediate social reform and utopias proper were often not far removed. It is in this period, too, that we begin to find a shift away from a concern with a limited demand and the satisfaction of only natural wants towards a conception of maximized production with the full employment of people and resources and a minimization of waste (goals to some extent shared by mainstream Mercantilism). Such times are evident in, for example, *A Description of the Famous Kingdom of Macaria* (1641), where most legislation is concerned with regulating the production of wealth, Peter Chamberlen's *The Poore Man's Advocate* (1649), which included a detailed scheme for the joint-stock employment of the poor to be supervised by public officials, Peter Plockhoy's *A Way Propounded to Make the Poor in These and Other Nations Happy* (1659), which proposed the resettlement into communities of an elite of artisans, husbandmen and traders, and John Bellers' *Proposals for Raising a Colleage of Industry* (1695), in which the wealthy would help to found communities where the poor were to support them while also providing a decent subsistence for themselves. In such plans, solutions to economic distress tended to focus increasingly upon isolated communities rather than the nation-state, and upon segments of the population rather than, for example, all the poor. It has been suggested (by J.C. Davis, 1981) that this implied a waning confidence in the ability of the state to tackle the problem of poverty, and certainly it seems evident that the Act of Settlement of 1662 transferred this burden to individual parishes and away from central government.

The period between 1700 and 1900 marks not only the great age of utopian speculation, but also the period in which economic practice and utopian precept become increasingly intertwined. In addition, it was here that a community of goods ceased to be the *sine qua non* of utopian ideas of property, and that the liberal view of the benefits of private property ownership itself was expressed in utopian form. This entailed a combination of utopian thought and the theory of progress, though in the genre as a whole the two are usually understood as contradictory. In both modern socialism and classical political economy, then, needs are perceived as virtually unlimited, and social harmony is contingent largely upon the fulfilment. The homage to *homo oeconomicus* is usually understood to have begun in Daniel Defoe's *Robinson Crusoe* (1719), and was at its most exalted in Richard Cobden and John Bright's mid-19th-century claims about the universal peace which would be incumbent upon the global extension of free trade. One of its first serious challenges was in John Stuart Mill's acceptance after 1850 of the desirability of a steady-state economy in which further economic development was avoided. Many 18th-century utopias were devoted to the notion of progress (e.g. Mercier's *L'An 2440* (1770) and Condorcet's *L'Equisse d'un Tableau historique des progrès de l'ésprit humain* (1794)). In others the critique of commercial society took various forms, such as Swift's gentle satire in *Gulliver's Travels* (1726), where the Houyhnhnms showed great disdain for shining stones and distributed their produce according to need, or Rousseau's more biting castigation of civilization in his *Discours sur l'origine de l'inégalité* (1755). Similar criticisms were developed into the foundations of modern communism in the writings of Raynal, Mercier, Mably, Morelly, Babeuf and in Britain, Spence and Godwin. In many of these the Spartan model was of some importance, and luxury seen as a principal source of working class oppression as well as general moral corruption.

Though the entire utopian edifice was severely shaken by the pessimistic prognosis of Malthus' *Essay on Population* (1798), the first half of the 19th century witnessed the widespread foundation of small 'utopian socialist' ideal communities which aimed to bring utopian goals into practice, and which could be essentially communistical (Robert Owen, Etienne Cabet) or semi-capitalist (Charles Fourier). Other plans concentrated upon the nation-state and the beneficial development of large-scale industry (Saint-Simon), a pattern which was to become increasingly dominant as the potential role of machinery in creating a new cornucopia became evident. (Some disenchantment with this view occurred later, however, for example in William Morris's *News from Nowhere* (1890), with its preference for rustic and artisanal virtues.) Considerably more attention came to be paid in the early 19th century (by Owen and Fourier, e.g.) to the disadvantages of too narrow a division of labour and the benefits of task rotation. At mid-century began the most compelling radical vision of the age in the works of Marx and Engels, whose plans qualify as utopian in the degree to which they inherited overly optimistic assumptions about human nature, technology and social organization in a future society in which private property and alienation were to be superseded. The last twenty years of the century found, at least in Britain and America, a virtually continuous outpouring of planned-economy utopias, of which the best known are Edward Bellamy's *Looking Backward* (1887), which included provisions for the abolition of money, equal wages and credit for all, and an industrial army,

W.D. Howells's *A Traveller from Altruria* (1894), and H.G. Wells's *A Modern Utopia* (1905), which made some effort to incorporate a conception of progress into the ideal image of the future, and included a mixed rather than wholly publicly owned economy.

In the 20th century utopianism has faltered in face of some of the consequences of modernity, and speculation has often taken the form of the negative utopia or dystopia. In the most famous of these, George Orwell's *Nineteen Eighty-Four* (1949), both capitalist aggression and inequality and communist despotism were criticized, with a central thesis of the work being the prevention of the majority enjoying the benefits of mass production via the deliberate destruction of commodities in war. More satirical of the hedonist utopia is Aldous Huxley's *Brave New World* (1932), though Huxley's later *Island* (1962) is a positive utopia which criticises the spiritual impoverishment of an overly-materialistic civilization. Late 20th century popular utopianism has included some works of science fiction, the libertarian speculation of Murray Rothbard and Robert Nozick (*Anarchy, State, and Utopia*, 1974), and the steady-state environmentalism of Ernest Callenbach's *Ecotopia* (1975). With the progressive extension of both machinery and the welfare state, utopias developing such themes optimistically have declined. To those stated with goods some of the attractions of the consumerist paradise have faded. Technological determinism has often seemingly rendered forms of economic organization unimportant. Two world wars and the spectre of nuclear catastrophe have dented confidence in human perfectibility, while half a century's experimentation with centrally planned communism has lent little credence to the view that this provides the surest path to moral and economic improvement. Nor is 'growth' any longer an uncritically accepted ideal even amongst those who have not yet experienced in effects. Nonetheless the utility of utopias to economic thought is undiminished, for they offer both illumination into important aspects of the history of economic ideas (especially in the areas of welfare and planning), as well as an imaginative leap into possible futures into which more positivist and empirically based thinking fears to wander. If 'progress' can be realized without 'growth', it will likely first persuasively appear in utopian form.

BIBLIOGRAPHY

Adams, R.P. 1949. The social responsibilities of science in *Utopia, New Atlantis* and after. *Journal of the History of Ideas* 10, 374–98.

Armytage, W.H.G. 1984. Utopias: the technological and educational dimension. In *Utopias*, ed. P. Alexander and R. Gill, London: Duckworth.

Boguslaw, R. 1965. *The New Utopians: A Study of System Design and Social Change*. Englewood Cliffs, NJ: Prentice-Hall.

Bowman, S. 1973. Utopian views of man and the machine. *Studies in the Literary Imagination* 6, 105–20.

Claeys, G. 1986. Industrialism and hedonism in Orwell's literary and political development. *Albion* 18.

Claeys, G. 1987. *Machinery, Money and the Millennium. From Moral Economy to Socialism*. Oxford: Polity Press.

Dautry, J. 1961. Le pessimisme économique de Babeuf et l'histoire des Utopies. *Annales Historiques de la Révolution Francaise* 33, 215–33.

Davis, J.C. 1981. *Utopia and the Ideal Society. A Study of English Utopian Writing 1516–1700.* Cambridge: Cambridge University Press; New York: Cambridge University Press.

Eurich, N. 1967. *Science in Utopia.* Cambridge, Mass.: Harvard University Press.

Farr, J. 1983. Technology in the Digger Utopia. In *Dissent and Affirmation: Essays in Honor of Mulford Sibley,* ed. A.L. Kalleberg, J.D. Moon and D. Sabia, Bowling Green: Bowling Green University Popular Press.

Flory, C.R. 1967. *Economic Criticism in American Fiction, 1792 to 1900.* New York: Russell & Russell.

Fogg, W.L. 1975. Technology and dystopia. In *Utopia/Dystopia?,* ed. P.E. Richter, Cambridge, Mass.: Shenkman.

Fuz, J.K. 1952. *Welfare Economics in English Utopias from Francis Bacon to Adam Smith.* The Hague: Martinus Nijhoff.

Gelbart, N. 1978. Science in French Enlightenment Utopias. *Proceedings of the Western Society for French History* 6, 120–28.

Goodwin, B. 1984. Economic and social innovation in Utopia. In *Utopias,* ed. P. Alexander and R. Gill, London: Duckworth.

Gusfield, J. 1971. Economic development as a modern utopia. In *Aware of Utopia,* ed. D.W. Plath, Urbana: University of Illinois Press.

Hall, A.R. 1972. Science, technology and utopia in the seventeenth century. In *Science and Society 1600–1900,* ed. P. Mathias, Cambridge: Cambridge University Press; New York: Cambridge University Press.

Hont, I. and Ignatieff, M. 1983. Needs and justice in the *Wealth of Nations*: an introductory essay. In *Wealth and Virtue: the Shaping of Political Economy in the Scottish Enlightenment,* ed. I. Hont and M. Ignatieff, Cambridge: Cambridge University Press.

Hudson, W. 1946. Economic and social thought of Gerrard Winstanley: was he a seventeenth-century marxist? *Journal of Modern History* 18, 1–21.

Hymer, S. 1971. Robinson Crusoe and the secret of primitive accumulation. *Monthly Review* 23, 11–36.

King, J.E. 1983. Utopian or scientific? A reconsideration of the Ricardian Socialists. *History of Political Economy* 15, 345–73.

Klassen, P.J. 1964. *The Economics of Anabaptism 1525–60.* The Hague: Mouton.

Krieger, R. 1980. The economics of Utopia. In *Utopias: the American Experience,* ed. G.B. Moment and O.F. Kraushaar, London: Scarecrow Press.

Landa, L. 1943. Swift's economic views and Mercantilism. *English Literary History* 10, 310–35.

Leiss, W. 1970. Utopia and technology: reflections on the conquest of nature. *International Social Science Journal* 22, 576–88.

Levitas, R. 1984. Need, nature and nowhere. In *Utopias,* ed. P. Alexander and R. Gill, London: Duckworth.

MacDonald, W. 1946. Communism in Eden? *New Scholasticism* 20, 101–25.

MacKenzie, D. 1984. Marx and the machine. *Technology and Culture* 25, 473–502.

Manuel, F.E. and Manuel, F.P. 1979. *Utopian Thought in the Western World.* Oxford: Basil Blackwell; Cambridge, Mass.: Harvard University Press.

Mumford, L. 1967. Utopia, the city and the machine. In *Utopias and Utopian Thought,* ed. F.E. Manuel, Boston: Beacon Press.

Novak, M. 1976. *Economics and the Fiction of Daniel Defoe.* New York: Russell & Russell.

Perrot, J.-C. 1982. Despotische Verkunft und ökonomische Utopie. In *Utopieforschung. Interdisziplinäre Studien zur neuzeitlichen Utopie*, ed. W. Vosskamp, Stuttgart: J.B. Metzlersche Verlagsbuchhandlung.

Pocock, J.G.A. 1980. The mobility of property and the rise of eighteenth-century sociology. In *Theories of Property, Aristotle to the Present*, ed. A. Parel and T. Flanagan, Waterloo: Wilfred Laurier University Press.

Sargent, L.T. 1981. Capitalist utopias in America. In *America as Utopia*, ed. K.M. Roemer, New York: Burt Franklin.

Schlaeger, J. 1982. Die Robinsonade als frühbürgerliche 'Eutopia'. In *Utopieforschung. Interdisziplinäre Studien zur neuzeitlichen Utopie*, ed. W. Vosskamp, Stuttgart: J.B. Metzlersche Verlagsbuchhandlung.

Schoeck, R.J. 1956. More, Plutarch, and King Agis: Spartan history and the meaning of *Utopia*. *Philological Quarterly* 35, 366–75.

Segal, H. 1985. *Technological Utopianism in American Culture*. Chicago: Chicago University Press.

Sibley, M.Q. 1973. Utopian thought and technology. *American Journal of Political Science* 17, 255–81.

Soper, K. 1981. *On Human Needs: Open and Closed Theories in Marxist Perspectives*. London: Harvester Press.

Springborg, P. 1981. *The Problem of Human Needs and the Critique of Civilisation*. London: George Allen & Unwin.

Steintrager, J. 1969. Plato and More's *Utopia*. *Social Research* 36, 357–72.

Taylor, W.F. 1942. *The Economic Novel in America*. Chapel Hill: University of North Carolina Press.

Thompson, N.W. 1985. *The People's Science. The Popular Political Economy of Exploitation and Crisis, 1816–34*. Cambridge: Cambridge University Press.

Welles, C.B. 1948. The economic background of Plato's communism. *Journal of Economic History* 8, 101–14.

Contributors

Armen A. Alchian Emeritus Professor of Economics, University of California, Los Angeles. 'Some economics of property rights', *Il Politico* 30(4), (1965); 'Information costs, pricing and resource unemployment', *Economic Enquiry* 7 (1969); 'Production, information costs and economic organization', *American Economic Review* 62 (1972); *Economic Forces at Work* (1977); 'Vertical integration, appropriable rents and the competitive contracting process', (with B. Klein and G.C. Crawford) *Journal of Law and Economics* 21 (1978); *Exchange and Production: Competition, Coordination and Control* (with W.A. Allen, 1983).

P.S. Atiyah Former Professor of English Law, Oxford University. Fellow of the British Academy. *The Rise and Fall of Freedom of Contract* (1979); *Introduction to the Law of Contract* (1981); *Promises, Morals and Laws* (1981); *Essays on Contract* (1987); *Form and Substance in Anglo-American Law* (with R.S. Summers, forthcoming).

James M. Buchanan General Director, Center for the Study of Public Choice, George Mason University, Virginia. Nobel Prize in Economics, 1986. *The Calculus of Consent: Logical Foundations of Constitutional Democracy* (with G. Tullock, 1962); *The Limits of Liberty: Between Anarchy and Leviathan* (1974); *Power to Tax* (with G. Brennan, 1980); *Liberty, Market and State* (1985); *Reason of Rules* (1985); *Economics: Between Predictive Science and Moral Philosophy* (with G. Brennan, 1988).

Gregory Claeys Lehrgebiet Auslandskunde und Anglistik, Hannover. 'Engel's *Outlines of a Critique of Political Economy* (1843) and the origins of the Marxist critique of capitalism', *History of Political Economy* 16(2), (1984); 'Industrialism and hedonism in Orwell's literary and political development', *Albion* 18 (1987); 'Justice, independence and individual democracy: the development of John Stuart

278

Mill's views on society', *Journal of Politics* 49(1), (1987); *Machinery, Money and the Millenium. Labour and Civilization in Early British Socialism* (1987).

Ralf Dahrendorf Warden, St Antony's College, Oxford. KBE; Fellow of the British Academy. *Class and Class Conflict in Industrial Society* (1959); *Society and Democracy in Germany* (1966); *The New Liberty* (1975); *Law and Order* (1985); *The Modern Social Conflict* (1988).

R.S. Downie Professor of Moral Philosophy, University of Glasgow. Fellow, Royal Society of Edinburgh. *Government Action and Morality* (1964); *Respect for Persons* (1969); *Roles and Values* (1971); *Education and Personal Relationships* (1974); *Caring and Curing* (1980); *Healthy Respect* (1987).

David D. Friedman John M. Olin Faculty Fellow, University of Chicago Law School. Member, Mont Pelerin Society. *The Machinery of Freedom* (1971); 'An economic theory of the size and shape of nations', *Journal of Political Economy* (1977); 'Reflections on optimal punishment' or 'Should the rich pay higher fines', *Research in Law and Economics* (1981); 'Efficient institutions for the private enforcement of law', *Journal of Legal Studies* (1984); *Price Theory; an Intermediate Text* (1986); 'An Economic Analysis of Alternative Damage Rules for Breech of Contract', *Journal of Law and Economics* (forthcoming, 1989).

Roger W. Garrison Associate Professor of Economics, Auburn University, Alabama. 'Austrian macroeconomics: a diagrammatic exposition', in *Austrian Economics; New Directions and Unresolved Questions* (ed. Louis M. Spadaro, 1978); 'Time and money: the universals of macroeconomic theorizing', *Journal of Macroeconomics* 6(2), (1984); 'Intertemporal coordination and the invisible hand: an Austrian perspective on the Keynesian vision', *History of Political Economy* 17(2), (1985); 'The Hayekian trade cycle theory: a reappraisal', *Cato Journal* 6(2), (1986); Phillips curves and Hayekian triangles: two perspectives on monetary dynamics', (with Don Bellante) *History of Political Economy* 20(2), (1988); 'The Austrian theory of the business cycle in the light of modern macroeconomics', *Review of Austrian Economics* 3 (1988).

J. de V. Graaff Emeritus Fellow, St John's College, Cambridge. *Theoretical Welfare Economics* (1958).

Ross Harrison Lecturer in Philosophy, Cambridge University; Fellow, King's College, Cambridge. *On What There Must Be* (1974); *Rational Action* (ed., 1979); *Bentham* (1985).

Robert F. Hébert Russell Foundation Professor of Entrepreneurial Studies, Auburn University, Alabama. 'A note on the historical development of the economic law of market areas', *Quarterly Journal of Economics* 86 (1972); 'Public economics at the Ecole des Ponts et Chaussées: 1830–1850', (with R.B. Ekelund)

Journal of Public Economics 1 (1973); *A History of Economic Theory and Method* (1975); 'Richard Cantillon's early contributions to spatial economics', *Economica* 48 (1981); *The Entrepreneur: Mainstream Views and Radical Critiques* (1982); 'Consumer surplus: the first hundred years', (with R.B. Ekelund) *History of Political Economy* 17 (1985).

Albert O. Hirschman Emeritus Professor of Social Science, Institute for Advanced Study, Princeton. Distinguished Fellow, American Economic Association; Member, National Academy of Sciences; Corresponding Fellow, British Academy; Talcott Parsons Prize for Social Science, American Academy of Arts and Sciences; Frank E. Seidman Distinguished Award in Political Economy; numerous Honorary Degrees. *National Power and the Structure of Foreign Trade* (1945); *The Strategy of Economic Development* (1958); *Journeys toward Progress: Studies of economic policy-making in Latin America* (1963); *Exit, Voice, and Loyalty* (1970); *The Passions and the Interests* (1976); *Rival Views of Market Society and Other Recent Essays* (1986).

Israel M. Kirzner Professor of Economics, New York University. *The Economic Point of View* (1960); *An Essay on Capital* (1966); *Competition and Entrepreneurship* (1973); *Perception, Opportunity and Profit* (1979); *Discovery and the Capitalist Press* (1985).

C.B. Macpherson Emeritus Professor of Political Science, University of Toronto. Officer, Order of Canada; Fellow, Royal Society of Canada; Fellow, Royal Historical Society. President, Canadian Political Science Association, 1963–4. *The Political Theory of Possessive Individualism: Hobbes to Locke* (1962); *The Real World of Democracy* (The Massey Lectures, Fourth Series) (1965); *Democratic Theory: Essays in Retrieval* (1973); *The Life and Times of Liberal Democracy* (1977); *Burke* (Past Masters Series), (1980); *The Rise and Fall of Economic Justice* (1985).

Peter Marshall Tutor in Philosophy, University College of North Wales. *William Godwin* (1984); *The Anarchist Writings of William Godwin* (1986); *Cuba Libre: Breaking the Chains* (1987).

Murray Milgate Associate Professor of Economics, Harvard University. *Capital and Employment* (1982); *Keynes's Economics and the Theory of Value and Distribution* (ed., with J. Eatwell, 1983); *Critical Issues in Social Thought* (ed., with C.B. Welch, 1989); 'The Legacy of Classical Social Thought' (with C.B. Welch), in *Critical Issues in Social Thought* (ed., with C.B. Welch, 1989).

D.H. Monro Professor of Economics, Monash University. *Godwin's Moral Philosophy: an interpretation of William Godwin* (1953); *Empiricisms and Ethics* (1967); *The Ambivalence of Bernard Mandeville* (1975).

Mancur Olson Distinguished Professor of Economics, University of Maryland. *The Logic of Collective Action* (1965); 'An economic theory of alliances', (with Richard Zeckhauser) *Review of Economics and Statistics* (1966); 'Positive time preference', (with Martin Bailey) *Journal of Political Economy* 89 (1981); *The Rise and Decline of Nations* (1982).

Alan Peacock Executive Director, David Hume Institute, Edinburgh. Fellow of the British Academy; President, International Institute of Public Finance (1966–69); honorary doctorates from the universities of Buckingham, Stirling and Zurich; KBE (1987). *Classics in the Theory of Public Finance* (with R.A. Musgrave, 1958); *The Growth of Public Expenditure in the United Kingdom* (with Jack Wiseman, 1962); *Welfare Economics, A Liberal Reappraisal* (with Charles Rowley, 1975); *The Economic Analysis of Government* (1979); *Public Choice Analysis in Historical Perspective* (forthcoming).

Nicholas T. Phillipson Senior Lecturer in History, Edinburgh University. Fellow, Royal Historical Society. *Scotland in the Age of Improvement* (ed., with R.M. Mitchison, 1970); *Universities, Society and the Future* (ed., 1983); *Hume* (1989).

John C. Robertson Fellow, Tutor and University Lecturer in Modern History, St Hugh's College, Oxford. 'The Scottish Enlightenment at the limits of the civic tradition' in *Wealth and Virtue: the shaping of political economy in the Scottish Enlightenment* (ed. I. Hont and M. Ignatieff, 1983); 'Scottish political economy beyond the civic tradition: government and economic development in *the Wealth of Nations*', *History of Political Thought* 4 (1983); *The Scottish Enlightenment and the Militia Issue* (1985).

Nathan Rosenberg Fairleigh S. Dickinson Jr. Professor of Public Policy, Stanford University; Member, National Academy of Sciences, Government-University-Industry Research Roundtable; Director, Center for Economic Policy Research (Stanford), Program on Technology and Economic Growth, 1987; Member, Board of Directors, National Bureau of Economic Research. Fellow, American Academy of Arts and Sciences; Fellow, American Academy for the Advancement of Science. *Perspectives on Technology* (1976); *The Britannia Bridge: The Generation and Diffusion of Technical Knowledge* (with Walter Vincenti, 1978); *Inside the Black Box* (1982); *How the West Grew Rich* (with L.E. Birdzell, Jr., 1986); *Adam Smith and the Stock of Moral Capital* (forthcoming, 1987); *The Organization of Innovative Activity* (with David Mowery, forthcoming).

Eugene Rotwein Professor of Economics, Queen's College, The City University of New York. Research Fellow, The Brookings Institution. 'On the methodology of positive economics', *Quarterly Journal of Economics* (1959); 'Economic concentration and monopoly in Japan', *Journal of Political Economy* (1964); *David Hume: Writings on Economics* (ed., 1970); 'The ideology of wealth and the liberal economic heritage; the neglected view', *Social Research* (1973);

'Empiricism and economic method: several views considered', *Journal of Economic Issues* (1973); 'Jacob Viner and the Chicago tradition', *History of Political Economy* (1983).

Alan Ryan Professor of Politics, Princeton University. Fellow, British Academy. *Russell: A Political Life; The Philosophy of John Stuart Mill* (1974); *The Idea of Freedom* (ed., 1979); *Property and Political Theory* (1984).

N.E. Simmonds University Lecturer in Law, Fellow and Director of Studies in Law, Corpus Christi College, Cambridge. *The Decline of Judicial Reason* (1984); *Central Issues in Jurisprudence* (1986).

A.S. Skinner Daniel Jack Professor and Clerk of Senate, University of Glasgow. Fellow, Royal Society of Edinburgh. Sir James Steuart, *Principles of Political Economy* (ed., 1966); Adam Smith, *The Wealth of Nations* (ed., with R.H. Campbell and W.B. Todd, 1976); *A System of Social Science*: Papers relating to Adam Smith (1979); *Adam Smith* (with R.H. Campbell, 1982).

Karen I. Vaughn Professor of Economics, George Mason University. Vice President, History of Economics Society (1988–9); Vice President, Southern Economic Association, (1986–7). *John Locke: Economist and Social Scientist* (1980); 'Economic calculation under socialism: the Austrian contribution', *Economic Enquiry* (1980); 'Does it matter that costs are subjective?', *Southern Economic Journal* (1980); 'Hayek's Ricardo effect: a second look', *History of Political Economy* (1986); 'The limits of homoeconomics in public choice and in political philosophy', *Analyse und Kritik* (1989).

C.B. Welch Lecturer in Social Studies, Harvard University. *Liberty and Utility: The French Ideologues and the Transformation of Liberalism* (1984); 'Jansenism and liberalism: the making of citizens in post-revolutionary France', *History of Political Thought* (1986); *Critical Issues in Social Thought* (ed., with Murray Milgate, 1989); 'Liberalism and social rights', in *Critical Issues in Social Thought* (ed. Murray Milgate and C.B. Welch, 1989); 'The Legacy of Classical Social Thought' (with Murray Milgate), in *Critical Issues in Social Thought* (ed. Murray Milgate and C.B. Welch, 1989); 'Democratic theory revisited', *American Political Science Review* (1989).

George Woodcock Emeritus Professor of English, University of British Columbia. Fellow, Royal Geographical Society. *Pierre-Joseph Proudhon* (1956); *Anarchism* (1962); *The Crystal Spirit: A Study of George Orwell* (1966); *Gabriel Dumont: The Métis Chief and His Lost World* (1975); *Peoples of the Coast: The Indians of the Pacific Northwest* (1977); *The Social History of Canada* (1988).

Stefano Zamagni Professor of Economics, University of Bologna; Adjunct Professor of Economics, Johns Hopkins University, Bologna Center. Member,

Academy of Sciences, Institute of Bologna; Member, Executive Committee of the Italian Economic Association. 'Efficiency, justice and morality in a market economy' in *Etica e Politica* (ed. W. Tega, 1984); 'Ricardo and Hayek effects in a fixwage model of traverse', *Oxford Economic Papers* (1984); 'Consumer theory in the last quarter of the century', *Economia Politica* (1986); 'From the theory of utility value to the theory of choice value', *Teoria Politica* (1987); *Microeconomic Theory* (1987); *An Historical Profile of Economic Thought* (1988).